SELF AND OBJECT CONSTANCY
CLINICAL AND THEORETICAL PERSPECTIVES

THE GUILFORD PSYCHIATRY SERIES
BERTRAM J. COHLER AND HENRY GRUNEBAUM, EDITORS

Self and Object Constancy: Clinical and Theoretical Perspectives
RUTH F. LAX, SHELDON BACH, AND J. ALEXIS BURLAND, EDITORS

Parenthood: A Psychodynamic Perspective
REBECCA S. COHEN, BERTRAM J. COHLER, AND
SIDNEY H. WEISSMAN, EDITORS

SELF AND OBJECT CONSTANCY

CLINICAL AND THEORETICAL PERSPECTIVES

EDITED BY

RUTH F. LAX, SHELDON BACH, AND J. ALEXIS BURLAND

THE GUILFORD PRESS

NEW YORK   LONDON

© 1986 The Guilford Press
A Division of Guilford Publications, Inc.
200 Park Avenue South, New York, N.Y. 10003

Printed in the United States of America

Library of Congress Catalog Card No. 85-27365
ISBN 0-89862-226-3

To Dr. Margaret Mahler—
independent thinker, researcher, and inspiring teacher

Contributors

SHELDON BACH, PhD, Clinical Professor of Psychology, New York University Postdoctoral Program in Psychoanalysis; Faculty and Board of Trustees, New York Freudian Society, New York, New York

HAROLD P. BLUM, MD, Clinical Professor of Psychiatry, New York University, New York, New York; Former Editor, *Journal of the American Psychoanalytic Association*; Executive Director, Sigmund Freud Archives

BERNARD BRANDCHAFT, MD, Supervising and Training Analyst, Los Angeles Psychoanalytic Institute; Assistant Clinical Professor of Psychiatry, University of California at Los Angeles, Los Angeles, California

J. ALEXIS BURLAND, MD, Training and Supervising Analyst (Adult and Adolescent/Child Curricula), Philadelphia Psychoanalytic Institute; Clinical Professor of Psychiatry and Human Behavior, Jefferson Medical College of Thomas Jefferson University, Philadelphia, Pennsylvania

RENATA GADDINI, MD, Associate Professor of Child Psychiatry, Department of Pediatrics, University of "La Sapienza," Rome, Italy; Full Member, Italian Psychoanalytic Society

ELEANOR GALENSON, MD, Clinical Professor of Psychiatry, Mt. Sinai School of Medicine, New York, New York

PETER L. GIOVACCHINI, MD, Clinical Professor, Department of Psychiatry, University of Illinois College of Medicine; Director, Chicago Psychoanalytic Study Group; Medical School and Residency Training, University of Chicago School of Medicine; Psychoanalytic Training, Chicago Institute for Psychoanalysis, Chicago, Illinois

SIMON GROLNICK, MD, Department of Psychiatry, North Shore University Hospital, Manhasset, New York; Columbia University Center for Psychoanalytic Training and Research, New York, New York

RUTH F. LAX, PhD, Associate Clinical Professor, Psychiatry and Psychology, Cornell Medical Center; Training and Supervisory Analyst, New York Freudian Society; Training and Supervisory Analyst, Institute for Psychoanalytic Training and Research, New York, New York

CONTRIBUTORS

MARGARET S. MAHLER, MD, ScD, The Margaret S. Mahler Psychiatric Research Foundation, New York, New York

JOHN B. McDEVITT, MD, Faculty, New York Psychoanalytic Institute; Chairman, Professional Advisory Committee, The Margaret S. Mahler Psychiatric Research Foundation, New York, New York

W. W. MEISSNER, SJ, MD, Clinical Professor of Psychiatry, Harvard Medical School; Training and Supervising Analyst, Boston Psychoanalytic Institute, Boston, Massachusetts

MARGARET HAMEL RAY, PhD, Training Analyst, New York Freudian Society; National Psychological Association for Psychoanalysis, New York, New York

DONALD B. RINSLEY, MD, Karl Menninger School of Psychiatry, Topeka, Kansas; Department of Psychiatry, University of Kansas School of Medicine, Kansas City, Kansas

HERMAN ROIPHE, MD, Department of Psychiatry, Mt. Sinai School of Medicine, New York, New York

JOSEPH SANDLER, MD, Sigmund Freud Professor of Psychoanalysis, Hebrew University of Jerusalem, Jerusalem, Israel; Freud Memorial Professor of Psychoanalysis, University College, London, England

ALBERT J. SOLNIT, MD, School of Medicine and Child Study Center, Yale University; Faculty, The Western New England Institute for Psychoanalysis, New Haven, Connecticut

MARJORIE TAGGART WHITE, PhD, Director, Seminar in Self Psychology; Faculty and Advisory Council, American Institute for Psychotherapy and Psychoanalysis; Supervisor of Doctoral Candidates in Psychology, Ferkauf Graduate School, Yeshiva University; Private practice of psychoanalysis, New York, New York

Preface

The chapters in this volume cover a spectrum of psychoanalytic views on the topic of self and object constancy. The pioneering research efforts in this aspect of early psychological development often derive from different data sources, use differing theoretical formulations, and are consequently expressed in different languages. Though such diversity may be initially confusing to the beginning student, it provides in the end a truer picture; and the experienced clinician should find the presentation of divergent viewpoints both seminal and enriching in their complementarity, offering a multidimensional perspective on the topic.

It is for this reason that we have not attempted to impose our own viewpoint regarding concepts, terminology, or developmental timetables. We feel that such attempts at correlation and standardization are premature, and we have therefore attempted simply to reflect the multiplicity of important viewpoints that characterize the current state of the art.

The Editors

Contents

SECTION III. SELF AND OBJECT

SECTION IV.   CLINICAL THEORY AND APPLICATION

Introduction

ALBERT J. SOLNIT

Periodically, and for good reason, the concept of object constancy is reviewed, and extended. To a significant extent this process reflects the continuing usefulness of this psychoanalytic concept, a construct that has practical applications as well as theory-building and explanatory value. Practical applications of this concept revitalize and refine it. At the same time such applications suggest what needs to be revised and how the theory can be elaborated and extended.

Even the controversies about when the child first begins to express the maturational capacity for object constancy and in what forms it can be demonstrated have been productive. Starting with Hartmann's (1952) concepts of the need-satisfying object and the constant object, there have been theoretical assumptions made on the basis of observational data, centering on when the child first gives behavioral evidence of recognizing the caregiving parent. The converse side of this perceptual-cognitive-emotional-behavioral response has been noted in those infants who show a fear-of-the-stranger reaction. This latter often is spoken of as the 8-months anxiety. In fact, as our observations have become systematic and comparable, we have come to recognize that each healthy, well-developing child will give clear behavioral evidence of recognizing the constant object, usually between 6 and 9 months of age; but we also know that all healthy children do not show a fear-of-the-stranger reaction—or that it is so short lived and so blended with other responses by the infant that we often fail to observe the reaction in the average expectable environment of the well-developing child.

It is clear, as Mahler, Pine, and Bergman (1975) have so vigorously demonstrated in their original research and as refined and restated by McDevitt and Mahler (Chapter 1, this volume), that "object constancy has its origins in infancy, begins to be attained in the third year, continues to develop throughout childhood and adolescence, and in all probability is

1

rarely completely attained" (McDevitt, 1975). As these and other authors have agreed, the process of object constancy is largely achieved through a synthesis of the child's predominantly libidinal attachment to the primary love-object and the child's cognitive capacities for person permanence and representational or symbolic functioning.

Thus, object constancy refers to the capacity to feel and use the psychological presence of the primary love-object even when he or she is not present or, if present, not approving; that is, object constancy depends on the internalization of a constant, well-cathected image of the primary love-object or objects. In healthy or normative development this emotionally charged presence is felt as approving, accepting, and as a source of realistic self-esteem. In deviant, stunted, or aggressively toned object constancy, whether characterized by deprivation, fragmentation, abuse, or the absence of a primary caregiving love-object, individuals are more likely to be unpredictable in their behavior or anxiously and insistently seek immediate, changing existential sources of affection, approval, and self-regard. Such persons tend to be less discriminating and less close or intimate in their personal relationships and in social and work situations.

When the primary caregiving person is sadistic and abusive, the child usually establishes a profound sadomasochistic primary attachment. Such relationships often lead to a destructive object constancy in which the psychological emotionally charged presence of the caregiving person is evoked mainly through the child provoking or arranging for the repetition of sadomasochistic social interchanges. Of course, such an exciting destructive presence and its impact on self-esteem may be defended against in a variety of intrapsychic dynamics and social behaviors. For example, such a person may ward off and avoid all or most such exciting, risk-taking behaviors, or the abused child, reacting against earlier life experiences and their effects, may become a rigid, dedicated parent or child-care provider.

Thus, the outcome of the object constancy process in an abused child is influenced and finally determined by many other developmental and life experience factors and patterns.

All too often,

[in] sadomasochistic relationships that characterize many of the attachments in abused children and their parents, object constancy is often associated with a provocative, pain-inflicting constant object. In these instances, tension reduction is preceded by storms of painful aggression as compared or contrasted to the gradual tension reduction associated with object constancy in which the love object representation is predominantly cathected with affectionate, pleasurable libidinal energies. These theoretical inferences are useful in explaining the persistent life-threatening attachment behavior displayed by many children who are violently abused physically and/or sexually. In such instances, early intervention is essential, not because there is an absence of attachment or object constancy, but because it often is life-threatening. (Solnit, 1982)

As Freud (1926) indicated, the human infant's helplessness at birth and the prolonged period of dependency is a vital explanatory link between the human's biological characteristics and the nature of the emotionally charged psychological relationships between the infant and the parents (the caregivers, the "life savers").

The object constancy process represents and fosters the infant's dawning capacity to move from physical and psychological dependency to increasingly independent capabilities. In a vital sense, object constancy enables the maturing, developing child to move away from the protective, approving, physical presence of the parent into a wider social setting with the internalized psychological presence of the parent as a supportive, comforting, encouraging inner resource. Object constancy is a capacity that is embedded in the ego, a foundation or precondition for other ego capacities. As our understanding increases it may be useful to characterize object constancy and its unfolding functions according to maturational changes, developmental vicissitudes, and the parental representations that are synthesized and re-created. In this sense object constancy is the context in which later ego identifications take place. These identifications become the bedrock for later socialization.

Under normative conditions the infant's craving and need for physical care, personal attention, and sustained affection becomes expressed through the child wanting to become inseparable and indivisible from the primary love-object. This primary identification with the caregiving parent is gradually transformed through maturation and development into a sense of separateness. Then individuation and separation enable the child to replace the merged primary identification with an internalized representation of that primary love-object. This internalized presence represents both an on-going secondary identification with the primary caregiver and the beginning of object constancy.

Toward the end of the 1st year of life the healthy human infant begins to unfold the capacity for object constancy. In the 3rd and 4th years of life this capacity is elaborated into a reliable, internalized function of object constancy together with the shaping of ego activity that reflects the child's identifications with the constant caregiving love-objects.

Identification is both a defense and adaptive mechanism through which a person consciously and unconsciously attempts to take over and integrate into his personality the attitudes and behavior patterns of parents and other important persons. These identifications, especially with primary love-objects, lead to a characteristic structuralization of ego formation in which the residues of the identifications with important love-objects are internalized and integrated into each person's unique personality. As this book suggests, we are in urgent need of studies that indicate the common roots and differential functions of object constancy and identification throughout the life cycle. To recapitulate, both identification and object constancy

3

enable the child to become increasingly independent, transforming passive into active modes of activity in proportion to newly acquired physical, emotional, social, and intellectual capacities. However, identification is a taking in of parental attitudes and behaviors so that the child can, in the process of internalization, modify and integrate the characteristics of a love-object in the service of progressive ego development. In comparison, object constancy is the internalized capacity to have available the primary love-object's psychological presence, normatively a loving, approving, protective resource.

In the 3rd and 4th years of life, with these inner resources, children are able to cope with separation from their parents (primary love-objects) and to become familiar with and trusting of the teacher as a bridge to the beginning of play, at first side-by-side with other children, and at a later age together with their fellow students. With the internalized psychological presence of the beloved, needed parent, the young child, feeling loved, wanted, and worthwhile, moves from separation and individuation into successive phases of a socializing development.

Thus, the common roots and significant differences between ego identifications and the process of object constancy are of great interest for those concerned with psychoanalytic developmental psychology. In this connection, object constancy is significantly modified and revised by the advent of superego structural and functional operations.

The Editors of this volume have recognized that it is time to present the many advancing sectors of experience and thinking in which object constancy provides a useful explanatory concept. The timeliness of this collection of essays is also a reflection of how psychoanalysts move toward a life-cycle perspective in the context of their empirical, clinical heritage.

The object constancy process indicates how the human infant, born helpless, moves away from helplessness without ever losing a certain awareness of that helplessness as an essential shaping, binding influence on the whole of his social self-definition. Just as one could not imagine leading one's life if there were no end to it—no dying at the end of it—so one cannot imagine living one's life without the internalized presence of those adults, the parents, who "saved" that child's life by caring for him when he was helpless.

This process is examined philosophically in a recent book by Richard Wollheim (1984), a philosopher and Kleinian psychoanalyst. In *The Thread of Life* he implies how essential the concept of object constancy is by examining what it means to be a person in terms of: (1) what is one's life as a whole; (2) how the conviction and expectation of death is a vital influence on the shape of our self-definition; and (3) how the awareness of the past influences the way one leads one's life in the present and in preparing for the future. As Wollheim says, "A person leads his life at a crossroads; at a point where a past that has affected him and a future that lies open meet in the present." Or as the philosopher Charles Taylor (1984) put it in a recent review of the Wollheim book: "A person lives under the influence of the past, which enters into his present state, while he is also self-concerned for his future state, the three relations cannot be dissociated from one another" (p. 52).

This philosophical perspective on the human lifespan is consistent with the psychoanalytic view of personality in which we shape ourselves significantly through our identifications with those who care for us from birth as we are enabled to care for ourselves and then for others. Taylor indirectly refers to this when he reflects that what "we are drawn to is living our lives through in a way that draws together our past and our future" (p. 53).

This ubiquitous human yearning and search for coherence, for a synthesis that can lead to a life worth living, is intrinsic to and expressed in elaborated ways by the essential human capacity of object constancy as a continuing process.

Dependent on the care, love, and approval of those who "save" our lives when we are helpless, this social "addiction" never leaves us though it changes form as we develop. It changes from dependency on physical-emotional care given by the primary love-objects to the quest for love and approval from those caregiving persons, and then from those who replace the original primary love-objects as each person lives out his life internally and externally. At the same time, this quest is associated with acquiring reality-tested self-approval and a sense of one's worth. However, the psychological presence of the original primary love-objects is a crucial part of each person's past that lives on in the residues of identifications with those persons. Continuity is maintained as the first-loved ones are replaced by future persons who are like the originals or who are intended to be *unlike* them.

Remembering and feeling the psychological presence of primary love-objects, past and present, approving and disapproving, loving and depriving, is how we carry our essential, emotionally charged person-rooted baggage from our past origins. It is one of the deeply felt, usually subtle sources of knowing the relative importance of striving for independence and self-worth as we move from childhood to adolescence and into the adult phases of our lives.

An individual may feel fragmented or tortured by the internalized presence of the constant object representations, rather than feeling approved, encouraged, steadied, and coherent. Such a person has a need, often a way of revisiting the past in order to review and accept it, especially in the light of opportunities to form new permanent relationships in late adolescence or early adulthood.

Psychoanalytic treatment can be an effective way of achieving this review, clarification, and acceptance. This enables the individual to reduce the baggage from the past so it will not dominate his present and future and, so that such persons can take charge of their lives, to recognize the choices they confront in the present and future.

Developmentally and as viewed in psychoanalytic treatment, object constancy is a milestone capacity in the development of object relations. Its achievement requires the intimacy and continuity of affectionate care which enables the child to move from need-satisfying limitations to the capabilities associated with object constancy, capabilities that can be characterized as ego functions. These are the ego functions that are expressed in memory, speech, thought as trial action, and in the elaboration of personal relationships which serve social-psychological needs.[1] Object constancy is a developmental capacity that provides the child with a sense of himself and his parents and enables him to become increasingly independent in forming new personal relationships, which in turn increasingly enable him significantly to shape his own social environment. Object constancy continues to unfold throughout the life cycle and to be responsive to life's events. (Solnit, 1982)

Thus, this book is responsive to the increasing sophistication and volume of research and teaching about parent-child interactional phenomena and the useful theory-building constructs that have resulted. In this connection the first two sections of the book examine theoretical and developmental aspects of the object constancy process with an emphasis on normative or healthy development. The third and fourth sections elaborate object constancy constructs in relation to deviant states and psychopathological conditions. A crucial part of the fourth section is presented in Ruth Lax's seminal contribution of studying how the psychoanalytic treatment process enhanced the recovery capacity of a man who had been suffering from the blighting effects of a developmental arrest.

Future research efforts that are suggested and encouraged by the clinical studies in this volume include:

1. The relative importance and specific roles of olfactory, visual, auditory, tactile, and kinesthetic components of such a capacity.
2. The cognitive components of object constancy and their relationship to the affective states that characterize object constancy.
3. The relationship between object constancy and the capacity for creating and exploiting transitional objects and other transitional phenomena.
4. How object constancy shapes and, in turn, is modified by the advent of superego structural and functional operations—an elaboration of ego-superego mutuality and conflicts.
5. How children extract and integrate the influence of several primary caregivers in an extended family setting.

---

1. Including the young child's need for continuity and permanency which supports age-appropriate fantasies that primary love-objects (parents) are omnipotent and omniscient.

6. The shape and shaping influence of object constancy at vital nodal points (normative developmental crises) throughout the life cycle.

Thus, this volume has provided a mapping of important and interesting areas that can be mined for the continuing yield from and advance of psychoanalytic theory and its applications.

REFERENCES

Freud, S. (1926). Inhibitions, symptoms and anxiety. *Standard Edition, 20*, 77-175.

Hartmann, H. (1952). Mutual influences of ego and id. In *Essays on ego psychology*. New York: International Universities Press, 1964.

Mahler, M., Pine, F., & Bergman, A. (1975). *The psychological birth of the human infant*. New York: Basic Books.

McDevitt, J. B. (1975). Separation-individuation and object constancy. *Journal of the American Psychoanalytic Association, 23*, 713-742.

Solnit, A. J. (1982). Developmental perspectives on self and object constancy. *The Psychoanalytic Study of the Child, 37*, 201-217.

Taylor, C. (1984). Design for living. *The New York Review of Books*, November 22, pp. 52, 53.

Wollheim, R. (1984). *The thread of life*. Cambridge: Harvard University Press.

Theoretical Considerations

CHAPTER ONE

Object Constancy, Individuality, and Internalization

JOHN B. McDEVITT
MARGARET S. MAHLER

I.

The attainment of a certain degree of object constancy, the achievement of a definite individuality, and a more enduring development of psychic structure—these are the three major tasks of the fourth and final subphase (from 24 to 36 months) from the point of view of the separation–individuation process. Behavioral data obtained in a research study of the separation-individuation process (Mahler, Pine, & Bergman, 1975; McDevitt, 1975a; Pine & Furer, 1963) provide the basis for inferences about the intrapsychic processes underlying each of these tasks.

Our primary aim will be to examine the beginning attainment of object and self constancy. An essential aspect of this examination will be a discussion of internalization and of the development of psychic structure.

Most authors believe that "libidinal" object constancy (Hartmann, 1952) is attained between 6 and 18 months of age (Cobliner, 1967; Fraiberg, 1969; A. Freud, 1965; Gouin-Décarie, 1965; Hoffer, 1952, 1955; Nagera, 1966; Spitz, 1965, 1966). Those who place it early in this age range use as their criterion the infant's libidinal attachment to the love object; those who place it at a later point add the establishment of some form of mental representation of the love object, employing Piaget's criteria for the emergence of the mental representation of inanimate objects at about 18 months of age.

In our view, however, "libidinal" object constancy only begins to be attained in the *3rd* year of life (Mahler, 1963, 1965, 1966, 1968; Mahler *et al.*,

Reprinted by permission from *The Course of Life: Psychoanalytic Contributions toward Understanding Personality Development* (Vol. I: *Infancy and Early Childhood*), S. I. Greenspan & G. H. Pollock (Eds.), Adelphi, MD: Mental Health Study Center, NIMH, 1980, pp. 407–423.

1975; McDevitt, 1975a). Although it is based on the child's libidinal attachment to the mother and on the cognitive achievement of person permanence and the symbolic function (Bell, 1970; Kaplan, 1972; Piaget & Inhelder, 1969), its eventual establishment depends on the gradual *internalization* of a constant, positively cathected image of the mother.

The basic difference between these two points of view is that the former sees the libidinally cathected, inner image of the external object as existing in the infant's cognitive or representational world, whereas the latter sees it as becoming internalized as a part of the structural organization of the psychic apparatus (Meissner, 1977; Rapaport, 1967). The cognitive or representational world constitutes an intrapsychic map of the external world; the internal world refers to the organization and integration of the intrapsychic structures themselves (Meissner, 1977; Sandler & Rosenblatt, 1962).

Since different aspects of object constancy emerge at different times, however, it may be profitable to look at the attainment of object constancy as a continuing process involving both precursors and degrees rather than as a specific stage in development. In this case both points of view are applicable to its development. We might say that object constancy has its origins in infancy, begins to be attained in the 3rd year, continues to develop throughout childhood and adolescence, and in all probability is rarely completely attained (McDevitt, 1975a).

According to the second viewpoint, only in the 3rd year do existing, cognitively stable, internal representations become *functionally* available to the child. They become functionally available as a result of an adequate resolution of the rapprochement crisis that occurs between 18 and 24 months. This resolution is brought about primarily by internalization. As a consequence, the mother can now be substituted for during her physical absence, at least in part, by the presence of an *internal* image that remains relatively stable irrespective of the state of instinctual need or inner discomfort. She will not be rejected (hated) or exchanged for another, even when she no longer provides satisfaction or when she is absent, provided the absence is not prolonged.

Object constancy implies several achievements: (1) A primarily positive attachment to the maternal representation has resulted from a reduction in the interpersonal and intrapsychic conflicts characteristic of the rapprochement crisis; (2) the "good" and "bad" aspects of the maternal representation have been united into a single representation, which brings about a lessening of ambivalence and a diminished tendency to regression and splitting of the object representation (Mahler, 1968; Mahler *et al.*, 1975; McDevitt, 1975a); and (3) "the maternal image has become intrapsychically available to the child in the same way that the actual mother had been libidinally available—for sustenance, comfort, and love" (Mahler, 1968, p. 222). There now exists a maternal representation, which is invested predominantly with libidinal as opposed to aggressive cathexis. Disappointment and rage become tempered and are tolerated better, since they are now counteracted to a greater degree by memories of the mother's loving as well as frustrating behavior (Pine, 1975).

These advances in the toddler's representational world are brought about by predominantly favorable identifications and introjections in his "internal," structural world (Hartmann, 1939; Meissner, 1973; Rapaport, 1967; Sandler & Rosenblatt, 1962; Schafer, 1968). These internalizations, to be discussed later, are, in our view, the most important determinants of the beginning attainment of object constancy.

II.

The gradual attainment of object constancy allows the senior toddler to tolerate his mother's absences for longer periods of time during the fourth subphase (24 to 36 months), provided he is in familiar surroundings. In fact, in our nursery-like research setting, the senior toddlers often preferred to play in the toddler playroom, leaving their mothers behind in the infant room.

When the child at this age chooses to play at some distance from his mother, he does not show the same lack of concern for her whereabouts characteristic of the practicing subphase (from 9 to 15 months). At that time (sensorimotor levels four and five) he organized reality by constructing the broad categories of action that are the schemes of the permanent object, space, time, and causality, substructures of the notions that will later correspond to them (Piaget & Inhelder, 1969). The child organized his universe on this practical level, and his mother's presence was taken for granted both in a sensorimotor and sensoriaffective way, unless the need for her arose by reason of hurt, frustration, or absence. She was experienced in a generalized, as opposed to a particularized, way at this time, prior to the acute awareness of her separateness in the rapprochement subphase (from 15 to 19 months) (Lichtenberg, 1977; McDevitt, 1977). By contrast in the fourth subphase (from 24 to 36 months), the toddler is very much aware of where his mother is and may have some idea of what she is doing; yet this awareness does not give rise to the concern over his mother's whereabouts that was present during the differentiation subphase (5 to 9 months) because of the infant's primitive self–object differentiation and during the rapprochement subphase (from 15 to 24 months), at which time, as will be discussed, the junior toddler becomes acutely aware of himself and undergoes a cognitive and affective decentering process (Piaget & Inhelder, 1969) in which he becomes acutely aware of his separateness, loneliness, and helplessness.

In the fourth subphase, when the mother chooses to leave the senior toddler for a brief time, he is better able to tolerate her absence. For example, if a child busily engaged in play is asked where his mother is or whether he misses her, he will usually provide a simple answer without needing to seek her out. The actual mother who served as a secure base from which to explore in the practicing subphase is now increasingly represented by a secure and stable mental image. The toddler is thus able to engage in a variety of activities indepedent of the actual mother (McDevitt, 1975a). By the end of the 3rd year of life, a sufficient degree of object constancy has ordinarily been attained for the child to tolerate separation well enough to be ready to enter nursery school and even to benefit by doing so (A. Freud, 1965).

The beginning attainment of object constancy contributes to other changes in the senior toddler. His sense of well-being is enhanced and there is a shift from self-centered, demanding, clinging behaviors to more mature, ego-determined object relations (A. Freud, 1965). He shows more consistent expressions of affection, trust, and confidence; has a greater capacity for empathy and concern; and is able to play cooperatively. In time these ego contributions to object constancy will lead to the development of mature object relations by a process akin to sublimation (Sandler & Joffe, 1966). The love object will come to be esteemed, valued, and treated with consideration.

III.

The establishment of object constancy is a slow, complex, multidetermined process. The capacity to maintain and to utilize effectively a stable mental representation of the libidinal object is the product of an interdependent relationship between the maturation, modulation, and fusion of libidinal and aggressive drives; the development of the ego, including the perceptual and memory apparatuses and the defensive and adaptive functions; and the real experiences of gratification and frustration in the child's life, particularly the degree of emotional availability of the mother and the quality of the mother–child interaction (McDevitt, 1975a). On the basis of these developments, particularly the latter, favorable identifications and introjections come into being.

We will mention only briefly some of the essential phase-specific, interdependent determinants of the development of object constancy that occur prior to the rapprochement crisis (for a fuller description including illustrative observational data, see Mahler *et al.*, 1975; McDevitt, 1975a). These include:

1. The occurrence of a specific libidinal attachment to the mother at approximately 5 months of age, indicating that a primitive "recognition memory" of the mother's face has been established on basis of pleasurable past experiences. Under favorable conditions, this attachment will grow and deepen as the child ages.
2. The establishment of trust and confidence in the mother through the regularly occurring relief of need tension. This has its onset in the late symbiotic phase and the differentiation subphase (from 5 to 9 months)

by way of gratifying experiences with the symbiotic, part object. In the course of the separation–individuation process, this relief is gradually attributed to the need-satisfying whole object (the mother) and is then transferred by means of internalization to the intrapsychic representation of the mother and to psychic structure (Mahler *et al.*, 1975).

3. The occurrence of satisfactory progress in the invariant, autonomous sequences in cognitive development during and following the sensorimotor phase (Piaget & Inhelder, 1969) and adequate development of concomitant levels of memory organization and mental representation (Kaplan, 1972). The mother is remembered from 3 to 5 months at times of recognition, from at least 8 months at times of biological and psychological need states, and at 15 to 18 months as the consequence of evocative memory with relative autonomy from external stimuli or internal need (Fraiberg, 1969; McDevitt, 1975a; Piaget & Inhelder, 1969).

4. The acquisition of such ego functions as reality testing, secondary-process thinking, sublimation, and neutralization, and tolerance for frustration, anxiety, and ambivalence.

5. The establishment of identifications ranging from primitive precursors in the form of merging and mirroring to later selective ego identifications. During the symbiotic phase mutual cueing between mother and child creates an indelibly imprinted configuration (Mahler, 1968) that becomes the *leitmotif* for the infant's becoming the child of his particular mother (Lichtenstein, 1961). Subsequent identifications both modify the sense of self and psychic structure and enrich object relations (McDevitt, 1977).

The strength of the attachment to the mother, the degree of trust and confidence, and the success of early identifications are necessary conditions for the resolution of the rapprochement crisis. Satisfactory resolution of this crisis is essential for the beginning attainment of object and self constancy in the fourth subphase (24 to 36 months).

IV.

The rapprochement crisis (18 to 24 months) occurs at a time when the toddler's cognitive, motor, and emotional development brings about a more precise awareness of the self as differentiated from the object and a more precise demarcation of self and object representations. The mother, the self, body parts, feelings and wishes, prohibitions, as well as complex relations among these, now become capable of mental representation and persist in the mind for progressively longer periods of time (McDevitt, 1975a). The junior toddler not only recognizes that he and his mother are separate beings, but he also begins to recognize that there are causes of events that exist outside himself, quite independent of his needs and wishes (Piaget & Inhelder, 1969).

On the one hand, the toddler wants to fully exercise his new-found feelings of autonomy and independence; on the other hand, he painfully feels the loss of his former sense of omnipotence and is distressed by his relative helplessness. Although he wants to share toys and activities with his mother, the toddler also shows an increasing possessiveness and jealousy of both his mother and inanimate objects, competing for and defending both as demonstrated by his frequent use of the word "mine."

The toddler cannot always have his mother's attention, the toys he desires, or the space he would like to occupy; he may become jealous of the interest his mother pays to siblings or other children. Forced to limit the toddler's activities and demands, the mother cannot restore his former sense of omnipotence, nor is she able to relieve his sense of aloneness and helplessness. The junior toddler comes to feel hurt, frustrated, and angry with his mother. As a result he is negativistic and provocative, or he clings helplessly to his mother.

It is at this time in the toddler's development, which coincides with the anal phase, that we see more focused, more active, more intentional, more differentiated, and more lasting expressions of object-directed hostile aggression (McDevitt, 1975a, 1978). At the same time we see the clear-cut onset of ambivalence. Angry thoughts and feelings now continue beyond the situation in which they originated. Conflicts no longer simply flare up and disappear; they seem to persist in the child's mind for longer periods of time whether the mother is present or absent, since by this age the mother can be brought to mind and remembered for increasingly longer periods of time, even when she is absent. Interpersonal conflicts begin to be transferred from the child's outer world to his internal, intrapsychic world. Anxiety and possibly aggression begin to be generated internally (McDevitt, 1971, 1975b, 1978).

At such times when aggressive forces outweigh libidinal forces, the toddler's representation of the mother becomes unstable. He experiences separation distress, attempts to maintain the stability of the object representation by coercion and by repeated contact with the mother, and may use the mechanism of "splitting of the object representation." When ambivalence and anxiety are intense, identification with and introjection of the "good" mother are not possible.

V.

If the toddler is fortunate in having a reasonably good relationship with his mother and other favorable conditions for development, he will proceed to higher levels of object and self constancy during the slow course of the resolution of the rapprochement crisis during the fourth subphase. Positive identifications with the parents are essential elements in this resolution. The junior toddler, for example, gradually resolves the actual and intrapsychic conflicts between his own wishes and his parents' prohibitions, as well as his feeling of helplessness and his wish to please his parents, by selectively identifying with them. If he is successful in these efforts, object constancy, individuation, sound secondary narcissism, and the development of psychic structure progress rapidly.

As we mentioned earlier, another essential determinant of object constancy is the intrapsychic quality of the maternal representation—one that produces in the child a sense of security and comfort, just as the actual mother had in the past. By "intrapsychic" or "internal" we refer not only to the "goodness" of the maternal representations and the maternal introjects but, most importantly, to their assimilation into the self-representation and into psychic structure by the process of identification. By means of identification, sufficient psychic structure is built up to permit the senior toddler to function to a limited extent independently and separately from his mother (see also Kohut, 1971; Tolpin, 1971).

The mother's optimal emotional availability is extremely important in the third subphase. It reduces ambivalence and interpersonal and intrapsychic conflicts. "It is the mother's love of the toddler and the acceptance of his ambivalence that enable the toddler to cathect his self-representation with neutralized energy" (Mahler, 1968). The relationship with the father becomes extremely important at this time (Abelin, 1971; Greenacre, 1966; Loewald, 1951).

The *father* seems to be associated with external reality, and successful autonomous functioning, rather than being a source of constraint and frustration or a source of maternal comforting—both of which may threaten the development of the child's initiative. The junior toddler's intense ambivalence and regressive tendencies seem to be specifically linked to the mother, whereas the father appears to be experienced as a powerful, "uncontaminated," helpful ally. He serves to dilute the ambivalence of the mother–child relation and helps the toddler to fight against regressive tendencies by encouraging autonomous development and serving as an important person with whom to identify. It may be that a satisfactory relation with the father is of major importance for the resolution of the ambivalent tie to the mother, and for the achievement of individuation.

If the toddler is not so fortunate in his development, and the rapprochement crisis leads to intense ambivalence and splitting of the object world into "good" and "bad," the maternal representation may be internalized as an unassimilated, dissociated, foreign body, as a hostile, "bad" introject. This outcome is most likely when (1) the love object is disappointing and unavailable or excessively unreliable and intrusive; (2) the child experiences the realization of his helplessness too abruptly and too painfully, resulting in a too-sudden deflation of his sense of omnipotence; (3) there has been an excess of cumulative or shock trauma (Mahler *et al.*, 1975); and (4) the child, more likely the little girl at this age, experiences to an unusual degree the narcissistic hurt of the castration reaction (Galenson & Roiphe, 1971; Roiphe, 1968). Under these conditions the behaviors characteristic of the rapprochement subphase more or less persist. They include excessive separation anxiety, depressive mood, passivity, and inhibitions on the one hand and demandingness, coerciveness, possessiveness, envy, and temper outbursts on the other.

In some instances the rapprochement crisis may persist as an unassimilated intrapsychic conflict. It may exist as an unfavorable fixation point, interfering with the development and the resolution of the Oedipus complex (Mahler *et al.*, 1975; McDevitt, 1967, 1971).

It does seem that hate as a form of aggression and as an aspect of ambivalence begins (or at least has its precursors) during the rapprochement (which encompasses the anal phase) and the fourth subphases (McDevitt, 1978). Although hate remains anaclitic longer than love (A. Freud, 1972), it now begins to persist in the mind as an enduring emotional reaction, tied to some degree to the maternal representation as is love. If hate is excessive, however, it will outweigh libido and hamper the development of self and object constancy. The toddler is now aware that the same person who gratifies him also frustrates him at other times. Frustration, particularly excessive frustration, turns interpersonal conflicts into temporary intrapsychic conflicts, since the ego now becomes increasingly intolerant of the simultaneous presence of incompatible feelings. As a consequence of these intrapsychic conflicts, we see the mechanisms of splitting and repression (Mahler & McDevitt, 1968; McDevitt, 1971, 1975a).

VI.

Although behavioral references are more elusive, the establishment of the self and self constancy follows a course of development similar to that of the beginning attainment of object constancy. For this reason the determinants contributing to the beginning attainment of object constancy prior to, during, and following the rapprochement subphase will not be repeated (see sections III, IV, and V). To these "similar" determinants, however, we must add more specific determinants. Of necessity this will involve some repetition of material in the previous chapter, although from a slightly different perspective.

If we compare the cathexis of the mother and of the self, we can readily see rather profound differences. The mother is specifically cathected with libido from 3 to 5 months at times of recognition, from at least 8 months on when she is remembered as a result of biological and psychological need states, and at approximately 14 to 18 months as the consequence of evocative memory. With respect to the self, the situation must be quite different. From the earliest months the organism that is to become the self must experience a variety of feeling states along the pleasure–unpleasure continuum within the framework of the mother–child dual unity. For example, in the research study of the separation–individuation process, from 3 to 4 months the children moved, stared at, examined, played with, and mouthed their fingers and hands, sometimes their toes and feet, with considerable interest and involvement. They were showing an increasing cathexis of and becoming more familiar with body parts. This was not dissimilar to the way in which they examined body parts and appendages (bracelet, brooch, etc.) of the mother. At the same time their vocalizations seemed to take on an affective and communicative meaning (unintended at this age), such as pleasure, cooing, or fussiness.

By 4 to 5 months an even greater attention to body parts (including those in the mirror) was observed along with a greater attention toward others visually and tactilely ("customs inspection") and to bright and colorful objects. The children began a process of observing the movement and the touching of their own body parts as they were observed in the mirror (similar to "customs inspection").

With the exception of the mirror image, the novelty of examining their own body parts had worn off by 8 months of age. Even in the mirror there was more interest in coordinated movements and facial expressions than in isolated body parts. All of the children became quite excited and smiled broadly when they saw and studied their mirror image. Their excited movements and smiles as seen by themselves in the mirror were reflected back to themselves, acting as a continuing source of stimulation.

These observations fit in with the hypothesis that the core of the beginning self is feelings within or about parts of one's own body (Greenacre, 1958; Mahler, 1958, 1968; Rose, 1966). The beginnings of these core feelings are not observable, however.

With the onset of the differentiation subphase (5 to 9 months), we inferred on the basis of our observations the experience of more discrete feelings associated with the beginning awareness of body parts as vaguely distinct from the part object. With the object there are at first positive or negative feelings at times of recognition. Within the baby there are from the beginning constant positive or negative internal feelings associated with sensorimotor activities and sensoriaffective states. These may or may not occur at times of interaction with the mother. The expression of these inner feelings is the main form of communication with the mother. They make it possible for her to physically and emotionally care for her infant.

The other major framework of self-orientation (Spiegel, 1959) is the gradual demarcation of the body-self from the object world. As the infant continues to experience and experiment with his body and body parts, he slowly distinguishes them from the body parts of others (parents, siblings, other children, dolls, and his own mirror image). From 12 to 18 months he slowly becomes aware that the body parts he sees in the mirror are his own, and by 18 months he is aware that the child he sees is indeed himself.

When his experiences in self-stimulation and self-movement occur side by side with the experiences of being touched, moved, and handled by his mother, he slowly becomes aware that the experiences are different. The experience of touching his own body is not the same as the experience of being touched by his mother. Similarly, the experience of moving part of his own body is not the same as having that part moved by his mother. In addition, the infant begins to perceive dimly the difference between the relief of inner tension by his mother and his own effort to comfort himself. Games with his mother also serve to delineate the infant's own body image from that of the mother. In these games we see comparative scanning, checking back, and, a little later, passive and then active peek-a-boo (Kleeman, 1967; Mahler *et al.*, 1975). These activities contribute to the building up of a self–body image, as do cuddling, molding, and stiffening in the mother's arms.

Later, in the practicing subphase, the child's encounters with the inanimate objects in the environment firm up and delineate his body–self boundaries. At the same time, the mother, in caring for her infant, libidinizes the practicing child's body boundaries.

The innate, maturational pressure toward individuation and autonomy is seen most clearly during the practicing subphase. As the infant explores his animate and inanimate world with all of his sensory modalities, he learns more and more about himself and his relation to the outside world. He learns that he can extend his arms and legs as he propels himself in space. He experiences pleasure or pain as he touches and explores, or he passively experiences the outer world as hard, unyielding, and at times hurtful. These experiences, along with the infant's identifications, contribute to the schema of the developing body and mental self. The nature of this schema at this age is practical, preverbal, sensorimotor, and sensoriaffective.

In the late practicing and rapprochement subphases, the toddler not only continues to build up a mental image of his own body; he also begins to develop an awareness of his mental self by a process similar to that described in sections III and IV. In addition to the development of representational thinking, this awareness depends on his ability to move toward and away from his mother; his distress at her disappearance, coupled with the realization that she will return, especially when he calls; and his mother's response or lack of response to his feelings, wishes, and activities. By the rapprochement subphase he clearly takes over the possession of his own body. Autonomy becomes all important; he resents the passive position, as in being diapered. A certain degree of negativisim is necessary to prevent regression and maintain the toddler's sense of autonomy.

During the third and fourth subphases, the integration of body parts coalesces, and there is an advance from the previous practical sensorimotor and sensoriaffective experience of the body self and the part object to a total (whole) representation of the mental self and of the object. This differentiation of the self and the object begins early in the rapprochement subphase. It can be inferred from the behaviors characteristic of this subphase described earlier, from children's play and attitudes to each other and from their imaginative play with dolls.

By 18 months of age or earlier the toddler has solidified the cognitive aspects of the sense of self. He begins to speak of himself in the first person or by using his own name. He recognizes himself as a person in the mirror and recognizes both himself and his mother in photographs. He distinguishes other people from himself by name, understands the pronouns "me" and "you," assigns ownership to various objects, and is conscious of himself as a person, as an "I." By the age of 2 years, he can speak in short sentences, using pronouns. By his third birthday, he has acquired hundreds, even thousands, of words, and he uses nearly all the syntactical forms of language in sentences of 12 to 15 words. By learning the names of things, he is able to internalize his environment symbolically so as to make possible its imaginative manipulation.

Not only has the senior toddler integrated more coherently body parts of both the self and the object, but he has also integrated these with his activities and the feelings, for example, "good" and "bad," that accompany these activities. By this time feelings and moods have become much more complex. For example, whereas the primary mood during the practicing subphase is elation, the toddler's mood during the rapprochement subphase is variable—frequently disgruntled, irritable, and depressed (Mahler, 1966).

By the fourth subphase the senior toddler's evolving sense of self includes his growing perceptions, his feelings and experiences, his capacities, and his awareness of his body and its functions. He likes to show off, to draw attention to himself, to seek admiration. He can now begin to reason and to play more imaginatively. There is more complex fantasy play, role play, and make-believe. At the same time play becomes more purposeful and constructive; it includes many detailed observations about the real world (Mahler, 1963).

With the firm establishment of free, upright locomotion and of representational intelligence (which culminates in symbolic play and speech during the rapprochement subphase), we see the final stage of the hatching process. At this time the toddler reaches the first level of individual entity.

As mentioned before, the establishment of a sense of self and self constancy is a slow, complex, multidetermined process, involving determinants similar to those described earlier for the establishment of object constancy. Of particular importance, of course, are the child's interactions and identifications with his parents, the development of progressively more complex levels of memory organization and mental representation, and the cognitive acquisition of the symbolic representation of the self.

How the senior toddler comes to feel about himself will also be determined by his interactions and identifications with his parents. For example, an important source of narcissistic libido, the quantity and quality of libidinization of the body–ego or body–self, is dependent on both early narcissistic supplies and the internalization of parental attitudes toward the child. In addition, each subphase makes its particular contribution to healthy or pathological narcissism (Mahler & Kaplan, 1977). While narcissistic reserves are built up from without by subphase-adequate mothering, the autonomous achievements of the practicing subphase are the main source of narcissistic enhancements from within. These include self-love, primitive valuation of the infant's accomplishments, and omnipotence. There is marked narcissistic gratification in practicing and exploring, in mastery and learning, in competence and effectiveness.

During the rapprochement subphase narcissism is particularly vulnerable as a consequence of the conflicts characteristic of the rapprochement crisis. If conditions for development are favorable, the senior toddler's realistic abilities and achievements, improved reality testing, and secondary-process functioning along with successful identifications enable him to overcome the sense of separateness, helplessness, and loss of omnipotence brought on by the rapprochement crisis. Successful self-assertion in the world of reality—as opposed to magical solutions of closeness, merging, or sameness—contributes significantly to a more realistic and satisfactory appraisal of the self in the fourth subphase and therefore to sound secondary narcissism, self constancy, and cohesiveness of the self.

Under favorable conditions of development the toddler may emerge from the rapprochement struggle by means of selective ego identifications with realistic self-esteem and self constancy. If conditions are unfavorable, however, hostile introjects may predominate over identifications, and the toddler may get caught up in an uncertainty about his identity as a viable separate being. Such uncertainty may be the effect of insufficient separation of the self-representation, particularly in terms of differentiation of self boundaries. As a result, fusion, or reengulfment, remains a threat against which the child continues to defend himself beyond the 3rd year (Mahler *et al.*, 1975). An unresolved severe rapprochement crisis leads not only to an uncertain sense of identity but also to diminished self-esteem. Aggression is unleashed in such a way as to inundate or sweep away the "good" object and with it the "good" self-representation (Mahler, 1971, 1972), as is indicated by early severe temper tantrums and by extreme attempts to coerce mother and father to function as quasi-external egos. Marked ambivalence continues to mar smooth development not only toward object constancy but also toward sound secondary narcissism and self constancy.

By the end of the third subphase, the child has accomplished the first level of identity formation. He has become aware of himself as a separate and viable entity. By the end of the 2nd year he also begins to accomplish the second level of identity formation: He becomes aware of his gender-defined self-entity as a boy or a girl. This level of identity formation will not be fully attained, however, until the phallic–oedipal phase.

Whereas both sexes enjoy the thrust of activity characteristic of the practicing phase, the rapprochement crisis may be more severe and may have a different quality in girls than in boys, since the discovery of the anatomic sexual difference, which occurs sometime between 16 and 21 months, is a much greater narcissistic blow to the little girl than to the boy. The discovery of the penis confronts the girl with something she lacks. This diminishes her self-esteem and makes her more vulnerable to abrupt deflation of her omnipotence. It also coincides with the emergence of the affect of envy. Early penis envy may account for the persistence of this affect in some girls.

For these reasons the task of becoming a separate individual seems more difficult for girls than for boys. They blame and are disappointed in their mothers; yet they make even more demands on them and become ambivalently tied to them. Boys, on the other hand, seem to be faced with castration anxiety only later, toward the end of the 2nd and in the 3rd year. They find it easier to function separately, to turn to the outside world or to their own bodies for pleasure and satisfaction, and to shift more readily to father as someone with whom to identify (Mahler *et al.*, 1975; see also Galenson & Roiphe, 1976).

VII.

In the two main tracks of the separation–individuation process, individuation versus intrapsychic separation, the ego's structuralization and the awareness of separateness are parallel developments. The processes of structuralization and internalization are closely related, and both depend on the quality of the child's object relations. These relations are the matrix out of which drives such as psychic representations and the ego differentiate (Loewald, 1971).

In this process the infant's view of his own and his parents' omnipotence must be replaced during the rapprochement crisis and its resolution by realistic achievement and realistic self-esteem, by a beginning shift from the pleasure to the reality principle and from the primary to the secondary process. Autonomous functioning ensures the beginning investment of the self with sound secondary narcissism, allows the ego apparatuses to attain secondary autonomy, and adds a measure of sublimation to the cathexis of the object world (Mahler *et al.*, 1975).

With the resolution of the rapprochement crisis, ambivalence diminishes, the "good" and "bad" maternal objects are unified into a single representation, and the defense mechanism of splitting is replaced by that of repression. For the first time we see intrapsychic conflicts and transient neurotic symptom formation (McDevitt, 1971; Nagera, 1966).

Extensive and enduring changes occur in psychic structure during the resolution of the rapprochement crisis. Not only do we see neurotic symptoms for the first time; the existence of sufficient psychic structure now makes child psychoanalysis possible, probably permits prediction with a greater reliability than previously, and helps to explain why reconstruction in the analytic situation, based on analytic data, can, as a rule, go back only as far as the rapprochement subphase.

Jacobson (1964) speaks of a compromise achieved by selective identification between the child's need to retain the symbiotic ties by aggressive, narcissistic expansion and independent ego functioning. She adds that under the influence of oedipal rivalry this conflict reaches its first climax toward the end of the oedipal period and is then resolved by superego formation (p. 50). We are suggesting that this same conflict reaches an earlier climax in the rapprochement subphase and is slowly resolved by the formation of psychic structure in the id, ego, and superego precursors. The identifications used to resolve the rapprochement crisis are probably forerunners to those used to resolve oedipal conflicts.

There now seems to be a clear differentiation not only between the self- and object representations but also between the id and the ego. The ego has acquired many functions: intentionality, early forms of postponement and inhibition of discharge, a resistivity against regression, and the beginning tolerance of frustrations, anxiety, and ambivalence.

There is also an integration of the "good" and "bad" aspects of the part object into one total (whole) object as well as an integration of body parts and "good" and "bad" aspects of the self into a whole self. Furthermore, during the fourth subphase there is an integration of self and object on a higher psychobiological and social level of development far removed from the earlier symbiosis of self and object. The self is experienced as an integral part of a larger whole, the family and society. This higher level of integration along with the development of object and self constancy relieves the toddler of threats of helplessness and loneliness characteristic of the rapprochement crisis. As a rule he no longer has to struggle against the danger of regressive symbiotic reengulfment. He has achieved internally and externally a close relationship with his love objects, while at the same time, he has achieved autonomy, individuation, self constancy, and cohesiveness of the self.

VIII.

In this chapter inferences have been made about some of the developmental steps that contribute to the gradual attainment of object and self constancy— in terms of both the cognitive development of stable object and self-representations and the stability of the cathexis and quality of these representations. These steps are brought about by the changing nature of the libidinal–narcissistic and aggressive cathexis of the love object and the self, the progressively more complex levels of memory organization and mental representation, and the emergence of numerous ego functions, particularly internalization.

The attainment of object and self constancy is a continuing process in the sense of being a developmental progression; yet the emergence of each aspect of development relevant to their attainment is phase specific. The most important of these aspects is the capacity to resolve the ambivalence and the "splitting" characteristic of the rapprochement crisis.

Mental health in preoedipal development depends on this resolution and on the continuing ability of the child to retain or restore his self-esteem in the context of relative libidinal object constancy. In the fourth subphase both inner structures—libidinal object constancy as well as a unified self-image based on true ego identifications—should have their inception. These advances may be disrupted, however, by struggles around toilet training and, particularly, by castration reactions. The latter are not only a blow to the narcissism of the little girl and a danger to the little boy's body integrity; they also reactivate fears of object loss (McDevitt, 1971, 1975a).

Under favorable conditions for development, a firm libidinal–narcissistic cathexis of object and self-representations has been established by the fourth subphase, the ego has exerted substantial control over the aggressive drive, and the "good" and "bad" aspects of the love object as well as the "good" and "bad" aspects of the self have become united in one concept. Major steps along the line of self–object objectivization, differentiation, and integration have been taken, and both the love object and the self are now perceived and represented in closer accordance with reality.

When conditions for development are not favorable, the rapprochement crisis may not be resolved satisfactorily. It may become a fixation point, with the persistence of excess ambivalence, "splitting," and intrapsychic conflict. As a result, the attainment of object and self constancy and the development of psychic structure are impaired, the resolution of oedipal conflicts is made more difficult, and either neurotic symptoms of the narcissistic variety may develop (McDevitt, 1967, 1971), or borderline symptoms may occur in latency and adolescence (Mahler *et al.*, 1975).

It seems to be inherent in the human condition that not even the most normally endowed child, with the most optimally available mother, can weather the separation–individuation process without crisis, come out unscathed by the rapprochement struggle, and enter the oedipal phase without developmental difficulty. The infantile neurosis may have its obligatory precursor, if not its first manifestation, in the rapprochement crisis (Mahler *et al.*, 1975). This crisis often continues far into the 3rd year and may overlap the phallic–oedipal phase, in which case it interferes with repression and with the successful passing of the Oedipus complex (see A. Freud, 1965; McDevitt, 1971; Nagera, 1966).

ACKNOWLEDGMENTS

This chapter is based in part on research supported by NIMH Grant MH-08238, USPHS, Bethesda, Maryland, and FFRP Grant C69-458, Foundation for Research in Psychiatry, New Haven, Connecticut, Margaret S. Mahler, Principal Investigator, John B. McDevitt, Co-Principal Investigator.

REFERENCES

Abelin, E. L. (1971). The role of the father in the separation–individuation process. In J. B. McDevitt & C. F. Settlage (Eds.), *Separation–individuation: Essays in honor of Margaret S. Mahler* (pp. 229–253). New York: International Universities Press.

Bell, S. M. (1970). The development of the concept of object as related to infant–mother attachment. *Child Development, 41,* 291–311.

Cobliner, W. G. (1967). Psychoanalysis and the Geneva School of genetic psychology: Parallels and counterparts. *International Journal of Psychiatry, 3,* 82–116.

Fraiberg, S. (1969). Object constancy and mental representation. *The Psychoanalytic Study of the Child, 24,* 9–47.

Freud, A. (1965). *Normality and pathology in childhood: The writings of Anna Freud,* 6. New York: International Universities Press.

Freud, A. (1972). Comments on aggression. *International Journal of Psycho-Analysis, 53,* 163–171.

Galenson, E., & Roiphe, H. (1971). The impact of early sexual discovery on mood, defensive organization, and symbolization. *The Psychoanalytic Study of the Child, 26,* 195–216.

Galenson, E., & Roiphe, H. (1976). Some suggested revisions concerning early female development. *Journal of the American Psychoanalytic Association, 24* (Suppl.), 29–57.

Gouin-Décarie, T. (1965). *Intelligence and affectivity in early childhood.* New York: International Universities Press.

Greenacre, P. (1958). Early physical determinants in the development of the sense of identity. *Journal of the American Psychoanalytic Association, 6,* 612–627.

Greenacre, P. (1966). Problems of overidealization of the analyst and of analysis. *The Psychoanalytic Study of the Child, 21,* 192–212.

Hartmann, J. (1939). *Ego psychology and the problem of adaptation.* New York: International Universities Press, 1958.

Hartmann, J. (1952). The mutual influences in the development of ego and id. In *Essays on ego psychology* (pp. 155–182). New York: International Universities Press, 1964.

Hoffer, W. (1952). The mutual influences in the development of ego and id: Earliest stages. *The Psychoanalytic Study of the Child, 7,* 31–41.

Hoffer, W. (1955). *Psychoanalysis: Practical and research aspects. The Abraham Flexner lectures* (Series 12). Baltimore: Vanderbilt University.

Jacobson, E. (1964). *The self and the object world.* New York: International Universities Press.

Kaplan, L. (1972). Object constancy in the light of Piaget's vertical decalage. *Bulletin of the Menninger Clinic, 36,* 322–334.

Kleeman, J. A. (1967). The peek-a-boo game: Part I. Its origins, meanings, and related phenomena in the first year. *The Psychoanalytic Study of the Child, 22,* 239–279.

Kohut, H. (1971). *The analysis of the self.* New York: International Universities Press.

Lichtenberg, J. D. (1977, December). *Factors in the development of the sense of the object.* Paper presented at the panel on object relations theory, meeting of the American Psychoanalytic Association, New York.

Lichtenstein, H. (1961). Identity and sexuality: A study of their interrelationship in man. *Journal of the American Psychoanalytic Association, 9,* 179–260.

Loewald, H. W. (1951). Ego and reality. *International Journal of Psycho-Analysis, 32,* 10–18.

Loewald, H. W. (1971). On motivation and instinct theory. *The Psychoanalytic Study of the Child, 26,* 91–128.

Mahler, M. S. (1958). On two crucial phases of integration of the sense of identity: Separation–individuation and bisexual identity (Abstract in panel on problems of identity, D. L. Rubinfine, reporter, 1957). *Journal of the American Psychoanalytic Association, 6,* 131–142.

Mahler, M. S. (1963). Thought about development and individuation. *The Psychoanalytic Study of the Child, 18,* 307–324.

Mahler, M. S. (1965). On the significance of the normal separation–individuation phase: With reference to research in symbiotic child psychosis. In M. Schur (Ed.), *Drives, affects, behavior* (Vol. 2, pp. 161–169). New York: International Universities Press.

Mahler, M. S. (1966). Notes on the development of basic moods: The depressive affect. In R. M. Loewenstein, L. M. Newman, M. Schur, & A. J. Solnit (Eds.), *Psychoanalysis—A general psychology: Essays in honor of Heinz Hartmann* (pp. 152–168). New York: International Universities Press.

Mahler, M. S. (1968). *On human symbiosis and the vicissitudes of individuation* (Vol. 1: *Infantile psychosis*). New York: International Universities Press.

Mahler, M. S. (1971). A study of the separation–individuation process and its possible application to borderline phenomena in the psycho-analytic situation. *The Psychoanalytic Study of the Child, 26,* 403–424.

Mahler, M. S. (1972). On the first three subphases of the separation–individuation process. *International Journal of Psycho-Analysis, 53,* 333–338.

Mahler, M., & Kaplan L. (1977). Developmental aspects in the assessment of narcissistic and so-called border-line personalities. In P. Hartocollis (Ed.), *Borderline personality disorders* (pp. 71–85). New York: International Universities Press.

Mahler, M., & McDevitt, J. B. (1968). Observations on adaptation and defense *in statu nascendi:* Developmental precursors in the first two years of life. *Psychoanalytic Quarterly, 37,* 1–21.

Mahler, M., Pine F., & Bergman, A. (1975). *The psychological birth of the human infant.* New York: Basic Books.

McDevitt, J. B. (1967). A separation problem in a three-year-old girl. In E. R. Geleerd (Ed.), *The child analyst at work* (pp. 24–58). New York: International Universities Press.

McDevitt, J. B. (1971). Preoedipal determinants of an infantile neurosis. In J. B. McDevitt & C. F. Settlage (Eds.), *Separation–individuation: Essays in honor of Margaret S. Mahler* pp. 201–226). New York: International Universities Press.

McDevitt, J. B. (1975a). Separation–individuation and object constancy. *Journal of the American Psychoanalytic Association, 23,* 713–742.

McDevitt, J. B. (1975b). Psychological disturbances during the first three years of life. In G. H. Wiedeman (Ed.), *Personality development and deviation* (pp. 89–109). New York: International Universities Press.

McDevitt, J. B. (1977, December). *The role of internalization in the development of object relations during the separation–individuation phase.* Paper presented at the panel on object relations theory, meeting of the American Psychoanalytic Association, New York.

McDevitt, J. B. (1978, February). *Separation–individuation and aggression.* Paper presented at the institute on recent advances in patterns of infant development: relevance for late life, Mesa, CA.

Meissner, W. W. (1973). Identification and learning. *Journal of the American Psychoanalytic Association, 21,* 788–816.

Meissner, W. W. (1977, December). *Internalization and object relations.* Paper presented at the panel on object relations theory, meeting of American Psychoanalytic Association, New York.

Nagera, H. (1966). *Early childhood disturbances, the infantile neurosis, and the adulthood disturbances—problems of a developmental psychoanalytical psychology.* New York: International Universities Press.

Piaget, J., & Inhelder, B. (1969). *The psychology of the child.* New York: Basic Books.

Pine, F. (1975). Libidinal object constancy: A theoretical note. *Psychoanalysis and Contemporary Science, 3,* 307–313.

Pine, F., & Furer, M. (1963). Studies of the separation–individuation phase: A methodological overview. *The Psychoanalytic Study of the Child, 18,* 325–342.

Rapaport, D. (1967). A theoretical analysis of the superego concept. In *The collected papers of David Rapaport* (pp. 685–709). New York: Basic Books.

Roiphe, H. (1968). On an early genital phase: With an addendum on genesis. *The Psychoanalytic Study of the Child, 23,* 348–365.

Rose, G. J. (1966). Creative imagination in terms of ego "core" and boundaries. *International Journal of Psycho-Analysis, 47,* 502–509.

Sandler, J., & Joffe, W. G. (1966). On skill and sublimation. *Journal of the American Psychoanalytic Association, 14,* 335–355.

Sandler, J., & Rosenblatt, B. (1962). The concept of the representational world. *The Psychoanalytic Study of the Child, 17,* 128–145.

Schafer, R. (1968). *Aspects of internalization.* New York: International Universities Press.

Speigel, L. A. (1959). The self, the sense of self, and perception. *The Psychoanalytic Study of the Child, 14,* 81–109.

Spitz, R. A. (in collaboration with W. G. Cobliner). (1965). *The first year of life.* New York: International Universities Press.

Spitz, R. A. (1966). Metapsychology and direct infant observation. In R. M. Loewenstein, L. M. Newman, M. Schur, & A. J. Solnit (Eds.), *Psychoanalysis—A general psychology: Essays in honor of Heinz Hartmann* (pp. 123–151). New York: International Universities Press.

Tolpin, M. (1971). On the beginnings of a cohesive self. An application of the concept of transmuting internalization to the study of the transitional object and signal anxiety. *The Psychoanalytic Study of the Child, 26,* 316–352.

CHAPTER TWO

The Earliest Internalizations

W. W. MEISSNER

INTRODUCTION

Recent years have seen an upsurge in interest and study of the earliest levels of infantile experience, particularly the earliest stages of neonatal development. As the pace of such investigation has quickened and deepened, our knowledge about infant behavior has increased manyfold, so that in the current context of our thinking about the beginnings of psychic life we are equipped with a considerable understanding of early patterns of behavior and interaction. Despite these efforts and the knowledge they have gained, our understanding of the beginnings of intrapsychic life remain relatively obscure—this due primarily to the unavoidable gap between the forms of naturalistic external observation employed in studies of infant behavior and our understanding of emerging psychic organization in the later development of the child, when forms of expression (verbal, graphic, motoric, etc.) have become available to the child as vehicles of intentionality and symbolic expression. Consequently, the question as to the origins of the inner world of psychic structure continues to present itself in problematic guise and continually challenges us to deepen our understanding of it.

The key issue in all of this is internalization. The evidence for an emergent psychic organization and for the influence of recognizable internalizations—in a sense more closely analogous to the referential base of these same terms in adult experience—can be found more clearly in the rapprochement crisis of the separation–individuation stage of development and even in fragmentary forms at earlier levels of differentiation and practicing (McDevitt, 1979). The argument of this chapter, however, will suggest that there is a residual gap in our understanding of the development of psychic structure from its earliest inception.

Under the clinical and theoretical impetus of object relations theorists, psychoanalysts have become convinced of the basic principle that the organization and shaping of the individual personality takes place under the significant and guiding influence of the individual's ongoing interaction with significant objects. It is the continuing internalization of aspects of those object relationships that shapes and molds the emergent characteristics of the individual's personality structure. While this principle can be amply validated in later developmental and clinical studies, the question remains open as to its applicability in the very beginnings of the organization and development of intrapsychic life. I will argue here that such internalizations indeed are an aspect of the very earliest levels of infantile experience and development and that without them we have no substantial basis for the understanding of the later development of these same capacities and their consequences in phases of childhood. The question is not whether there are such processes at work in the very beginnings of psychic life, but what is their nature and how do they influence psychic development.

Unfortunately, Freud has not left us very well off in regard to these issues. His views about various forms of internalization were slow to emerge (Meissner, 1970), and the major focus of his interest fell on the origin and patterning of identifications that played a role in and served as the basis of oedipal development. Concern with preoedipal developments was by no means a matter of central interest for him. In fact, he left us with a somewhat uncertain and confused picture of these early oedipal internalizations. His most explicit statement on the subject describes the earliest identification as "the original form of emotional tie with an object" (Freud, 1921). This earliest form of internalization was loosely connected with the infantile level of oral incorporation based on and following the primitive oral model of psychosexual development. This notion of primary identification was used as the basis of understanding the process by which the distinction between inner experience and the outer world was to arise, but at the same time was conceived of as taking place prior to any self–object differentiation.

The focus in the present discussion will be on aspects of psychic development and the patterns of internalization that can be defined and described prior to self–object differentiation. Consequently, in reviewing the literature the emphasis will be on the aspects of the developmental process that illuminate or reflect the underlying patterning of internalizations, and we will limit our consideration to the 1st year of life. By the end of the 1st year, self–object differentiation, in the sense of the differentiation of maternal and self-images, has already been established in the normal course of events, and the child is already well launched into the early stages of separation-individuation.

Some preliminary comments about internalization may be useful at this point. The object relations view of development has impressed on us the realization that the patterning of intrapsychic development depends in part, even in large measure, on the sequence and quality of the infant's object experience. Ultimately, the question has to do with the process by which structure is formed, how it comes into being, how it is modified, and what the role of the relationship with the external object plays in the organization of such intrapsychic structure. Ultimately, our notions of how structure is formed are metaphoric but not entirely so, since our concepts of structure contain immediate reference to specifiable aspects of psychic organization, differentiation, sequencing, patterning, and the enduring qualities and characteristics of the activity of the mind.

In this frame of reference, then, the processes of structuralization and internalization are intimately linked and interdependent. We need to be specific about this understanding of internalization. It does not simply refer to the translation of some element or aspect from the external realm of experience, whether perceptual or otherwise, to the internal realm. Its meaning in the psychoanalytic frame of reference is quite specific and technical. We can accept Roy Schafer's (1968) excellent definition as a useful working definition for the purposes of our inquiry. He writes: "Internalization refers to all those processes by which the subject transforms real or imagined regulatory interaction with his environment, and real or imagined characteristics of his environment, into inner regulations and characteristics" (p. 9).

Some additional clarifications should be made. Certain forms of internal experience do not fall under the aegis of this definition. For example, perceptual processes can be said to give rise to an inner image of an external object, but perception or the cognitive apparatus allied to perception cannot be said to be a form of internalization. By the same token, the complex processing that gives rise to object representations also remains in the cognitive or representational frame of reference and does not yet constitute internalization. While these processes and their products may be "inner" in some sense, in the sense that they constitute some part of the subject's inner world, they have not yet become a part of his functioning self. What is internalized, therefore, by implication has become a part of the structure of the self and has been integrated into the structural organization of the psychic apparatus.

The basic definition here was first formulated by Hartmann and later emphasized by Rapaport (1957), that is, the distinction between the "inner world" and the "internal world." Thus, the inner world was a sort of intrapsychic map of the external world that was interpolated between receptors and effectors and provided a medium through which the ego could regulate its interaction with the external environment. The internal world, by way of distinction, referred to the organization and integration of intrapsychic structures that composed the psychic apparatus. Consequently, the inner world is primarily cognitional and representational and must be carefully distinguished from the internal world which is essentially structural. A similar distinction was made by Sandler and Rosenblatt (1962) in contrasting the significance of the representational world with intrapsychic structure as such.

In this sense, then, internalizations are equivalently structural modifications of the self-system. The status of the concept of the self in psychoanalytic theory is as yet lacking in specificity and definition. However, in terms of the present discussion, I will regard the self-system as part of the internal world such that it can be effectively described in structural terms. In this approach, which is at variance with perhaps the dominant view of the self among psychoanalysts as representational, the self is constituted as a supraordinate intrapsychic organization, epiphenomenal in nature, and includes the familiar tripartite structures as subsystems. Nonetheless, the self is not simply reducible to the functional or structural terms of these suborganizations. Consequently, the self-organization is experienced in terms different from any of the structural subsystems, engenders qualities and functions not simply reducible to the respective functions of the component systems, and serves as a locus for the organization and integration of the functioning of these respective subsystems in which equivalently the whole exceeds the sum of its parts. The self-representation ultimately reflects this structural organization and its component elements, but it does not constitute them (Meissner, 1979).

Thus conceived, it is immediately evident that the self-system arises out of and is shaped in terms of sequential internalizations that take place throughout the course of development. Such internalizations are complex processes that develop out of and reflect the vicissitudes of the developmental matrix at each point of its evolution. Such internalizations then form a channel or a derivative of the integration (or relative lack of integration) of multiple and complex developmental influences. Our effort in the present study is to trace and articulate some of the patterns of influence that are distilled into patterns and sequences of internalization.

NATURE OF THE DEVELOPMENTAL PROCESS

Before we move on to a more specific consideration of aspects of development, a few comments may be made regarding the developmental process itself. From the very beginning, neonatal behavior is organized into distinct and recurrent forms of action. The implicit psychological structure at this level takes the form of reflex schemata that ensure that behavior will be repeated in relatively stable form. As the result of ongoing experience, new schemata are acquired that advance the infant another small step along the pathway of increasing adaptation and interaction with his environment (Wolff, 1963). The emergence and consolidation of such schemata lead in the direction of progressive development and differentiation. Anna Freud (1980) has suggested that when the appropriate constitutional and environmental ingredients are available in optimal degree, development emerges along three lines leading toward a gradual distinction between soma and psyche, between the child's own and the mother's body, and between self and object.

The emphasis in early studies tends to fall on perceptual and sensorimotor development. However, as Sander, Stechler, Julia, and Burns (1971) have noted, the effects of such early learning may not be limited to those dimensions, but may in addition be concerned with establishing overall regulatory mechanisms that pertain to the activity of the infant in relation to his environment and are fundamental to the emerging capacity for adaptive functioning. In this sense the early instability of action patterns regulated only by reflex schemata are enlarged on by the experience of repetition in specific contingencies that arise between various states of the infant and the sequence of particular caretaking activities. Thus, even in the very first days of life the opportunity is provided for establishing certain stable patterns in the interaction between infant and caretaker (Sander *et al.*, 1971).

The path of development is quite variable, however, and manifests considerable individual differences. Different infants will respond to similar or nearly identical stimulus conditions with quite different responses. The same developmental transitions may be achieved through different routes as a function of the infant's achieved action patterns at any given point and the manner of the mother's response in dealing with the child's activity (Escalona, 1963). In general, the course of development follows an epigenetic sequence that is marked by the progressive emergence and differentiation of various aspects of the infant's capacity to function and interact. While general patterns of such sequential development can be described, there are marked variations that characterize individual infants even within the range of normal developmental potentialities. The pathological deviations from the normal program increase the spectrum of variability considerably.

In general, the course of development traces a path from the infant's condition as a biological entity toward the emergence and articulation of increasingly identifiable psychological capacity. Along with this general trend, there is a tendency to view the course of development in terms of a progressive shift from relative passivity to increasing activity and autonomy and from levels of relative lack of differentiation in the capacity to act and respond to increasingly differentiated and progressively more articulated patterns of response. There has been, however, a progressive shift of emphasis in the literature over the last few years, earlier studies tending to emphasize the biologic beginnings of human life along with the characteristics of relative passivity and lack of differentiation in neonatal functioning. More recent studies have shifted the emphasis to the opposite poles and have placed greater emphasis on the presence of psychological organization, the relative capacity for attentive activity, and a more articulated view of the organization and differentiation of neonatal functions even from the very beginning.

Consistent with this more recent emphasis, the view of the infant as involved in a process of interaction with the caretaking person, usually and particularly the mother, has received increasing reinforcement and substantiation. For example, Sander's (1962, 1969, 1980) studies of neonatal behavior have defined a process of interaction and mutual regulation that characterizes the mother–child interaction from the very beginning. Similarly, Weil (1970) has described the emergence of a "basic core of fundamental trends" based on the interaction between the infant's congenital equipment and early experiential factors, particularly the interaction in the earliest mother–child relationship, which establishes early patterns of regulatory stability.

One of the conceptual difficulties encountered in this regard arises in relation to our understanding of object relations at this stage of development. Much of the developmental literature has taken its lead from object relations theorists who have insisted on the fact of the infant's relationship with the mothering object from the very beginning. The difficulty arises, however, of connecting this fact of early infantile experience with our more evolved and developed notions of object relationship. As I have pointed out elsewhere (Meissner, 1979), there can be little doubt that the interaction between the mother and her infant is real enough. Mother and child are related in some real and fundamental sense. The question of whether in the child's mind there is any differentiation between his own sense of himself and the representation of the object-mother is quite a different question. While we have no observational resources that allow us to infer such an intrapsychic distinction in the neonate, it seems to me at the same time a mistaken notion to infer such intrapsychic relationship on the basis of a real observed external relationship. In the present discussion, then, I will try to preserve the distinction between object relatedness, which characterizes the real, external, observable relation between mother and infant, and object relationship, which implies a further stage of intrapsychic development involving the formation of self and object representations and the differentiation between them. Part of the conceptual problem lies in the connection between these two levels and modes of object involvement and in formulating the manner in which the effects of object relatedness form the fundamental basis for the emergence and development of the subsequent capacity for object relationships.

DEVELOPMENTAL INFLUENCES

The first question has to do with what the infant brings to his developmental experience. What is the basic stuff, the material, on which the developmental process works? Much of what we see in the newborn is an aggregation of perceptual functions and motoric reflexes (Paine, 1965). Some of these reflex schemata reflect the neurologic immaturity of the newborn (the Babinski reflex, tonic neck reflexes, automatic grasping and walking, the Moro reflex) and do not disappear until additional neurologic maturation takes place, usually within a few months. Some of these reflexes undoubtedly are phylogenetic vestigia, but others have adaptive value, as, for example, the role of rooting and sucking reflexes in feeding or that of the tonic neck reflexes in juxtaposition of mouth and fingers. Nonnutritive sucking seems to play an important role in calming restless infants and has a tension-reducing effect (Silverman, 1980).

One of the early important contributions to the study of individual differences was the description of a continuum of congenital activity types that characterize the relative behavioral disposition of the newborn infant. Fries and Woolf (1953) described a range of such activity types covering a relatively normal span of quiet, moderately active, and active types, and extending to more pathological forms at the extremes of the range of activity, that is, both hypo- and hyperactive dispositions. The level of activity and the disposition to reactivity that characterizes the infant's neurologic organization undoubtedly plays an important role in determining the emerging patterns of interaction with caretaking figures.

As Escalona (1962) would later point out, the understanding of such activity types must be tempered by an appreciation of a variety of state variables that characterize the same infants as well as the interaction of these variables with environmental influences. In fact, the consistency of such activity types is not as well maintained as originally thought, since the maintenance of such behavioral dispositions is more closely related to the variety of stimulus conditions. Of the behavioral characteristics that can be defined at birth, including activity level, sensory thresholds, and more general characteristics as vigor and tempo, there is little behavioral evidence that suggests that any of these early behavioral characteristics tend to remain stable. Escalona's own work (Escalona & Heider, 1959) points more in the direction of patterns of substantial change than of behavioral stability.

In addition to activity types, infants can also vary considerably in degree of sensitivity and receptivity to external stimuli. Infants may demonstrate unusual degrees of sensitivity in any of the sensory modalities (Bergman & Escalona, 1949). In such cases the infant's own response capacities are not sufficient to protect him from the harmful effects of excessive stimulation, so that the role of the mother as a sort of secondary or supplemental stimulus barrier becomes increasingly important (Boyer, 1956). When the protective barrier is inadequate, either as the result of its inherent failure or the inadequacy of maternal protection, the stimulus is provided for premature ego formation, which can be both fragile and incomplete (Bergman & Escalona, 1949). Boyer (1956) has even hypothesized that excessive anxiety at this early stage serves to elevate perceptual thresholds, thus providing a model for defensive protection against stimuli and withdrawal from the environment, as would presumably have been the case in infants suffering from hospitalism.

There are, in fact, a fairly large number of variables that tend to demonstrate a considerable degree of individual differences from infant to infant and play a significant role in predisposing the child to a given form of developmental experience and in eliciting a certain pattern or quality of response from the mother or other caretaking figures. Such variables would include the frequency and the length of periods of alert inactivity and availability to external stimulation; the capacity for singular or global response to stimulation as opposed to a more multiple response; the capacity to respond to multiple or competing external stimuli; the influence of the infant's internal state on behavior and sensory responsiveness; the distinctness with which the infant's state is expressed or communicated to caregivers; differences in instinctual drive endowment; the degree of mode reliance or extent to which organ modes are expressed and generalized; the relative degree of dedifferentiation; the degree of self-consistency and of behavioral disorganization to internal need-states; and differences in psychosexual dispositions in terms of early patterns of mouthing, sucking, activity or passivity, masturbation, and the like (Alpert, Neubauer, & Weil, 1956; Korner, 1964; Korner & Grobstein, 1976). Such variations have both long- and short-term implications, influencing the immediate patterning of the mother–child interaction, as well as acting as determinants in part of the longer-range course and sequence of normal development (Korner & Grobstein, 1976) and its deviations (Weil, 1956).

Despite these more or less innate and biologically given patterns of variability, more recent contributions have emphasized the difficulty of differentiating constitutional variables from the effects of environmental influences. While innate abilities must be regarded as significant contributing factors that exert a continuing influence on behavior, the designation of innate patterns of functioning and their relevance for later development have not been altogether satisfactory (Blank, 1964). Increasing emphasis has been placed on the interplay between such innate factors and caretaking practices. For example, the rhythm and organization of both arousal and inhibitory systems, which lay the basis for early regulatory patterns affecting the sleep–wake cycle and the hunger cycle, can be considerably modified by the arousing or calming response of the mother to the stimulus provided by the infant's alert and attentive gaze (Bennett, 1971). Thus, the disentangling of constitutional and environmental factors remains difficult and problematic. While prematurely born infants could be shown to have significant deficits in cognitive organization, it was also found that prematures tended to come from grossly inhibiting environments more frequently than controls. The behavioral deficit was not only a matter of maturational difficulties but seems also to have reflected the impact of psychological stress factors that resulted in inhibition of development (Caplan, Bibace, & Rabinovitch, 1963).

In this more interactional view, then, while constitutional and innate factors play an undeniably important role, greater emphasis is placed on the interplay of such factors with the caretaking environment. Sander (1980) has emphasized the infant's finding of an ecological niche that allows for a profound revision in the temporal organization of disparate functions as a result of the organizing and integrating interaction with the mother. As Sander (1980) puts it:

On the basis of present investigations of newborn physiology, it is conceivable now to regard the new baby as a composite of semi-independent physiological subsystems, each with its own rhythm. . . . They must become harmonized and coordinated *within* the new baby, and in turn, tuned-up with the regular periodicities of the world and of the people who make up the baby's world. (p. 179)

A similar emphasis has been endorsed by other theorists of infant development (Greenspan & Lieberman, 1980; Weil, 1970).

Such congenital endowments and variations do not play a direct role in internalization, but rather provide the foundation or the material basis on which further developmental processes including internalizations take place. Given activity types or sensory sensitivities enter immediately into the patterning of interaction with the caretaking objects, and through the effects set up within that interaction play out their influences on the patterning of subsequent internalizations. In addition, innate patterns of activity or responsivity play a more direct role in establishing the quality of the infant's experience, which both conditions and shapes the internalizing processes as they take place.

The patterns of activation and subsequent development of the innate capacities of the infant play an important role in the developing pattern of internalizations. Any number of authors have stressed, in opposition to earlier views, that the infant is, in fact, an active agent and participant in his developing interaction with the environment, rather than, as was previously thought, a more or less passive recipient of internal stimuli (Ainsworth, 1969; Emde, 1980; Goldberg, 1977; Stechler & Carpenter, 1967). The infant shows a quite developed capacity for differential responsiveness, particularly to certain forms of human stimulation (Graves, 1980). This differentiation is sufficient to justify the view that the newborn infant is, in fact, preadapted for selective attention to human stimulation, and has a repertoire of innate behaviors that serve to reinforce and facilitate effective adult–infant interaction.

Thus, the infant's cry is one of the most powerful stimuli for eliciting adult attention, and qualitatively different forms of crying serve effectively to elicit different kinds of adult response (Goldberg, 1977). In addition, the efficacy the infant experiences in exerting control over his environment seems to play an important developmental role. When the capacity for such effectiveness is realized, a positive basis is contributed to the emergence of the core of the infant's self. By the same token, when the infant is unable to effect a degree of influence, predictability, and comprehension, the result is narcissistic trauma and developmental impediment (Broucek, 1979). Thus, the baby's capacity to shape the caretaker's behavior and to participate in establishing a degree of mutuality with the caregiver is both the basis for the development of such feelings of efficacy in relationship to the emerging sense of self and can be effectively facilitated or impeded by the response of the caregiver (Brazelton, 1980).

An additional perspective is added to these considerations by the notion that, as self-organizing processes take place in early developmental phases, organization takes place around elements or information inherent in stimulus input. Thus, if the dimensions of stimulation are reduced to those of novelty and familiarity without taking into consideration the meaning of that information to the organism, we are left with an incomplete model of perceptual and adaptive organization. A novel stimulus may be more than simply alerting, since the manner of receiving and processing new information remains dependent on the background against which it is perceived. By the same token, a stimulus that is familiar is not simply nonnovel, but already has an experiential history and thus a meaning. The differential response at about 4 weeks to the human facial configuration suggests a relative tuning to the meaningful characteristics of that stimulus configuration in preference to other inanimate stimuli (Stechler & Carpenter, 1967).

The question of stimulus selectivity and optimal levels of activation has been related to the notion of the stimulus barrier. Freud (1920) had originally proposed the notion of *Reizschutz* as an innate barrier whose purpose was to protect the immature infant psyche from excessive levels of stimulation. Benjamin (1965) had developed the idea by distinguishing between a passive stimulus barrier, which characterized the infant in the earliest weeks of life and reflected a relative absence of a capacity to process incoming stimuli due to the lack of functional neurologic connections, and a later maturationally more mature active barrier.

At about 3–4 weeks there occurred a maturational crisis, marked by a relative sudden increase in sensitivity to both external and internal stimulation. Benjamin postulated that subsequent to this maturational spurt, the infant was in a relatively vulnerable position in that his capacity to respond to stimulation had been increased without commensurate development of protective mechanisms. This increased vulnerability put excessive demands on the capacity for the mother to respond to the infant's needs and thus serve a supplemental function in protecting the infant against excessive stimulation (Benjamin, 1965; Boyer, 1956). This period of relative vulnerability was followed at about 8–10 weeks by the emergence of the capacity in the infant to protect himself from excessive stimulation by his own active efforts. Benjamin referred to this as the "active stimulus barrier."

A later experimental reevaluation of Benjamin's formulations has found good experimental support for the notion of the passive stimulus barrier. However, the neuromaturational spurt, which increases sensitivity to stimulation without an increase in inhibitory or regulatory mechanisms, must be qualified by the fact that there is also an increase in the coordination of sensory input and motor response that provides the infant with the means of pleasurable discharge. Although the autonomous means of protection against stimulation are lacking, the infant does have a more integrated channel for processing of stimulus input. The subsequent reorganization at 8–10 weeks does not find any clear supporting evidence. Rather, the active stimulus barrier does not seem to become effective until well into the 4th month. At 8–10 weeks there are a variety of changes in responsivity that are followed in about a month by the emergence of functioning inhibitory and regulatory mechanisms that can serve for reducing the impact of stimulation (Tennes, Emde, Kisley, & Metcalf, 1972).

The ability to organize and maintain alertness and response to stimulation undergoes a progressive development. The capacity for visual attending progresses from an almost complete lack of visual following in the first hours of life to a capacity for fleeting attention, leading to increasingly sustained periods of visual attention and visual fixation within the subsequent weeks and months (Fish, 1963). Within a few months the primary direction of attention to the human facial gestalt becomes a predominant feature, and marks a turning point in development from the predominance of more passive reception to a more active perceiving function (Spitz, 1955). The infant is thus an observer from the beginning. Very early in life infants manifest a clear preference for patterned and more complex visual stimuli. Even in the first few weeks during nursing, for example, the infant's gaze is fixed on the mother's face, probably because of the more interesting complexity of stimulus patterns it presents, and also because in the first few months the infant's eyes have a fixed depth of focus at about 13 centimeters, the approximate distance to the mother's face during the nursing.

In this context the infant also shows increasing responsiveness to the sound of the human voice (beginning around 3–6 weeks) and eye-to-eye contact (beginning around 2–3 weeks), particularly with the mother (Silverman, 1980). The emergence of this more selective pattern of scanning and of visual fixation takes the place of the previously more endogenous pattern of eye movement (Emde, 1980). Thus, in terms of perceptual capacity there is a shift from the relatively passive to the increasingly active, and from a level of the predominance of proprioceptive sensory modalities in which sensory experience is primarily coenesthetic to the increasing maturation of distance perception, which is more diacritically organized (Spitz, 1955). This shift in perceptual capacity has been linked to a shift in libidinal cathexis marked by an increasing outer direction and attention to aspects of the external environment (Mahler & McDevitt, 1980).

A similar pattern of progressive activation can be seen with regard to the smiling response. The earliest pattern of smiling seems to be predominantly endogenous, occurs randomly and in response to nonspecific stimulation or even in sleep, and seems to be primarily correlated with central nervous system (CNS) discharge. During sleep it seems to be correlated with rapid-eye-movement (REM) states, and tends to occur with greater frequency in premature infants (Spitz, Emde, & Metcalf, 1970). Alert smiles begin to occur within a few weeks, especially in response to the sound of the human voice (Sroufe & Waters, 1976). Blind babies in this same period will respond to sound stimuli, but the response becomes rapidly selective and attuned to the mother's voice (Freedman, 1980).

At about 2 months, the smile becomes specific and responsive to external stimulation; it begins to take on a social significance and a selectivity primarily in response to the facial gestalt (Shapiro & Stern, 1980). The infant's smile, then, begins to enter into a process of reciprocity and begins to play a more active role in the eliciting and reinforcement of caretaker behaviors, complementing its earlier function of merely maintaining a novel stimulus situation. At about 8–12 weeks, the exogenous smiling response can be predictably elicited by the "essential sign gestalt," the most potent stimulus being the mother's face (Spitz *et al.*, 1970). Thus, the smiling response becomes another vehicle of the infant's active participation in his interaction with his environment and becomes an aspect of his evolving competence to effect responses and achieve a degree of control over the environment (Sroufe & Waters, 1976). The need for optimal levels of stimulation, neither too much nor too little, seems to be a primary requirement in all sensory modalities, even in tactile sensation (Shevrin & Toussieng, 1965). The question as to whether an increase or stimulation in other modalities can compensate for defects in a given sensory modality remains unresolved.

There is a progression from passivity to activity in regard to the capacity for motility also (Mittelman, 1960). Restriction of motility in early months will create a distress reaction. But in the early months of a child's experience passive motility predominates and has a relatively soothing effect. Being carried and rocked, as the baby so often is, carries with it the implications of being taken care of by a benevolent power and resonates with the strains of omnipotence and autoerotic gratification of this early period.

Motility can also be active, as in the relatively nonadaptive forms of reflex grasping or random body movements or even autoerotic rhythmic motor patterns. But here again, motility only gradually gives way to a capacity for action that involves some adaptive interaction with the environment and serves the purposes of developing mastery, of testing reality, and contributes to the development of object relations, aggression, self-esteem, and the differentiation of self and object.

A normal progression in the development of motility and the capacity for independent action depends to a great extent on the quality of the interaction with the mother. When the infant becomes capable of locomotion, following the mother is the most frequent response to separation, more to mothers who are sensitive to the infant's needs than otherwise. When mothers are relatively insensitive the more frequent response is crying. Infants who manage to attain a balance between attachment and exploratory behaviors toward the end of the 1st year demonstrate less ambivalence in their relationship to the mother, and tend to have enjoyed an increased amount of satisfying face-to-face interaction with the mother in the first few months of life. Mothers of such children who are relatively free to act and explore tend to be more responsive to their infants' cries and more sensitive to signals in the early feeding situation (Lamb, 1976).

The infant also gradually develops a capacity for self-stimulation. The role of the development of autoerotic activity is interesting in this regard, since it serves a function partly compensatory for the lack of stimulation from the environment, but at the same time demonstrates the development of a capacity that is a function of the child's meaningful interaction with his objects. Spitz's (1949, 1962) early studies of genital play in children raised in environments of varying deprivation (private families, foundling home, and a hospital nursery) conclude that where there was no emotional involvement between mother and child autoerotic activity was also missing, and that the closer the mother–child bond the more frequently was autoerotic activity, particularly genital play, observable.

Autoerotic activity, even if it can be viewed in the context of the need to maintain homeostatic equilibrium through the medium of self-stimulation, still does not do away with the role of the mother as a contributing factor or regulating influence on the achievement of that homeostatic balance (Nagera, 1964). Thus, while autoeroticism serves in a sense as a substitute of a part of the body for the absence of the mother (A. Freud, 1953), it also expresses and reflects the infant's enlarging capacity to provide his own stimulation, to gain some mastery over internal states, and to become an increasingly effective agent in both internal self-regulation and dealings with the environment. This capacity itself is a function of and a derivative of meaningful and developmentally facilitating object relations.

An important component of the developing infant's capacity to engage with, control, and manipulate his environment and of his increasing engagement in meaningful relationships with objects is the progressive development of aggression. The early precursors of aggression are manifested in forms of crying and distress and serve primarily as a vehicle of essential communication to the object, which serves to elicit appropriate responses from those objects (Emde, Gaensbauer, & Harmon, 1976). The highpoint of the infant's specific libidinal attachment to the mother at about 5 months is followed by increasing efforts to differentiate and detach himself from the mother in the interest of exploring the world. The mother's efforts to restrain this exuberant and often dangerous exploration is met by anger and struggle against the mother's restraints. This anger toward and attacks against the mother emerge at about 8–10 months, whereas previously attacks against the object with intent to hurt could not be observed (McDevitt, 1980; Spock, 1965). This capacity for directing anger against the mother was a function of a more stable libidinal cathexis of the mother and development of the capacity to experience anger in a more organized fashion. Moreover, the anger always occurred in connection with unpleasureful restriction or frustration of activity, and as soon as the obstruction was removed the anger subsided. Anger at this level was stimulus bound, short-lived, and restricted to specific eliciting conditions.

Gradually, defensive modifications of aggression become observable, particularly in terms of the displacement, restriction of aim, sublimation, and fusion with libido of aggressive impulses. The infant would become playfully teasing, or would begin to displace anger at the mother toward a doll or even turn it against himself. Patterns of inhibition, withdrawal, or negativism begin to be seen. The rapid alternation between loving affection and angry attacks has been described as "ambitendency" (Mahler & McDevitt, 1968). By 12 months of age the infant's object-directed anger had become more differentiated, integrated, and complex, without as yet manifesting any deliberate intent to hurt. Under optimal conditions, anger could be used constructively in the service of facilitating distancing and promoting self–object differentiation. When conditions were unfavorable—as in the case of overly controlling, intrusive, or anxious mothers—the infant's excessive anger, frequently accompanied by anxiety, tended to interfere with optimal distancing. Such infants would often show patterns of excessive avoidance or excessive clinging to the mother (McDevitt, 1980; Mittelman, 1960).

Such patterns undoubtedly reflect the premature differentiation of aggression related to a failure of need-satisfying responses from the object. The consequence is an increased cathexis of the object with aggression, an increased titer of ambivalence and a perception of the object as frustrating and bad (Rubenfine, 1962). The difficulties posed by an excessive titer of aggression and ambivalence for the accomplishing of distancing behaviors in the practicing subphase also contribute to difficulties in self–object differentiation (McDevitt, 1980). It is not until the child enters the rapprochement subphase with its more differentiated and stable representations of both self and object that aggression can be expressed in a more sustained fashion and begins to approximate forms of aggression at more adult levels, including the intent to hurt.

In all of these dimensions of development that we have described, there is a progressive differentiation and activation of inherent developmental potentialities. The impulse to suck, for example, in the early weeks of life shows little discrimination among sources of oral stimulation. By 3–4 months, however, there is considerable discrimination and little is left to chance: The sucking response is elicited preferentially by the appropriate nutritive stimuli, the breast or bottle. This reflects the developing parameters of perceptual differentiation, memory functioning and motor control (Hoffer, 1949, 1950).

The gradual shift toward increasing activity and environmental engagement and interaction has also been traced with regard to the peek-a-boo game (Kleeman, 1967). The evolution of this infantile play reflects the emergence of other developmental influences. The game begins passively, with the adult playing peek-a-boo with the child, beginning usually somewhere between the 4th and 9th months. The game gradually shifts to a more active form in which the infant begins to play an active part somewhere between the 6th and 11th month. The onset tends to correlate with critical developmental periods, particularly the beginnings of differentiation subphase and early suggestions of self–object differentiation. The shift to a more active form corresponds to the move out of the differentiation subphase and is connected with the development of the well-known 8th-month anxiety. In fact, at this stage the game may serve a useful purpose for establishing mastery over both separation and stranger anxiety (Kleeman, 1967). This latter development corresponds to a more general developmental shift reflecting a more intensified and specific attachment to caregiving objects and the increasing capacity for a fearful response corresponding to the emergence of stranger and separation anxiety (Emde, 1980).

In all of these developmental parameters, we can identify certain specifiable developmental patterns. In the 1st year the infant's behavior shifts from a relatively endogenous base to a more exogenous orientation, that is, instead of behavioral states being determined primarily by internal need states and stimulus conditions, the infant gradually and increasingly becomes more responsive to the influence of external stimuli. Rather than being the passive recipient or observer or external influences, the infant increasingly demonstrates his growing competence and effectiveness in exercising control over his environment and in eliciting certain patterns of stimulus input. In addition to his growing competence in effecting changes in his environment, there is also a comparable increase in his capacity for internal self-regulation. This reflects not only neuropsychological maturation but also a dawning and enlarging awareness of self-as-agent and an increasing degree of experience and experiment with the infant's own body as an instrument for gratification and modification of internal states. Thus, while at the very beginning the economic demands for homeostatic regulation and for maintenance of an optimal level of stimulation are the predominant factors, and the infant's adaptive resources are mobilized for these purposes, there is a gradual shift during the 1st year from a decreasing concern with such fundamentally physiologic needs toward increasingly intense and complex patterns of social interaction. In all of these areas the infant becomes an increasingly active and effective agent in promoting the shifts in developmental patterning. As we shall see in detail later, each of the aspects of these shifts in developmental patterning have important implications for the nature and quality of the infant's internalizations, which accompany and in part promote these same pattern shifts.

Undoubtedly, the most significant arena within which these developmental parameters are elaborated is that of the mother–child interaction. From the moment of birth the temporal reorganization of rhythms of activation and quiescence begins to take place and is shaped to the usual diurnal cycle. In describing the emergence of an interactive regulative system between infant and caregiver, Sander (1980) makes the following points: Birth itself is a profound rupture in mechanisms of temporal organization in the fetal–maternal system; the developing ecological niche of the newborn must provide for reestablishing a pattern of temporal organization regulating new exchanges between neonate and his environment; individual differences in periodicities and rates of change in the first days of life on the part of the infant interacting with individual differences in the caretaker result in specific patterns of 24-hour exchange between them; the specificity of regulative fittedness between particular infant and particular caregiver can reach an appreciable degree by the 10th day of life; and the later adaptive use of sensorimotor functions is influenced by the earlier role such functions play in establishing the regulatory coordination in the mother–child system.

Sander (1962, 1969) has also described a sequence of stages in developing mother–child regulation. He calls the first stage, which takes place in the first 3 months, a period of "initial adaptation." The focus here is on the stable regulation of basic biologic processes such as feeding, sleeping, and elimination. Optimally, the routine between mother and child settles down to a regular and predictable pattern and is accompanied by some sign of the baby's preferential response to her ministrations. When the affective tone is predominantly positive and pleasant, one may see the emergence of the smiling response with its first suggestions of social interaction. The specific issue in this phase has to do with the degree of adaptation established between mother and child, such that the mother's behavior becomes specifically appropriate to the baby's internal states and the cues he may give concerning it.

Sander calls the next phase that of "reciprocal exchange"; it extends from the 4th to the 6th month approximately. The emphasis here falls on active reciprocal play between mother and infant, particularly around the spontaneous development of smiling play. This provides a degree of delight and mounting exuberance for both participants and reflects the pattern of reciprocal coordination in all areas of caretaking activity between them. This emerging collaboration affects all caretaking activities such as diapering, dressing, or even spoon feeding. The issue, then, is the extent to which the interaction between mother and child includes reciprocal sequences of interchange between them, back and forth, and with alternating patterns of active and passive stimulus and response.

The next phase covers the subsequent 3-month period and finds the infant becoming more vigorous in expressing initiative in bids for attention, social exchange, motor exploratory and manipulative activities, or in general expressing his own preferences. Sander refers to this period as that of "early directed activity" or "initiative." Optimally, the mother's response is capable of attending to, recognizing, and responding to these initiatives of the child and being able to maintain respect for the unique individuality they are beginning to express. The issue, then, becomes the degree to which the child's initiative can be successful in establishing areas of reciprocity in his interaction with the mother. The last few months bridging from the end of the 1st year into the 2nd are marked by the advent of locomotion and an enlargement of the infant's capacity to direct his own activity and express specific intentions by it. This is the period of "focalization," particularly on the mother, and provides an opportunity for the child to determine the extent to which the mother remains available to him. This would correspond to Mahler's "practicing period."

Other observers have noted the relative instability of behavior patterns in early infancy and the degree to which psychophysiologic homeostasis is easily upset. Behavior is often marked by frequent oscillations between regressive and progressive trends (Cytryn, 1968). The rhythm and organization of both arousal and inhibitory systems is gradually stabilized and expressed in part in the sleep–wakefulness–hunger cycle. Particularly important is the alert inactive state, since it is in this phase of the infant's alertness cycle that visual discrimination and possible simple forms of learning may begin to take place (Bennett, 1971). The mother's role in reinforcing or inhibiting such periods of alert attention is vital in terms of a balance between calming and arousing responses (Greenspan & Lieberman, 1980; Silverman, 1980). The extent to which periods of alert attention without excessive or distressing arousal can be maintained serves the interests of further adaptation and developmental progression.

In his own genial way, Erikson (1980) has described these early patterns of routinization and interactional regulation under the rubric of ritualization. The regularities of cleaning, feeding, and putting to sleep may seem stereotypical, but they are also highly individual reflecting the synchrony and adaptation occurring between a particular individual infant and his caretaker. Thus, patterns of periodicity are imposed on libidinal and physical needs, and the infant's disparate experiences begin to be made coherent by the interaction with his mother. The mother is thus more than a generalized caregiver; she must become the mother of a special kind and in a special way of this infant. This first human ritualization both fulfills a series of fundamental needs and duties, but also supports the joint need for both infant and caretaker for mutuality of recognition.

The importance of reciprocity has been variously emphasized. The mother's feeding style, for example, the manner of holding, the presentation of the breast or bottle, the pacing and consistency, all shape the infant's sensorimotor adaptation to the feeding situation. Later on, the emergence of playfulness presents opportunities for mastery of the mother as the holding environment, for developing initial degrees of mastery and autonomy, and form the basis for the infant's emerging style of dealing with instinctual derivatives and the external environment. Such emerging stylistic characteristics form the basis for ways of relating to objects, adapting to external stimuli, and developing learning and cognitive styles. Moreover, they emerge out of mutual processes of participation and interaction and even imitation involving both parent and child (Call & Marschak, 1966).

The responsive caregiver consequently provides a matrix of social support in which the baby's capacity to become more active and to participate in the interaction by beginning to shape the caretaker's behavior provides the basis for that sense of satisfying mutuality that allows play for the infant's growing sense of efficacy and capacity in dealing with and controlling his environment. Where that process of exchange and interaction is short-circuited, whether through maternal inadequacies or depression or by an inherently unresponsive baby, feedback patterns are interrupted, the relationship becomes dysynchronous, and there is a lack of adaptive fit, which can have severe developmental consequences. A lack of response in the child can interfere seriously with the mother–child interaction and even in extreme cases elicit anger and rejection from the parents as is often the case with brain-damaged children (Brazelton, 1980).

Emphasis has been placed on the role of visual contacts as one of the cardinal attachment behaviors and serving a particularly important function in the evolving interaction between mother and child. Not only is visual contact under voluntary control, but it also plays an increasing role in forming the mother–infant tie. As Stern (1971) has noted, true eye-to-eye contact begins at about 6 weeks and has a dramatic effect on the mother, making her feel that she is relating to a responsive person and thus contributing greatly to the enhancement of the interaction. Any infant refusal of eye-to-eye contact at this juncture can be deeply felt by the mother. Moreover, the face-to-face position seems to be necessary for the emergence of the normal smiling response. Erikson (1980) has also emphasized the importance of the developing eye-to-eye relationship as part of an essential dialogue necessary for the infant's psychological development.

All of this is reminiscent of Winnicott's (1960, 1967) emphasis on the mirror role of the mother. He asks, "What does the baby see when he looks at the mother's face?" He answers that the baby sees himself or, alternatively, that what the mother looks like as she looks at her baby is related to what she sees there. This giving back on the part of the mother to the baby of the baby's own self strikes an important note for the understanding of primitive levels of internalization and continues to have implications for later aspects of development when patterns of internalization become more elaborate and the child becomes increasingly less dependent on the return from others as a vehicle for shaping his own sense of self.

At this juncture the mother's capacity to acknowledge and respond to the infant in terms of his own emerging individuality, rather than in terms of her own expectations, anxieties, or projections, becomes vital in influencing the pattern of internalizations. The emotional matrix set up between mother and child becomes the medium for interconnecting patterns of externalization and internalization that serve as initial phases or precursors of later and more evolved forms of projective–introjective interaction. What the mother externalizes via projection can serve as the basis of the infant's internaliza-tion—for well or for ill. This model of interaction is familiar from more mature contexts of familial interaction (Meissner, 1978a) and personality functioning (Meissner, 1978b), as well as well-known clinical phenomena (Meissner, 1981).

These earliest levels of synchrony and mutual communication between mother and child serve as the basis for an emerging and increasingly elaborate sense of mutuality (Murphy, 1980). Much of the quality of the interaction between parent and child depends on the extent and the areas within which mutuality can be established. Certainly, parental attitudes can be influenced by the child's developmental patterns and can stimulate different reactions often mobilizing unconscious reactions and attitudes in the parents. The intermeshing of individualities on both sides of the equation, child and parent, is often a complicated matter. The cuddling child will elicit a different response from the mother than the child that refuses comforting or is difficult to quiet.

The variabilities in such interaction have been described in a number of cases by Coleman, Kris, and Provence (1953). The mother whose child is seen as a child-lover at her breast and as her exclusive possession begins to fail as the toddler begins to assert his independence. Or similarly the mother who views the child as a narcissistic extension of herself will find difficulty in accepting the child's independence, thus provoking opposition and struggle. For a mother whose child had been unsatisfactory from birth, the difficulties in caretaking only seemed to reinforce her own tendency to project her dissatisfaction with herself onto the child. Her attitude changed only when the child began to turn more actively toward her; the greater degree of differentiation allowed the mother to begin to read cues that she had previously ignored. Insofar as the child was responded to less as part of herself, he was less subject to attack and more subject to understanding. Another mother never wanted her female child and felt unable to handle her, viewing her as a rival. Here again, the child's increasing independence made it more possible for the mother to respond in developmentally helpful ways. Thus, the basic equipment that a child brings to the mothering situation can influence what may be frustrating for a particular mother.

At this early level the child's basic equipment is as significant as the mother's caring response in determining the balance of gratification and frustration. That balance has an important effect on the emerging pattern of internalizations insofar as where the balance of experience in the mother-child interaction is gratifying, it fosters the emergence of patterns of imitation and progressively leads in the direction of more positive identifications. Where the balance is in the direction of frustration, however, there tends to develop a confluence and integration of memory islands tinged with experiences of frustration, anxiety, and pain, which contribute to the formation of a bad maternal part-image and correspondingly defensive forms of internalization (Mahler & Gosliner, 1955; Ritvo & Solnit, 1958).

Such findings have put considerable emphasis on the role of the presence and availability of the mother as an important factor in the child's developmental experience. The child's initial dependence and increasing attachment to the mother plays an important role in normal development, but also increases progressively the threat of the loss of the object with its undesirable and even disastrous consequences. The necessity for the availability and constancy of the object, even for the maintenance of early homeostatic conditions, is abundantly established. The object is an indispensable element in the titration of pain and pleasure, which is so important to early adaptation. Early disorders in object relationships can reveal themselves in developmental emotional retardation, in physical sleep dysfunction, and even in gastrointestinal disorders. When the caretaking object is lost, there can occur a heightening of self-interest, a withdrawal of interest from the frustrating object, and a readiness for substitution. Loss of the object at this early phase, when the relieving of discomfort and satisfying of need are primary, elicits a predominantly aggressive response. It is only later in emotional development, when attachment to the object has become sufficiently strong, that the phenomenon of mourning and depression can be identified as a result of object loss. In very young children who experience object loss through separation or deprivation, or in cases where an adequate object relationship has failed to develop, the clinical picture demonstrates the infantile vicissitudes of aggression rather than depression (Rochlin, 1961).

Similarly, Weil (1970) has emphasized the critical role of the mutual adaptation of mother and child in laying the groundwork for basic parameters of the child's emerging personality. She writes:

The early interaction between the infant's equipment and the mother's attunement results in a basic core, which may range from greater harmony and potential for ego structuring and ego strength to considerable imbalance and vulnerability. The infant begins the symbiotic phase with this basic core, in which the mother's care-taking has already attentuated or aggravated the original trends. (p. 457)

Further, the characteristics of this basic core tend to persist as a fundamental layer that is extended through the subsequent phases of separation–individuation and psychosexual development and continues to influence the organization and texture of these developments.

The infant's intensifying sense of dependence and attachment to the mother brings with it the corresponding threat of loss and usually is manifested in forms of stranger anxiety. This is the familiar 8th-month anxiety originally described by Spitz (1945, 1946). The development of this pattern of anxiety is a function of increasing cognitive elaboration, the emergence of a capacity for object permanence in Piaget's sense. However, there is no general agreement that stranger anxiety (even if it occurs at 8 months) is a sign of the development of object constancy or that it indicates a preference for animate over inanimate objects (Shapiro & Stern, 1980). It seems more likely that the infant's capacity to accept separation from the mother is a function of the infant's own inherent endowment in conjunction with the pattern of interaction between mother and child, which allows for a greater degree of independence and autonomy. Thus, the so-called 8th-month anxiety may, in fact, occur at any age at which the baby is able to differentiate the mother from a stranger, but has not yet achieved sufficient environmental mastery to be confident in dealing with new objects and new faces. The danger encountered by the infant is consequently probably not specifically age related, but rather belongs to a transitional period where differentiation occurs in a context of limited mastery. The capacity to master this anxiety may be an important index of development in the last quarter of the 1st year (Murphy, 1980). From this point of view, then, the so-called stranger anxiety or 8th-month anxiety can be taken as a sign of increasing individuation and differentiation (Weil, 1956).

Perhaps the clearest evidence of the importance and significance of the infant's relationship with the caretaking object in the 1st year of life comes from Spitz's early studies of hospitalism and subsequent studies that have developed the theme of the effects of object loss and its sequelae on infant development. Spitz's early studies (1945, 1946) described the effects of the deprivation of maternal care. The lack of consistent mothering care, in infants raised in a foundling home situation, led to severe developmental retardation, marked deviations from normal developmental patterns, and bizarre stereotyped behaviors. Such deprived infants seemed to show progressive deterioration, which eventually led to psychosomatic deficits, including diminished resistance to disease and increased mortality. Infants raised in the nursery context, in which the deprivation of mothering was not as severe, showed a much decreased incidence of both mortality and morbidity.

The common factor seemed to have been the removal of the mother after a period of about 6–8 months of contact with the child. This led to the development of the syndrome, which was entirely lacking when the mother was not removed. This pattern of developmental arrest, the loss or inhibition of the capacity to function and an irreversible personality distortion, came to be described as "anaclitic depression" (Spitz & Wolf, 1946). In general, these studies indicated that if the relationship to the love object had been satisfactory, it was much more difficult to find a substitute; that the severity of the depression seemed to be worse with the loss of a good mother–child interaction; but that depression was often lacking when the loss was of a mother–child interaction that had been unsatisfactory. Even under the nursery conditions, which were not as severely depriving as in the foundling home, if there were no return of the object or replacement of it by a substitute, the depression became rapidly worse and led to a kind of stuporous, unresponsive, and withdrawn state.

Subsequent studies of the effects of institutionalization when accompanied by object deprivation have simply underlined the point. In their observations of such institutionalized children, Provence and Ritvo (1961) have observed that the deprivation in mothering produces certain identifiable effects on patterns of growth: Specifiable apparatuses for functioning seemed to appear on schedule, but were nonetheless delayed in the infant's capacity to bring them under ego control and to utilize them adaptively, and the integration of behaviors into more complex action units seemed delayed and distorted and lacked the richness and subtlety of mere normal development.

In contrast to the playing period of more normal children, these institutionalized children showed a general tendency to manipulate toys less, showed no evidence of toy preference, and little displeasure when toys were removed. There was a delay in the development of the concept of the object, little spontaneous play, little elaboration or enjoyment or zest in play, and perhaps most noteworthy, no formation of transitional objects. They conclude that the lack of adequate mothering in this early period of development introduces an inappropriate balance between comfort and discomfort, which impedes the formation of memory traces of the object that would contribute to more permanent development of more permanent object cathexis; that consequently the displacement to inanimate objects is not normal; and that the mechanism of displacement is not adequately structuralized or energized. The conclusions support and reinforce the importance of the continuing contribution from interaction with significant objects as essential to developmental progression (Blank, 1964; Provence & Ritvo, 1961).

A similar conclusion can be drawn from Solnit's (1970) study of infants hospitalized with infantile diarrhea. The treatment of the infectious process by hospitalization and isolation involved an interruption of maternal care and a form of emotional deprivation. Solnit concluded that such deprivation and isolation only intensified the debilitating effects of the diarrhea and led to progressive marasmus and death in a number of instances. Where substitute emotional supplies could be provided in the form of constant and attentive nursing, recovery was facilitated and the rate of morbidity and mortality minimized. The nurse-substitute provided a substitute need-satisfying love object who was able to administer plenteous libidinal infusions, which made it possible for the infant to respond to physiologic treatment.

It is difficult to know what the operative factors are in the failure experienced by such children in the face of object loss, and their revival when the object is replaced or substituted. Arguing on an economic basis, a number of authors have suggested that in the face of the loss of the object or the failure of the mother's protective function there is a compensatory increase of perceptual thresholds resulting in a pattern of withdrawal from stimulation or a failure to respond (Boyer, 1956; Shrevin & Toussieng, 1965). Economic questions of levels of activation and optimal intensities and forms of stimulation may, in fact, play a significant role in the understanding of these conditions, but more frequently the emphasis is put on the qualities of the object relationship itself. Mahler has emphasized that the presence and interaction with the need-satisfying mother is a prerequisite for normal growth through the symbiotic phase and that loss of the object during this phase (extending from 2 to 3 months, peaking at about 6 months, and fading out by the end of the 1st year) has devastating consequences, particularly in disrupting the shift from enteroceptive to distance perception, and in the transition from primary to secondary narcissism. The infant can recover from object loss in the symbiotic phase, if the separation is not premature or excessively long; otherwise, the damage can be irreparable (Mahler, 1961, 1965).

A particular case of selective deprivation can be found in the case of blind children—a sort of experiment of nature. The visual track forms a preferred channel of communication and feedback in the mother–child dyad for the normal-sighted infant, but in the case of the child without sight this channel is interrupted. The important feedback connection that is established through eye-to-eye and face-to-face contact that provides the important mirror function described by Winnicott is entirely lacking (Burlingham, 1964). The lack of visual stimulus creates a developmental lag as well as the demand for more intensive degrees of stimulation from the mother through other sensory modalities. Auditory and tactile cues become particularly important, but do not seem to be as arousing or effective as the visual.

Such children often reveal a pattern of behavior abnormality that is referred to as "blindisms," that is, rhythmic movements of rocking, swaying, twisting, or waving arms, that may also be seen in sighted children when they are deprived of motility (Burlingham, 1965). These children will also show certain patterns of relatively autistic behavior, delay in speech and motor behavior, increased susceptibility to separation anxiety, and diminished capacity for the development of object constancy (Call, 1971). Differences in the capacity to play have also been noted, particularly in the transition from the predominance of play with the mother's body to the development of transitional objects and play with cuddly toys. The blind baby remains in the first stage longer and requires an increased degree of tactile play with the mother's body and subsequently with the child's own body in order to make the transition (Burlingham, 1967).

Blind children have been observed to have a relatively high incidence of deviant and relatively undifferentiated personality structure and even at times gross abnormalities in ego development (Fraiberg, 1968, 1971). The tendency for blind babies to be relatively quiet and unresponsive increases the tendency for the child to remain without adequate stimulation. When the level of interaction is intensified, the usual "dialogue" between infant and caretaker begins to take place (Fraiberg, 1968). It is not that the blind baby is unresponsive in the early period; he can demonstrate a smile in response to the sound of the mother's voice in the early weeks, quite similar to that of sighted babies. There is frequently the capacity to show discomfort when the blind baby is being handled by a stranger, probably on the basis of postural and tactile cues. Tactile cues in the exploration of objects with hands and fingers become extremely important, and between 6 and 8 months the blind baby shows a clear preference for the mother when confronted with her and a stranger. But the smiles are not as frequent as in sighted babies or as spontaneously joyful.

Toward the end of the 1st year, however, blind babies show a marked difference from sighted ones in that they do not initiate affectionate games or patterns of interaction with significant figures. At about the same time, there is also a developmental impasse in motor development insofar as the baby seems to have developed the capacity for locomotion but cannot put this capacity into operation. Consequently, creeping and independent walking are significantly delayed. Fraiberg (1968) links this developmental lag with the problems of reaching for and grasping objects and the difficulties the blind baby has of locating an object on the basis of sound cues alone. By way of comparison to the sighted child, the blind baby exists in a sensory void in which objects can only be located by tactile contact, which is often accidental or random. The lack of information about the world beyond the child's own body makes his adaptation to that world all the more difficult (Fraiberg, 1968). Consequently, the prolonged period through which the infant passes before he is able to reach and locate external objects on the basis of sound cues delays not only the capacity for locomotion but also the progressive cognitive differentiation which allows for the establishment of self–object differentiation and the gradual acquisition of the capacity for permanent cathexis of objects and ultimately object constancy (Wills, 1970).

One of the most significant contributing elements to the success of the mother–child interaction and to the development of the dialogue between them is the mother's capacity to respond to the infant's needs and to sense what is being communicated to her in the interaction. This is a function of the mother's own attributes and her inherent capacity to generate such responses. Particularly important are her perceptiveness and flexibility with respect to specific needs and her willingness and ability to act on the given cues. In addition, her ability to differentiate the infant from herself and from her own internal needs plays an important role (Cytryn, 1968).

To a certain extent these mothering capacities are related to the mother's own developmental experience and patterns of internalization that underline her own personality structure (Jackson, Klatskin, & Wilkin, 1952). The predominance of the mother's own psychological needs and illusions over the baby's can be seen as reflecting a fixation to a traumatic core relationship with the mother's own mother. The interaction with the child can serve as a stimulus to activate pathogenic introjects in the mother that derive from the less desirable and less healthy aspects of her own involvement with her own mother in the preceding generation. As such pathogenic internal structures are mobilized, they play into the interaction with the child in ways that can be destructive and frustrating both for the homeostatic regulation of internal discomfort in the infant as well as for other aspects of his developmental progression (Tischler, 1979). These underlying dynamics can serve as the basis for anthropomorphic fantasies in the mother that determine the selection of cues to which she can be responsive and influence the meaning that she attributes to them (Bennett, 1971). The interaction of such unconscious fantasy material in the parent with the inborn characteristics of the child has been traced by Coleman *et al.* (1953) in a number of cases. The child is often attributed a set of characteristics or personality traits on the basis of projections derived from the parents' own internal conflicts and introjective organization.

The problems here are related to the process of gradual separation of the infant in the mother's mind from the mother's own sense of herself. An important variable is the mother's capacity to recognize and to adjust to the inborn rhythm of the child's own needs and characteristics, which serve as the initial basis for his emerging individuality. The child begins to show the first signs of individuation at 3 or 4 months in terms of the development of posture, molding, stiffening, and so on. The mother's unconscious fantasies, conscious expectations, and anxieties can play a critical role in facilitating or hindering the child's optimal development (Mahler, 1963).

The influence of such maternal attitudes, both conscious and unconscious, on the development of the child have been variously described, but an excellent detailed description in one mother–child pair has been provided by Kaplan (1964). In this case the mother's inability to tolerate arousal and the need to ward off stimuli led to a pattern of mothering marked by casualness, emotional detachment, minimal handling, and an attempt to protect the child from exposure to arousing stimulation. This created an ambience of sensory impoverishment and equivalently interposed an early barrier to the shift of libidinal cathexis from the child's self to surrounding objects. By 16 weeks little Daphne was relatively unresponsive, rarely looked at the people around her, was obviously more comfortable with inanimate objects than with people, found great difficulty in accepting change, was unable to tolerate any new stimuli, and showed a behavior pattern of diminished bodily activity and increased passivity and finger sucking. By 23 weeks she was immobile, showed little tendency to reach for objects, was unresponsive and floppy, showed no adaptive postural responses, but showed a marked degree of persistent finger and toe sucking. The mother's persistent attempts to protect the child from stimulation produced a diminished cathexis of external objects and an increased level of autoerotic activity, which was utilized in the service of screening out contact with the environment and the objects in it.

One of the fascinating aspects of this dimension of the psychological influences that come to bear on the child's development is the whole question of the impact of pregnancy on the mother and what the nature of the fantasies are that may be elicited by it. Over 30 years ago Coleman *et al.* (1953) commented:

Throughout pregnancy an apparently new and yet unconsciously prepared network of fantasies tends to develop—or more correctly, older fantasies tend to be refocused or reactivated. These fantasies, however different from individual to individual, are impressively grouped around well-known common themes. (p. 23)

The authors go on to note that in the experience of parenthood in the interaction with the developing child there is a reenactment of the parents' relationship to their own parents either by repetition or by avoidance.

The impact of pregnancy itself has been studied by Bibring and her associates (Bibring, 1959; Bibring, Dwyer, Huntington, & Valenstein, 1961). In studying pregnant mothers Bibring noted that these women had seemed relatively healthy before the onset of pregnancy, but as the pregnancy progressed they presented a more disturbed and regressive picture than other patients, and at times almost seemed borderline in personality organization. However, with these same patients therapeutic results seemed to be achieved quite readily and easily. Bibring argued that the pregnancy itself created a psychological upheaval for the mother, which had to have important effects on the mother's adaptation to the baby and on the patterning of that interaction.

The pregnancy created a shift in the woman's libidinal position, with an increased libidinal concentration on herself and her own body, including the child in her womb. With quickening, however, the baby begins to be experienced as a new object now within the mother's self, and the basis is laid for establishing a new relationship to a more separate object. The baby at this point is invested with the fusion of narcissistic and object libidinal strivings, reflecting an amalgamation of the mother's libidinal investments in the child who remains in some sense both a part of herself and at the same time an object that is part of the outside world, as well as part of the mother's own sexual mate. Consequently, it can be said that the psychological crisis of pregnancy sets the stage for the mobilization of the mother's own introjective components so as to provide a ready vehicle for the production of projections, which are then imposed on the child in the mother–child interaction.

An added consideration is that pregnancy creates a shift in the balance of emotional forces within the family system, as well as within the mother herself. The progression of the husband–wife couple into the triad of father–mother–child brings with it emotional shifts and developmental pressures and stresses that impinge on the capacity of the mother to adjust to and integrate the pregnancy and early mothering experience. The impact of the newborn child on the family system stirs responses and counterinfluences that inevitably affect the mother's involvement with her infant. This applies with differences of emphasis not only for the firstborn, but for each new arrival. The role of the father assumes central importance in this regard. On this basis Belsky (1981) has recently argued for the necessity of integrating the efforts of developmental psychology with family sociology.

SEPARATION–INDIVIDUATION AND THE DEVELOPMENT OF OBJECT RELATIONS

The framework of developmental phases provided by Margaret Mahler (1963, 1968; Mahler, Pine, & Bergman, 1975) provides a convenient context for discussing the evolution of object relationships and their role in development. The first 1 or 2 months of life constitute the autistic phase, during which awareness of surroundings is limited except for brief episodes of alert awareness prompted by biologic needs that put the infant into contact with the responsive mothering persona. During this period there is an association built up between the mother's face and pleasurable sensations and relief from internal distress. The appearance of social smiling in the 2nd or 3rd month marks the shift to the second phase, the *symbiotic phase*, during which the infant shifts from the predominantly coenesthetic and inner-directed organization of the autistic phase to an increasing interest in the external world and particularly in the perceptual gestalt provided by the mother. This latter is gradually incorporated into the infant's own emerging body image and self-representation. This is a period of increasing interest in the external environment and is marked by an increase in eye-to-eye contact, smiling and cooing, as well as by increasing curiosity and exploratory activity.

The labeling for these early phases is unfortunate, since they provide a form of pathological metaphor to describe early normal development. To an extent these concepts rest on a pathological reconstruction that reflects an earlier set of convictions about early infantile mental life. Current studies have shifted the emphasis to a better appreciation of the infant's capacity for adaptedness and attentive response, which counters the emphasis on passivity and withdrawal inherent in the pathological metaphors (e.g., autism and symbiosis). The separation–individuation process, however, seems more descriptive of ensuing patterns of mother–child interaction.

After several months of intense social interaction, particularly with the mother, the infant enters the beginnings of the separation–individuation process itself and begins to "hatch" from the symbiotic orbit. This subphase of *differentiation* is characterized by a shift from the illusion of permanent, inner-directed, symbiotic fusion with the mother to a more outwardly directed, differentiated, exploratory interest in the external environment. Somewhere in the 4th–6th months, the infant has gained a sufficient degree of differentiation between self and object that he will cry or reach out for the mother when she leaves the room, but will also develop an intense interest in strangers, frequently making a busy comparison between the mother's face and the stranger's. This interest in the stranger tends to gain an increasingly negative quality leading to a pattern of frowning, fussing, or crying in the presence of strangers in around the 7th–9th month.

Spitz's early studies of the so-called 8th-month anxiety recognized it as a function of the development of the sufficient self–object differentiation to allow for an emerging fear of the mother's loss. He concluded that stranger anxiety was a necessary feature of normal development. However, there is considerable variation in the occurrence of this phenomenon. Where the developmental progression has been positive and has served to establish an adequate foundation in basic trust, and particularly where exposure to other caretaking persons besides the mother has been a feature of early experience, the reaction of stranger anxiety may be relatively modest (Mahler *et al.*, 1975). Emde *et al.* (1976) have shown that the infant's distress reaction is connected with the expectation of seeing his mother's face in the context of an approaching person, only to see a strange face instead. The 8th-month stranger anxiety reflects not only a level of cognitive differentiation and an increasing attachment to the mother but also demonstrates a shift in emotional differentiation that allows for the capacity for fearfulness that had not been possible previously.

In the last few months of the 1st year, the next subphase of separation-individuation, namely, the *practicing period*, takes effect. This is marked by an intense degree of curiosity and interest in exploring the environment, retaining the mother as a base of security from which the infant can venture out on explorations and to which he can return when necessary. The emergence of locomotor capacities, at first crawling and then walking, combine with this burgeoning curiosity to form the basis for the exercise of increasingly independent ego capacities that draw the infant away from the maternal orbit. It is also a period of increasing awareness of the degree of separation from the mother and marks the beginnings of the child's individuation out of the representational fusion between mother and self into a more independent and autonomous functional sense of self. This is also the period, as Winnicott (1953) observed, in which the development of transitional objects and transitional phenomena occurs, as aids to the infant to console himself in the face of separation and to a degree restore the illusion of union with the mother.

As has been frequently observed, the infant's early relationship with the mother is marked by the capacity of the mother to satisfy the infant's internal needs (Hartmann, 1952; Hoffer, 1952). At the earliest stage of development, the drives and inner need-states are imperative and are dominated by the pleasure principle, such that there is an inherent demand for immediate satisfaction and relief. As Anna Freud (1952) has pointed out, these demands have to be modulated and brought under control before the infant can develop the capacity to maintain cathexis of the object, even under conditions in which satisfaction is not forthcoming. It is the development of this capacity that allows for an increasing degree of separation from the mother. In her view it is possible to exchange objects in the very earliest months of life provided the necessary need-satisfaction is maintained, but by about 5 months the degree of specific and focal attachment to the object increases so that any separation from the object tends to produce a reaction of acute distress.

As the relationship with the mother is transformed from one of primary need-satisfaction to increasing attachment, the image of the mother ceases to be associated only with states of need-dependency and with conditions of need-satisfaction, and the infant becomes capable of a more consistent and permanent level of libidinal cathexis in which the maternal representation is maintained in stable and consistent fashion regardless of need-satisfying conditions (A. Freud, 1953). While experiences of need-satisfaction lead to the development of a good object representation, the experience of need-frustration lays the basis for the formation of a bad object representation. An adequate degree of frustration, along with adequate levels of satisfaction in the relationship with objects, serves as a stimulus to appropriate degrees of separation. In addition, without a measure of frustration and delay, the stimulus may be lacking for the development of ego functions and for the increasing differentiation of self and object.

The capacity to discharge aggression against the object may be compromised, resulting in turning aggression against the self. Consequently, where need-satisfaction is inadequate, there may be a premature differentiation of the aggressive drive, resulting in hypercathexis of perception with aggressive derivatives, premature separation from the object, and excessive formation of frustrating and bad object representations. The infant's emerging psychic structure in such instances may be overburdened with conflict rather than the achievement of need-satisfaction and tension discharge. This can result in severe disturbance in the infant's relationship with the mothering object, even in the first 6 months, and would similarly tend to intensify subsequent separation and stranger anxiety (Rubenfine, 1962).

Particularly during the symbiotic phase, the relationship to the mother has this predominantly need-satisfying character. The mother is equivalently seen as an extension of the self. As the stage of need-satisfaction progresses, the object is only transiently recognized as in some degree separate only at moments of increased need, as when the infant is feeling the pangs of hunger; but as satisfaction of the need occurs, the object sinks back into its fused condition and ceases to exist until the need arises once again. In this sense the need-satisfying function takes precedence and predominance over the role of the object (Edgcumbe & Burgner, 1972). The transition from such need-satisfying relationships to a more mature form of object relationship, in which the infant is capable of maintaining his or her awareness of and relationship to a specific object regardless of the state of need-satisfaction, opens the way to the state of object constancy. In their discussion of early object relations, Burgner and Edgcumbe (1972) describe various aspects of object constancy. They include:

... perception (especially the ability to differentiate between self and object, to organize stable representations of self and object, and to maintain a perceptual image of the object in its absence); stability of cathexis (the capacity to invest drive energy, especially libidinal, in a particular preferred object representation); the capacity for neutralization and fusion of drives directed to a specific object; the capacity to maintain a positive (loving) emotional attachment to a particular object regardless of frustration or satisfaction of needs, drive pressures, and wishes; the capacity to tolerate ambivalent feelings toward the same object; the capacity to value the object for qualities not connected with its ability to satisfy needs and provide drive satisfactions. (pp. 319–320)

In other words, the achievement of object constancy marks a level of the development of obejct relationships in which there is not only a permanent and consistent formation of an object representation but also indicates that the organization and functioning of the infant's own sense of self has achieved a degree of internal consistency and stability that allows for the maintenance of self–object differentiation and sufficient inner organization to allow the infant to maintain a consistent view of himself as related to the object regardless of the object's capacity for responding to felt inner needs or distress.

This formulation would seem to apply to a later developmental stage than our present concern. Such libidinal object constancy may evolve in the 2nd year. The "object constancy" of the 1st year involves the establishing of the libidinal tie to the mother as reflected in the increasingly selective and exclusive attachment to the mother, independent of need or need-satisfaction, and possibly also the onset of separation and/or stranger anxiety. This early constancy can be seen as a preliminary stage in the development of the later libidinal object constancy as described by Edgcumbe and Burgner (1972). Fraiberg (1969) has attempted to distinguish these forms of constancy in terms of the cognitive elements, the earlier form reflecting the establishment of recognition memory, the latter the capacity for evocative memory.

The transition out of total need-dependency toward object constancy is a vital aspect of the "hatching" process which begins separation–individuation out of the symbiotic maternal relationship. An important aspect of this developmental step is the emergence of transitional objects and transitional phenomena originally described by Winnicott (1953). As later suggested by Tolpin (1971), the transitional object becomes the vehicle for the gradual process by which certain characteristics and functions originally provided for the child by the external caretaking object become internalized, that is, are transformed by the emergence of an internal psychic structure that carries out the same function in the service of maintaining internal homeostatic balance. For Tolpin, following Kohut, the basis of the process is narcissistic, but in fact it may have broader and more far reaching implications.

A significant aspect of this emerging developmental paradigm is that the infant begins to use an object (in Winnicott's sense, to "create" an object), that is, to endow some object in the external world with a similar capacity to that originally experienced in the relationship with the mother. The mother's original role of soothing and quieting the child is transferred to the blanket or the cuddly toy so that it begins to possess the soothing and tension-relieving functions originally exercised by the mother. The child creates such an object usually when he has sufficiently emerged from the symbiotic orbit and begins to perceive the mother as the increasingly separate but important vehicle for comfort and relief from distress. The transferal facilitates the child's initiative toward increasing independence from the mother insofar as, in virtue of his replacement of the mother to some extent by the soothing, tension-relieving blanket or toy, he has gained a means of calming and soothing himself that does not require the presence or participation of the mother. This developmental progression also serves the interests of shifting the basis of the child's involvement in the world from relative passivity to increasing activity and control. The dependence and often addictive attachment to such transitional objects often fades corresponding to the degree to which the child develops an increasingly internalized capacity for self-soothing and internal regulation.

The process of separation from the mother is a gradual one involving a series of minute losses through separation and surrender of symbiotic dependence and through gradual degrees of transitional dependence toward increasing self-dependence and emerging individuality. Tolpin (1971) writes:

By preserving the mental organization associated with the "good-enough" mother who mediates structure while it is lacking "inside," the blanket eases the stress of transition to object constancy. . . . At the same time, it promotes internalization of the mental structure on which object constancy depends—the inner structure now performs for the self some of the equilibrium-maintaining regulations which depended at first on the need-satisfying object. Circumscribed losses of the mother in her role as need-satisfying (structure-mediating) soother or regulator not only are inevitable and unavoidable during infancy; they are also necessary in optimal doses if mastery of separation from her and individuation of the psyche are to occur. (p. 328)

By the same token, a parallel process of assimilation and internalization of the mother's anxiety-relieving functions also contributes to the elaboration of ego functions that facilitate internal regulatory capacities and subserve the emerging function of signal anxiety in the service of the organization of appropriate defenses and the preservation of the self.

The internalization of these functions proceeds smoothly and effectively in the context of good-enough mothering and an appropriate titration of degrees of frustration–gratification and separation–dependence. The mother's failure to support or facilitate this process can prove traumatic and frustrate developmental objectives leaving the child excessively dependent, or threateningly isolated, or vulnerable to overwhelming and disrupting anxiety.

Hand in hand with this developing pattern of the infant's experience and relationships to objects, there is a gradual emergence and articulation of the infant's sense of self as a separate entity. Certainly, the earliest experiences of repeated satisfaction–frustration in relationship to the mother contribute to a gradual building up of the infant's growing sense of the mother as, at first globally and then more discretely, separate from himself. Moreover, as Hoffer (1950, 1952) and Geleerd (1956) have pointed out, the differential experiences of the infant's touching parts of his own body, or being touched by others, or touching others, particularly the mother, provide an important vehicle for facilitating this gradual sense of differentiation. Gradually, the organization of memory deposits and early associations forming discrete islands of pleasure and pain at first connected with the mother's pleasure-giving and distress-relieving ministrations serve as the basis for early part-images of the self and the beginnings of discriminations from the mother (Mahler & Gosliner, 1955).

Early explorations of the infant's own body as well as the mother's and an increasing cathexis of body parts, the so-called "customs inspection," provide the basis for a core of the emerging sense of self and a gradual demarcation of the body self from the object world (McDevitt & Mahler, 1980). As a number of observers have pointed out (McDevitt & Mahler, 1980; Murphy, 1980; Tolpin, 1971), as the child gains an increasing capacity for active participation and as his inherent capacities for mastery and competence in dealing with objects, both animate and inanimate, in his environment grows, his sense of self is increasingly shaped and reinforced. Even the earliest experiences of participatory activity, the capacity to elicit even on the simplest level certain responses from his environment that prove satisfying and rewarding, serve as the initial building blocks for an emerging sense of self-as-agent. This rudimentary sense of self emerges in step-by-step progression as the developmental process evolves. Moreover, as we shall see in a moment, this emerging sense of self is fed by the progressive steps of internalization that underlie and are implicit in the same developmental process.

PATTERNS OF INTERNALIZATION

As can readily be appreciated from this review, internalization reflects and touches most of the important aspects of the developmental process. What aspects of internalization, then, can we specify amid the complexities of developmental progression? The infant is embedded in a matrix of object relations (object related) from the very moment of birth, if not before (Graves, 1980). From the very beginning, then, internalization processes are taking place and result in the laying down of building blocks of structural aspects of the infant psyche and components of the emerging self.

If we return for a moment to our working definition, our focus here is on those specific processes by which the infant subject transforms the regulatory interactions with his environment and particularly with the caregivers in his environment into inner regulations and characteristics. From the very beginning of this process, the infant is interacting with his environment and assimilating from it as well as accommodating to it. In the earliest interchanges with the mother, when the first regulatory patterns are being established and the infant is finding an "ecological niche," the patterning of communications between mother and child is intense, complex, and has profound effects. Our current understanding of the complexity of this interaction makes it clear that considerably more is at stake and more involved than issues of mere homeostatic regulation.

The basis of the process even at this most primitive level is by no means reductively physiologic, but involves important communications of affect that intermesh with physiologic variables, but have considerable impact on the infant's evolving sense of well-being and security (Pine, 1981). When the good-enough mother responds sensitively and comfortingly to her infant's distress, she is not simply restoring a physiologic state of homeostasis and relieving the tension related to the infant's distress, but she is, by the same actions, communicating a set of affects and attitudes toward the infant which qualify the infant's experience in the interaction.

The issues, then, are not simply quantitative (economic), but also involve important meaning-impregnated affective experiences, which the infant experiences within the fusion of the mother–child unity as somehow related to himself. In other words, hand in hand with the physiologic replacement, there is an affective infusion generated by the mother within the complex interaction between them, which the infant experiences, however globally and indistinctly, as somehow his own. This is the "mirroring function," which Winnicott has described so well, in which the child experiences himself as he is experienced by the mother. In this sense, then, the importance of all of the parameters of early management of the cycle of waking–sleeping, feeding–eliminating and the patterns of regulatory exchange that evolve in connection with them, as well as the issues of optimal levels of stimulation in all sensory modalities, carry with them the added impact of this sensoriaffective level of communication and include as one important aspect of their developmental significance the internalization dimension. Thus, these early affective components, which arise within the context of the interaction and relatedness to the mother, become a part of the infant's emerging inner world and are gradually consolidated along with other aspects of his emerging psychic structure.

Lichtenstein (1977) has focused on the mirroring aspect of this primitive relatedness. What emerges dimly in the mirror is not so much a primary love object (mother) as the child's own image as reflected in the mother's own needs vis-à-vis the child. What is internalized is a sense of primary identity that becomes a basic organizing principle for further emerging patterns of internalization. The child begins to experience his own existence as it is reflected in and through the mother's responsive libidinal cathexis of the child.

With regard to the infant's earliest self-experience, Dare and Holder (1981) have recently provided us with a summarizing statement:

We believe that under normal conditions the earliest self-experiences are almost totally determined by the nature of the mother/infant relationship. It is a necessity that the mother and newborn baby adapt to each other. Different babies have different "personalities" and temperaments, as well as varying adaptive capacities. The infant's adaptive capacities are, of course, considerably more limited than those of the mother. Winnicott (1965) has remarked that the infant's first view of himself is the reflection of what he sees in his mother's eyes. In other words, the mother can be understood as acting like a mirror, reflecting the first qualities of the infant's self onto the infant. When she smiles and cuddles the infant closely, the emergent self-image will be associated with feelings of warmth, safety and of being cherished. When the mother is withdrawn, depressed or angry, the emergent self is experienced as fragile, unloved and unvalued. Later, of course, the child whose mother is consistently negative towards him may come to regard himself as the cause and source of the mother's unhappiness or hostility.

We would speculate that the first disjointed experiences of that which is later to become the "self" are essentially affective, deriving from bodily sensations and the interactions with the mother. At this early point in development, such experiences lack the degree of organization with regard to time and space as well as the cognitive elements which will eventually accrue to a cohesive self-representation. (p. 327)

The importance of this dimension of the infant's early experience is amply underlined by studies of the effects of object loss or deprivation at this level. These effects have been amply documented in studies of anaclitic depression, hospitalism, and even the effects of transient separation.

This pattern of communication and interaction becomes increasingly more complex and evolves in the direction of increasing activity and initiative on the part of the infant. The earliest internalized components derive from the state of the infant's object relatedness, particularly with primary caregivers, but this gradually evolves in the direction of an increasing sense of interaction with and relationship to a separate object. As the infant's experience of the object becomes increasingly distanced and gradually separate (Brodey, 1965), the experience of feeding or being fed or not being fed is gradually disengaged and connected with the presence or the absence of a feeder, so that only gradually are certain regulatory functions connected with the presence or absence of the object.

As the infant's capacity to differentiate the significant others who are interacting with him enlarges, there is a corresponding increase in the complexity and differentiation of internalizations. At this point the infant tends to show an increase in initiatives and an increasing organization and differentiation of emotional components, such as affiliation, fear, curiosity, and exploration. By the same token this burgeoning capacity to take initiative and to organize behavioral and feeling states is simultaneously enriched by and facilitates the infant's capacity to internalize (Greenspan & Lieberman, 1980). It is at this point that the capacity to imitate and to bring imitation to the service of increasing intentionality becomes important.

Imitation plays a particularly important role in the infant's emerging capacity to internalize. Imitative behaviors can be observed even in the earliest weeks of life. These primarily involve movements of the mouth, tongue, and head and have a quality of mimicry, which seems to facilitate the pleasureful interaction between child and adult. At this earliest level such behavior undoubtedly reflects an inherent capacity for mimicry and seems to serve important uses in the maintenance of and eliciting of certain kinds of pleasureful adult response (Abravanel, Levan-Goldschmidt, & Stevenson, 1976), and reflects part of the infant's preadaptive repertoire of behaviors that elicit and reinforce his interaction with adults. Moreover, the infant's tendency and apparent capacity for imitative behavior can be facilitated or hindered by the pattern of response from the parent (Call & Marschak, 1966). Where the interaction with the parent or caregiver is mutually pleasureful and optimally arousing, the tendency for such imitative responses is facilitated and encouraged. This also begins to take place in the evolving pattern of playfulness between child and caregiver and can be clearly identified as an evolving pattern in early childhood games like the peek-a-boo game (Kleeman, 1967). Such imitative behaviors are quickly brought to the service of the child's increasing initiative and the urge to mastery.

It is important, however, to realize, as Spitz (1958) has noted in connection with the mirroring of prohibitive gestures and in connection with superego development, that true imitation of parental gestures begins to occur in the second half of the 1st year, but these have a mimicking quality as echo-like reproductions of the adult gesture. They tend to be immediate responses and mirror a gesture initiated by the adult. The pattern of such imitative behaviors, however, rapidly shifts from a basis in mirroring or mimicry and becomes increasingly reflective of the infant's growing initiative and is rapidly placed in the service of his capacity to elicit responses from his environment and thus to gain increasing competence and mastery.

It is useful to remember that imitation itself is not a form of internalization but is rather a complex form of learning based on modeling (Meissner, 1972). Consequently, imitations in the developmental context may serve as inducements to or precursors of internalizations that both accompany and follow as a natural consequence the imitative behavior but are not identical. By the same token, imitative behaviors may reflect underlying patterns of internalization or may serve defensive functions as a vehicle for inhibiting or preventing further identification (Meissner, 1974).

In the normal course of events, when the affective experience with the object is predominantly positive and constructive, the conditions prevail for eliciting and facilitating the infant's capacity to both constructively imitate and internalize. The patterns of emerging initiative and competence that the infant develops, often in rapid and remarkable fashion toward the end of the 1st year, lay the basis for an increasing capacity for positive and constructive identifications with loved and admired adult objects. Imitation plays a transitional role insofar as it is a vehicle through which external capacities or characteristics of significant objects can become a functional part of the infant's own capacity. But while imitation remains a matter of behavioral patterns, identification reaches beyond to include qualities and characteristics of the object itself or the object relationship. Consequently, the behavioral modifications of imitation imply no enduring structural change in self-organization (Meissner, 1972).

Even in the 1st year of life, and possibly quite early in the 1st year, the infant has the capacity for internal psychic organization and synthesis based on the modeling of an external object. This capacity for identification emerges simultaneously with the capacity for differentiation between self and object images and is rapidly brought into the service of developing competence and mastery. The infant's emerging capacity for initiative and autonomous behavior provides another facilitating basis for this identificatory capacity.

However, the emergence of this capacity can be short-circuited or diverted by those vicissitudes in the infant's object relationships that introduce frustration in excessive degree, heightened anxiety, insecurity, loss, abandonment, or other growth-inhibiting or growth-frustrating determinants. The effect of such vicissitudes can be a subverting of the infant's inherent identificatory potential with the result that forming structures are organized in terms of defensive needs or are overly influenced by and vulnerable to drive derivatives. Consequently, the internalizations that occur in these defensively overburdened contexts tend to underlie pathological personality configurations and remain continuously susceptible to degrees of drive-determined dysfunction and vulnerable to regressive pulls and defensive distortions (Meissner, 1971).

The earliest levels of affective interaction in the mother–child dyad have an influence on inchoate and emerging patterns of internalization. The predominance of harmonious, adaptive, and mutually reinforcing interactions between mother and infant, particularly having to do with affective communications although not exclusively, allows for a relatively unencumbered assimilation of elements from the object-related sphere to the infant's emerging sense of self. The "primary identity" has embedded in it affective reverberations of comfort, security, well-being, and positive anticipation and expectation as the infant begins to approach the external world. The effects of such good-enough mothering, or perhaps more precisely good-enough mother–child interacting, is to provide optimal stimulus to the child's growing capacity to assimilate, imitate, take initiative, and achieve increasing degrees of mastery and competence in his ability to respond to and engage with his environment. The inherent capacity for self-actualization and for integrating aspects of given objects in the process of selectively and adaptively shaping a sense of self is given optimal stimulus and support. These aspects of early internalization point in the direction of an emerging capacity for positive and constructive identifications.

Where the process falters, the ground is laid for a gradual accretion of impediments to the capacity to internalize aspects of objects and object relations as an expression of the initiative, adaptive selectivity, and creative integration in the formation of the self. Even the earliest elements of disquiet, disequilibrium, excessive frustration, or significant failures of the mother to respond in need-satisfying and adaptive ways to the child's distress leaves a sense of lack, discomfort, and dis-ease within the infant's rudimentary experience of self. The affective tone is negative rather than positive. The sense of trust is shifted in the direction of mistrust, insecurity, uncertainty. The emerging capacity for dealing with the environment is cast in doubt and is unreliable, halting, and uncertain. The progression toward an increasing sense of mastery and competence falters. The affective coloration to the emerging sense of primary identity is negative and insecure. In this sense the basis is laid for the tendency in the later course of development toward introjection as the predominant modality of internalization, rather than identification.

A crucial point in the development of internalization comes with the infant's hatching from the symbiotic orbit. At this juncture, the element of loss becomes an operative part of the developmental process. The diminishing of symbiotic dependence and the gradual course of separation and individuation calls into play compensatory internalization processes that enable the child to assimilate aspects and functions of the caretaking objects. The advance in internalization provides the internal components for increasing individuation and serves basic needs for a sense of inner competence and capacity and for the maintaining of narcissistic equilibrium. At this point the beginnings of the form of internalization that we can later recognize as introjection (especially in the rapprochement and oedipal phases) enter the picture. To the extent that earlier affective assimilations have left a core of positive residues, the introjective components will build on a relatively positive base. Where the residues are excessively negative or ambivalent, the quality of emerging introjects tends toward increased aggression, poorer integration, faulty internalization, permeation with unintegrated drive derivatives, greater degrees of conflict, and the need for defensive maintenance. Such introjects are more poorly structuralized and have an increased regressive potential. They are also more susceptible to externalization and can function as core elements of pathological personality organization (Meissner, 1978b).

The emergence of transitional objects and related transitional phenomena are a function of the availability of processes of introjection and, correspondingly, projection. These are the intrapsychic processes by which transitional objects are created, transformed, and gradually internalized. When negative or conflictual elements, even from the earliest levels of infantile experience, contaminate these processes, the child's capacity to form and utilize transitional objects in the service of optimal psychic growth, effective separation–individuation and increasing autonomy can be compromised—even severely so. Transitional phenomena may not develop, or may be subverted into the formation of fetishistic (Greenacre, 1969) or even autistic objects (Tustin, 1980).

By way of conclusion, then, the argument presented in this chapter would suggest that in the 1st year of life, and even in the very first object-related experiences of the newborn infant, internalizing processes are at work and constitute the heart of the developmental progression. Moreover, specifiable internalizing processes function at a more primitive level, in the form of precursors, than their more evolved and differentiated counterparts in later stages of development. At the most primitive level, the process is incorporative, particularly in that it predominates in the period in which mother and child are fused in a dyadic unity in which there is neither self nor object. The mother's affective relation to the child is at the same moment his own, and is gradually assimilated into the islands of experience that become increasingly organized and stable and form the first rudiments of the self-organization.

As these affectively colored rudiments are extended to later forms of internalization, they are progressively integrated with the continual flow of internalizations. The balance of libidinal, narcissistic, and aggressive components influences the pattern of subsequent internalizations and determines the extent to which positive or negative (pathogenic) introjections take shape and come to dominate the organization of the self, or the extent to which positive patterns of identification will provide the basis for more positive, autonomous, adaptive, and cohesive elements as the essential building blocks of a healthy and mature self-organization and personality structure (Meissner, 1971, 1972, 1981).

ACKNOWLEDGMENTS

I am indebted to Drs. Eveoleen Rexford and Suzanne van Amerongen for their critical reading of an earlier draft of this chapter and for their helpful suggestions.

REFERENCES

Abravanel, E., Levan-Goldschmidt, E., & Stevenson, M. B. (1976). Action imitation: The early phase of infancy. *Child Development, 47,* 1032-1044.

Ainsworth, M. D. S. (1969). Object relations, dependency, and attachment: A theoretical review of the infant-mother relationship. *Child Development, 40,* 969-1025.

Alpert, A., Neubauer, P. B., & Weil, A. P. (1956). Unusual variations in drive endowment. *The Psychoanalytic Study of the Child, 11,* 125-163.

Belsky, J. (1981). Early human experience: A family perspective. *Developmental Psychology, 17,* 3-23.

Benjamin, J. D. (1965). Developmental biology and psychoanalysis. In N. S. Greenfield & W. C. Lewis (Eds.), *Psychoanalysis and current biological thought* (pp. 57-80). Madison: University of Wisconsin Press.

Bennett, S. L. (1971). Infant-caretaker interactions. In E. N. Rexford, L. W. Sander, & T. Shapiro (Eds.), *Infant psychiatry: A new synthesis* (pp. 79-90). New Haven: Yale University Press, 1976.

Bergman, P., & Escalona, S. K. (1949). Unusual sensitivities in very young children. *The Psychoanalytic Study of the Child, 3/4,* 333-352.

Bibring, G. L. (1959). Some considerations of the psychological processes in pregnancy. *The Psychoanalytic Study of the Child, 14,* 113–121.

Bibring, G. L., Dwyer, T. F., Huntington, D. S., & Valenstein, A. F. (1961). A study of the psychological processes in pregnancy and of the earliest mother–child relationship: I. Some propositions and comments. *The Psychoanalytic Study of the Child, 16,* 9–24.

Blank, M. (1964). The mother's role in infant development. In E. N. Rexford, L. W. Sander, & T. Shapiro (Eds.), *Infant psychiatry: A new synthesis* (pp. 91–103). New Haven: Yale University Press, 1976.

Boyer, L. B. (1956). On maternal overstimulation and ego defects. *The Psychoanalytic Study of the Child, 11,* 236–256.

Brazelton, T. B. (1980). Neonatal assessment. In S. I. Greenspan & G. H. Pollock (Eds.), *The course of life: Psychoanalytic contributions toward understanding personality development* (Vol. I: *Infancy and early childhood,* pp. 203–233). Adelphi, MD: Mental Health Study Center, NIMH.

Brodey, W. M. (1965). On the dynamics of narcissism: I. Externalization and early ego development. *The Psychoanalytic Study of the Child, 20,* 165–193.

Broucek, F. (1979). Efficacy in infancy: A review of some experimental studies and their possible implications for clinical theory. *International Journal of Psycho-Analysis, 60,* 311–316.

Burgner, M., & Edgcumbe, R. (1972). Some problems in the conceptualization of early object relationships: II. The concept of object constancy. *The Psychoanalytic Study of the Child, 27,* 315–333.

Burlingham, D. (1964). Hearing and its role in the development of the blind. *The Psychoanalytic Study of the Child, 19,* 95–112.

Burlingham, D. (1965). Some problems of ego development in blind children. *The Psychoanalytic Study of the Child, 20,* 194–208.

Burlingham, D. (1967). Developmental considerations in the occupations of the blind. *The Psychoanalytic Study of the Child, 22,* 187–198.

Call, J. D. (1971). Infant observation and longitudinal study: Implications for mental health and primary prevention of mental disorders in high-risk situations. In E. N. Rexford, L. W. Sander, & T. Shapiro (Eds.), *Infant psychiatry: A new synthesis* (pp. 7–14). New Haven: Yale University Press, 1976.

Call, J. D., & Marschak, M. (1976). Styles and games in infancy. In E. N. Rexford, L. W. Sander, & T. Shapiro (Eds.), *Infant psychiatry: A new synthesis* (pp. 104–112). New Haven: Yale University Press, 1976.

Caplan, H., Bibace, R., & Rabinovitch, M. S. (1963). Paranatal stress, cognitive organization and ego function. In E. N. Rexford, L. W. Sander, & T. Shapiro (Eds.), *Infant psychiatry: A new synthesis* (pp. 251–263). New Haven: Yale University Press, 1976.

Coleman, R. W., Kris, E., & Provence, S. (1953). The study of variations of early parental attitudes: A preliminary report. *The Psychoanalytic Study of the Child, 8,* 20–47.

Cytryn, L. (1968). Methodological issues in psychiatric evaluation of infants. In E. N. Rexford, L. W. Sander, & T. Shapiro (Eds.), *Infant psychiatry: A new synthesis* (pp. 17–25). New Haven: Yale University Press, 1976.

Dare, C., & Holder, A. (1981). Developmental aspects of the interaction between narcissism, self-esteem and object relations. *International Journal of Psycho-Analysis, 62,* 323–337.

Edgcumbe, R., & Burgner, M. (1972). Some problems in the conceptualization of early object relationships: I. The concepts of need-satisfaction and need-satisfying relationships. *The Psychoanalytic Study of the Child, 27,* 283–314.

Emde, R. N. (1980). Toward a psychoanalytic theory of affect: II. Emerging models of emotional development in infancy. In S. I. Greenspan & G. H. Pollock (Eds.), *The course of life: Psychoanalytic contributions toward understanding personality development* (Vol. I: *Infancy and early childhood,* pp. 85–112). Adelphi, MD: Mental Health Study Center, NIMH.

Emde, R. N., Gaensbauer, N., & Harmon, R. J. (1976). *Emotional expression in infancy: A behavioral study* (Psychological Issues, Monograph 37). New York: International Universities Press.

Erikson, E. H. (1980). Elements of a psychoanalytic theory of psychosocial development. In S. I. Greenspan & G. H. Pollock (Eds.), *The course of life: Psychoanalytic contributions toward understanding personality development* (Vol. I: *Infancy and early childhood*, pp. 11–61). Adelphi, MD: Mental Health Study Center, NIMH.

Escalona, S. K. (1962). The study of individual differences and the problem of fate. In E. N. Rexford, L. W. Sander, & T. Shapiro (Eds.), *Infant psychiatry: A new synthesis* (pp. 46–67). New Haven: Yale University Press, 1976.

Escalona, S. K. (1963). Patterns of infantile experience and the developmental process. *The Psychoanalytic Study of the Child, 18,* 197–244.

Escalona, S. K., & Heider, G. (1959). *Prediction and outcome.* New York: Basic Books.

Fish, B. (1963). The maturation of arousal and attention in the first months of life: A study of variations in ego development. In E. N. Rexford, L. W. Sander, & T. Shapiro (Eds.), *Infant psychiatry: A new synthesis* (pp. 207–219). New Haven: Yale University Press, 1976.

Fraiberg, S. (1968). Parallel and divergent patterns in blind and sighted infants. *The Psychoanalytic Study of the Child, 23,* 264–300.

Fraiberg, S. (1969). Libidinal object constancy and mental representation. *The Psychoanalytic Study of the Child, 24,* 9–47.

Fraiberg, S. (1971). Intervention in infancy: A program for blind infants. In E. N. Rexford, L. W. Sander, & T. Shapiro (Eds.), *Infant psychiatry: A new synthesis* (pp. 264–284). New Haven: Yale University Press, 1976.

Freedman, D. A. (1980). Maturational and developmental issues in the first year. In S. I. Greenspan & G. H. Pollock (Eds.), *The course of life: Psychoanalytic contributions toward understanding personality development* (Vol. I: *Infancy and early childhood*, pp. 129–145). Adelphi, MD: Mental Health Study Center, NIMH.

Freud, A. (1952). The mutual influences in the development of ego and id: Introduction to the discussion. *The Psychoanalytic Study of the Child, 7,* 42–50.

Freud, A. (1953). Some remarks on infant observation. *The Psychoanalytic Study of the Child, 8,* 9–19.

Freud, A. (1980). Child analysis as the study of mental growth. In S. I. Greenspan & G. H. Pollock (Eds.), *The course of life: Psychoanalytic contributions toward understanding personality development* (Vol. I: *Infancy and early childhood*, pp. 1–10). Adelphi, MD: Mental Health Study Center, NIMH.

Freud, S. (1920). Beyond the pleasure principle. *Standard Edition, 18,* 7–64. London: Hogarth Press, 1957.

Freud, S. (1921). Group psychology and the analysis of the ego. *Standard Edition, 18,* 65–143. London: Hogarth Press, 1957.

Fries, M. E., & Woolf, P. J. (1953). Some hypotheses on the role of the congenital activity type in personality development. *The Psychoanalytic Study of the Child, 8,* 48–62.

Geleerd, E. R. (1956). Clinical contribution to the problem of the early mother–child relationship: Some discussion of its influence on self-destructive tendencies and fugue-states. *The Psychoanalytic Study of the Child, 11,* 336–351.

Goldberg, S. (1977). Social competence in infancy: A model of parent-infant interaction. *Merrill-Palmer Quarterly, 23,* 163–177.

Graves, P. L. (1980). The functioning fetus. In E. N. Rexford, L. W. Sanford, & T. Shapiro (Eds.), *Infant psychiatry: A new synthesis* (pp. 235–256). New Haven: Yale University Press, 1976.

Greenacre, P. (1969). The fetish and the transitional object. *The Psychoanalytic Study of the Child, 24,* 144–164.

Greenspan, S. I., & Lieberman, A. F. (1980). Infants, mothers and their interaction: A quantitative clinical approach to developmental assessment. In S. I. Greenspan & G. H. Pollock (Eds.), *The course of life: Psychoanalytic contributions toward understanding personality development* (Vol. I: *Infancy and early childhood*, pp. 271–312). Adelphi, MD: Mental Health Study Center, NIMH.

Hartmann, H. (1952). The mutual influences in the development of ego and id. *The Psychoanalytic Study of the Child, 7*, 9–30.

Hoffer, W. (1949). Mouth, hand and ego-integration. *The Psychoanalytic Study of the Child, 3/4*, 49–56.

Hoffer, W. (1950). Development of the body ego. *The Psychoanalytic Study of the Child, 5*, 18–23.

Hoffer, W. (1952). The mutual influences in the development of ego and id: Earliest stages. *The Psychoanalytic Study of the Child, 7*, 31–41.

Jackson, E. B., Klatskin, E. H., & Wilkin, L. C. (1952). Early child development in relation to degree of flexibility of maternal attitude. *The Psychoanalytic Study of the Child, 7*, 393–428.

Kaplan, S. (1964). A clinical contribution to the study of narcissism in infancy. *The Psychoanalytic Study of the Child, 19*, 398–420.

Kleeman, J. A. (1967). The peek-a-boo game: I. Its origins, meanings, and related phenomena in the first year. *The Psychoanalytic Study of the Child, 22*, 239–273.

Korner, A. F. (1964). Some hypotheses regarding the significance of individual differences at birth for later development. *The Psychoanalytic Study of the Child, 19*, 58–72.

Korner, A. F., & Grobstein, R. (1967). Individual differences at birth: Implications for mother–infant relationship and later development. In E. N. Rexford, L. W. Sander, & T. Shapiro (Eds.), *Infant psychiatry: A new synthesis* (pp. 68–78). New Haven: Yale University Press, 1976.

Lamb, M. E. (1976). Proximity seeking attachment behaviors: A critical review of the literature. *Genetic Psychology Monographs, 93*, 63–89.

Lichtenstein, H. (1977). *The dilemma of human identity*. New York: Jason Aronson.

Mahler, M. S. (1961). On sadness and grief in infancy and childhood: Loss and restoration of the symbiotic love object. *The Psychoanalytic Study of the Child, 16*, 332–351.

Mahler, M. S. (1963). Thoughts about development and individuation. *The Psychoanalytic Study of the Child, 18*, 307–324.

Mahler, M. S. (1965). On early infantile psychosis: The symbiotic and autistic syndromes. In E. N. Rexford, L. W. Sander, & T. Shapiro (Eds.), *Infant psychiatry: A new synthesis* (pp. 220–226). New Haven: Yale University Press, 1976.

Mahler, M. S. (1968). *On Human symbiosis and the vicissitudes of individuation*. New York: International Universities Press.

Mahler, M. S., & Gosliner, B. J. (1955). On symbiotic child psychosis: Genetic, dynamic and restitutive aspects. *The Psychoanalytic Study of the Child, 10*, 195–212.

Mahler, M. S., & McDevitt, J. B. (1968). Observations on adaptation and defense in statu nascendi: Developmental precursors in the first two years of life. *Psychoanalytic Quarterly, 37*, 1–21.

Mahler, M. S., & McDevitt, J. B. (1980). The separation–individuation process and identity formation. In S. I. Greenspan & G. H. Pollock (Eds.), *The course of life: Psychoanalytic contributions toward understanding personality development* (Vol. I: *Infancy and early childhood*, pp. 395–406). Adelphi, MD: Mental Health Study Center, NIMH.

Mahler, M. S., Pine, F., & Bergman, A. (1975). *The psychological birth of the human infant*. New York: International Universities Press.

McDevitt, J. B. (1979). The role of internalization in the development of object relations during the separation–individuation phase. *Journal of the American Psychoanalytic Association, 27*, 327–343.

McDevitt, J. B. (1980, November). *Separation–individuation and aggression.* A. A. Brill Memorial Lecture, New York Psychoanalytic Society.

McDevitt, J. B., & Mahler, M. S. (1980). Object constancy, individuality, and internalization. In S. I. Greenspan & G. H. Pollock (Eds.), *The course of life: Psychoanalytic contributions toward understanding personality development* (Vol. I: *Infancy and early childhood,* pp. 407–423). Adelphi, MD: Mental Health Study Center, NIMH.

Meissner, W. W. (1970). Notes on identification: I. Origins in Freud. *Psychoanalytic Quarterly, 39,* 563–589.

Meissner, W. W. (1971). Notes on identification: II. Related concepts. *Psychoanalytic Quarterly, 40,* 277–302.

Meissner, W. W. (1972). Notes on identification: III. The concept of identification. *Psychoanalytic Quarterly, 41,* 224–260.

Meissner, W. W. (1974). The role of imitative social learning in identificatory processes. *Journal of the American Psychoanalytic Association, 22,* 512–536.

Meissner, W. W. (1978a). The conceptualization of marriage and family dynamics from a psychoanalytic perspective. In T. J. Paolino & B. S. McCrady (Eds.), *Marriage and marital therapy: Psychoanalytic, behavioral, and systems theory perspectives* (pp. 25–88). New York: Brunner/Mazel.

Meissner, W. W. (1978b). *The paranoid process.* New York: Jason Aronson.

Meissner, W. W. (1979). Internalization and object relations. *Journal of the American Psychoanalytic Association, 27,* 345–360.

Meissner, W. W. (1981). *Internalization in psychoanalysis* (Psychological Issues, Monograph 50). New York: International Universities Press.

Mittelmann, B. (1960). Intrauterine and early infantile motility. *The Psychoanalytic Study of the Child, 15,* 104–127.

Murphy, L. B. (1980). Psychoanalytic views of infancy. In S. I. Greenspan & G. H. Pollock (Eds.), *The course of life: Psychoanalytic contributions toward understanding personality development* (Vol. I: *Infancy and early childhood,* pp. 313–363). Adelphi, MD: Mental Health Study Center, NIMH.

Nagera, H. (1964). Autoerotism, autoerotic activities, and ego development. *The Psychoanalytic Study of the Child, 19,* 240–255.

Paine, R. S. (1965). The contribution of developmental neurology to child psychiatry. In E. N. Rexford, L. W. Sander, & T. Shapiro (Eds.), *Infant psychiatry: A new synthesis* (pp. 26–45). New Haven: Yale University Press, 1976.

Pine, F. (1981). In the beginning: Contributions to a psychoanalytic developmental psychology. *The International Review of Psycho-Analysis, 8,* 15–33.

Provence, S., & Ritvo, S. (1961). Effects of deprivation on institutionalized infants: Disturbances in development of relationship to inanimate objects. *The Psychoanalytic Study of the Child, 16,* 189–205.

Rapaport, D. (1957). A theoretical analysis of the superego concept. In M. M. Gill (Ed.), *The collected papers of David Rapaport* (pp. 685–709). New York: Basic Books, 1967.

Ritvo, S., & Solnit, A. J. (1958). Influences of early mother–child interaction on identification processes. *The Psychoanalytic Study of the Child, 13,* 64–91.

Rochlin, G. (1961). The dread of abandonment: A contribution to the etiology of the loss complex and to depression. *The Psychoanalytic Study of the Child, 16,* 451–470.

Rubenfine, D. L. (1962). Maternal stimulation, psychic structure, and early object relations: With special reference to aggression and denial. *The Psychoanalytic Study of the Child, 17,* 265–282.

Sander, L. W. (1962). Issues in early mother–child interaction. In E. N. Rexford, L. W. Sander, & T. Shapiro (Eds.), *Infant psychiatry: A new synthesis* (pp. 127–147). New Haven: Yale University Press, 1976.

Sander, L. W. (1969). The longitudinal course of early mother-child interaction—cross-care comparison in a sample of mother-child pairs. In B. M. Foss (Ed.), *Determinants of infant behavior* (Vol. IV, pp. 189-227). London: Methuen.

Sander, L. W. (1980). Investigation of the infant and its caregiving environment as a biological system. In S. I. Greenspan & G. H. Pollock (Eds.), *The course of life: Psychoanalytic contributions toward understanding personality development* (Vol. I: *Infancy and early childhood*, pp. 177-201). Adelphi, MD: Mental Health Study Center, NIMH.

Sander, L. W., Stechler, G., Julia, H., & Burns, P. (1971). Primary prevention and some aspects of temporal organization in early infant-caretaker interaction. In E. N. Rexford, L. W. Sander, & T. Shapiro (Eds.), *Infant psychiatry: A new synthesis* (pp. 187-204). New Haven: Yale University Press, 1976.

Sandler, J., & Rosenblatt, B. (1962). The concept of the representational world. *The Psychoanalytic Study of the Child, 17,* 128-145.

Schafer, R. (1968). *Aspects of internalization.* New York: International Universities Press.

Shapiro, T., & Stern, D. (1980). Psychoanalytic perspectives on the first year of life—the establishment of the object in an affective field. In S. I. Greenspan & G. H. Pollock (Eds.), *The course of life: Psychoanalytic contributions toward understanding personality development* (Vol. I: *Infancy and early childhood*, pp. 113-128). Adelphi, MD: Mental Health Study Center, NIMH.

Shrevrin, H., & Toussieng, P. W. (1965). Vicissitudes of the need for tactile stimulation in instinctual development. *The Psychoanalytic Study of the Child, 20,* 310-339.

Silverman, M. A. (1980). The first year after birth. In S. I. Greenspan & G. H. Pollock (Eds.), *The course of life: Psychoanalytic contributions toward understanding personality development* (Vol. I: *Infancy and early childhood*, pp. 147-175). Adelphi, MD: Mental Health Study Center, NIMH.

Solnit, A. J. (1970). A study of object loss in infancy. *The Psychoanalytic Study of the Child, 25,* 257-272.

Spitz, R. A. (1945). Hospitalism: An inquiry into the genesis of psychiatric conditions in early childhood. *The Psychoanalytic Study of the Child, 1,* 53-74.

Spitz, R. A. (1946). Hospitalism: A follow-up report on investigation described in Volume I, 1945. *The Psychoanalytic Study of the Child, 2,* 113-117.

Spitz, R. A. (1949). Autoerotism: Some empirical findings and hypotheses on three of its manifestations in the first year of life. *The Psychoanalytic Study of the Child, 3/4,* 85-120.

Spitz, R. A. (1955). The primal cavity: A contribution to the genesis of perception and its role for psychoanalytic theory. *The Psychoanalytic Study of the Child, 10,* 215-240.

Spitz, R. A. (1958). On the genesis of superego components. *The Psychoanalytic Study of the Child, 13,* 375-404.

Spitz, R. A. (1962). Autoerotism re-examined: The role of early sexual behavior patterns in personality formation. *The Psychoanalytic Study of the Child, 17,* 283-315.

Spitz, R. A., Emde, R. N., & Metcalf, D. R. (1970). Further prototypes of ego formation: A working paper from a research project on early development. *The Psychoanalytic Study of the Child, 25,* 417-441.

Spitz, R. A., & Wolf, K. M. (1946). Anaclitic depression: An inquiry into the genesis of psychiatric conditions in early childhood, II. *The Psychoanalytic Study of the Child, 2,* 313-342.

Spock, B. (1965). Innate inhibition of aggressiveness in infancy. *The Psychoanalytic Study of the Child, 20,* 430-433.

Sroufe, L. A., & Waters, E. (1976). The ontogenesis of smiling and laughter: A perspective on the organization of development in infancy. *Psychological Review, 83,* 173-189.

Stechler, G., & Carpenter, G. (1967). A viewpoint on early affective development. In J. Helmuth (Ed.), *Exceptional infant: The normal infant* (pp. 165-189). New York: Brunner/Mazel.

Stern, D. N. (1971). A microanalysis of mother–infant interaction: Behavior regulating social contact between a mother and her 3½-month-old twins. In E. N. Rexford, L. W. Sander, & T. Shapiro (Eds.), *Infant psychiatry: A new synthesis* (pp. 113–126). New Haven: Yale University Press, 1976.

Tennes, K., Emde, R., Kisley, A., & Metcalf, D. (1972). The stimulus barrier in early infancy: An exploration of some formulations of John Benjamin. *Psychoanalysis and Contemporary Science, 1,* 206–234.

Tischler, S. (1979). Being with a psychotic child: A psychoanalytic approach to the problems of parents of psychotic children. *International Journal of Psycho-Analysis, 60,* 29–38.

Tolpin, M. (1971). On the beginnings of a cohesive self: An application of the concept of transmuting internalization to the study of the transitional object and signal anxiety. *The Psychoanalytic Study of the Child, 26,* 316–352.

Tustin, F. (1980). Autistic objects. *International Review of Psycho-Analysis, 7,* 27–39.

Weil, A. P. (1956). Some evidences of deviational development in infancy and early childhood. *The Psychoanalytic Study of the Child, 11,* 292–299.

Weil, A. P. (1970). The basic core. *The Psychoanalytic Study of the Child, 25,* 442–460.

Wills, D. M. (1970). Vulnerable periods in the early development of blind children. *The Psychoanalytic Study of the Child, 25,* 461–480.

Winnicott, D. W. (1953). Transitional objects and transitional phenomena. In *Playing and reality* (pp. 1–25). New York: Basic Books, 1971.

Winnicott, D. W. (1960). The theory of the parent–infant relationship. In *The maturational processes and the facilitating environment* (pp. 37–55). New York: International Universities Press, 1965.

Winnicott, D. W. (1967). Mirror-role of mother and family in child development. In *Playing and reality* (pp. 111–118). New York: Basic Books, 1971.

Wolff, P. H. (1963). Developmental and motivational concepts in Piaget's sensorimotor theory of intelligence. In E. N. Rexford, L. W. Sander, & T. Shapiro (Eds.), *Infant psychiatry: A new synthesis* (pp. 172–186). New Haven: Yale University Press, 1976.

CHAPTER THREE

Self Constancy: The Elusive Concept

MARJORIE TAGGART WHITE

Self constancy, like the proposition that "all men are created equal" seems to be a concept we have taken for granted as a self-evident idea requiring no further examination, once it was enunciated. However, self constancy, like the so-called self-evident truth about the creation of equal men, contains at least two far-reaching and unsubstantiated hypotheses: In the case of mankind's equal creation, both creation and equality are assumed, and these are, in fact, conditions we really know nothing about. In the case of self constancy we are referring to a state—constancy—which, at best, can be thought of as the ideal of mature development, both with respect to the self and its accompanying concept, object constancy. As for the self, Kohut's far-reaching and controversial formulations of the new self psychology (1977) have vividly demonstrated how unclear and yet vitally important the concept of the self can be, let alone the condition of its constancy, which might now be equated or at least compared with Kohut's description of "a stage of the cohesive self—that is, the growth of the self experience as a physical and mental unit which has cohesiveness in space and continuity in time . . ." (1971, p. 118).

Wallerstein (1981), in summing up his discussion and reservations at the panel on "The Bipolar Self" at the American Psychoanalytic Association, New York, December 1979, said: "I want very much to acknowledge the salutory impact on our field of this new focus on the self, on the psychology and the pathology of the self, as a central dimension of our understanding of human development."

It is from this viewpoint of the centrality of the self that I would like to explore the development of the concept of self constancy. Insufficient self constancy or an alarming lack of it with a concomitant decline in functioning or a total collapse indicates, by contrast, the relatively smooth competence, the self-possession that characterize the presence of self constancy.

In one clinical illustration a 17-year-old girl in high school was called upon to recite Hamlet's soliloquy in class. The girl had carefully memorized and rehearsed it and was looking forward to impressing her English teacher with her performance. As she began she flashed a pleased smile at him to indicate her appreciation that he had called on her. He gave her a chilling frown, which shook her self-confidence so that she could only rattle off the lines, casting to the winds all her preparation to make her recital dramatic and moving. When she had finished, her teacher said sarcastically, "Miss Martin has an excellent memory but perhaps she had better save it for computers rather than for drama!" Miss Martin assumed a sphinx-like air, staring off into space. She was not able to concentrate on what else was going on in class and stared coldly at the teacher as she dashed past him when class was over, not hearing his belated apology when he saw how stricken she was. By the time she reached home she had lost her voice. She could only speak in a whisper and with considerable pain, so that her family never heard about the abortive soliloquy. She did not go for the final examination in her English class and transferred to another high school for her senior year, where she kept a low profile and just managed to graduate, after having been an honor student up to the time of the collapse of her self-esteem—what Kohut would have called probably a fragmentation of her self that included a rather extensive failure of ego functioning.

Her image of herself was so devastated by the experience of the teacher's rejection and criticism that she was never able to explore, until she came into analysis, just what it was she thought the teacher frowned at when she smiled appreciatively at him. It was the unexpectedness of the frown that caused her self constancy to plummet. She had been the "golden girl" in the class, the one who was always an A-plus student and the leading lady for any special project. She had been so taken aback by the unexpected frown that she lost all her vaunted ability to pull herself together in a crisis. She literally forgot her position in class, her tested abilities, and who she was, so to speak, in space and time. The collapse of her self constancy was so unexpected for the teacher that he was shocked, rattled, and angry at her for disappointing him and, as he thought, for being unprepared and not even trying to ad lib a good performance. It seemed to me, as the analyst, that his frown might have had to do with a feeling that her initial flashing smile was not an appropriate way to start a suicidal soliloquy and that she, as a really good and potential actress, should have known this. There may also have been some anxiety at the sexual attraction and adoration he sensed in the flashing smile, feelings that the girl was able to recall as if they belonged to someone else, someone who had not dropped, as it were, into this emotional graveyard empty of hope. It was the perfectionism in the teacher winning out over the man she loved that made her feel uncared about, pushed aside as if she were a 3-year-old again.

Her father had too often been completely insensitive to her feelings if she failed in any way to come across with perfection. Her father's frown had always made her despair of ever really pleasing him, despair she thought she had left behind when she fell in love with her English teacher and tried to be perfect for him. One of the goals of treatment turned out to be the development of a stable sense of self-worth that would not collapse at the hypercritical reactions of love objects. To the extent that a stable sense of self-worth can be said to imply the attainment of a state of self constancy, then one of the treatment goals for this patient involved the development of self constancy. However, if regression to an infantile state involving orality and symbiotic needs is regarded as a defense against an oedipal problem, then the supraordinate goal of treatment, presumably, would be the resolution of the oedipal conflict with the concomitant establishment of higher level defenses.

This question of the appropriate treatment goal and the appropriate techniques for attaining the goal is very much implied in Wallerstein's (1981) discussion of the goals of analysis. He says that a harmonizing framework can be brought to bear upon seemingly opposed views of psychoanalytic technique. Wallerstein then refers to the issue of either-or or both-and, which he sees as the application of Waelder's (1936) principle of over-determination and multiple function. Each of the interpretative concepts offered by Kohut (1979) could have an appropriate role in the overall analytic work. When and how would then involve the suitable use of the tools of empathy and introspection that Kohut has helped to bring to our attention.

One could even question how much the more substantial and more enduring result that eventuated from the second analysis of Mr. Z was a matter of an improved theory and how much a question of better empathy, guided certainly by the broader understanding that arose from the new concepts of the psychology of the self.

Wallerstein seems to be raising a basic issue with respect to both theory and technique. It is the issue, diagnostically, as to whether there is a failure of development in psychotic or so-called borderline states and whether, because of this developmental deficit, a different technical approach is needed in treatment to help repair the deficit—that is, to start immobilized developmental processes going again—and that such a mobilizing process is needed for growth to resume. That impaired psychological development could resume (given the chances for derailment shown by Spitz, Mahler, Winnicott, Jacobson, and Kohut), with the what-will-arise-can-be-dealt-with approach implied in Wallerstein's version of Waelder's (1936) multiple function approach, seems highly unlikely and threatens to take us back to the days when Knight (1954) first wrote of the need for a concept of the borderline.

In connection with Wallerstein's and Kohut's recognition of the importance of empathy, Fleming (1975) also said:

It seems to me we have tended to take object responsiveness for granted and in so doing, have not given the feedback system in the relationship the proper significance or studied in detail the characteristics of the feedback that are effective. . . .

Fleming also pointed out that Mahler focused on the reciprocal nature of the relationship between mother and child. Fleming asked if it could be possible that the therapeutic "alliance" duplicated the ego operations presumably occurring in the development of object constancy. She also asked whether the descriptions we use, such as "development of an observing ego," actually apply to "the beginnings of new self-image" along with introjecting an image of the analyst. Fleming cited Mahler in regard to how the mother's responses to her toddler's efforts to move out of his symbiotic relationship can foster or slow down this process of development.

Fleming then raised an essentially controversial issue by asking if the structural changes sought in psychoanalysis could be facilitated by reactions from the analyst, apart from interpretations. She said that her experience with the clinical phenomena that usually appear in psychoanalytic therapy had persistently led her in this direction. "An adult patient is not a baby, and an analyst is not the parent," she reminded us. Nevertheless, the need in many adults often gives rise to the functional relationship between mother and child, namely, the "diatrophic feeling" which the analytic process needs for sustenance and success (Spitz, 1956; Gitelson, 1962; Fleming, 1972).

Fleming suggested that in the organization of differentiated images of object and self, "*the important element is the feeling of being approved of, of being valued*" [italics added]. She felt that the content of the message was even more important than the source. Fleming thought that the mothering person also was pleased with the child and had a libidinal investment in how he or she responded. She pointed out that we could have a kind of relatedness in which knowing that "I mean something to you which also pleases me" could affect the shape of the mental representation of both the object and the subject in the "transaction" (Sandler & Rosenblatt, 1962).

Fleming has shown in clinical material that the development of a more cohesive self-image emerged from the establishment of more object constancy with respect to the evocable mental representation of the analyst that led to the evocable memory of a patient's early loss of his mother. The patient had been separated from his mother when he was 5 years old, because of the mother's severe illness. After the patient had been able to find out where the analyst lived, he was able to say to the analyst "I need you to be with me to know how I feel about myself" (p. 754).

My own patient's response was similar in that she needed to check that I felt positively about her in order for her to be able to talk at all, of course involving her traumatic experience with the disappointing, idealized love-object, her high school English teacher. It seems to me that the responsive attitude in both cases contributed to the building of internal structure, which eventually aided both patients in arriving at the higher developmental level of self and object constancy. This achievement involves mysteries and unknowns. But then in the realm of self development, which involves all of the amazements and questions of creativity, we are constantly facing the unknowns.

Would more object responsiveness to the elusive images of the self, as Kohut and Fleming suggested, foster a more visible and cohesive "true" self? Both Winnicott and Mahler have stressed the private quality of the "true" or "core" self. Winnicott (1963) has said: "In health there is a core of personality that corresponds to the true self. I suggest that this core never communicates with the world of perceived objects and that the individual person knows that it must never be communicated with or be influenced by external reality." Winnicott also pointed out that while "healthy" persons enjoy communicating, each individual is also "permanently unknown" and "unfound."

Mahler, Pine, and Bergman (1975) go on to say that the developmental task of the usual "separation-individualization process" is to establish "a measure of object constancy" together with "a measure of self constancy," in order to produce a lasting individuality. This involves attaining two levels of identity: (1) being aware of existing in a separate and individual capacity and (2) beginning to be aware of a self-identity based on gender (pp. 223-224).

Mahler's questions relating to the development of a measure of self constancy, together with Winnicott's ideas of a presumably constitutional protection of the self core, imply a kind of pessimism about the possibility of the expression of self constancy. Yet, in so many artistic communications there has been the thrust of the baring of the artist's self responding in often unbelievable ways to the impact of both external and internal stimuli. So that the question of self constancy (as Mahler et al., 1975, expressed it in very guarded terms as a "measure of self constancy") becomes a very complicated concept involving all of the biologic, psychological, creative, and moral aspects of the self but also the effect of object relations impinging upon the self-experience in manifold ways.

Insistence upon the self-experience is heard in the Egyptian *Book of the Dead* (Van Doren, 1934) dating from 3500 B.C. One poem has the remarkable title, "He Holdeth Fast to the Memory of His Identity":

> In the Great House, and in the House of Fire,
> On the dark night of counting all the years,
> On the dark night when months and years are numbered—
> O let my name be given back to me!
> When the Divine One on the Eastern Stairs
> Shall cause me to sit down with him in peace,
> And every god proclaims his name before me—
> Let me remember then the name I bore! (p. 238)

How self constancy is related to the conscious self and to the unconscious are vital questions arising from the Nobel Prize-winning research on the dual hemispheres of the brain, awarded in 1981 to Roger Sperry, Torsten Wiesel, and David Hubel for studies carried out in the past 25 years. Restak (1982) notes that Sperry and his colleagues showed in "split-brain" subjects the specialization of each hemisphere for carrying out particular functions.

For example, the right hemisphere deals with nonverbal processes (e.g., drawing, spatial awareness) while the left hemisphere specializes in language.

Sperry takes the thought-provoking position, according to Brown (1980), that "consciousness is an emergent property of the brain, evolving from interactions of the simpler elements and properties of the brain in such a way that the nature of consciousness cannot be predicted from the interactions" (p. 122).

Brown cites Sperry (1969) maintaining that mental phenomena composed of neural events are seen acting dynamically in brain organization and also interacting at their own level in brain function. Mutual interaction between the neural and the mental events seems evident. Moreover, subjective properties are viewed as top-level causal determinants. Thus, mind can be said to move matter in the brain.

Brown stresses that Sperry's research indicates a different explanation, namely, that the two hemispheres provide different mental operations to the "development of self-awareness and intention." The nondominant hemisphere seems to function in analyzing and synthesizing concepts and then directing *appropriate* behavior. The dominant hemisphere, however, adds the elements that involve consensual discrimination and the synthesizing of individual being, that is, awareness. Both sorts of mental operation, in order to become conceptual and appropriate, require a continuous information interchange between the hemispheres. To produce a coin, for example, when asked to come up with an unavailable dollar bill means that the appropriate response could arise only through suitable concept formation on the one hand and some kind of self-awareness on the other. Only by recognizing an appropriate response *and* by having an awareness—and not necessarily a conscious awareness—of the unique self able to carry out the response could such an action take place.

Brown suggests that we may never know completely how much consciousness is bound up with language. She proposes, however, that if speech potentialities are only in the dominant hemisphere, the split-brain patients' failures to be self-aware of their own actions could also mean that speech is tied exclusively to the mechanisms for self-awareness and not inevitably to other aspects of consciousness. An unconscious awareness of one's own body seems necessary, Brown points out, for coordinated, purposeful actions. Moreover, with the great redundancy of brain circuits, split-brain patients might eventually acquire self-awareness "just as chimpanzees have learned human symbols." Brown stresses that we do not need conscious awareness to arrive at advanced syntheses of environmental demands and appropriate responses. Such syntheses are subjective and biological and are stored in and retrieved from memory.

The right hemisphere, devalued in the foregoing as an "automaton," is regarded as the seat of perception, visual imagery, kinesthetic, visuospatial, imaginative, and synthetic perceptual functions. One could make a case for the importance of all these functions to the experience of the self. The tendency to devalue vital functions connected with self-experience reflects the historical yet puzzling tendency to minimize the importance of the self and to maximize the importance of objects.

Although Freud (1905, 1911, 1914) warned against the overvaluation of the love-object as an invitation to infatuation and a weakening of one's powers of judgment, he was also skeptical about the advisability of caring for oneself. In summarizing, in the Schreber case, the paranoid defenses against homosexuality (1911), he offered a final rejection of the threatening proposition, "I do not love at all—I do not love any one," which Freud then saw, "since . . . one's libido must go somewhere," as meaning "I love only myself," that is, "megalomania, which we may regard as a *sexual overvaluation of the ego*" (p. 65).

Three years later Freud (1914) seemed less devaluing of self-love when he defined normal narcissism, not as a perversion, but rather as a libidinal component of "the instinct of self-preservation," (p. 74) which "every living creature" seems to display (p. 74). Freud, almost warmly, even spoke of primary narcissism as the state in which "'His Majesty the Baby'" feels himself to be the "core of creation" (1914, p. 91). Yet this omnipotent position fairly soon turns into object-love, which insofar as longing and deprivation are concerned, lowers self-esteem; while being loved, having it returned, and also possessing the loved one, raises self-regard again (1914). Such a need to be loved and to possess the love object in order to raise one's self-regard would certainly be termed a narcissistic need for attention, according to classical psychoanalysis. Yet the only other alternative Freud offered in 1914 was that such a love would be like the early condition in which object–love and ego–libido could not be differentiated (1914).

Today, this would be regarded as a regression to an infantile symbiotic state, from the standpoint of psychoanalytic developmental psychology. Freud himself remained pessimistic about the possibilities of successfully treating pathological narcissism. He found that patients suffering from such a disorder did not develop the usual transference neurosis and that they often seemed close to psychosis. The importance of the object, as compared with the self, even when Freud used the term "ego" as presumably meaning the self, can be seen in Freud's recommendation for dealing with the loss of a love object, namely, for the self to take on or identify with some of the characteristics of the lost object, a process that Freud sees as a part of normal mourning (1917, 1923).

Given the ambiguous valuation Freud put upon the concept of the self, it is surprising that Hartmann in "Comments on the Psychoanalytic Theory of the Ego" (1950) accorded an implied equality, respecting both representation and cathexis, to the concept of the self along with the concept of the object. Hartmann noted that narcissism and the libidinal cathexis of the ego was and still is widely regarded as equivalent in psychoanalytic literature. Hartmann also pointed out that sometimes Freud refers to the cathexis of the body, or of the self as the libidinal cathexis of the ego. A clear distinction between such terms as ego, self, and personality is not always made in analysis, Hartmann said. However, he stressed that it is necessary to differentiate between these concepts in order to regard consistently the problems raised by Freud's structural psychology. With respect to the term narcissism, two opposites often seem to be combined according to Hartmann: One meaning of narcissism refers to the self (one's own person) in contrast to the object. The second meaning refers to the ego (as a psychic system) in contrast to the other substructures of personality.

Hartmann stressed that the "opposite of object cathexis is not ego cathexis, but cathexis of one's own person, that is, self-cathexis" (Hartmann, 1952). In regard to self-cathexis, it is not implied where this cathexis is located, that is, in the id, ego, or superego. Hartmann notes that while "narcissism" is found in all three psychic systems, there is usually opposition to or reciprocity with object cathexis. He proposed that it "therefore will be clarifying if we define narcissism as the libidinal cathexis not of the ego but of the self" (p. 163). He suggested applying the term "self-representation" as the opposite of object representation.

Hartmann also pointed out that the term "ego libido" may often mean a cathexis of one's person rather than a cathexis of one's ego. He noted that many times when we say there has been a withdrawl of libido or that ego cathexis has replaced object cathexis, what we really mean is that a withdrawal into the self has occurred in the first instance. In the second instance, he suggested that we say that either self-love or a neutralized form of self cathexis has replaced object cathexis.

I noted in an earlier paper (White, 1980) that "in this seemingly simple change in terminology, Hartmann makes it possible to think of the self or self-representations as content of the ego, just as object representations are also regarded as content of the system ego" (p. 6). I also pointed out that the implications seemed profound not only in regard to narcissism but also to internalization and identification.

Yet Hartmann did not continue to give the concept of the self the same weight as the concept of the object. Fraiberg, in her paper "Object Constancy and Mental Representation" (1969), noted that Hartmann first used the term "object constancy" in 1952. This was the first time the term was employed in the psychoanalytic literature in this context. For Hartmann, object relations would include object constancy, which must imply, for the ego, some neutralization of aggressive as well as libidinal energy. He also suggested that it could imply a promotion of neutralization.

It is noteworthy that Hartmann, in his 1952 paper, did not connect his new concept of object constancy with a comparable concept of self constancy. This omission is even more striking in his next discussion of object constancy (1953). As Fraiberg (1969) noted, Hartmann here "links his use of the term 'constancy' to Piaget's 'object concept.'"

In his 1953 discussion of object constancy, Hartmann noted that at first the object is only a continuation of the child's activity, as Piaget (1937) pointed out. In other words, Hartmann perceived that the infant does not differentiate between his actions in relation to the objects and the objects themselves. In Piaget's words (1937), "The object is still only a prolongation of the child's activity during those processes that lead to a distinction of object and self." Hartmann proposed that the child also comes to differentiate between his activity and the object toward which it is directed. The earlier activity stage, Hartmann suggested, could be correlated with magic action and probably represented a "transitory step" in ego development, occurring between simple discharge and real ego-directed and organized action. Piaget's findings, Hartmann concluded, agree rather well with analytic findings and this meant, metapsychologically speaking, that, from then on, there was a difference between the effect of an object-directed ego function and the impact of the object representation.

In the foregoing discussion, Hartmann underlined the importance of object constancy, again with no consideration of the possible importance of self constancy. His focus on the separation of self and object is understandable in the light of his previous (1950) proposal that self cathexis, not ego cathexis, is the opposite of object cathexis and that the term "self-representation" might be used "as opposed" to object representation. Even in his 1950 paper the emphasis is really on the separation of the self and object representations. If we then think of the term "opposed" in relation to self and object representations, there is the implication of conflict between the self's needs and wants and those of the object. Freud, in his 1914 paper, had already limned this struggle, even in the concept of the narcissistic object choice.

Especially in Hartmann's 1953 paper, "On the Metapsychology of Schizophrenia," where he is struggling to comprehend schizophrenia in relation to ego functions, it is not surprising that Hartmann would emphasize the child's learning to distinguish between his or her activity and the object toward which this activity is directed, that is, the reality of the permanence of the object, namely, its "objectivation" and the object's difference from the child per se and the child's activity. All of these distinctions may be impossible for the schizophrenic to make. However, there is little apparent interest on Hartmann's part, in what is happening with the child; for example, what does the child's activity mean to the child if he or she cannot yet distinguish his or her activity from the object toward which it is directed? and how *does* the child learn to make this distinction? It may be that we have been spoiled by the kind of questions, observations and inferences that Spitz, Mahler, and Kohut have raised with respect to the details of *how* the child develops, all of which could presumably contribute to the understanding of what the self-images and self-representations of the child contain and what part they play in a constant image of the self just as a constant image of the object is involved in object constancy.

Perhaps in line with a growing trend to consider the concept of self as meriting full investigation and foreshadowing Heinz Kohut's self psychology, Edith Jacobson, in 1954, in her first version of "The Self and the Object World," said, "Normal ego functioning presupposes a sufficient, evenly distributed, enduring, libidinous cathexis of both object- and self-representations" (p. 94). This would appear to put self-love or self-valuation on an equal footing with object-love or object-valuation, a development which Freud and Hartmann did not recognize as desirable or necessary. In an earlier paper of mine (White, 1980), I traced the implication of Jacobson's position as suggesting, "in terms of an evenly distributed libidinal cathexis between self- and object-representations, that normally we love ourselves as much as we love others" (p. 20). Jacobson's concept of a 50-50 distribution of libidinal cathexis between one's self and the loved one constituted a departure from Freud's economy of love, where he saw "being in love" as having less self-regard and much more regard for the loved one. Jacobson seemed to be suggesting that a healthy self-esteem is a necessary foundation for enduring love. Jacobson (1954) also recognized that to approach another person libidinally requires not only a hypercathexis of the object, but also "the spur of a concomitant, libidinous hypercathexis of the self-representations which will encourage and guarantee the success of the action" (p. 94). Such a hypercathexis would extend to the body parts and organs in the action. The whole self, as an entity, would also be hypercathected. This would lead to feelings of increased self-confidence, thus stimulating, Jacobson believed, both the executive organs and the action. The idea of hypercathexis of the self, of increased self-confidence as a vital and perhaps essential aspect of successful object relations, underlines again the need for healthy narcissism as indispensable for mature object relations.

While Jacobson implied that the concept of self constancy was the logical accompaniment to object constancy, she did not use the term "self constancy" until 1964 in the book version of *The Self and the Object World*. However, in her 1954 version of this work, she describes the development of "a realistic concept of the self" in terms that seem quite appropriate to the concept of self constancy, as an alternative to object constancy.

Jacobson pointed out that her concept of the self at first is similar to primitive object images and therefore is not stable. Emerging from sensations close to our perceptions of the gratifying part-object, the self-concept seems fused and confused with object images at first. Basically, it appears as a constantly changing series of self-images reflecting the constant fluctuations of the primitive mental state, according to Jacobson.

Advancements in psychosexual and ego development, along with maturing physical abilities, emotional and ideational processes, reality testing, and growing capacities for perception, self-perception and introspection, all accompany the growth of self-images. The latter images become organized and integrated into fairly realistic concepts of the object world and of the self, Jacobson suggested.

She saw a realistic concept of the self as mirroring both the physical and mental assets and limits of one's bodily and mental ego. This included appearance, anatomy and physiology as well as our conscious and preconscious feelings and thoughts, wishes, impulses and attitudes, of the self's physical and mental activities. She concluded that while all these specific features will have corresponding psychic representations, "a concept of their sum total, i.e., of the self as a differentiated but organized entity, will simultaneously develop" (1954, pp. 86–87).

This idea of Jacobson's of a concept of all the specific aspects of a developing self, coming to be embodied in a "differentiated but organized entity," would seem to approach the elusive self constancy for which we have been searching. The term "self constancy" as the subjective equivalent of "object constancy" finally sneaks in, as a footnote to Spiegel's (1959) paper "The Self, the Sense of Self, and Perception." Spiegel says that through

the ego's tendency to achieve constancy of internal perception through pooling, it achieves both a constant frame of reference and a constant ratio of single self-representation . . . and thus a constant self-feeling. Fisher (1959, p. 99) has suggested placing this *self constancy alongside of object constancy (love objects) and perceptual constancy (inanimate objects)* [italics added].

Charles Fisher made this suggestion in regard to self constancy, according to Spiegel's bibliography, in the discussion of this paper at the New York Psychoanalytic Society in 1959.

Jacobson's and Spiegel's interest in aspects of the self per se as a concept can be seen as precursors of over two ensuing decades of intensified focus on the self and its concomitant problems of narcissism. This focus has been highlighted by Kohut's "self psychology" (1977), which posits a "supra-ordinate self," impressively conceptualized clinically, to replace drive theory, while retaining as crucial, the concept of the "selfobject," that is, "objects which are themselves experienced as part of the self" (1971). Kohut later (1977) compared modern physics' fundamental claim that "the means of observation and the target of observation constitute a unit that, in certain respects, is in principle indivisible." He noted that this conclusion can make an equal claim, namely, that the presence of an empathic or introspective observer can similarly affect the psychological field (cf. Habermas, 1971; Kohut, 1959). Stressing the need for parental empathy, that is, selfobject empathy, Kohut said that a child's sexual arousal upsets related to his seeing parental sexual intercourse, for example, can mask the much more important failure of the parents' appropriate empathic responses to the child's need for mirroring and for a target for his idealizing needs (1977, p. 187). In a further elaboration of this view of the selfobject concept, he noted that, in regard to the child's need for mirroring and for someone to idealize, what a child needs is neither perfect empathic responses from the selfobject nor exaggerated admiration. The matrix for the development of a healthy self in a child, Kohut said, is the selfobject's capability to respond with appropriate mirroring at least some times. What makes for pathology is not an occasional failure, but the selfobject's chronic incapacity to respond appropriately, which arises from his or her own problems with respect to the self.

Kohut stressed that it is the optimal frustration of the child's healthy narcissistic needs that, through transmuting internalization, leads to the consolidation of the self. This provides the basis of self-confidence and basic self-esteem that sustains a person throughout life. The endopsychic narcissistic resources of normal adults will continue to need the mirroring of his self by selfobjects. He will also continue to require targets for his idealization. No allegation of immaturity or psychopathology must, therefore, be made from the fact that another person is used as a selfobject. Kohut believed selfobject relations occur on all developmental levels and in psychological health as well as in psychological illness (1977, pp. 187-188).

P. Ornstein (1981) points out that studying the vicissitudes of the narcissistic line of development has shown that archaic selfobject relations and functions develop in to more mature selfobject relations and functions. Concomitant with this development, he also cites the well-known emergence of object love.

Ornstein adds: "From the vantage point of the bipolar self, however, once we conceive of the drives as constituents of the self, our primary attention is focused on the development of the total self (without losing sight of its constituents)" (1981). When both the mirroring and idealizing poles of the bipolar self are adequately developed, the self achieves the capabiltiy of becoming a relatively independent center of initiative which is the "true object" of the classical framework. Thus giving primary attention to the development of the bipolar self does not cancel out the differentiation and separateness that occur all along the way.

P. Ornstein also points out that recognizing the fact that specific selfobject needs continue to exist throughout the life cycle is not at all incompatible with the equally necessary focus on the corresponding growth of the ability to perceive the relative independence of the other. Optimally, in health, the self may oscillate between these two modes of relating to its object (1981, p. 358).

As I noted earlier, in 1975 Mahler *et al.* brought forward the term "self constancy," as necessarily and logically implied by object constancy. At the same time Lichtenberg (1975) expanded on Kohut's concept of self in terms of self-experience or the "sense of self" in an effort to trace developmentally Kohut's concept of self cohesion. The question of how self-cohesion is related to self constancy naturally arises.

The development of a cohesive self, according to Kohut (1971), involves the mother's joyful response to the whole child (e.g., calling him by name as she clearly enjoys being with him and seeing what he is doing) supports at the appropriate phase, the development from autoerotism to narcissism—from the stage of self nuclei (i.e., the fragmented self) to the cohesive self. Kohut defines the cohesive self as involving "the growth of the self experience as a physical and mental unit which has cohesiveness in space and continuity in time" (1971, p. 19). The preceding stage of narcissism involves isolated mental and physical functions which, of course, are not to be considered as morbid but as appropriate to such an early phase of development.

Kohut stressed that the capacity to enjoy individual body parts and their functions along with single mental activities remains after the cohesive self experience has been well developed. Adults as well as children do not fear fragmentation in enjoying the individual body and mind, Kohut points out, because they realize these body parts and their functions belong to a stable total self.

The awareness of the self's reality arises from a firm cathexis with narcissistic libido, essential to its cohesiveness. Kohut found this led to a subjective feeling of well-being and also to an improved functioning of the ego, shown, for instance, in a patient's increased capacity for work and greater work efficiency.

Lichtenberg (1975) describes the cohesion of the sense of self as a "potent organizing factor in the mental life of the child." He places the beginning feeling of a sense of cohesion at the second half of the 3rd year of life, that is, toward the end of the separation-individuation phase as defined by Mahler. Elaborating on self cohesion, Lichtenberg sees the cohesiveness of the sense of the self as mirrored in a greater integration in ego functioning. Since cohesiveness is an experience, he believes that the sense of a cohesive self as a feeling of being "all together" relates to a more globally experienced feeling of early basic trust, safety, and well-being.

Parents may experience the child at three and a half as having become really "human" through an awareness of the child's desire to retain this cohesive feeling. Lichtenberg suggests that parents may intuitively help the child put up with unavoidable disruptions that threaten his new-found cohesive sense, for example, too much arousing play, overly intense teasing by older siblings, prolonged exposure to the behavioral demands of the adult world.

In approaching the psychoanalytic concept of the self, Lichtenberg distinguishes between an experiential realm where the self can be understood empathically and the nonexperiential realm in which the tripartite psychic structure functions. Like Glover (1932) and Kohut (1974), he sees the sense of self arising in infancy as islands of experience that are gradually formed into more ordered groupings of images. Lichtenberg (1975) describes the component groups of self-images as containing self-images of one's body and self-images with objects seen as definitely separate. He also includes grandiose self-images in association with idealized self-objects. All these images become blended into a sense of self that involves unity and continuity in state, time, and space.

Lichtenberg, as noted earlier, cites the disruptions that cause the child's new-found cohesive sense of self to be lost. The possibility of disruption and loss points to the difference between a cohesive sense of self and self constancy. The practice of pairing self and object constancy (once self constancy was even considered) has led to the assumption that self constancy is a kind of reflection of object constancy.

A search for a comprehensive definition of object constancy, however, leads us to Edgcumbe and Burgner's valiant effort (1972) to synthesize the aspects of object constancy set forth since Hartmann's initial conceptualization: They conceptualized the growth of object relationships with respect to the eventual establishment of *"perceptual object constancy"* along with the eventual establishment of the *"libidinal tie to the primary object."* These developments make possible moving away from the *"stage of the need-satisfying relationship"* and provide the basis for the growth of the *"capacity for constant relationships."* Within the latter, the relation of the drives and affects to the object representation are of major importance. They have further differentiated between the connection to the *primary libidinal object* and subsequent ties to love *objects* (Edgcumbe & Burgner, 1972).

Kernberg (1975) uses terms such as "normal narcissism," "self-continuity," "self-integration," and "ego identity" to describe what appears to be the concept of self constancy, with an emphasis on the interaction of self and object representations within the structure of the ego. Kernberg, following Hartmann, equates normal narcissism with the libidinal investment of the self. The self is viewed as an intrapsychic structure composed of many self representations and the affects which color them. Self representations are seen as "affective-cognitive structures." They reflect the person's view of himself in a range of interactions, for example, with significant others in real situations and in fantasy with internal representations of significant others, that is, with object representations. The self as part of the ego is also seen as containing ideal self-images and ideal object-images.

Kernberg sees the normal self as integrated, since "its component self representations are dynamically organized into a comprehensive whole." As with "good" and "bad" object representations, the self constitutes an integration of "good" and "bad" self-images based on the libidinal and aggressive early self-images or the integration of both good and bad self-images into a realistic self-concept, which Kernberg sees as a requirement for the acceptance of a normal self. He sees this as explaining the paradox that the integrating of love and hatred is necessary for normal love.

Noting that this approach accords with Sandler and Rosenblatt's "representational world" (1962) and Erikson's "ego identity" (1956), Kernberg (1975) proposes that clinically, an integrated self includes a self-experience with historical continuity also including co-existing areas of functioning in different kinds of psychosocial interactions.

With respect to normal narcissism as the libidinal investment of the self, Kernberg (1975) notes that self-esteem or self-regard is "not simply a reflection of 'instinctual cathexes': it always reflects a combination of affective and cognitive components, with the predominance of diffuse affective components at more primitive levels of regulation of self-esteem, and a predominance of cognitive differentiation with 'toned-down' affective implications at more advanced levels of regulation of self-esteem."

Kernberg notes that because the structures influencing the instinctual investment of the self include aggressive interactions, the regulation of normal narcissism can be understood only in terms of the relative predominance of libidinal over aggressive investment by these same intrapsychic structures.

In a recent paper, Mahler (1981) also focuses on the interplay of aggressive with libidinal elements in a mother-daughter relationship with respect to the use of aggression to foster disengagement and distancing for, first, successful separation-individuation and, later, to maintain individual identity. Mahler stresses that "even if we avoid the issue of whether aggression is or is not a primary instinctual drive . . . the source of aggression is the growth process and all the mechanisms of life itself," as Greenacre (1960), Spitz (1953), and Winnicott (1963) have implied and explicated. She adds that maturation of the neuromuscular apparatus results from growth which is "most independent of the environment."

Mahler (1981) describes how, at 19 months of age, a little girl (Cathy) switched from an "elated practicing phase" where elation was predominant to an increasing fear of closeness to her mother. Her aggression intensified against the mother in the service of eliminating the dangerous primary or total identification with her, which was a threat to Cathy's self-identity. As Mahler points out this pull toward symbiotic fusion was especially great because of her father's absence until she was 2 years old, which Mahler believes made it especially difficult for Cathy to shift from primary to selective identification with her mother.

Mahler notes that selective identification is a most important mechanism for the achievement of a child's separation-individuation. In the process, there is usually a dilution so to speak, of the mother-child symbiotic dual-unity stage by a distribution of cathexis to father and siblings in the family.

Mahler has also suggested that the attainment of self constancy may include a lack of continuing consciousness of the self. She says that the consciousness of the self and absorption without awareness of the self are two poles between which the normal adult seems to move with varying ease and different degrees of alternation or simultaneity.

Here Mahler seems to imply that the self-representations can be so well integrated structurally that the availability of the reliable, constant self can be taken for granted. Stolorow and Lachmann (1980) relate such integration to self constancy. They say that the establishment of a cohesive self-image reflects "the consolidation of differentiated and integrated representations" of the self. The cohesive image of the self "is temporarily stable and has an affective coloration more or less independent of immediate environmental supports." Such "self constancy," the authors note, has been described in terms of "the subjective sense of identity (Erikson, 1956) and the continuity of self-esteem (Jacobson, 1964; Kohut, 1971)" (p. 4).

The maintenance of self constancy can be seen in terms of the interplay between self-esteem, defined by Stolorow and Lachmann (1980) as a complex state embodying cognitive-affective factors, and narcissism, defined as embodying the mental operations which regulate self-esteem ("the affective coloring of the self representation") and maintain the cohesion and stability of the self representation (pp. 20-21). The authors compare functional narcissism to a thermostat, which regulates and stabilizes room temperature against a host of forces which threaten it with imbalance.

Stolorow and Lachmann point out that self-esteem is vulnerable to the pressure of many internal and external influences. But when self-esteem is dangerously lowered, or destroyed, then narcissistic activities arise in order to restore and stabilize it. With respect to Joffe and Sandler's idea (1967), narcissism viewed as serving self-esteem regulation is potentially compatible with intense object relationships, which may be serving the same end.

Freud's original idea (1914), that self-esteem, as the libidinal investment of the self, decreased with object-love and increased in withdrawal from disappointing objects is contradicted, according to Joffe and Sandler (1967) and Stolorow and Lachmann (1980), by the well-established clinical fact that object relations can both increase and greatly undermine self-esteem, depending on the nature of the self-object interaction. Hartmann's concept of the "average expectable environment" (1939) as a crucial factor in adaptation, Mahler's emphasis on the importance of the mothering person's holding behavior (Mahler et al., 1975) in the broadest sense for the libidinization of the baby's body and his or her eventual capacity for sound secondary narcissism and object love, Kohut's formulation of the process of "transmuting internalization" (1971) of soothing and confirmatory experiences for the child's physical, affective, and cognitive self-development all recognize the farreaching impact that the primary mothering object has upon the neonate's "ideal shape of the self-image . . . that is, a self-image which will yield the greatest degree of narcissistic gratification and well-being" (Sandler & Rosenblatt, 1962, p. 144).

A poignant confirmation of the power of the mothering person's reactions and withdrawal of positive confirmation upon a child's acceptance and enjoyment of his or her body-self being observed is presented in Amsterdam and Levitt's (1980) paper "Consciousness of Self and Painful Self-Consciousness." The authors hypothesize that maternal disapproval of genital play and exhibitionism acounted for the impressive change (90%) in a sample of 88 children who, in their 1st year (6–12 months) clearly delighted in their mirror image and in the 2nd year (14–24 months) increasingly showed self-consciousness and embarrassment, with 90% warily withdrawing from their mirror image.

A second, videotaped study of maternal and contextual determinants of self-consciousness was increased with the admiring attention of a live stranger than when given no particular attention or when exposed to his simultaneous video image. It appears, therefore, to be that the focus of another's direct admiring attention will probably arouse more self-conscious feeling than being the center of one's own attention, at least on closed-circuit TV (Amsterdam & Levitt, 1980, p. 72).

Citing Galenson and Roiphe's finding (1974) that spontaneous and active genital play is enjoyed by children of both sexes in the second half of the 1st year, Amsterdam and Levitt (1980) propose that disturbing self-consciousness arises as children are either quietly stopped and distracted, or more directly punished for showing off their bodies (nakedness) and for any interest displayed in their genitals, ranging from even looking to active playing. So the child learns that pleasurable sensations from within, in response even to his own ministrations are not only rejected by mother and other adults, but may also be forbidden when they are present. Thus, the child learns by command, as it were, to inhibit genital sensations, let alone exploration in the presence of others. This seems to occur at precisely the same time as he also experiences affective self-consciousness before the mirror. Amsterdam and Levitt stress the significance of both these behaviors following the mastery of walking, the pleasurable and unself-conscious exhibition of the naked body, and the intentional touching of the genitalia.

The authors stress, in relation to Kohut's work, that even the best-matched union of mother and child can be upset with the arrival of specific genital activity. "One of the first narcissistic injuries in the mother-infant relationship may be the mother's . . . prohibition of genital play," the authors propose. "The child's dream of his own perfection is thus destroyed, and . . . his own bodily sensations now produce shame" (pp. 77–79).

Amsterdam and Levitt stress that while shame, fear, anger, and disgust play crucial roles in the development of the self-concept, "too little attention and emphasis have been given to the positive emotions" (1980). In addition to the delight and curiosity typically accompanying the child's initial exploration of his own and others' bodies, they cite both Mahler's (Mahler et al., 1975) and Kohut's (1977) emphasis on the expansive narcissism and triumphant self-assertiveness associated with the attainment of upright locomotion.

Amsterdam and Levitt (1980) suggest the excessive emphasis on shame, fear, and guilt in building self-consciousness is inherited from the anti-sexual, anti-self, Judaeo-Christian tradition, with its emphasis on the inferiority of the body and the superiority of the spirit. They also note that the

Anglo-Saxon Calvinistic culture intensifies shame about the body and individuation, with its stress on a rigid posture suggesting the social demand to be upright and above everyone. They point out that we are expected to stand erect in a specific way, and also to control our eyes, mouth, noses, hands, feet, and genitals. Could such a culture generate much besides shame, fear, and guilt from the earliest bodily sense of self? As a final deprivation, they remind us that pride is one of the seven deadly sins, and we are taught not to show off, or even boast about ourselves (1980, p. 80).

Recognizing the disparagement of concern for oneself in Western religion and philosophy, Kohut (1972) stressed that the hypocrisy toward narcissism needs to be overcome today just as urgently as sexual hypocrisy needed to be overcome a century ago. He added that our ambitions, including our urge to dominate, should not be denied. He accepted our yearning to shine and to merge into omnipotent figures. But this involved, as he pointed out, an acknowledgement of the legitimacy of these narcissistic stirrings, just as we have acknowledged the acceptability of our object-instinctual strivings. Kohut stressed that, as it has been found, in the systematic therapeutic analysis of narcissistic personality disturbances, our archaic grandiosity and exhibitionism can be transformed into realistic self-esteem and into enjoying ourselves. Also, as Kohut found, "our yearning to be at one with the omnipotent selfobject can change into the socially useful, adaptive, and joyful capacity for enthusiasm and for admiration of the great after whose lives, deeds and personalities we can permit ourselves to model our own" (Kohut, 1972).

Earlier I proposed (White, 1980) that it is the positive cathexis of the self-representations developed through attuned mothering that activates ego functions, including the individuation of the child. In regard to self constancy, I also suggested that while object constancy seems to require acceptance of the object's needs, despite the frustrations, including self inhibitions, this may impose, we also have to think of the need for self-constancy involving possibly "'synchrony'—a stability of self-regulation" (Schwaber, 1980, pp. 216-217). Self-feelings, positive or negative, con-interest in narcissism is recognizing a broader recognition of the developmental need for healthy self relations and is anticipating a new era in therapeutic technique as well as in theory (White, 1980, p. 22).

Such a new era in technique and theory conceivably could give greater recognition to the importance of fostering the development of positive self constancy involving possibly "'synchrony'—a stability of self-regulation," (Schwaber, 1980, pp. 216-217). Self-feelings, positive or negative, constructive or destructive, appear to be deeply involved in the activity of the brain's limbic system including the hypothalamus; such self-feelings have already been found to increase or decrease the efficacy of the body's immunologic system, in connection with terminal diseases linked with stress and including cancer (Pelletier, 1977; Simonton & Mathews-Simonton,

1978). That psychotherapeutic technique focused on developing a positive self constancy together with object constancy could also ameliorate significantly high-risk and often incurable stress-related diseases is perhaps an achievable goal in the foreseeable future.

It cannot be emphasized too strongly that we are dealing with an as yet incomprehensible interaction between conscious and unconscious aspects of the mind and the fantastic 15-billion cell complexity of the brain to produce discernible changes in feeling and behavior and in physiologic changes of a life-saving efficacy. Simonton and Mathews-Simonton report on the efficacy of guided fantasy focusing on strengthening belief in the recuperative powers of one's own immunologic system, leading to startling remissions in cancer cases medically declared terminal. Similar results in stress-related illnesses, such as heart ailments, are being increasingly reported (Pelletier, 1977). In addition, the widening interest in the significance of what perhaps now deserve to be called self relations (White, 1980) as separate from, although not necessarily antagonistic to, object relations opens up broadening perspectives for both individual and social aspects of integration. Furthermore, there is the literally breathtaking vista of the incredible powers of the human mind interacting with the human brain toward the most delicate control of the body as well as of the brain (Brown, 1980).

In connection with the complexities of self relations in response to object relations, both positively and negatively, we have the whole as yet unresolved problem of how one's feelings and needs in relation to oneself can be somehow modulated (as in an orchestra playing together) to the gratifications and problems presented by other people. (I have to remind the human race that this is the essential issue in the possibility of nuclear annihilation, and of the likely necessity of turning away from war as a self-destructive human institution for settling power and real estate problems.)

Earlier in this chapter I alluded to Mahler's (Mahler *et al.*, 1975) suggestion that the attainment of self constancy may include the possibility of "absorption without awareness of self" as a polarity that a normal adult could move to from a "consciousness of self." Bach took up this issue (1980), recognizing that it is involved in the human capacity to be aware of both self-feelings and a sensitivity to the feelings of one or more objects. In other words he is concerned with the integration of both self and object constancy. Bach (1980) says that the child confronts the double or complementary task of "establishing a sense of self as a center for action and thought, and of viewing this self in the context of other selves as a thing amongst things" (p. 175). Two different perspectives on the same self are required, Bach suggests, namely both a subjectification and an objectification. Perhaps a multiplicity exists, he points out. A vivid clinical example of what Bach has in mind involves an actor describing an experience he had in the theater as a member of the audience. Sitting back, way at the top, the players from on high seemed perfect, faultless, "as if *they* were acting and what I did was something else entirely" (Bach, p. 177). He said he felt worthless and despondent about himself. During intermission, a friend offered him a seat in the front row. The actor could now see the makeup, the actors sweating, the mistakes in footwork. Feeling that they clearly were doing the same thing he did, the actor could identify with the actors as he hadn't been able to before, and he found himself learning from what he was seeing.

Bach (1980) points out that the patient could not make the transition from objective to subjective awareness, until he was helped to do so by changing his physical distance and perspective. Other patients have also reported being able to move from one mode of awareness to another by changing a physical position, by becoming active rather than passive, and by a change from the symbolic to the concrete.

The exploration of the "elusive concept" of self constancy, therefore, can heighten our awareness of the profound complexities in experience and understanding with which the interaction and integration of subjectivity and objectivity confront us. As Bach suggests, the individual's experiencing of himself as a "who," based on primarily subjective data, and his recognition of himself as a "what" derived from objective extrinsic data, is a paradoxical experience. It is certainly necessary, as Bach maintains, to believe that these two different experiences represent "some invariant supraordinate meaning or symbolic creation" called the "self."

Kohut offered us a solution of this paradox of self constancy by proposing the development of a cohesive, core self, that is, a "nuclear self" which provides the basis for our awareness of being "an independent center of initiative and perception, integrated with our most central ambitions and ideals and with our experience that our body and mind form a unit in space and a continuum in time" (Kohut, 1977, p. 177). As we know too well, it is the temporary or permanent sense of losing this self constancy that provides the soil upon which pathology flourishes.

REFERENCES

Amsterdam, B. K., & Levitt, M. (1980). Consciousness of self and painful self-consciousness. *The Psychoanalytic Study of the Child, 35*, 67-83.

Bach, S. (1980). Self-love and object-love: Some problems of self and object constancy, differentiation and integration. In R. F. Lax, S. Bach, & J. A. Burland (Eds.), *Rapprochement: The critical subphase of separation-individuation* (pp. 171-197). New York: Jason Aronson.

Brown, B. B. (1980). *Supermind: The ultimate energy.* New York: Harper & Row.

Edgcumbe, R., & Burgner, M. (1972). Some problems in the conceptualization of early object relationships. Part II: The concept of object constancy. *The Psychoanalytic Study of the Child, 27*, 315-333.

Erikson, E. (1956). The problem of ego identity. In *Identity and the life cycle* (*Psychological Issues*, Monograph 1, pp. 101-171). New York: International Universities Press, 1959.

Fleming, J. (1972). Early object deprivation and transference phenomena: The working alliance. *Psychoanalytic Quarterly, 41*, 23-49.

Fleming, J. (1975). Some observations on object constancy in the psychoanalysis of adults. *Journal of the American Psychoanalytic Association, 23*, 743-759.

Fraiberg, S. (1969). Object constancy and mental representation. *The Psychoanalytic Study of the Child, 24*, 9-47.

Freud, S. (1905). Three essays on the theory of sexuality. *Standard Edition, 7*, 135-243.

Freud, S. (1911). Psycho-analytic notes on an autobiographical account of a case of paranoia (dementia paranoides). *Standard Edition, 12*, 9-82.

Freud, S. (1914). On narcissism: An introduction. *Standard Edition, 14*, 73-102.

Freud, S. (1917). Mourning and melancholia. *Standard Edition, 14*, 237-258.

Freud, S. (1923). The ego and the id. *Standard Edition, 19*, 12-68.

Galenson, E., & Roiphe, H. (1974). The emergence of genital awareness during the second year of life. In R. C. Friedman, R. M. Richart, & R. I. Vande Wiele (Eds.), *Sex differences in behavior* (pp. 223-232). New York: Wiley.

Gitelson, M. (1962). On the curative factors in the first phase of analysis. In *Psychoanalysis: Science and profession* (pp. 311-341). New York: International Universities Press, 1973.

Glover, E. (1932). A psycho-analytic approach to the classification of mental disorders. In *On the early development of mind* (pp. 161-186). New York: International Universities Press.

Greenacre, P. (1960). Considerations regarding the parent-infant relationship. *International Journal of Psycho-Analysis, 41*, 571-584.

Hartmann, H. (1939). *Ego psychology and the problem of adaptation.* New York: International Universities Press, 1958.

Hartmann, H. (1950). Comments on the psychoanalytic theory of the ego. In *Essays on ego psychology* (pp. 113-141). New York: International Universities Press, 1964.

Hartmann, H. (1952). The mutual influences in the development of ego and id. In *Essays on ego psychology* (pp. 155-181). New York: International Universities Press, 1964.

Hartmann, H. (1953). On the metapsychology of schizophrenia. In *Essays on ego psychology* (pp. 182-206). New York: International Universities Press.

Jacobson, E. (1954). The self and the object world: Vicissitudes of their infantile cathexes and their influence on ideational and affective development. *The Psychoanalytic Study of the Child, 9*, 75-127.

Jacobson, E. (1964). *The self and the object world.* New York: International Universities Press.

Joffe, W., & Sandler, J. (1967). Some conceptual problems involved in the consideration of disorders of narcissism. *Journal of Child Psychotherapy, 2*, 56-66.

Kernberg, O. (1975). *Borderline conditions and pathological narcissism.* New York: Jason Aronson.

Knight, R. P. (1954). Borderline states. In C. Friedman & R. P. Knight (Eds.), *Psychoanalytic psychiatry and psychology* (pp. 97-109). New York: International Universities Press.

Kohut, H. (1971). *The analysis of the self.* New York: International Universities Press.

Kohut, H. (1972). Thoughts on narcissism and narcissistic rage. *The Psychoanalytic Study of the Child, 27*, 360-400.

Kohut, H. (1974). Remarks about the formation of the self. In P. H. Ornstein (Ed.), *The search for the self* (Vol. 2, pp. 737-770). New York: International Universities Press.

Kohut, H. (1977). *The restoration of the self.* New York: International Universities Press.

Kohut, H. (1979). The two analyses of Mr. Z. *International Journal of Psycho-Analysis, 60*, 3-27.

Lichtenberg, J. D. (1975). The development of the sense of self. *Journal of the American Psychoanalytic Association, 23*, 453-484.

Mahler, M. S. (1981). Aggression in the service of separation-individuation: Case study of a mother-daughter relationship. *Psychoanalytic Quarterly, 50*, 625-638.

Mahler, M. S., Pine, F., & Bergman, A. (1975). *The psychological birth of the human infant.* New York: Basic Books.

Ornstein, P. H. (1981). The bipolar self in the psychoanalytic treatment process: Clinical-theoretical considerations. *Journal of the American Psychoanalytic Association, 29*, 353-375.

Pelletier, K. R. (1977). *Mind as healer, mind as slayer.* New York: Delacorte Press/Seymour Lawrence.

Piaget, J. (1937). *The construction of reality in the child.* New York: Basic Books, 1954.

Restak, R. M. (1982, Summer). The brain. *The Wilson Quarterly, 6,* 89-113.

Sandler, J., & Rosenblatt, B. (1962). The concept of the representational world. *The Psychoanalytic Study of the Child, 17,* 128-145.

Schwaber, E. (1980). Self psychology and the concept of psychopathology: a case presentation. In A. Goldberg (Ed.), with summarizing reflections by H. Kohut, *Advances in self psychology* (pp. 215-241). New York: International Universities Press.

Simonton, O. C., & Matthews-Simonton, S. (1978). *Getting well again.* Los Angeles: Tarcher.

Sperry, R. W. (1969). A modified concept of consciousness. *Psychological Review, 76,* 532-536.

Spiegel, L. A. (1959). The self, the sense of self, and perception. *The Psychoanalytic Study of the Child, 14,* 81-107.

Spitz, R. A. (1953). Aggression: Its role in the establishment of object relations. In R. M. Loewenstein (Ed.), *Drives, affects, behavior* (pp. 126-138). New York: International Universities Press.

Spitz, R. A. (1956). Countertransference. *Journal of the American Psychoanalytic Association, 4,* 256-265.

Stolorow, R. D., & Lachmann, F. M. (1980). *The psychoanalysis of developmental arrests.* New York: International Universities Press.

Van Doren, M. (Ed.). (1934). Egyptian book of the dead (3500 B.C.). He holdeth fast to the memory of his identity. *An anthology of world poetry* (p. 238). New York: Reynat & Hitchcock.

Waelder, R. (1936). The principle of multiple function: Observations on over-determination. *Psychoanalytic Quarterly, 5,* 45-62.

Wallerstein, R. S. (1981). The bipolar self: Discussion of alternative perspectives. *Journal of the American Psychoanalytic Association, 29,* 377-394.

White, M. T. (1980). Self relations, object relations and pathological narcissism. *Psychoanalytic Review, 67,* 3-23.

Winnicott, D. W. (1963). Communicating and not communicating, leading to a study of certain opposites. In *The maturational processes and the facilitating environment* (pp. 179-192). New York: International Universities Press.

The Emergence of the Sense of Self

CHAPTER FOUR

Comments on the Self and Its Objects

JOSEPH SANDLER

Although the search for close-fitting and unambiguous definitions in our field is a most important and commendable enterprise, it is inevitable that we need to use some terms that carry a variety of different meanings, even though we might feel dissatisfied with the lack of clarity inherent in the concept. In a sense such concepts are "pliable" and context dependent. Concepts of this sort serve us well, until they become overstretched, at which point an acceptable reorganization of the concept may, and usually does, emerge. The concept of *self* is *par excellence* a pliable one, whose exact meaning at any one time will depend on the particular context in which the term is used. Unfortunately, as things are at present, any precise definition of "self" will of necessity exclude certain meanings of the term that we need for communicating with one another. The extent of contemporary discussion about the self indicates an increasing degree of "strain" within the concept, and major aspects of the meaning of the concept do need to be separated.

It is generally accepted that the term *das Ich* was used by Freud to refer to both the self (in a variety of meanings) and to the ego as a "structure" in the sense of a large-scale psychological organization. Conscious of the problems generated by using the ambiguous term "ego," a concept which had reached the limit of its elasticity, a distinction was made between concepts of the ego and the self in the USA after World War II. Following a suggestion of Hartmann (1950), Edith Jacobson put forward a concept of self-representation that had the same theoretical status in relation to the ego as had object representation (Jacobson, 1954). By distinguishing between ego and self, some of the phenomena of narcissism and masochism could be better understood, and love or hate for oneself could be seen more clearly as paralleling love or hate for the object.

The psychoanalytic notion of the self introduced by Hartmann and Jacobson is essentially a concept of a self-representation. Such a concept of representation links the ideas of self and the older ideas of body image and body schema, although the self is a broader concept than either. From a number of points of view, the self can be regarded as being (among other things) an elaboration or extension of the body schema or of the body image (see Sandler, 1962, for a full discussion of this topic). Such a view probably corresponds to one of the meanings of Freud's remark that "The ego is first and foremost a body ego" (1923), provided that for "ego" we now read "self." One could say that the self-representation can be looked at as a self-schema, an extended body schema, about which Henry Head said many years ago:

The sensory cortex is the storehouse of past impressions. They may arise into consciousness as images, but more often . . . remain outside central consciousness. Here they form organized models of ourselves which may be called schemata. Such schemata modify the impressions produced by incoming sensory impulses in such a way that the final sensations of position or of locality of the body rise into consciousness charged with a relation to something that has gone before. (1926)

It should be noted that the concept of self-representation has at least two main facets and that the term as I shall use it here encompasses both. The sense of the first is conveyed by what one might call the self-schema, a structural organization formed in exactly the same way as Head described the development of the body schema. It is an organized psychological structure that exists outside consciousness, and indeed, I would say, outside subjective experience, in the so-called nonexperiential realm of the mind (Sandler & Joffe, 1969).

The second major aspect of the meaning of self-representation is the *phenomenal* or *experiential* one, in which the self-representation can be considered to be the image and subjective experience of ourselves that we have at any given moment. Thus if we have a fantasy involving ourselves, the self-representation in that fantasy is, while we are having the fantasy, an experiential representation of ourselves, usually in interaction with others, that is, with object representations that parallel the self-representation. Such a subjective experience may be conscious, but it may equally be unconscious, for the notion of unconscious experience is a central one in psychoanalytic thinking.

Just as we build up and differentiate self-representations during the course of development, so do we construct object representations, that is, organized schemata and images of the object in our world. This has been put as follows (Sandler, 1962):

From the concept of the self representation . . . it is not a difficult step to make the further extension to representations which correspond to all the non-self components of the child's world. As the child gradually creates a self representation, so he builds up representations of others, in particular of his important love and hate objects. In the beginning the representations which he constructs are those which are linked with need satisfaction, but he gradually creates schemata of many other things, activities and relationships. He does all of this as a consequence of the successive experiences of his own internal needs and their interaction with his external environment. He gradually learns to distinguish between "inner" and "outer," a distinction which he cannot make in the earliest weeks and months of life, where the main differentiation between experiences must be based on whether they provide pleasure or pain. Incidentally, this is why I have avoided the use of the term "inner" or "internal" world for the representational world, for these terms . . . refer to only a part of the child's representational world—that part which a child learns to localise as being inside himself.

The concept of the representational world has been an extremely useful tool for the more refined conceptualization and clarification of psycho-analytic concepts (Sandler, 1962; Sandler & Rosenblatt, 1962). It allowed a new approach to the understanding of processes of internalization, to the superego (Sandler, 1960b), the ego ideal (Sandler, Holder, & Meers, 1963), and to a variety of other clinical as well as theoretical problems such as childhood depression and processes of individuation (Joffe & Sandler, 1965; Sandler & Joffe, 1965). In the application of what can be called a esentational point of view, it is convenient to speak of the particular "shape" of a self- or object representation "to denote the particular form and character assumed by that representation or image in the representational world at any one moment" (Sandler & Rosenblatt, 1962). The idea of the "shape" of a representation allows us to use a convenient shorthand in diagrammatic representations to illustrate, for example, the changes that take place in the representational world when different mechanisms of defense are applied to unconscious psychic content.

The child who feels angry at one moment, and the subject of attack at another, shows a change in the shape of his self representation—or alternatively his self image (be it conscious or unconscious) has changed. Moreover, the shape of an unconscious self representation may be differentiated from that shape which is permitted access to consciousness or motility. Thus we can speak of the child who has an unconscious aggressive wish to attack an object as having a particular shape of his self representation—the unconscious image of himself attacking the object—which is not ego syntonic and which is only permitted to proceed to consciousness or motility once its shape has been changed by means of defensive activity on the part of the ego. . . . The self representation can assume a wide variety of shapes and forms, depending on the pressures of the id, the requirements of the external world and the demand and standards of the introjects. Some shapes of the self representation would . . . evoke conflicts if they were allowed discharge to motility or consciousness, and the defence mechanisms are directed against their emergence. (Sandler & Rosenblatt, 1962)

As self-representations can be considered to be sensorimotor in nature, *identification* can be regarded as a change in the shape of a self-representation based on the model of another. So if a little child walks like her mother, we can say she changes the shape of her self-representation on the basis of an object representation (or an aspect of that representation), that is, on the basis of an image of her mother walking. (I do not distinguish here between identification and imitation, which can be differentiated by other criteria.) Of course, identifications are never complete, but can be, to varying degrees, partial, temporary, or enduring and (after a point relatively early in development) can occur throughout life.

The sort of identification just described has been referred to as secondary identification. In this process the boundaries between the self and the object remain intact. The object is still perceived as an object, but the shape of the self-representation has been changed. Incidentally, the term "self boundary" is far more appropriate in this context than "ego boundary." So-called primary identification, in which there is a fusion or confusion between self- and object representation, involves the absence or breakdown of functioning self boundaries. This phenomenon occurs very early in life, before boundaries between self and object have been established, and later as a regressive manifestation in certain psychotic states.

Although the terms *introjection* and *identification* have often been used synonymously, it is possible to differentiate the two in a meaningful way in terms of the representational world. So-called "early" introjection can be seen as the process of building up the inner world of representations, a product of the "organizing activity of the ego" (see Hartmann, 1939; Sandler, 1960b). Introjection, of the sort which is thought to result in the formation of an organized superego, can be regarded as the process of attributing to certain object representations a special status, so that they are felt to have all the authority and power of the real parents. The child then reacts, when his parents are absent, as if they were present. This does not mean that he copies them any more than before, for that would be the process of identification. Of course, identification can (and often does) accompany introjection of the type described, but from a theoretical point of view the two processes should be sharply differentiated. *Incorporation* refers to the actual taking into the body of substances or things from the outside, but fantasies or thoughts of incorporation (usually referred to simply as "incorporation," which is very confusing) involve the shape of the self-representation being changed so that it now encloses a representation of something which is "nonself." In one sense thoughts or fantasies of incorporation represent displacements from one part of the representational world to another.

The workings of the mechanisms of defense can be illustrated conveniently in terms of changes in the representational world. Thus the mechanism of *projection*, from a representational point of view, becomes a transfer of some aspect of the self-representation to an object representation. The unconscious image of oneself attacking an object, for instance, is transformed into a conscious image or thought of the object attacking the self. The "attacking part of the self" is projected (i.e., displaced within the representational world) onto the object representation. The defense mechanism of *displacement* is reflected simply in a change in the direction of an activity, originally directed toward one object, toward another. So the child who has a wish to attack his mother, whom he also loves, can deal with his conflict of ambivalence by directing his attacking wishes toward a sibling or other convenient person. In *reaction formation* the shape of the self can be changed (in certain respects) into its opposite, so that an unconscious image of a sadistic self becomes one of a kind, caring self; or an unconscious dirty, messy self-representation is changed into one which is neat, clean, and meticulously tidy. All the mechanisms of defense can be viewed with profit in representational terms.

In a 1963 study of the ego ideal, we put forward the view in the Hampstead Index project that the concept of ego ideal had been stretched beyond its useful limits, and proposed that we make use of the motion of an ideal self in many of the contexts in which the idea of the ego ideal had been used (Sandler *et al.*, 1963). The ideal self represented a shape of the self which was the most desirable, in either instinctual or narcissistic terms, at any one time. It could change from moment to moment, depending on the state of the individual's unconscious impulses and on his sources of narcissistic supply, as well as on many other factors. The state of the self-representation at any moment was referred to as the "actual" self. The existence of a discrepancy between actual self and ideal self, at any point in time, was regarded as providing a motivating force for appropriate adaptive ego activity. If the gap between actual self and ideal self is too great, then it is experienced as pain of one sort or another (Joffe & Sandler, 1965; Sandler & Joffe, 1965).

The representational approach allows us to see the close relationship between the various mechanisms of defense and the ideal shape of the self. The mechanisms operate to bring about a change in the self-representation, so that it becomes one that is more acceptable to the individual, arouses less conflict and unpleasure, and is more consistent with his internal standards (which may or may not be related to his superego introjects). The mechanism of reaction formation, seen in this way, clearly involves an identification with an ideal—in the example given it is the ideal of being clean and tidy.

Ideal shapes of the self can be simply states of instinctual wish fulfillment, or may be shapes of the self that the individual regards as being most desirable to his objects or to his introjects. So the shape reflecting the "good child" desired by the parents at any one time may be quite different from the shape of the self that represents the fulfillment of an instinctual wish of one sort or another. Indeed, we can look at psychic conflict, as unconsciously sensed by the ego, as being conflict involving different ideal shapes of the self, the ego being motivated to identify with different ideal self-representations. This is well illustrated by the frequent conflicts that exist for the ego (Sandler, 1974) in regard to reaching an ideal state of instinctual satisfaction (the "instinctual" ideal) and reaching an ideal shape of the self that is felt by the ego as being held up to it by an introject. Much of the ego's activity can then be seen as being concerned with the finding of compromise representational solutions, so that, as far as possible, the conflicting tendencies will be satisfied. We can also look at the changes that occur in therapy, from a representational point of view, in terms of discrepancies between actual and ideal self-representations. If, for example, we are dealing with someone who is depressed, who has had a depressive reaction to a painful gap between his actual self (as he sees it) and his ideal self, then we can think in terms of therapeutic interventions that predominantly affect his (conscious or unconscious) view of his actual self and those that affect his ideal self (e.g., impossibly high standards of conduct or attainment associated with "strict" superego introjects).

At any one time we have a whole system of ideal selves that are derived from different sources. One may be closely related to the aims of an unconscious instinctual wish, another may be linked to superego standards, others with the ideals of the real parents or of the group of which we are a part, and so on. The ideal we fashion from all of these self-representations will be a function of many forces. Above all, the roles played by sources of well-being and self-esteem are highly significant. It has often been said half-jokingly that the superego is that part of the mental apparatus that is soluble in alcohol, and the truth in this statement comes from the fact that alcohol (like many other drugs) provides an alternate feeling of well-being, so that the need to appease the superego—that is, to identify with the ideal self felt to be held up by the superego, the need to gain the feeling of internal parental approval—is temporarily diminished or absent.

One way of looking at the superego (Sandler, 1981) is to see it as referring to phantom companions who exist in the unconscious part of the representational world. These are companions who are unconsciously treated and reacted to as if they were really present, but who do not normally appear in recognizable form above the threshold of normal perception. Having a superego is like living with such phantom companions, who are tolerated because they are not only felt to criticize but are also felt to provide approval and support. Of course, if we can embody such phantoms in external figures or in external institutions, we will do so, and will relate to these institutions and figures as if they were the superego introjects. In therapy we see such processes of externalization occurring over and over again, and these may provide one of the avenues for the therapeutic intervention to find an effective way into the mind of the patient. The analyst or therapist then becomes a source of new ideal shapes of the self, and it is probable that every psychoanalytic interpretation carries with it a new ideal, even if that ideal only reflects the view that it is permissible to tolerate and even enjoy all sorts of wishes in fantasy, even if they are not appropriately translated into action. The therapist who says to his patient, "Well, of course you would like to kill me, because you are angry with me," conveys an ideal to the patient that it is permissible to have such a wish, permissible in the area of wishes and fantasies to tolerate a "child" part of oneself as a normal state of affairs.

At this point I should like to go back to something touched on earlier, that is, the parallel between self and object. I am convinced that the most useful way to look at the notion of self is to maintain the strictest possible parallel between the ideas of self and object, and to examine, as far as we can, the parallel between the two in different contexts. So, for example, if we think of the notion of identity, we can understand the concept of identity relatively easily in relation to an object, for the object has a name, endures in time, is perceived by us again and again. We recognize objects as existing, not only in space but also in time, and because of this we can abstract a notion of identity in relation to the object. We do not have a problem about saying, "This is Mr. Smith. We know things about him because we know his past, and he is not Mr. Jones." If we then transfer this concept of identity to the self, it becomes clear that whatever we can say about the object with regard to identity can also be said about the self (A.-M. Sandler, 1977). It is as if the self-representation is the representation of a companion, an object we have grown up with, one that shows relatively slow changes over time, and is immediately recognizable. The self is our oldest and closest object, and because of this its identity is normally well known to us. (This raises all sorts of philosophical problems, but these can safely be left to the philosophers.) Similarly, self-esteem can be taken as the counterpart of esteem for the object, self-love as parallel to love for the object, and so on.

Psychoanalytic theory has traditionally placed enormous emphasis on the role of the instinctual drives and drive derivatives in its theory of motivation. The part played by such drives in mental life is central to psychoanalytic thinking, but more and more noninstinctual factors are being admitted into our understanding of the way people function. For example, it seems to be very clear now that, whatever the role of urges toward instinctual drive satisfaction may be, an overriding consideration for the individual is to preserve a feeling of safety. If the threat to his safety is too great, he will give up the striving toward the gratification of his drives (Sandler & Joffe, 1969). Freud was aware of this when he wrote of the self-preservative drives of the ego (Freud, 1910), and Anna Freud (1936) has written of the need to preserve the integrity of the ego as a motive for defense.

In addition to instinctual drive satisfaction and the need to preserve a background feeling of safety (Sandler, 1960a), there has been increasing emphasis in recent years on the individual's need to regulate his supplies of well-being and self-esteem to preserve what can be called his narcissistic balance. It is now possible to see many disturbances of childhood and of adult life in terms of pathological attempts to regulate feelings of safety and well-being (Joffe & Sandler, 1967).

If we pick up on the formulation of Anna Freud in *The Ego and the Mechanisms of Defence* (1936) that the motives for defense are neurotic anxiety, superego anxiety (guilt), realistic (reality-based) anxiety, and threats to the integrity of the ego, we can develop a basis for a psychoanalytic theory of motivation that puts feeling states at the center of the stage (Sandler, 1972).

The drives can be regarded as stimuli that disturb the basic feeling state and mobilize instinctual wishes, but there are also wishes of other sorts, prompted by other factors, which have to take their place as important psychological motives. We can think in particular here of wishes to apply one or other mode of defense, such wishes being stimulated by the motivating power of unpleasant affective states referred to by Anna Freud. Narcissistic imbalance brought about by wounded self-esteem can provide the affective basis for the creation of unconscious wishes of one sort or another.

The striving for pleasant feelings of all sorts must be given the same weight as the avoidance of unpleasure in the psychoanalytic theory of motivation. In this context a differentiation has to be made between the erotic satisfaction gained in the process of instinctual drive gratification, and the "after-satisfaction" experienced as a *result* of the instinctual gratification. The two are substantially different. The baby sucking at the breast obtains an erotic satisfaction gained in the process of instinctual drive gratification and the "after-satisfaction" experienced as a *result* of the instinctual gratification. The two are substantially different. The baby sucking at the breast obtains an erotic oral satisfaction, but the blissful feeling experienced by the child after his feed is a satisfaction of a vastly different quality. I do not want to dwell too long on the possibilities for a revised psychoanalytic theory of motivation, except to say that in my view, a model of the sort I have mentioned seems to be a necessary consequence of the line of thought initiated by Freud's revision of the theory of anxiety in *Inhibitions, Symptoms and Anxiety* (1926).

It is possible to understand more of the complexities of object relationships by taking the view that wishes do not only involve self-representations but also object representations and representations of the interaction between self and object. Again, these wishes need not be only instinctual, but may be motivated by factors such as the need to preserve feelings of safety and to redress narcissistic wounds. From very early in his life, the interaction between the child and his mother provides feelings of safety and security, and Margaret Mahler (1978) has described how the child manages to develop a capacity for separateness from the mother via the process of "checking back to mother," in which he allows himself to move away from her, while constantly turning back in order to gain supplies of reassurance and affirmation. The obtaining of what Mahler has called "refueling" remains as an essential part of object relationships and this process continues into our social life, where by unconscious convention, we normally provide one another with minute signals of affirmation and reassurance. In general, it is now not difficult for us to make a link between the concept of the wish, instinctual or otherwise, and the concept of object relationship (Sandler & Sandler, 1978).

It has been pointed out that the wish contains representations of self, object, and the interaction between the two. As wish fulfillment comes about when the wished-for state is reached, what is gained is not only a particular state of the self-representation, but a state in which self and object interact. The individual will do all he can to satisfy his wishes in a direct or indirect way, and he will do so through a process of actualization (Sandler, 1976a, 1976b; Sandler & Sandler, 1978). He will attempt to change the external world or himself so that he can bring about a situation in which the wish is satisfied. A very large part of the process of actualization involves the manipulation of objects so that they conform to the role implicit in the wish, and a great deal of "trying out" of what has been called the individual's "role-responsiveness" (Sandler, 1976b) occurs as part of normal social life. The process of actualization, as it relates to unconscious wishes and the associated object relationships can best be seen in the psychoanalytic situation, where transference is now generally regarded as involving more than the distortion of the patient's picture of the analyst, including as well attempts on the part of the patient to manipulate the analyst into playing a particular role (Sandler, Dare, & Holder, 1973). The effect of this manipulation can be felt and assessed in the countertransference (Sandler, 1976b).

REFERENCES

Freud, A. (1936). *The ego and the mechanisms of defence.* London: Hogarth Press, 1954.

Freud, S. (1910). The psycho-analytic view of psychogenic disturbances of vision. *Standard Edition, 11.*

Freud, S. (1914). On narcissism: An introduction. *Standard Edition, 14,* 73–102.

Freud, S. (1923). The ego and the id. *Standard Edition, 19,* 3–66.

Freud, S. (1926). Inhibitions, symptoms and anxiety. *Standard Edition, 20,* 77–178.

Hartmann, H. (1939). *Ego psychology and the problem of adaptation.* New York: International Universities Press, 1958.

Hartmann, H. (1950). Comments on the psychoanalytic theory of the ego. *The Psychoanalytic Study of the Child, 5.*

Head, H. (1926). *Aphasia and kindred disorders of speech.* New York: Macmillan.

Jacobson, E. (1954). The self and the object world: Vicissitudes of their infantile cathexes and their influence on ideational and affective development. *The Psychoanalytic Study of the Child, 9,* 75–127.

Joffe, W. G., & Sandler, J. (1965). Notes on pain, depression and individuation. *The Psychoanalytic Study of the Child, 20.*

Joffe, W. G., & Sandler, J. (1967). Some conceptual problems involved in the consideration of disorders of narcissism. *Journal of Child Psychotherapy, 2,* 56–66.

Mahler, M. (1978). *The psychological birth of the human infant.* New York: Basic Books.

Sandler, A.-M. (1977). Beyond eight-month anxiety. *International Journal of Psycho-Analysis, 58,* 195–207.

Sandler, J. (1960b). On the concept of superego. *The Psychoanalytic Study of the Child, 15,* 128–162.

Sandler, J. (1962). Psychology and psychoanalysis. *British Journal of Medical Psychology, 35,* 91–100.

Sandler, J. (1972). The role of affects in psychoanalytic theory. In *Physiology, emotion and psychosomatic illness* (Ciba Foundation Symposium 8, New Series). Amsterdam: Elsevier/Excerpta Medica.

Sandler, J. (1974). Psychological conflict and the structural model: Some clinical and theoretical implications. *International Journal of Psycho-Analysis, 55,* 53-62.

Sandler, J. (1976a). Dreams, unconscious fantasies and "identity of perception." *International Review of Psycho-Analysis, 3,* 33-42.

Sandler, J. (1976b). Countertransference and role-responsiveness. *International Review of Psycho-Analysis, 3,* 43-47.

Sandler, J. (1981). Character traits and object relationships. *Psychoanalytic Quarterly, 50,* 694-708.

Sandler, J., Dare, C., & Holder, A. (1973). *The patient and the analyst.* London: Allen & Unwin.

Sandler, J., Holder, A., & Meers, D. (1963). The ego ideal and the ideal self. *The Psychoanalytic Study of the Child, 18,* 139-158.

Sandler, J., & Joffe, W. G. (1965). Notes on childhood depression. *International Journal of Psycho-Analysis, 46,* 88-96.

Sandler, J., & Joffe, W. G. (1969). Towards a basic psychoanalytic model. *International Journal of Psycho-Analysis, 50,* 79-90.

Sandler, J., & Rosenblatt, B. (1962). The concept of the representational world. *The Psychoanalytic Study of the Child, 17,* 128-145.

Sandler, J., & Sandler, A.-M. (1978). On the development of object relationships and affects. *International Journal of Psycho-Analysis, 59,* 285-296.

CHAPTER FIVE

The Relationship of Winnicott's Developmental Concept of the Transitional Object to Self and Object Constancy

SIMON GROLNICK

But I am constant as the northern star,
Of whose true-fix'd and resting quality
There is no fellow in the firmament.
—Shakespeare, *Julius Caesar*

For, such as I am, all true lovers are;
Unstaid and skittish in all motions else,
Save in the constant image of the creature
That is belov'd.
—Shakespeare, *Twelfth Night*

There is nothing in this world constant but inconstancy.
—Jonathan Swift, *A Cricical Essay upon the Faculties of the Mind* (1707)

There is no Death; what seems so is transition.
—Henry Wadsworth Longfellow, *Resignation* (1849)

INTRODUCTION

In this chapter I hope to apply Winnicott's concept of the transitional object (Winnicott, 1951) to Mahler's concepts of self and object constancy (Hartmann, 1952; Mahler, Pine, & Bergman, 1975). This presumes a functional relationship between the two bodies of knowledge, at least from the developmental point of view. Since both D. W. Winnicott and Margaret Mahler and her co-workers (Pine, Bergman, McDevitt, Furer, etc.) can be considered to be within the developmental school of modern psychoanalysis, it might be expected that various links can be established. Mahler *et al.* refer to Winnicott and the transitional object frequently; while, even though his writing ceased in 1971, and Mahler's greatest influence on the psychoanalytic scene occurred during the past decade, Winnicott referred to Mahler's work both in his collected papers and in *Playing and Reality*.

An important issue should be addressed before I proceed. Are these formulations at the same conceptual and methodological levels, so that they can be related to each other in a *consistent* manner? This question cannot be answered easily. Do Mahler and Winnicott share a rather specific view of early development? Winnicott's and Mahler's work can be subsumed under what Werner and Kaplan (1963) termed the "organismic-holistic" and the developmental approach. Werner and Kaplan wrote, ". . . within the organismic-holistic assumption, every behavioral act, whether outward bodily movement or internalized cognitive operation, gains its significance and status in terms of its role in the overall functioning of the organism. The holistic assumption itself pertains to the 'reciprocal relationship between an organism and its environment.'" According to Werner and Kaplan, the developmental orientation assumes that "organisms are naturally directed towards a series of transformations—reflecting a tendency to move from a state of relative globality and undifferentiation and undifferentiatedness towards states of increasing differentiation and hierarchic integration." Implicit in this basic orientation is the principle of spirality. With Hegel (1831), Freud (1965), and Hartmann (1952),

. . . it must be maintained that with the attainment of higher levels, lower levels of functioning are not lost. [In fact:] Under normal circumstances, such lower levels of functioning (both in terms of means and ends) are subordinated to more advanced levels of functioning; they may come to the fore again under special internal or external conditions, for example, in dream states, in pathological states, under intoxication by certain drugs, or under various experimental conditions. They also, and characteristically, may come to the fore when the organism is confronted with especially difficult and novel tasks: in such cases, one often finds a partial return to more primitive modes of functioning before progressing upwards to full-fledged higher operations; we may refer to this tendency as a manifestation of the *genetic principle of spirality*. (Werner & Kaplan, 1963, p. 8)

While Piaget was concerned primarily with cognitive development, within their holistic frame of reference, Werner and Kaplan could not see the relationship between the inner and the outer in a dualistic manner and, of necessity, took affective, interactional, and developmental considerations into account. It is most significant that they found a close affinity with Winnicott's work on the transitional object, designating the transitional object as "protosymbol," a stage in the development of nonverbal and verbal symbols. They saw, as did Winnicott, the primitive symbol emerging from the only partially differentiated mother-child relationshp. "It is a pre-symbolic situation in which there is little differentiation in the child's experience between himself, the other (typically the mother), and the referential object" (Werner & Kaplan, 1963). Essentially, this is the same manner in which Winnicott conceived the transitional object to emerge from or to be created from the dyadic, dual unity, that is, the first primitive triangulation. My reading of the body of Mahler's separation-individuation process places her well within the framework of Werner and Kaplan and, implicitly, Winnicott.

Kohut (1971), working in a similar area, attempted to differentiate his theoretical system from that of Mahler's separation-individuation sequence, as well as from Winnicott's transitional object. His comments can be used as another frame of reference. Kohut felt that Mahler's formulations "belong in the sociobiological framework of direct child observation," where, according to Kohut, the child is a "psychobiological unit which interacts with the environment." In contrast, Kohut characterized his own observational method as the construction of the "inner life" of adults "on the basis of transference reactivations." He saw his formulations as psychoanalytic metapsychology, defined, in his case, "by the position of the observer who occupies an imaginary point *inside* the psychic organization of the individual with whose introspection he empathically identifies (vicarious introspection)" (1971, p. 219). Kohut was aware of the closeness of some of his formulations with Winnicott's, and devoted a paragraph in *The Analysis of Self* (1971) to relating his "selfobject" with Winnicott's transitional object. (Actually, Kohut and some of his followers referred to the selfobject as the "transitional selfobject.") Kohut granted that Winnicott's transitional object concept attempts to grapple with the issues of the archaic object, but, similar to his comments on Mahler's methodology, he viewed Winnicott primarily as an infant observer and considered the transitional object a *descriptive* entity in contrast to his own explanation of the phenomena (of selfobjects) as "metapsychological terms" (1971, p. 33).

It is ironic that it was Tolpin (1971), one of Kohut's followers, who placed Winnicott's transitional object rather solidly into the metapsychological realm, as well as the mainstream of American developmental psychoanalysis, when she disagreed with Winnicott (who wrote that the transitional object eventually fades away) and claimed that by the process of Kohut's "transmuting internalization," the transitional object normally transforms into an internalized, self-comforting psychic structure. Winnicott himself was a pragmatic man, and not a rigorous methodoligist. When he did mention this problem, he ironically professed a methodology similar to that described by Kohut—his formulations were based primarily on the work he did with adult patients in analysis. ("Indeed it is not from the direct observation of infants so much as from the study of the transference in the analytic setting that it is possible to gain a clear view of what takes place in infancy itself" [Winnicott, 1960, p. 54].) It would seem to me that Winnicott actually utilized both areas, the empathic field of adult analysis and the observation of children, working back and forth between one and the other. This is most appropriate, as the main content of his contribution involves an important developmental phase and ego process that interplays *between* reality and fantasy, *between* the objective and the subjective poles.

Actually, Winnicott did make a related statement on this subject at the end of a short paper written in 1957, "On the Contribution of Direct Child Observation to Psycho-Analysis":

Psycho-analysis has much to learn from those who make direct observations of infants, and of other and infants together and of small children in the environment in which they naturally live. Also, direct observation is not able of itself to construct a psychology of early infancy. By constantly co-operating analysts and direct observers may be able to correlate what is deep in analysis and what is early in infant development. (Winnicott, 1957, p. 114)

It seems to me that this is the same position that Mahler and her co-workers take, in spite of Kohut's (and I might say classical, conflict-theory analyst Charles Brenner's) belief that infant observation and adult psychoanalysis exist in two unrelated realms.

SOME ESSENTIAL ASSUMPTIONS ABOUT WINNICOTT'S CONCEPT OF THE TRANSITIONAL OBJECT

It is now necessary to restate and clarify some aspects of Winnicott's widely known but difficult concept of the transitional object. To better assimilate the content of this chapter, certain assumptions would be helpful for the reader to maintain, either through experience, belief, or, perhaps, a suspension of disbelief.

Winnicott's concept is ambiguous by definition because it attempts to bring discursive, even explanatory, considerations into an area of flux, paradox, and abstract processing; it is an area, the "intermediate area" as he termed it (Winnicott, 1971), that he tries to crystallize, to cross-section a process as it oscillates, interplays and transforms to progressive or regressive forms. Basically, the transitional object concept can be looked at in some of, and no doubt more than, the following ways:

1. *The transitional object as an actual object that the child possesses* (in the phenomenon as an actual, perceived, visual, auditory, or rhythmic experience). He has the illusion that it was created by him and that it is part of both his own self and body image and that of his primary caretaker's; that it is *both* an object and a partially internalized, partially stable, psychological function that would be considered by many as a primitive or proto-psychic *structure*, one that would involve an early sense of self-integrity, self-reliance, and self-comfort, and an internalized precursor of the formation of affectively laden verbal and nonverbal symbols.

2. *The transitional object as part of a long developmental line*, which was delineated in a gradual and somewhat haphazard manner throughout

Winnicott's writings and formally described by Anna Freud (1965), "from the body to the toy and from play to work." Since the transitional object can be seen quite early, at ages 4 months or even before, it undergoes a long developmental pathway. The archaeology of this pathway ranges from the primitive to the most sophisticated, and is characterized by complex mixing of layers, challenging the observer's attempts to reconstruct the story of the civilizing of the "little savage." The earliest attachments to a transitional object or phenomenon (a phenomenon is a nonobjectual perception, such as a tune, a voice, a word, a visual image, or a rhythm) are, in part, operating at the level of the conditioned response as well as at the drive (libidinal or aggressive) or at the positively or negatively tinged affective level. Spitz (1965a, 1965b), who has taught us so much about early object relations and mother-child dialogue, was working, before he died, on the transformational, organizing aspects of the transitional object. In a short article, a virtual manifesto titled "Bridges" (1972), he wrote about the earliest "bridge":

I consider, furthermore, the conditioned reflex the first implementation (the first on the psychic level) of the tendency to coherence, that tendency which is present in all congeneric living matter. The conditions for such coherence are coextensiveness and simultaneity of percept and affect during one and the same process. Under the pressure of the need to survive, this affective coextensiveness introduces the time-binding factor of duration.

(The importance of the sense of time—past, present, and future—and its relation to the transitional object and to object and self constancy will be discussed later in this chapter.)

From its early conditioned reflex, sensorimotor origins, during the early and middle part of the first year, to its protosymbolic status during the rapprochement period of the second year of life, to its ultimate fate in internalized function and in the spheres of the symbolic capacities of the playful imagination, the transitional object has traversed an odyssean journey.

3. *The transitional object as a crystallized element of a much broader process*, what Gilbert Rose (1978, 1980) has termed the "transitional process." Transitional process "arises out of the importance modern conceptual models assign to shifting boundaries as opposed to stable structure." In this view, "reality is no longer seen as a steady backdrop, but is, instead, viewed as a dynamic oscillation of figure and ground; and the organism as a whole is looked at as an open system continuously engaged in mutual development with the outside." Rose (1980, pp. 112-115) writes that the transitional process implies that (1) the dynamic equilibrium between a relatively fluid self and reality is not limited to the transitional object of childhood, but continues into adulthood; (2) the adaptation of everyday life and the originality of creative imagination both represent a continuing

"transitional" interplay between self and reality; (3) in this interplay between self and reality, a greater accommodation to reality characterizes adaptation, and a greater reshaping of reality characterizes creative imagination; (4) to the extent that creative imagination must also accommodate to reality, it is adaptive, and to the extent that adaptation selectively integrates elements of reality, it may be thought of as creative; (5) both adaptation and creative imagination are on the same continuum in that both abstract elements to "create" an *Umwelt* comprising a necessarily selective mix of self and reality.

4. *The capacity of the human object to be considered as a whole or in part a transitional object.* This controversial thesis is an important part of my argument, since, if true, a therapist working within such a transference field could play an important structure-building role.

Winnicott made conceptualizing in this entire area more difficult for us when he said in his original paper (1951) that the mother *could* be a transitional object. If criteria for the transitional object were that it be (1) inanimate and (2) a substitute for the mother, how could the mother *be* a transitional object? In his reprinted classical paper (1971), Winnicott described two brothers and their uses of a transitional object. The older brother's difficulty was subsumed under the rubric, "distortion in use of transitional object." He was difficult to wean. "He never sucked his thumb or his fingers" and when he mother weaned him, "he had nothing to fall back on. He had never had a bottle or a dummy or any other form of feeding. He had a very strong and early *attachment to the mother herself*, as a person, and it was her actual person that he needed." The brother acquired a stuffed rabbit at the age of 12 months, but Winnicott did not regard this as a true transitional object because it was never, "as a true transitional object would have been, more important than the mother, an almost inseparable part of the infant." The boy later developed asthma. He had been weaned at 7 months, after which he developed asthma. The rabbit was not given up until he was 5 or 6 years old. Though Winnicott thought the patient came within the wide definition of the term normal, or healthy, he still had a "very powerful attachment" to his mother and had not married. In a chart elaborating the case history of the two brothers, Winnicott included the two brothers and the rabbit under the heading "transitional object," even though he designated the "type of child" as "mother-fixated."

When Winnicott referred to the possibility that a mother could be a transitional object, what did he mean? I think that the time of the original article (the early 1950s) and the kind of conceptual thinking that went into it must be taken into account here. Winnicott was still influenced by the object relations psychology of Melanie Klein, even though he was beginning to differentiate himself from it. He was not then, nor later, a metapsychologist, and in addition, the whole concept of the representational world and a clear understanding of the qualities of a self and an object representation were not well ensconced in the psychoanalytic literature. Winnicott *did* attempt a metapsychological discrimination when in his original paper he said that the "transitional object is *not an internal object* (which is a mental concept). It is a possession. Yet it is not (for the infant) an external object either" (original italics). It is this intermediate, for some, ambiguous position of the concept that becomes difficult, perhaps by definition. However, Winnicott was clear that the transitional object for the brother (his mother), was *not* healthy, and that the mother fixation prevented him from investing the "*solitude à deux*" onto the stuffed rabbit. The rabbit could not become a developmentally active furthering possession. Today we would probably designate a prolonged attachment to the mother symbiotic, perhaps some would term it fetishistic. Of course a part of the mother's body, such as her ear lobes or hair, could be used as a kind of transitional object. But Winnicott and Gaddini (1978) eventually worked out the alternative concept of the "precursor object," as contrasted to the true transitional object. The precursor object could be a pacifier, a bottle, a part of the mother's body. But it is not yet a true, developmentally alive transitional object since it cannot fulfill the criteria of being controllable by the child and having been chosen under the illusion that the *child* initiated the choice.

All this becomes even more complicated when dealing with adults. There have been a number of contributions to the psychoanalytic literature which conceptualize the therapist or analyst as a transitional object. This is usually restricted to borderline and psychotic patients or patients with basic difficulties in self and object constancy. Modell (1981) described "transitional object relations" as one of the criteria for the borderline patient. Searles (1976), Greenbaum (1978), Greenson (1978), Solomon (1978), Horton (1976), and others have all written of the patient's use of the analyst as a transitional object. They refer to the patient who has not as yet established truly internalized self and object relations and, more frequently than not, show an impoverishment of their affective symbolic and creative life (unless they happen to be highly creative on a constitutional basis).

These formulations involve the concept of a regression or a fixation to a transitional object "phase." Here only partial internalization of self and object representations have occurred, as well as only partial internalization of self-comforting and self and body images; of course all this in an individual who usually has experienced cognitive maturation and has achieved the capacity to abstract and to symbolize cognitively. However, to symbolize cognitively and to symbolize *affectively and cognitively* are not the same. I believe we are dealing here with a phenomenon that is analogous to, and in some ways homologous to, the difference between cognitive and affective (or Mahler's "emotional") object constancy.

Winnicott (1971) and Green (1975, 1978) have both discussed the less than neurotic, presymbolic patient. Winnicott saw adult play, that is, developmental play, analogous to early child play (the work of childhood), as the necessary condition for these patients to be able to use the traditional methods of classical psychoanalysis, that is, the interpretation of meaning through the process of free association. Winnicott put it thus:

> The general principle seems to me to be valid that psychotherapy is done in the overlap of the two play areas, that of the patient and that of the therapist. If the therapist cannot play, then he is not suitable for the work. If the patient cannot play, then something needs to be done to enable the patient to become able to play, after which psychotherapy may begin. (1971, p. 54)

In my experience, the patient who either temporarily or permanently uses the therapist or analyst as a transitional object can be differentiated from the patient who uses the therapist or analyst as a narcissistic object. Usually the analyst who is treated as a transitional object experiences intense feelings, feelings of being owned, cuddled, "sniffed out," and being observed microscopically. (This differs from the use of the analyst as a narcissistic object, which usually evokes therapist boredom.) From the developmental standpoint, the patient is attempting to realize (actualize) the combination of his perceptions and projections within the therapist. This projection-introjection process, in the setting of a solid enough alliance ("transitional" though it may be), allowing the possibility for the process of transmuting internalization of self and object representations to occur, is one way of understanding how the transitional object (here the presence of the therapist) can assist the patient to establish a higher degree of self and object constancy. Of course, how much this is possible in each therapist–patient dyad is limited by a multiplicity of variables.

An unmarried phobic, creative young woman required several years of modified therapy using some of Winnicott's play techniques. She experienced a lack of continuity to her relationships with her self and others, and sometimes felt hopelessly alone. Also there had been interference with the internalization of a stable nurturing modality. She tried to use her creativity and many transitional object and fetishistic derivatives (stuffed animals, her hair, pet dogs, birds, and so on) to experience a sense of continuity. As she became more able to trust me, the treatment evolved into a more classical one and she could reveal much she had not previously disclosed to anyone, including four therapists. Typically, progressions in her treatment and in her life were followed by regressive periods during which she would feel estranged, occasionally suicidal, and at home sometimes she would curl up into a ball and hold a stuffed animal. However, each time she emerged from these states (which did not disrupt her day-to-day functioning) she felt stronger, more open, and more related to others and myself. Once, during this spiraling developmental growth, while going through a period of anxiety and aggression toward me, she reported that she found herself (literally) picturing *me* but using *her own* words emerging from *my* mouth to comfort herself and see herself through what she considered to be a crisis. Later, this combined image was more and more bilaterally depersonalized as the image slowly turned into thought. The patient described a growing desire, and then the ability, to be alone. She was able to become increasingly interested in intellectual pursuits long forsaken, and subsequently began to consolidate a professional identity. Gradually, what was "us" became "her."

This combined therapist-patient comforter seems to be a newly generated transitional phenomenon that could serve as a stabilizer during the ups and downs of the developmental arena created within the analytic situation. Fortunately this patient had "good enough" reality testing so that she could use me as *both* a security object and a transference figure. As the analysis became more traditional many erotic elements in the transference emerged. They corresponded to a rich, sadomasochistic, and sexual fantasy life; but these could be analyzed only after the patient's self and object representations were more fully consolidated and stabilized. To sum up, she was first allowed to play in the presence of someone else (Winnicott, 1958), then feel safe enough to utilize me as a transitional figure and ultimately, more and more as a symbolic, transference figure. All along, internalizations of our developmental relationship contributed to her developing fuller, more stable self and object representations. This did not occur in clear-cut phases, but as I have indicated, in a complex, spiraling manner.

A skin-cutting, suicidal, borderline patient of mine had many transitional-fetishistic object supports that functioned as primitive comforters, body completers (Kestenberg & Weinstein, 1978), and self-animators. She presented with anorexia nervosa at the age of 16, and after 13 months of hospitalization and the attainment of normal weight, she practiced both wrist cutting and bulimia. The latter was intensely multidetermined, and allowed her, in a regressive form, the to-and-fro-ness of the rapprochement period and the inner and outer movement between inside and outside. Hence the food represented an inanimate, transitional object-like comfort, filling and, in reverse, a holding nurturing figure that, when inside, was experienced as fusing and dangerous, necessitating a controllable, immediate expulsion from the body-self by the induction of vomiting. This patient's treatment has consisted of developmental considerations alternating on occasion with the necessity for the formal interpretation of conflicts at a more structured and oedipal level. However, the primary consideration has been the attempt to create a developmental field in which more structure, reliable and "constant" self and object representations can be built. Treatment is slow and laborious but the alternatives are portentous: either a literal suicide or a death of the true self or a (probably impossible) return to her premorbid "good little girl," false-self personality. This patient who is developmentally more primitive than the previous patient requires refuelling episodically even though it would seem structure is gradually being formed. She is of normal weight, can remain alone for longer periods of time and is moving closer to a symbolic mode.

I hope these clinical examples will demonstrate that, where development is still open, and self and object constancy are not well established, new development can be enhanced, often slowly and painstakingly by the transitional object functions that are invested in both the person of and the patient's imagery of the therapist and his interpretative actions. At the same time, the therapist, in a facilitating developmental role (Fleming, 1975), including his holding environment functions (Winnicott, 1971), allows the patient to have the stabilization of nonhuman transitional object and fetishistic derivatives during the stormy regressive periods that are, by definition, inevitable in a therapeutic field of this nature.

It is clear, I believe, that the concept of a person being invested with transitional object qualities is a plausible one. It is this very shift from the vitalized inanimate world back to the human world (when accomplished in a good enough therapeutic situation) that represents a distinct developmental advance. Hopefully, this developmental "nesting place" that has been created by therapist and patient alike can lead to the kind of true structural change that leads to a greater degree of both self and object constancy.

5. *The capacity of the transitional object to be considered as part of the self.* Again, a most controversial concept. When viewed in light of the development of the category of the precursor object, there is less of a problem. It is a kind of primitive part-object. As I have mentioned, Gaddini and Winnicott (Gaddini, 1978) worked out this concept: ". . . we have termed *precursors* (of transitional objects) those objects that, while they have the capacity to console the child, have not been discovered or invented by the child. *They are provided by the mother, or are parts of the child's or the mother's body.*" Precursor objects include the tongue, the fingers, the pacifier, the bottle used as a pacifier, the child's wrist, the back of the child's hand, the back of the mother's hand, and the child's hair, ears, or nevi. Clearly, the precursor object, *especially* when it is part of the infant's body, is not an illusory, "self-created," controllable, developmentally alive, and enabling object. When it does not give way to a true transitional object, then, as Gaddini has demonstrated (1978), the danger of early psychosomatic illness is heightened. I might add that other possibilities are increased body narcissism, hypochondriasis, and fetishism.

However, the concept of the person regarding himself or his body as a transitional object has been emerging in the literature. In an interesting series of case reports titled "The Self as a Transitional Object," Natterson (1976) mentions several male homosexual patients who regarded their bodies as dolls. John Kafka (1969), in a paper titled "The Body as Transitional Object: A Psychoanalytic Study of a Self-Mutilating Patient," wrote: ". . . I described a rather ill young woman who had been hospitalized for two years. Her symptoms consisted primarily of cutting herself and interfering with wound healing." Kafka conceptualized the patient's treatment of her skin as an inanimate object that she tried to animate with the warm feeling of the blood on her skin. Interestingly, she used worms soaked in ink to make a kind of "found art," creating, in another manner, an object transitional "between living and dead matter." Kafka felt that he and the patient were in an alive, developmentally oriented treatment, and clearly took the transitional object facilitation of further development into account by considering the sadomasochistic investment of both the body surface and transitional space. As Kafka put it, "In analysis, the ebb and flow of the sadomasochistic transference and countertransference may be conceptualized as a factor contributing to the reformation of a more integrated, more bodily ego syntonic membrane and thus contributes to the eventual elimination of the symptom."

If one conceptualizes an object relations field (rather than a conflict structural one), there are other examples of how nonconcrete *aspects* of the self can be endowed with transitional object-derived qualities. This has been written about particularly in the area of transitional phenomena. Volkan (1973) has described a patient who used what he termed "transitional fantasies" to maintain an omnipotent view of the world. Actually, in 1962, Joseph Solomon wrote an article, "The Fixed Idea as an Internalized Transitional Object," showing that patients "cling" to obsessional and delusional ideas as if they were transitional objects. In the introduction to *Playing and Reality* (1971), Winnicott acknowledged his puzzlement about the idea of an "internalized version" of his pet subject. Winnicott wrote, "I am not sure how far I am in agreement with Dr. Solomon, but the important thing is that with a theory of transitional phenomena at hand many old problems can be looked at afresh." While many (e.g., Brody, 1980) object to these extensions of the transitional object concept, when looked at in the broader sense of Rose's *transitional process*, I feel these extensions can be especially useful both clinically and technically. For example, a dream may be treated as a transitional phenomenon. Earlier (Grolnick, 1978) I described a patient who was fetishistically involved in his girlfriends' pinky fingers. In his analysis he utilized a part of his self (a plethora of dreams) not as a resistance, but as transitional phenomena with which, through the dream retelling and analysis, he controlled and equilibrated the distance between us. When these dreams, which preoccupied the early part of the analysis, were interpreted in the traditional manner as resistance, the "resistance" only intensified. Understanding developmental significance of transitional phenomena aids the analyst in his interpretive work, as well as his therapeutic stance.

It becomes evident that when the self or an object can be invested with transitional object qualities, the concept of the transitional object inevitably broadens. However, many workers in the field are beginning to realize that it *is* a broad concept. Rose (1978, 1980) has articulated this most explicitly and unapologetically. It involves a *process* view of the mind, a true appreciation of paradox (not only conflict), a realization that the duality of "inner" and "outer" is only conceptual, and that the transitional fields that are set up both intrapsychically and extrapsychically (within the body, the human, and nonhuman environments) are continuously in flux. They must be taken into account by both the psychoanalytic practitioner as well as by the psycho-analytic theory-builder.

In sum, I am describing one important way of looking at the intrapsychic processes. There are others, but this vantage point seems to have a particular usefulness, especially for therapists who are treating patients who have suffered from the effects of developmental difficulties.

Thus, the transitional object concept can be looked at from a number of points of view, similar to the concept of the various metapsychological points of view. The descriptive, metapsychological, developmental, object relations, symbolic, and process frames all seem helpful and necessary to grasp a complex phenomenon that must be teased out from the multi-dimensional flux of day-to-day experiencing and developing. What we can do to retain conceptual clarity is to attempt to identify which frame is being utilized at any given time.

A SAMPLING OF EARLY REPORTS IN THE NONPSYCHOANALYTIC LITERATURE ON THE ROLE OF THE INANIMATE WORLD IN THE ESTABLISHMENT OF THE SENSE OF SELF AND OTHER

Philosophers, and the psychologists they evolved into during the late 19th century, were frequently deeply involved in understanding how the infant develops a sense of self; from early on they were aware of the distinction between the subjective self (or sense of self) and the so-called "objective self." It is interesting to note that in the psychoanalytic literature, probably because of its original objectivist and determinist leanings, the principal emphasis was on the development of a sense of the *object* and the *objective*, "realistic" world. Though "psychological reality" was considered the basic domain of psychoanalysis, it was the object rather than the self-representation, or the self, that preoccupied psychoanalysis for so many years. It is only now, in the past decade or two, that interest in the self-representation and the sense of self has burgeoned.

A perusal of some of the pre- or nonpsychoanalytic literature on this subject is of special interest. James Sully was an early theologian turned philosopher who became one of the first child psychologists. His *Studies of Childhood* (1896) achieved contemporary fame, was cited several times by Freud. Sully was aware of how the child's interaction with the environment aided the development of a sense of self and other. In a number of ways Sully anticipated the work of Winnicott, Mahler, Spitz, and Piaget. For example, Sully wrote about the child's first encounter with the environment:

In this first clash of his will with another's he knows more than the brute's sensual fury. He suffers consciously, he realizes himself in his antagonism to a world outside him. It is probable, that even a physical check bringing pain, as when the child runs his head against a wall, may develop his consciousness of self in its antagonism to a non-self. This consciousness reaches a higher phase when the opposing force is distinctly apprehended as another will. (1896, p. 235)

Sully (1881) described the importance of the child's treasured objects, how they represent and foster healthy illusion. Then he tried to show the developmental line of the treasured object and the imaginary companion, a relationship that has been noted by Greenacre (1969), Nagera (1981), and Bach (1971). For Sully the "invention of fictitious persons fills a large space in child-life." He spoke of a "warm grasp of living reality in this solitary play, where fictitious companions perfectly obedient to the little player's will take the place of less controllable tangible ones."

Sully stressed the powers of the imagination (translated without too much difficulty into the concept of the transitional process). He wrote of the "realizing power of the imagination" and of language. The real world becomes more real by virtue of its animation by the imagination and is differentiated, as has been mentioned, by the child's interaction and impact with that real world. Sully reported and elaborated on Preyer's (1882) description of the use of the mirror in assisting the child to develop a sense of self. Of course, this early work has now become increasingly sophisticated in the more abstract concept of mirroring as elaborated by Kohut (1971) and Winnicott (1971). Sully went further when he described the "imaginative vivication" of the doll which can become a "permanent companion and pet": "Clusters of happy associations gather about it, investing it with a lasting vitality and character." Sully repeatedly stressed the importance of imagination, play, and story telling, of permanent material and imaginary companions, in the development of the child's sense of self and his capacity for creative living. Similar to Winnicott, he also repeatedly stressed how important it is for the mother and the family to respect these phenomena and not interfere with their normal unfolding.

Sully also stressed the naming of the object to help provide it a sense of reality. The very imagination itself "derives support from sense [sensation]" and "leads to a habit of projecting fancies and giving them an external and local habitation. In this way the idea receives a certain solidity and fixity through its embodiment in the real physical world." Sully recognized the interplay between the real and the fanciful world. The world of actuality is validated by imaginative animation, and the intrapsychic world is given a sense of reality and identity by its projection into the world of actuality. In the late 19th century, Sully saw, as did Winnicott and Spitz later, that crystallizations of this process, transitional objects and phenomena, are both organizers and indicators of the process.

In the classic *Mind, Self and Society* (1934), the social psychologist George Mead (in the footsteps of William James) explored the formation of the sense of self and the capacity to objectify the self. Interaction with the family and society, and the role of play as an important mediator were stressed. Mead was primarily interested in the cognitive and social determinants of the sense of self, and understated the importance of and the specificity of the mother-child dyadic interaction. He wrote: "Anything— any object or set of objects, whether animate or inanimate, human or animal, or merely physical—toward which he (the human organism) acts, or to which he responds, socially is an element in what for him is the generalized other; by taking the attitudes of which toward himself he becomes conscious of himself as an object or individual, and thus develops a self or personality."

Charles H. Cooley, especially in his *Human Nature and the Social Order* (1902), came closer to a modern psychoanalytic, developmental perspective. A typical Cooley observation is "as a rule the child associates 'I' and 'me' at first only with those ideas regarding which his appropriative feeling is aroused and defined by opposition." Characteristically, Cooley wrote as if he did observe children carefully, rather than "human organisms," and was first concerned with "feelings," tinged both positively and negatively, and with the creative imagination. His writings were closer than Mead's to Sully's and Winnicott's.

This sampling of the nonpsychoanalytic literature should show that the ingredients for seeing the importance of the inanimate world in shaping the sense of self and object and their lasting nature have been available for some time. It is clear that a certain bias existed that both Sully, at the turn of the century, and Winnicott, over a half century later, had to combat. The idea that an inanimate, nonhuman object could be an important part of the child's development was resisted by parents as well as professionals. When Winnicott wrote that, at times, the transitional object could be *more* important than the mother (he meant when there was a conflict with the mother), the idea was resisted by psychoanalysts. Winnicott's first task was to translate Wulff's (1946) "fetish object," a pathological entity, into his own healthy, developmentally progressive concept of the transitional object. My sense of it is that a tragic sense and capacity for empathy (Schafer, 1976) in certain observers allow them to recognize the imposing task that development places upon both the infant and the mother in this complex society, especially since the advent of separate sleeping arrangements between children and parents (Ariès, 1960). One senses certain moralistic overtones in objections to the "helpers" described by Winnicott, helpers who were translated into "crutches" or, more contemporaneously, fetish objects.

PHENOMENON OR EPIPHENOMENON

Thus it should be acknowledged that the psychoanalytic literature does not reflect a universal agreement with my major thesis that the transitional object plays a substantial role in furthering the development and internalizing process in the average Western-nurtured and -raised baby. For those who feel skeptical or who wish to be aware of dissenting opinions, the alternate view should be cited. Sperling (1963) maintained that the "morbid attachment to an inanimate object is an indication of an arrest in the development of object relationship and fixation to part-object relationship. It is the quality of the relation with his mother that determines how a child treats his objects, animate or inanimate, and whether he needs to cling to an inanimate object, whatever name be given to it." (Greenacre [1970] openly disagreed with this view, maintaining that the transitional object was normal and that it furthered development.) Dickes (1978) at first agreed with Sperling but later felt that nonaddictive attachments, if they appeared within the years of the separation-individuation process, were not pathological. Bowlby felt that transitional objects were not decisive in the developmental process. In a personal communication, Selma Fraiberg wrote in 1973, ". . . I am one who does not attribute great significance to the transitional object in the scheme of early human object relationships. In my own clinical experience it is not an indicator of the quality of the libidinal tie to the mother. In general, I find that the empirical work in this area is very weak."

Fraiberg, however, was quite interested in the fact that in cultures in which the babies sleep with other family members, transitional objects, as we know them, are virtually absent. This is in agreement with anthropological observers and with studies carried out by Gaddini (1978) on lower-class modern Roman families. One might easily conclude from these observations that "normal" development precludes the overt transitonal *object*. One could easily account for the presence of imaginative thinking, creativity, and art in these cultures on the basis of the *transitional process*, which involves the very nature of interrelationship within the mind of intrapsychic and outer reality. However, these anthropological observations warrant another point of view (see also Hong, 1978). Since the overt transitional object is a manifestation of Western, separate beds and separate bedroom living conditions, the transitional object becomes a *necessary* cultural presence to substitute for the presence of the other during the long, regressive, object and self-image loss involved in sleeping alone (Grolnick, 1978; Grolnick & Lengyel, 1978). The authentic "capacity to be alone" (Winnicott, 1958), with its implied internalized and abstracted object, may then be *culture specific*. In a society where babies do *not* sleep alone, a highly developed capacity to be alone would be maladaptive. Of course, this raises the important implication that certain qualities of so-called self and object constancy might be culture bound. More specifically, the "unnatural" sleeping arrangements that have prevailed in the West only during the past few hundred years (Ariès, 1960) may have necessitated an adaptive increased internalizing of a comforting and completing modality. This complex psychological, social, and anthropological area requires considerable thought and study.

Winnicott described an important developmental line running throughout life. He provided us with a new conceptual tool to understand and study the genesis of a firm yet flexible sense of self and object that has the capacity to be self-evoked and to tolerate relative prolonged absence of reinforcement from the outside. [Until Winnicott's original (1951) description of the transitional object concept and his ultimate demonstration of its role in separation, boundary and symbol formation, and the consolidating of self and object representations (1971) the principal function of the "fetish object" (as Wulff [1946] designated it) was to shore up *defects* in the self or the object world.] When constitutional or traumatic rearing experiences resulted in defects in intrapsychic structure, transitional, fetishistic, or prosthetic (Bak, 1974) objects were used by the adult in an adaptive manner. The objects were either directly libidinized (true fetishes in the adult) or indirectly libidinized as fetishistic objects. An extreme example of the latter would be a young man I saw at one time, who presented with rather substantial defects in self and object constancy. When he began treatment, he was unable to put himself to sleep without sucking his thumb and fingering the satin binding of his blanket. Another example is a borderline young man in his 20s who would inadvertently find himself rubbing the lower edge of his pants cuff while he made rhythmic movements of his tongue against his cheek. His "habit" extended back as far as he could remember. The literature now abounds with descriptions of how patients use amulets, rabbits' feet, cigarettes (and the whole act of smoking), pets, tunes, and the like, as fetishistic (Greenacre, 1970) supports to patch faults in the body ego.

That these primitive, external ego defect supports can begin to blend into the symbolic, or at least the primitive symbolic, should be clear to us in the following clinical example, which was reported more extensively in a previous publication (Grolnick, 1978). A man (mentioned above; see p. 117) in his 30s, when he associated to the color pink which had appeared in a dream, recalled that he had had a pink blanket as a young child. He then reported for the first time in his analysis that he loved to feel the pinkies of his dates; in fact, he utilized the feel of the young woman's pinky as a criterion with which to judge her desirability. One could justifiably point to the fetishistic elements here, but it does seem that a certain transformation, small as it may be, had occurred. Elements of personal taste, even aesthetic taste, primitive as they were, seemed to enter into the content of his object representations.

Victor Rosen (1964) demonstrated, in a difficult patient with whom he worked, how the patient's original transitional object, over which he had struggled with his mother, became an organizing factor in his character style and the development of his aesthetic sense, both of which became aspects of his bohemian life-style. Here the transitional object and its qualities contributed importantly to sustaining aspects of the self-representation.

The following is an example of a patient for whom a transitional object later appeared in the qualities of her *object* representations. It served as a relatively fixated substitute object (Beres, 1965) but also was able to assume developmental progressive functions for the patient. A young married woman had been given a wire haired terrier puppy as a pet when she was not quite 2 years of age, apparently on the occasion of the birth of a younger sibling. The dog slept on her pillow for the next 16 years, until it died. The dog developed transitional object qualities for her; certainly the gift served as a compensation for a loss. In addition, her mother was characterized as nonempathetic and intrusive; fetishistic elements were probable from the start but the pet seemed to provide a kind of developmental stabilizer. However, the transitional object side becomes interesting in her young adult years. The patient had married a man of the same religion and race (Caucasian) who was similar in character to her mother. He was domineering, even tyrannical, insisting that the patient turn herself into a bleached blonde, mini-skirted doll for him, while at the same time demanding that she launder, starch, and iron his shirts, even though she had a full-time job. The marriage became stormy, but she felt utterly unable to leave him, even though she no longer loved him. She acquired a most unlikely lover (considering her cultural and religious background and past history)—a tall, husky, athletic black man who continuously kept her guessing as to whether or not he was faithful to her. She loved his wiry hair, and, even though she deplored his "promiscuous tendencies," she was clearly intrigued by them. That her dog's name had been "Skippy" lent further credence to the appearance of the qualities of the transitional object pet in the qualities of her object representation and choice, although this was on a totally unconscious basis. In a late adolescent surge of development in part supported by my presence, she was able to use the relationship with her lover as a bridge toward her own independence. At the same time, the influence of the relationship with her lover enabled her to resist the narcissistic enthrall-ment that had turned her into the bleached blonde doll. She began to dress in a more individualistic manner and felt that she was more of a person. Eventually she obtained a divorce from her husband and seemed to be open to a new object choice after she broke off the relationship with the lover.

Clearly, this patient demonstrated the transformation of what may very well have been a transitional phenomenon metamorphosing into a true fetishism (a syndrome that has been only rarely reported in females in the psychoanalytic literature). However, the spectrum between the function of a healthy, developmentally progressive transitional object and a pathological, fixed, fetishistic or true fetish object must be carefully delineated. What is important is that in the absence of "optimal" good-enough mothering, the transitional object or phenomenon can assume more adaptive functioning, as in the instance of the patient with the little dog. The perceptive and apperceptive mother (Winnicott, 1971) can be equilibrated by the child's transitional experience. Identifications with the object in both self and object representations are likely to occur. The self qualities can become character traits and the object representational qualities can become factors that influence the choice of the qualities of the object. Fetishistic and transitional object derivatives can easily interweave.

A short psychobiographical sketch shows rather graphically how a transitional phenomenon ultimately evolved into qualities of *both* self and object representations. George Sand, in her *Histoire de Ma Vie* (1854), provides us with a treasure of information. She relates how she had been told that as an infant she was accustomed to put herself to sleep by strumming on the strings of a little lyre that was affixed to her crib. When she was an older, prepubescent child, she had a rather deep investment in an imaginary companion she could hear but not see, a friend she called "Echo." Then, as an adolescent, she created an imaginary god called "Corambé." Her own words best describe him:

He was pure and charitable as Jesus, radiant and beautiful as Gabriel; but it was needful to add a little of the grace of the nymphs and the poetry of Orpheus. Accordingly he had a less austere form than the God of the Christian, and a more spiritual feeling than those of Homer. And then I was obliged to complete him by investing him on occasion with the guise of a woman, for that which I had up to this time loved the best, and understood the best, was a woman, my mother. And so it was often under the semblance of a woman that he appeared to me. In short, he had no sex, and assumed all sorts of aspects. . . . Corambé should have all the attributes of physical and moral beauty, the gift of eloquence, the omnipotent charm of the arts—above all, the magic of musical improvisation. I wished to love him as a friend, as a sister, while revering him as a God. I would not be afraid of him, and to this end I desired that he should have some of our errors and weaknesses. I sought that one which could be reconciled with his perfection, and I found it in an excess of indulgence and kindness. (in Sully, 1896)

George Sand composed a thousand sacred songs for Corambé, and she sang them for him at a secret shrine she established in a little wood in her grandmother's garden. One day an actual playmate came to look for her and discovered her in her secret grove. Sand wrote later on: "From the instant other feet than mine had trodden his sanctuary, Corambé ceased to dwell in it. . . . it seemed to me as if my ceremonies and my sacrifices were from this time only childishness, that I had not in truth been in earnest. I destroyed the temple with as much care as I had built it."

Needless to say, the adult version of the story concludes with George Sand (née Aurore Dupin) cross-naming and cross-dressing (a longstanding, rather stable quality in George Sand's self representation) and in her choice of her ultimate love object, Chopin, the quintessence of the esthetic, romantic musician.

FROM COLORING SELF AND OBJECT REPRESENTATIONS TO FACILITATING THEIR CONSOLIDATION AND STABILITY

I hope I have made plausible some of the ways an original relationship with a transitional object or phenomenon can become internalized into both self and object representational qualities. Now it is necessary to show how these qualities as well as transitional object functions, along with a myriad of others, can be *stabilized* to the point where there is a sense of continuity in time and a capacity to evoke the self or object representations without too much help from the external world.

A consideration of the "gap" between Mahler's object constancy and Piaget's object permanence is pertinent here. The differences between Piaget's sixth stage of inanimate object permanence and Mahler's fourth phase, "on the way to emotional object and self constancy," have been rather clearly delineated, especially since the publication of an article by Fraiberg (1969). Generally, Piaget's *object constancy* is dated approximately from the beginning to the middle of the second year of life, while the latter is timed usually at the end of the third year. It is just this "gap" that becomes important in considering the role of transitional object and phenomena in the establishment of self and object constancy.

As is suggested by this year-and-a-half "lag," the toddler is faced with a greater developmental task when he attains the capacity to evoke spontaneously an image of the loved (and hated) other than when he accomplishes the same with a relatively unfamiliar inanimate object. Spitz (1965a), Metcalf and Spitz (1978), Fraiberg (1969), Mahler *et al.* (1975), and others have cited the difficulties in the laying down of organized, integrated, and more or less "permanent" or "constant" representations of the mother, a person with her own needs, quirks, and inconstancies. Under the most optimal of circumstances, the mother and her caretaking functions are subject to greater or lesser fluctuations, leading to outer conflict with her. This "outer" conflict, due to spiraling processes of accommodation, assimilation, and internalization, gradually creates inner conflict, what could be considered at the early toddler stage as object relations conflict (Modell, 1981). *It is at this critical point that the more controllable transitional object enters to aid the toddler in the process of establishing object and (as we shall see) self constancy.* As Winnicott repeatedly writes, the child, in a progressive regression, with the use of the transitional object, is able to create the *illusion* of the presence of the mother, to fill in the gaps of the external *and* the internal presence of the mother. If the animated transitional object is the first true possession of the child, it is owned in a manner that the mother can never be owned (unless psychosis intervenes). As Greenacre (1969, 1970) has written, by utilizing the transitional object, the child can adjust and titrate the discrepancies in the relationship with the mother. The transitional object then serves as an *adjunct* of the developmental process. Kestenberg and Weinstein (1978) have conceptualized transitional objects as having their origins as "adjuncts to drive satisfaction during nursing. . . . However, as restorers and maintainers of body integrity, they may gain independence from drive aims and drive objects and are used by some children who do not engage in nutritive sucking. Sometimes their function becomes more clearly related to allaying anxiety and to the defensive working through of a loss."

The literature is filled with metaphors describing the helpful, ancillary role transitional objects and phenomena play in development: adjuncts, way stations, comfort stations, comforters, guardians. This all makes sense if one accepts the premise that this piece of the nonhuman world is truly an *influencer* of the course of development; a psychic organizer as designated by Metcalf and Spitz (1978).

However, the psychoanalytic literature now reflects something more: the belief that Winnicott's developmental line is operative in *structural development*. Perhaps the most definitive statements on the role of the Winnicott line in the development of self and object constancy have been made by Metcalf and Spitz (Metcalf, 1975; Metcalf & Spitz, 1978). Therefore, I shall quote liberally from their work.

In a paper titled "The Transitional Object: Critical Developmental Period and Organizer of the Psyche," Metcalf and Spitz (1978, pp. 101-105) wrote:

We maintain that on the way from recognition memory, active from about six months, to the predominance of evocative memory, achieved toward the end of the second year of life, the establishment of "transitional phenomena" and the transitional object represents a stage of its own.

When the need for the mother arises, the transitional object serves as a quasi-evocative stimulus. With the help of the completion gradient, this stimulus evokes the total affect-gestalt, "mother," with the unique meaning of security. It is out of this impact of developmental process on ongoing maturation, that we observe the epigenesis of evocative memory. It is this process and this structuring that enables the child to endow one inanimate thing from his surround (a blanket, a soft toy, etc.) with an essential attribute of the libidinal object: *security*. A new structure arises, purely psychological and by nature devoid of all actual need-gratification: the transitional object. As a result of a psychological operation, the transitional object is transformed into a quasi-need.

The going to sleep transition represents a danger to the ego and demands the intervention of mother (a glass of water, a tuck-in, singing, presence), and when that is not available, the transitional object is called upon to evoke her memory and replace her.

With the emergence of what Metcalf and Spitz considered the fourth psychic organizer, a new "modus operandi" develops:

The emerging capacity to bring about interchanges between cognitive mental structures in the form of thought processes and interactions between these mental structures and objects or individuals in the surround. . . . In exchanges with the libidinal object (the real, living mother), conflict arises incessantly and actually forms the fabric, the tissue of object relations. . . . The transitional object will carry even over into the often tempestuous vicissitudes of object relations the climate of that golden age in which the unambivalent signal, "need-gratification," represented the relief of need-tension. We therefore feel justified in postulating the establishment of the transitional object as a *specific stage in the progress from recognition of a sign gestalt to evocation through a volitional act of mentation.* It is a stage in the natural history of object development.

Metcalf and Spitz proceed to show that after the stage of the formation of libidinal object constancy (they tend to date it somewhat earlier than Mahler's "on the way to object constancy"), the transitional object remains as a "prosthesis for evocative memory," aiding the individual in the lifelong process of reorganizing and consolidating object (and I would add self) representations with the overall establishment of a state of reasonably stable object (and self) constancy.

In her pivotal paper on the internalization of comforting and signal anxiety functions, Tolpin (1971) was rather explicit concerning the role of the transitional object in the establishment of object constancy:

. . . transmuting internalization of regulatory functions mediated by the "good enough" mother of the separation phase (the narcissistically perceived maternal image and its functions) and the "assistant" (the transitional object) gradually leads to psychic structure which enables the child to satisfy some of his own needs; the freedom from exclusive dependence on the need-satisfying object conferred by this structure is indispensable for the achievement of object-constancy. (p. 332)

Of course, throughout the paper Tolpin alluded to the importance of the transitional object in the ultimate cohesiveness and continuity of the self. Also, anticipating Metcalf and Spitz (at least in the literature, as far as I could ascertain), Tolpin wrote, "Since the blanket is such a visible indicator of the structure-mediating, growth-facilitating mother–infant bond appropriate to the separation phase, I have suggested that the transitional object (and phenomenon) be included among the other visible signs which Spitz described as psychic organizers" (p. 348).

In an important article on development of the sense of self, Lichtenberg (1975) points to the hierarchical stages involved. He includes Tolpin's (1971) suggestions about transmuting internalizations of interactions with the transitional object as an intermediate stage in the development of an internalized sense of self. Then, in discussing depersonalization, Stolorow and Lachmann (1980) described a patient's use of a tape recorder during his sessions as a "transitional self object which signaled a partial internalization of the analyst's mirror function [and] enabled him to regain a sense of conviction about his own substantiality and helped him to restore self-cohesion in the wake of narcissistic injuries." Greenacre (1970) wrote of the transitional object's capacity to "carry multiple reassuring illusions, and in this way consolidate the stable perceptive appreciation of many new objects both animate and inanimate." Bach (1980), in a paper considering self and object constancy, wrote, "In the early phases of treatment [of patients with developmental difficulties] the analyst will be required as a kind of transitional object to bridge the gap not only between the self and the other, but also between the subjective and objective worlds." He described "the gap between the subjective self and the objective self and the importance, especially in therapy, of allowing transitional experiences along the way to the development of self-constancy." Then, "I am in agreement with Winnicott that from a certain perspective what is required is the acceptance of paradox. And it appears that this acceptance can only take place in a context of basic trust, that is, the expectation that the facilitating environment and its feedback bear some trustworthy, invariant relationship to our phenomenal world, so that the construction of a reliable, continuous, and meaningful 'self' is possible." Throughout his paper, Bach interweaves the opportunities and challenges of Mahler's rapprochement subphase and Winnicott's transitional object as intermediate stages in the development of both self and object constancy.

SOME PERTINENT LITERATURE ON ADOLESCENCE

This sampling of the recent literature demonstrates an increasing acceptance among developmentally oriented psychoanalysts of the important role of transitional objects and phenomena in early development and in the further stabilization and consolidation of self and object representations. This point is reiterated in the psychoanalytic literature on adolescence. For the last two decades, adolescence has been thought of as featuring a recrudescence of separation-individuation conflicts.

Peter Blos, in his classic *On Adolescence* (1962), referred to the transitional object in two places and to Winnicott in three. While he did not stress the specific use of transitional objects and phenomena by the adolescent or (as models) by the therapist, Blos did write about the importance of the adolescent diary: "The diary stands between daydream and object world, between make-believe and reality, and its content and for change with the times; for material that was once kept as an anxiously guarded secret today is openly expressed."

Settlage (1972), in an article titled "Cultural Values and the Superego in Late Adolescence," showed how literal and imaginative play in the adolescent functions as an area that "offers both a needed relief from the otherwise unremitting strain of moderating between the demands of inner and outer reality, and an area for creative thought and problem solving." Settlage deemed adolescence a crucial period in which Winnicott's intermediate area aids in continuation of the developmental process, a successful negotiation of which, in turn, enables the adolescent to leave late adolescence with the "moral and ideological acquisitions" that are "assessed and shaped into the values which are to govern one's immediate future as an adult."

In a paper on developmental space, Bergman (1978) makes specific reference to Winnicott's potential space concept. She gives the example of how the child's clothes take on symbolic (I would say also transitional) meaning during the rapprochement phase. The struggles between the parent and the rapprochement (and older) child over clothing become important developmental events with the potential for the furtherance of the separation-individuation process and internalization of self and object representations. Bergman cites a specific instance of an adolescent boy who used his torn jeans in a developmentally adaptive manner.

In his paper titled "Transitional Phenomena in the Analysis of Early Adolescent Males," T. Wayne Downey (1978) showed in the most definitive manner (at this writing) the importance of the transitional object in the assessment and treatment of the adolescent and the establishment of a more reliable inner representational world. Downey put it this way: "In a general sense . . . the transitional object is a transference object, . . . carrying with it important aspects of mother which have not yet been completely internalized but which are in the process of internalization into a constant mental representation." In the course of his paper, Downey pointed out how the therapist can join the transitional world of the adolescent caught in separation-individuation anxiety by accepting and empathically understanding the transitional object attachments of his patient to "clothing, living space, artistic media, . . . a record, or a film. . . . The adolescent's need for experiences with pronounced transitional components seems as strong as the toddler's." It is difficult to disagree with Downey.

THE TRANSITIONAL PROCESS, TIME, AND SELF AND OBJECT CONSTANCY: A THEORETICAL SUGGESTION

In this chapter I have attempted to demonstrate in a variety of ways that transitional objects and phenomena are a vital part of the developmental separation-individuation process that leads to establishment of reasonable degrees of self and object constancy. The bulk of the relevant literature accepts Mahler's fourth subphase of separation-individuation as being a developmental, structural achievement, but, as Mahler et al. (1975) wrote, these structures "represent merely the beginning of the ongoing developmental process" (p. 118). More recently, the phrase "self constancy" has taken the place of what Mahler et al. called "the consolidation of individuality." In trying to differentiate Piagetian from Mahlerian object constancy, Burgner and Edgcumbe (1972) suggested using the term "the capacity for constant relationships" in place of "object constancy."

It seems to me that these refinements represent attempts to avoid the sense of fixity in the terms object (and self) *constancy* and reflect an intrinsic difficulty in this theoretical area. I think most of us would agree that a so-called mature adult does not carry an internal, *fixed* image of either an original or a secondary loved object. Internalization and structuralization never "terminate." Autonomy and individuation are always in a feedback system with dependence and the *need* to externalize and *realize* fantasy and imagination. A love affair, for example, consists of many internalized aspects of object love, but at the same time, the reality of the loved one's personality and bodily self is equally important. One could say the same about the "normal" narcissism. One's body is loved in direct terms at the same time the internalized sense of self and an internalized body image are in a complementary relationship with this more concrete need.

Thus, it can be claimed again that oscillating transitional process modes are present throughout life (Rose 1978, 1980; Kestenberg & Buelte, 1977). In this sense, within Western civilization, the transitional object is not only a facilitator of a so-called "higher" level of internalized self and object "constancy," but also is internalized at less "metabolized levels," having retained some of its *original* qualities, even though these are functioning at a new level. Another way of saying this is that Winnicott was describing some of the roots of our capacity, to form healthy illusion, and to tolerate and importantly, *appreciate* paradox, presence and absence, the concrete and the abstract. These capacities are linked, in part, with the development of the imagination (which requires both internal fantasy and external perception) and the capacity to suspend disbelief. We are also involved here with the capacity to form a transference (its "let's pretend" qualities) and with psychological mindedness itself. No doubt the sense of tragedy and irony (Schafer, 1976) is also involved.

In addition, the transitional object is linked with time as is the concept of object constancy. "Transitional objects serve the preservation of the old, within the newness of the present, into the future" (Kestenberg, 1971). Colorusso (1979), in a paper titled "The Development of Time Sense," wrote, ". . . the transitional object also provides the child with a vehicle for elaborating his experience of time, for we can conceive that the existing memories of already past experiences are externalized into this in-between space where they are compared and correlated with the current and more consciously perceived experiences with the mother and the emerging self. The infant plays, as it were, with past and present images of self, object and object relatedness, as they are on their way toward stable intrapsychic representation (Settlage, 1972, p. 76)." Colorusso elaborates: "Mother's presence represents *present*; her mental representation when apart becomes the *past*, and the anticipation of returning to her foreshadows the *future*. With the eventual withdrawal of the transitional object and the achievement of object-constancy, there is a repression of much of the equation *mother equals time.*"

I would now add to these cogent formulations that it is important for us to understand what kind of time experience we mean when we speak of "constancy." The quote by Swift, "There is nothing in this world constant but inconstancy," is consistent with modern relativistic conceptions of time (Rose, 1980). Loewald (1972), in his paper titled "The Experience of Time," referred to the opposite poles of time, "the experience of eternity where the flux of time is suspended" versus the "experience of fragmentation, where one's world is in bits and pieces none of which have any meaning." This continuum oscillates throughout life and can be subsumed under "subjective time," as compared to "objective" or clock time. There are exceptions. In his important contribution *Of Time, Passion and Knowledge*, Fraser (1975) writes, "There are no existential paradoxes of time in the lives of horses, dogs, savages, children, and saints: life and death, for example, form an unquestioned unity."

But most of us live our lives in an interplay between the continuum of subjective time and objective time; we must "live with" the ominous maxim, "here today, gone tomorrow." I would suggest that a "good-enough" internal environment of self and object representations includes the capacity to progress and regress. The *constancy of inconstancy* and in turn the *inconstancy of constancy*, interspersed with reasonable amounts of constancy, are close to the experience the mature adult must undergo and adapt to during a long, complex life cycle. It is relevant that Louise Kaplan (1972) has formulated "a concept of object-constancy, as well as memory, structured according to levels of organization, with object constancy having to be re-acquired in more complex and integrated ways at successive phases of development."

The various child, adolescent, and adult developmental phases provide opportunities for new adaptive levels of self and object constancy. However, it is the transitional process and its vicissitudes that provide the possibility for moment-to-moment, minute-to-minute, day-to-day, year-to-year, and phase-to-phase adaptation to the dialogue between fixity and flux to which we are all subjected, in our relations both with the world and others, and with ourselves. At times, for most of us, actual transitional objects and transitional phenomena (sometimes bordering on the fetishistic end of the spectrum) are necessary to adjust the balance.

REFERENCES

Ariès, P. (1960). *Centuries of childhood: A social history of family life.* New York: Vintage Books, 1962.

Bach, S. (1971). Notes on some imaginary companions. *The Psychoanalytic Study of the Child*, *26*, 159-171.

Bach, S. (1980). Self-love and object love: Some problems of self and object constancy, differentiation and integration. In R. Lax, S. Bach, & J. A. Burland (Eds.), *Rapprochement: The critical subphase of separation-individuation*. New York: Jason Aronson.

Bak, R. C. (1974). Distortions of the concept of fetishism. *The Psychoanalytic Study of the Child*, *29*, 191-214.

Beres, D. (1965). Symbol and object. *Bulletin of the Menninger Clinic*, *29*, 2-23.

Bergman, A. (1978). From mother to the world outside: The use of space during the separation-individuation phase. In S. Grolnick & L. Barkin (Eds.), in collaboration with W. Muensterberger, *Between reality and fantasy: Transitional objects and phenomena*. New York: Jason Aronson.

Blos, P. (1962). *On adolescence: A psychoanalytic interpretation*. New York: The Free Press of Glencoe.

Brody, S. (1980). Transitional objects: Idealization of a phenomenon. *Psychoanalytic Quarterly*, *49*, 561-605.

Burgner, M., & Edgcumbe, R. (1972). Some problems in the conceptualization of early object relationships: Part II. The concept of object constancy. *The Psychoanalytic Study of the Child*, *27*, 315-333.

Colorusso, C. (1979). The development of time sense—from birth to object constancy. *International Journal of Psycho-Analysis*, *60*, 243-251.

Cooley, C. (1902). *Human nature and the social order*. New York: Charles Scribner & Sons.

Dickes, R. (1978). Parents, transitional objects and childhood fetishes. In S. Grolnick & L. Barkin (Eds.), in collaboration with W. Muensterberger, *Between reality and fantasy: Transitional objects and phenomena*. New York: Jason Aronson.

Downey, T. W. (1978). Transitional phenomena in the analysis of early adolescent males. *The Psychoanalytic Study of the Child*, *33*, 19-46.

Fleming, J. (1975). Some observations on object constancy in the psychoanalysis of adults. *Journal of the American Psychoanalytic Association*, *23*, 743-759.

Fraiberg, S. (1969). Libidinal object constancy and mental representation. *The Psychoanalytic Study of the Child*, *24*, 9-47.

Fraser, J. T. (1975). *Of time, passion and knowledge: Reflections on the strategy of existence*. New York: George Braziller.

Freud, A. (1965). *Normality and pathology in childhood*. New York: International Universities Press.

Gaddini, R. (1978). Transitional object origins and the psychosomatic symptom. In S. Grolnick & L. Barkin (Eds.), in collaboration with W. Muensterberger, *Between reality and fantasy: Transitional objects and phenomena*. New York: Jason Aronson.

Green, A. (1975). The analyst, symbolization and absence in the analytic setting (on changes in analytic practice and analytic experience). *International Journal of Psycho-Analysis*, *56*, 1-22.

Green, A. (1978). Potential space in psychoanalysis: The object in the setting. In S. Grolnick & L. Barkin (Eds.), in collaboration with W. Muensterberger, *Between reality and fantasy: Transitional objects and phenomena*. New York: Jason Aronson.

Greenacre, P. (1969). The fetish and the transitional object. *The Psychoanalytic Study of the Child*, *24*, 144-164.

Greenacre, P. (1970). The transitional object and the fetish with special reference to the role of illusion. *International Journal of Psycho-Analysis*, *51*, 442-456.

Greenbaum, T. (1978). The "analyzing instrument" and the "transitional object." In S. Grolnick & L. Barkin (Eds.), in collaboration with W. Muensterberger, *Between reality and fantasy: Transitional objects and phenomena*. New York: Jason Aronson.

Greenson, R. (1978). On transitional objects and transference. In S. Grolnick & L. Barkin (Eds.), in collaboration with W. Muensterberger, *Between reality and fantasy: Transitional objects and phenomena*. New York: Jason Aronson.

Grolnick, S. (1978). Dreams and dreaming as transitional phenomena. In S. Grolnick & L. Barkin (Eds.), in collaboration with W. Muensterberger, *Between reality and fantasy: Transitional objects and phenomena*. New York: Jason Aronson.

Grolnick, S., & Lengyel, A. (1978). Etruscan burial symbols and the transitional process. In S. Grolnick & L. Barkin (Eds.), in collaboration with W. Muensterberger, *Between reality and fantasy: Transitional objects and phenomena*. New York: Jason Aronson.

Hartmann, H. (1952). The mutual influences in the development of ego and id. In *Essays on ego psychology: Selected problems in psychoanalytic theory*. New York: International Universities Press, 1964.

Hegel, G. (1831). *The philosophy of history*. New York: Wiley, 1944.

Hong, K. (1978). The transitional phenomena: A theoretical integration. *The Psychoanalytic Study of the Child, 33*, 47-79.

Horton, P. (1976). The psychological treatment of personality disorder. *American Journal of Psychiatry, 133*, 262-65.

Kafka, J. (1969). The body as a transitional object: A psychoanalytic study of a self-mutilating patient. *British Journal of Medical Psychology, 42*, 207-212.

Kaplan, L. (1972). Object constancy in the light of Piaget's vertical *décalage. Bulletin of the Menninger Clinic, 36*, 372-384.

Kestenberg, J. (1971). From organ-object imagery to self- and object-representations. In J. B. McDevitt & C. F. Settlage (eds.), *Separation-individuation: Essays in honor of Margaret Mahler*. New York: International Universities Press.

Kestenberg, J., & Buelte, A. (1977). Prevention, infant therapy, and the treatment of adults. *International Journal of Psychoanalytic Psychotherapy, 6*, 339-396.

Kestenberg, J., & Weinstein, J. (1978). Transitional objects and body-image formation. In S. Grolnick & L. Barkin (Eds.), in collaboration with W. Muensterberger, *Between reality and fantasy: Transitional objects and phenomena*. New York: Jason Aronson.

Kohut, H., (1971). *The analysis of self: A systematic approach to the psychoanalytic treatment of narcissistic personality disorders*. New York: International Universities Press.

Lichtenberg, J. (1975). The development of the sense of self. *Journal of the American Psychoanalytic Association, 23*, 453-484.

Loewald, H. (1972). The experience of time. *The Psychoanalytic Study of the Child, 27*, 401-410.

Mahler, M., Pine, F., & Bergman, A. (1975). *The psychological birth of the human infant: Symbiosis and individuation*. New York: Basic Books.

Mead, G. (1934). *Mind, self and society*. Chicago: University of Chicago Press.

Metcalf, D. (1975, April 19). *René Spitz and the biophysiology of early infant development: The inception of dreaming*. Paper presented to North Pacific District Branch, Western Canada District Branch APA, Vancouver, British Columbia.

Metcalf, D., & Spitz, R. (1978). The transitional object: Critical developmental period and organizer of the psyche. In S. Grolnick & L. Barkin (Eds.), in collaboration with W. Muensterberger, *Between reality and fantasy: Transitional objects and phenomena*. New York: Jason Aronson.

Modell, A. (1981). *Self psychology as a psychology of conflict: Comments on the psychoanalysis of the narcissistic personality*. Paper presented at the winter meetings, American Psychoanalytic Association, New York.

Nagera, H. (1981). *The developmental approach to childhood psychopathology*. New York: Jason Aronson.

Natterson, J. (1976). The self as a transitional object: Its relationship to narcissism and homosexuality. *International Journal of Psychoanalytic Psychotherapy, 5*, 131-142.

Preyer, W. (1882). *Die Seele des Kindes*. New York: Appleton.

Rose, G. (1978). The creativity of everyday life. In S. Grolnick & L. Barkin (Eds.), in collaboration with W. Muensterberger, *Between reality and fantasy: Transitional objects and phenomena*. New York: Jason Aronson.

Rose, G. (1980). *The power of form: A psychoanalytic approach to aesthetic form*. New York: International Universities Press.

Rosen, V. (1964). Some effects of artistic talent on character style. *Psychoanalytic Quarterly*, *33*, 1-24.

Sand, G. (1854). Histoire de ma vie (M. E. Joël, trans.). In J. Sully, *Studies of childhood*. New York: Longmans, Green, 1896.

Schafer, R. (1976). *A new language for psychoanalysis*. New Haven: Yale University Press.

Searles, H. (1976). Transitional phenomena and therapeutic symbiosis. *International Journal of Psychoanalytic Psychotherapy*, *5*, 145-204.

Settlage, C. (1972). Cultural values and the superego in late adolescence. *The Psychoanalytic Study of the Child*, *27*, 74-92.

Solomon, J. C. (1962). The fixed idea as an internalized transitional object. *American Journal of Psychotherapy*, *16*, 632-644.

Solomon, J. C. (1978). Transitional phenomena and obsessive-compulsive states. In S. Grolnick & L. Barkin (Eds.), in collaboration with W. Muensterberger, *Between reality and fantasy: Transitional objects and phenomena*. New York: Jason Aronson.

Sperling, M. (1963). Fetishism in children. *Psychoanalytic Quarterly*, *32*, 374-392.

Spitz, R. (1965a). The evolution of dialogue. In *Drives, affects, behavior* (Vol. 2). New York: International Universities Press.

Spitz, R. (1965b). *The first year of life*. New York: International Universities Press.

Spitz, R. (1972). Bridges: On anticipation, duration, and meaning. *Journal of the American Psychoanalytic Association*, *20*, 721-735.

Stolorow, R., & Lachmann, F. (1980). *The psychoanalysis of developmental arrests: Theory and treatment*. New York: International Universities Press.

Sully, J. (1881). *Illusion: A psychological study*. New York: Appleton.

Sully, J. (1896). *Studies of childhood*. New York: Longmans, Green.

Tolpin, M. (1971). On the beginnings of a cohesive self: An application of the concept of transmuting internalization to the study of the transitional object and signal anxiety. *The Psychoanalytic Study of the Child*, 26.

Volkan, V. (1973). Transitional fantasies in the analysis of a narcissistic personality. *Journal of the American Psychoanalytic Association*, *21*, 351-376.

Werner, H., & Kaplan, B. (1963). *Symbol formation*. New York: Wiley.

Winnicott, D. W. (1951). Transitional objects and transitional phenomena. In *Collected papers: Through pediatrics to psychoanalysis*. New York: Basic Books, 1958.

Winnicott, D. W. (1957). On the contribution of direct child observation to psycho-analysis. In *The maturational processes and the facilitating environment*. New York: International Universities Press, 1965.

Winnicott, D. W. (1958). The capacity to be alone. In *The maturational processes and the facilitating environment*. New York: International Universities Press, 1965.

Winnicott, D. W. (1960). The theory of the parent-infant relationship. In *The maturational processes and the facilitating environment*. New York: International Universities Press, 1965.

Winnicott, D. W. (1971). *Playing and reality*. New York: Basic Books.

Wulff, M. (1946). Fetishism and object choice in early childhood. *Psychoanalytic Quarterly*, *15*, 460-471.

CHAPTER SIX

Self Constancy and Alternate States of Consciousness

SHELDON BACH

If we ask ourselves naively how the phenomenal sense of self constancy, of being the same person from day to day, is maintained throughout a lifetime, we are instantly beset with fascinating questions. Why indeed do we not awaken one morning like Gregor Samsa to the realization that we are an insect or why, like Chuang Tzu, are we not constantly haunted by the question of whether we are Chuang Tzu who dreamed he was a butterfly, or a butterfly dreaming he is Chuang Tzu?

And yet, although we live in a world of continual flux and are constantly recycled over shorter or longer periods of time, we must account not only for our feeling of constancy within flux but also for our sense that we are capable of change at all. Our subjective feelings of identity, vitality, and growth seem to depend on some interactional process, some integration achieved in the course of separation–individuation.

Whether we emphasize the dynamic, economic, structural, or genetic aspects of self constancy; whether we conceive of it as a fantasy about the self, as a homeostatic self-regulating mechanism, as an ego function, or as an identity theme imprinted from infancy, we tend to regard it as a configuration with a relatively slow rate of change over time (Rapaport, 1967). This contrasts with drives or forces, processes which, by definition, have relatively rapid rates of change over time.

In traditional psychoanalytic thinking the drives guarantee change; the structures guarantee continuity. If we regard self constancy as some sort of structural capacity, we might imagine it as the ability to integrate a relatively stable and continuous sense of self regardless of the state of drive activation or environmental press. Our definition should satisfy both the need to experience ourselves as the same or constant and the need to experience ourselves as growing or alive.

It is not at all clear what dimensions of functioning must remain stable and continuous in order to produce a phenomenal sense of self constancy, although there are two most commonly mentioned parameters. The first is bodily constancy, a sense of body cohesiveness in space and time, which would seem to relate to the achievement of well-defined self- and object representations. The second is affective constancy, a sense of emotional continuity and well-regulated self-esteem, which would seem to relate to the achievement of integrated good and bad self-representations. Presumably, affective constancy is a later achievement than bodily constancy, if only because it seems more dependent on the advent of the symbolic process.

But in point of fact, we could list as many constancies as we could ego functions. Historically, the concept derives from early attempts by experimental psychologists to explain the puzzling observation that objects remain recognizably themselves although the impinging retinal stimulation may change radically from moment to moment. What they discovered was that perception is a process involving relationships, and that constancy is a learned configuration corresponding to probabilities in the world "out there."

As analysts, however, the function that interests us above all else is the capacity of the patient to utilize the analytic process, that is, the ability to engage a transference relationship in such a way that it becomes ultimately analyzable. Since a transference relationship is essentially illusory, and the ability to analyze it requires a degree of reality testing, I believe that the function in question is the capacity to move freely, voluntarily, and consciously between the realms of illusion and reality, or playing and reality (Winnicott, 1971), or subjectivity and objectivity (Bach, 1980), or not-real and real experiences (Steingart, 1984), or, in general, between the realms of the inner and the outer world.

This ability to maintain a homeostasis between the self-world and the object world, to be "both fully 'in' and at the same time basically separate from the world 'out there'" (Mahler, 1972), seems to be a major component of the phenomenal sense of self constancy. It is this component that is at the core of Chuang Tzu's dilemma about whether he is a man dreaming he is a butterfly or a butterfly dreaming he is a man; and since it involves the distinction between fantasy and reality, or between alternate states of consciousness, I propose to call it the function of state constancy. State constancy involves the capacity to move freely along a continuum of alternate states and yet, when necessary, to locate ourselves on this continuum with respect to consensual reality. It involves an ability to give in to our subjective experience, while at the same time retaining the capacity to observe and orient ourselves in reality. I believe that a useful way to think of this is to imagine the development of a higher level integrative state that tolerates and allows free access to affective memories of alternate states; a kind of supraordinate reflective awareness that permits of multiple perspectives on the self.

While reality testing has always been considered a developmental achievement, it is sometimes achieved at the expense of an inner world, a fantasy life, the ability to love, or the ability to lend oneself to a transference experience. In such cases, of course, we would view this as a conflicted achievement; the more complete achievement would be the capacity to conceive of oneself as the *same* self throughout a multitude of ego states. What I am describing is a supraordinate state of consciousness that develops out of an integrative capacity. This capacity makes possible the development of analyzability and also identifies it, and the methods of actualizing this ability are an important part of the theory of psychoanalytic technique.

I propose now to illustrate this concept with two clinical examples: the first, a woman whose reality testing was not in question but whose state constancy *was* and who, consequently, was not available for analysis; and the second, a man whose reality testing was far from secure but who, nevertheless, was able to lend himself to the analytic process.

CASE 1: ALTERNATE FEELINGS AND ALTERNATE FIGURES

A 50-year-old woman came for consultation because the recent death of her husband after a long and happy marriage had thrown her into a panic. She was well dressed, trim and alert, and a very attractive, intelligent, and perceptive woman.

Initially, she complained of an obsessive thought that she had killed her husband. We found this obsessive thought to have two roots: that he had killed himself because she had treated him badly in the final year of his illness, and that he had injured *her* through his death and by the authoritarian manner in which he had stifled her throughout their marriage.

The patient complained of an inability to mourn, though in fact she missed her husband terribly. It soon became clear that while she was depressed by her loss, she was also elated by her new-found freedom. It seemed quite impossible for her to believe in the reality of both of these contradictory feelings; either she should be elated or she should be depressed, but ambiguity was too much for her to bear.

In this connection she noted that from early childhood she had been unable to tolerate ambiguous situations: She would become extremely anxious and do everything possible to avoid them. As an example, she mentioned reversible figures; it made her panicky just to look at them. If she didn't *know* the figures were ambiguous she experienced no panic but, even when she knew, she generally couldn't permit the figures to reverse—it was either two faces or a vase—how could it be both? In the course of describing her panic reaction to the figure–ground reversals, she misspoke herself and while intending to say, "I cannot bear *not* to know where I am," she in fact said, "I cannot bear to *know* where I am."

This woman's mother was a narcissistic *grande dame* of the old school—a demanding, perfectionistic, and moralizing woman who knew exactly what was right and wrong in all details of dress, deportment, and duty. The patient feared her, depended on her, and hated her from as far back as she could remember and compliantly sacrificed autonomy in order to retain her mother's love. Though feared and hated, the mother was experienced as necessary for the patient's very existence.

Typically, the issue was resolved when the patient left home, against her mother's wishes, to marry her husband, a man who in so many ways resembled the mother. But whereas the dependency–autonomy conflict had always remained alive with her mother, it became submerged with the husband. He too became the vital center of her life, but now she willingly complied with his demands, and her autonomy could find expression in managing their home and pursuing their many interests.

The first cracks in this edifice began to appear after the children left home when the patient, past 40 years of age, began to feel that her life was meaningless if she couldn't find something else to do. For a few years she alternated between anxiety and depression, unwilling to seek help because this would mean there was something wrong with *her* when in fact she was now beginning to feel that she had been kept in subjugation throughout her life.

One day, while having a routine checkup, her doctor made some suggestive remarks to her. On succeeding visits he would sometimes behave like a lover and at other times he would treat her distantly, as though she were simply another patient. She could not clarify this situation in her mind and feared she was having "delusions"; she became obsessed with every detail of their meetings and was soon in a panic. Eventually she told her husband of the situation and appealed for help. At this point he was very ill and suggested she see a psychiatrist, a suggestion she resented and resisted. The marriage rapidly deteriorated. She became angry and querulous and couldn't find the love within her to "help him die in peace," although she made valiant efforts to do so and bitterly reproached herself for the failure. Shortly after his death, she came for a first consultation, wracked with anguish, panic, and guilt.

Despite her tormented condition, she was unable to commit herself to any treatment plan, and we agreed to an extended consultation. With unusual perceptivity she was able to explain that she feared her dependency and was determined not to add me to the long list of mother, husband, doctor, and others whom she needed, loved, complied with, rebelled against, and hated.

At the beginning she was enormously impressed by my flexibility and understanding. She repeatedly thanked me for the help I was giving her, and within a few weeks she began to experience relief from her anxiety, obsessive thoughts, insomnia, and depression. Predictably, in the 17th session, at the point where she was feeling relatively normal again, trouble arose.

She thought she caught me stifling a yawn, was not certain whether her perception was correct or "a delusion," and asked me about it. She noted that she had an extreme sensitivity to any sign of boredom or lack of interest; if she were certain I had yawned, she would be obliged to "put an end to our conversations."

Typically, she would not be put off by any discussion of her feelings or of what the incident might mean to her. She insisted on a yes or no answer, while admitting that she might very well not believe me. She would tolerate no analogy with her "delusions" about the doctor, no empathy with how she must have felt then or be feeling now, no curiosity as to why *my* perception of reality should count more than hers, and especially no discussion of her angry feelings. I suggested that since she was here already, she might perhaps stay until the end of the hour. To this she readily agreed "out of common courtesy." In fact, she came back for 3 more hours while we tried to work this through.

We began with the fact that once before, about 3 weeks earlier, she had expressed fears that I might be bored and stifling a yawn, a clear misperception on her part. I had tried at the time to relate this to her "delusion," but she insisted that she had "more important matters" to discuss. We both understood that she had still been too needy to risk a confrontation.

It now appeared that her exquisite sensitivity to inattention was a function of her dependency on objects such as her mother, her husband, her doctor, and me. Not feeling autonomous in the world, she experienced her mental stability as entirely dependent on the stability of the object, whether "good" or "bad." She was, in perceptual language, field-dependent. Just as, perceptually, she was obliged to stabilize her world by keeping the ambiguous figure from reversing in order to ward off panic, she was likewise obliged to keep the people in her life clear and unambiguous, although in some way she knew that this was a distortion of reality. She had little freedom to play with her fantasy, or to entertain the idea that things *might* be other than what they *must* be.

I reminded her of the slip she made, saying, "I cannot bear to know where I am," when she had meant to say, "I cannot bear *not* to know where I am." To know where she was had always been defined by knowing where the other person was; ambiguity about the other person's position, just as variations in figure–ground, led to panic because then she was indeed obliged to know where *she* was. She was afraid to define herself in terms of her own feelings, which were dangerous, ambivalent, and difficult to integrate. Here we spoke at length about her anger at her husband and, in particular, about her decision to tell him of her flirtation while he was dying. She was very upset by this, but seemed to despair of ever changing. It was easier to think of her marriage as either perfect or disastrous, of her mother or husband as either benevolent or despotic, of her reaction to the death as either depression or elation, of me as either perfect or fatally flawed, and of her role in life as either dependent or totally autonomous. We discussed all this in relation to her wish to terminate the consultation, and she was able to observe that the consultation reproduced not only the pattern of the relationship with her doctor but the pattern of her marriage as well.

She was nevertheless determined to stop, if only I would assure her of my availability should need arise. This I did, and we parted on apparently friendly terms. Some months later I received a note from her saying that she had been mourning but was otherwise doing well, and expressing gratitude for my help. Two years later I heard quite accidentally that she was engaged in a successful business venture and was "looking like her old self again."

Discussion of Case 1

This brief vignette of what might be called a typical case of "love addiction" has a number of interesting aspects. Clinically, one is impressed by the awesome rapidity with which, in an extended consultation lasting only a few weeks, the transference and countertransference grew to such fever pitch and reproduced with such complexity the core of so many important earlier relationships. Of course, the patient had become frightened of her growing love and hate for me and the ambivalence conflict this aroused. Having raised the possibility that *I* might not love her or be worthy of her love (if I yawned), she had then rejected me, thus actively mastering the trauma passively experienced when the doctor rejected her. The "delusional" affair with the doctor was in itself a response to abandonment by her dying husband, just as confessing the affair to him was both a hateful abandonment of him before he could leave her and an invitation to rescue and reject her. This invitation was reenacted with me, but this time *she* left first, whereas I had promised to wait forever. Thus she had spared herself the likelihood of narcissistic mortifications and conflicts around aggression in a real therapeutic relationship by exchanging it for the fantasy of "all and forever" in an imaginary relationship with me. In fact, several years later, she confided to the referring internist that she often thought of me, was reassured by my availability, but had never gone into treatment because she was "afraid of falling in love."

From time immemorial the virtues of love have been extolled by such diverse parties as biblical prophets, Provençal poets, and country rock singers. Love is the most widely desired of any state of consciousness, with the possible exception of sleep. Why in the world should anyone be afraid of falling in love?

Although this patient might have maintained that her fear was based on the probable lack of sexual gratification, one is not overly impressed with this argument. The greatest loves in history were, after all, sexually frustrated: Romeo and Juliet, Tristan and Iseult, Eloise and Abelard. Of course, these loves were reciprocated, whereas the patient certainly feared that hers would not be, and unrequited love seemed more horrendous than unconsummated love. But if consummation were not the goal, then why should respect, affection, and helpfulness not have sufficed instead? Was this woman one of those "children of nature" of whom Freud speaks, those who "are accessible only to 'the logic of soup, with dumplings for arguments'"? (Freud, 1915a, p. 167).

To my mind, the patient's real fear was about the nature of her love, which seemed to her totally disabling and more akin to a state of hypnotic surrender than to a state of mature love. She seemed afraid that in the course of treatment she would develop a regressive state of consciousness from which she would be unable to extricate herself. In this regressive state she would have surrendered herself; that is, the parameters of voluntary action, reflective awareness, and logical thought organization would be so attenuated that she would feel "possessed," unable to act on her own initiative and unable to reflect objectively on her own actions. She would feel entirely dependent upon the will of another. This state in many ways replicated her early relationship with her mother, and while secretly desired it was also greatly feared.

I must digress for a moment on this fear of total surrender, so often encountered when we attempt to do analytic work with those patients who would generally be seen as narcissistic, borderline, or psychotic. What they seem to fear is a "malignant regression" (Balint, 1968), a regression to "resourceless dependence" (Khan, 1972), or, simply, a pathological regression as opposed to a regression in the service of the ego. Gill and Brenman (1959) have noted that regressions in the service of the ego are characterized by:

1. A definite beginning and end
2. Reversibility, with a sudden and total reinstatement of the previous ego organization
3. Terminability under emergency conditions by the person unaided
4. Being entered into only when the person judges the situation to be safe
5. Being voluntarily sought by the individual
6. Being active rather than passive relative to pathological regression.

Gill and Benman (1959) note, and this is a fact of considerable clinical importance, that the degree to which the personality is engulfed, or the degree to which autonomous apparatuses continue to function, does *not* distinguish between the two kinds of regression.

Of course the first three characteristics of having a definite beginning and end and being reversible and self-terminable are conclusions after the fact. How are we or the patient to predict this in advance? The other characteristics all pertain to voluntary action by the patient; he voluntarily submits himself to regression because he has some confidence that it is in fact reversible. With these patients it is of the utmost clinical importance that the regression be engaged voluntarily and that they feel free to discuss their anxieties and to control the situation, as, for example, by sitting up at their discretion. Any hint of pressure from the analyst in any direction is fraught with dangers for a pathological regression.

I have elsewhere described two patients who presented after previous treatments which had ended traumatically (Bach, 1980). They were both terrified of regressing once more, and both

. . . tended to become anxious and panicky the more comfortable a situation appeared. They suffered from a kind of "signal contentment" which warned them that some important aspect of subjective or objective reality was being omitted and that sooner or later some catastrophic reversal would ensue in which black would become white, happiness become misfortune and the world be turned inside-out again. Like Alice, they felt they had stepped through the looking-glass and could never be quite certain again. (Bach, 1980, p. 188)

It is clear that such a fear—of figure and ground reversing, of black becoming white, and good becoming bad, a fear of reality reversal—was literally present in the woman I saw in consultation. Yet the other two patients both managed to engage the transference regression and conclude relatively successful analyses. How can we understand the differences?

In terms of environmental situation, none of these women had a prominent supportive figure in their lives, which made the transference that much more dangerous. In addition, they all suffered from a profound inability to mobilize rage and aggression around object failure, this being a major factor in their fear of enslavement to the object. Mrs. Smith, my consultee who refused treatment, had led an apparently normal and successful life until the beginning of her husband's illness. My other two patients, although quite successful in their professional endeavors, had both displayed rather severe pathology at one time or another. Nonetheless, they had both lived in a variety of realities and could no longer deny discordant subjective experiences, even though dissociated or alternating. Mrs. Smith, in appearance so much more "normal," had bought this normality at the price of constricting her experience.

The crucial element, then, would seem to be a particular kind of rigidity, namely: the degree to which alternate areas of experience, affectivity, and thought are split off, dissociated, or held in abeyance. These areas involve playing, subjectivity, fantasy, illusion, humor, and make-believe, that is, those areas that are indexed as being not-real (Steingart, 1984), not belonging to the normal, alert, waking state of consciousness. Simply put, I am saying that in assessing analyzability, one should pay attention to patients' experiences with alternate states of consciousness and their capacity to permit themselves such experiences; to enjoy them, to survive them, and to integrate them as part of their self-concept. This is the capacity I refer to as state constancy. But let me return to the clinical material.

If we compare the sessions of Mrs. Smith, my consultee, with the sessions of Richard, a patient I shall now present, we notice a marked difference in the use of language, fantasy, and the ability to play with ideas. This despite the fact that Richard's reality testing was considerably less secure than Mrs. Smith's, and that historically Mrs. Smith had led a relatively normal life whereas Richard was more "disturbed" and appeared to have undergone confusional and psychotic episodes.

CASE 2: HURRY UP PLEASE, IT'S TIME

One may commonly observe that certain people experience a mild sort of anxiety when confronted with a digital timepiece. I first noted this in the final months of treatment of a 35-year-old man as he began to give up the illusion of living in endless narcissistic time and develop a sense of urgency about living in finite real time. The date for termination had been fixed a year and a half previously by the patient himself and yet, typically, it was not until the end was almost upon us that he began to experience intimations that *it might really happen*. Considerable experience with Richard and other patients of this type had led me to believe that a frontal assault on the affective denial of termination would not prove useful, since in one sense he knew that we were finishing and talked about it frequently, but in another way could not really believe that it would happen. What I was hoping for, I can now understand, was not an abdication or surrender of the realm of illusion and fantasy, but its reelaboration and reintegration into a larger hierarchic perspective.

To the best of our understanding, and we discussed this often enough, it was not that we had totally missed some unconscious fantasy to which he desperately clung; it was, so far as we could gather, that he knew we were ending in July but both did and did not believe that it would really happen.

This is a typical example of what I have more generally called "retrospective reality testing" in these patients, referring to the fact that sometimes until the action, acting-out, or event actually occurs, discussion of the conflict or consequence tends to be sterile, since the belief in the reality of the prospective event always remains in question. Freud pointed to a similar situation in his remarks on death (1915b) and on splitting of the ego in fetishism (1940). I believe this relates to a peculiar attitude toward time and reality, which involves not only unconscious fantasies of narcissistic reunion, invulnerability, and living "alongside of the real world," but also related cognitive difficulties in integrating the subjective sense of one's aliveness with the objective knowledge of one's vulnerability and mortality. Ultimately, this involves a difficulty with integrating alternate states of consciousness and their thought processes, that is, a difficulty with state constancy.

In any case, about a year before the prospective termination, my patient Richard became very interested in the philosophy of time and spent many hours in the library reading on the subject. He had no difficulty in relating this to his anxieties and disbelief about termination, but felt that there was some underlying flaw in his grasp of the concept. At about this time he lost his watch and replaced it with a digital timepiece. One aspect of the complicated meaning this held for him was an attempt to remain timelessly attached to me by denying his responsibility and participation in the passage of time. Digital time to him seemed absolute, imperative, and coercive; it does not require or permit imagination or "figuring out" as does the reading of an ordinary analog clock face. It is not manipulable; one cannot fudge the time to make it a little earlier or later if one wants. It enters consciousness as a command from without, a given, and does not require the participation of the observer. For Richard this meant that it encouraged passivity and irresponsibility; the termination was not of his doing but was an act of God, my voice speaking through his timepiece. But at the same time this renunciation of responsibility filled him with anxiety lest he be imposed upon, subjugated, and annihilated. Thus, fearing activity lest he fail and be responsible, and fearing passivity lest he be manipulated and attacked, he was repeating at termination a central conflict that had brought him into analysis, and which he had attempted to resolve by living alongside of his real life and watching it unfold as if it were happening to someone else.

At this point he feared terminating analysis before he was perfect, just as he feared turning in his already long overdue book manuscript because he knew *that* was less than perfect. Somehow, one of us would have to remain perfect; either he or I, the book or the analysis, or else what was there to believe in? How could he orient himself? He wanted to take a morally superior position, to be above the fray, to remain aloof and angry and perfectionistic, but he knew that in fact the results could only be ambiguous. Both he and I, the book and the analysis, were only human and full of faults: "You hate them but you also love them; it's relative, like time." He had a dream:

A huge digital clock with many windows and numbers going all different ways. I can't make any sense out of it, and I open the back and there are more windows and numbers; a knob marked SET with numbers; another marked CUE with numbers, and then yellow and red wires in very intricate and tangled connections. Deep in the center of all this, I finally discover what's moving it: an old-fashioned wind-up alarm clock with bells on top.

He felt that the dream was an angry satire of my efforts, the analysis, and himself but, as he worked it over, he slowly came to feel that it was also an embracement and acceptance of things as they were. He continued to speak in the time metaphor:

Digital time is unyielding, it's absolute, but the hands on an analog watch never stop at any particular time, it's an unfolding. . . .

Digital time is the here and now; it allows for change from moment to moment but each reading is only itself. How can you be sure that the next reading will really be 1 second or 1 minute after that one? It requires a certain trust, a trust that something will remain the same even in the process of change, that there will be a continuity behind or beneath the change. You remember how I used to feel that when I turned on the water tap, blood might come out? I used to marvel at how certain you seemed when you came into the waiting room that you would find *me* there and not someone else—a plant or a monster. . . . Now I rarely think about those things . . . I guess I've developed some sense of trust that things will remain the same. . . .

Analog time not only gives you the time but it shows you the past and the future—what time it was and what time it will be. It gives you a vision of the whole, an overview of the situation.

With digital time I feel that I live in the moment and can change, but I have to trust that the continuity will be there. . . . And I think that the continuity is you . . . the giver of 50 minutes and the taker away . . . you become inexorable time—the killer.

I know that I'll miss you, that we're both going to die, that I've loved you and hated you and that I still do. . . . Is it inevitable that leaving should be a question of kill or be killed?

At another time he drew in the air with his forefinger five sixths of a circle, representing the transit of the minute hand over a 50-minute period. He indicated that the measure he was using was not the arc of the almost complete circle, but the arc of the incomplete portion. I remarked that his cue was not what is there but what *isn't* there. His associations clearly pointed to the presence or absence of the penis, and his attempts in fantasy to remain a woman rather than face the consequences of possessing a penis and acting like a man. Analog clocks, it occurred to him, have hands, but with digital clocks there are no hands, only a frightening gap between moments of time.

This material intertwined with musings about analog time as the merging mother, life-giver, and transitional object, versus digital time as the castrating father yet representative of reality, of accomplishment in the real world, and termination of the analysis. Emerging from this came some feeling that he called "relativity":

How to live in the moment, yet live in the flux of time; how to be separate from the world yet live in it; how to be lost in yourself yet still be able to find where you belong in the big picture; how to be form and content. . . .

There's always the other side . . . classical art concentrates on the form or structure and leaves you to supply the emotional content . . . the romantics concentrate on the emotional content and leave you to supply the form . . . it's back and forth like figure and ground. . . .

What I'm looking for is a resolution of all the oppositions . . . not really a resolution but a recognition and acceptance of relativity . . . it's more than just accepting that there are men and there are women and I only have one chance at it—I can't be both. . . . It's inside of *me,* the man and the woman. . . . You really can't tell the dancer from the dance . . . it oscillates, depending on what you're looking for and what you're willing to supply.

I think you just have to go ahead with some confidence in the process, that it will turn out all right. It may sound mystical, but it feels right to me. . . . I think I'd better hurry up now because it's time. . . .

Although the above reflections on time and termination were excerpted from notes made over the last year of treatment, I think they give a fair picture of the back and forth in the material. Themes from all parts of the analysis seemed to be dredged up in the whirlpool of the termination, to be reworked and in some way reintegrated. The impression, in fact, was of being in a time machine where one could move from one epoch or developmental level to another, speed up the process one hundred-fold, or slow it down to a crawl. Perhaps all of this was connected to fantasies of rebirth, which now made their appearance, as they sometimes do during the terminal phase of analysis. In any case the preoccupation with time eventually diminished, as did the anxiety about his digital watch.

But what impressed me most of all was a mutuality that developed in our sense of time without any direct discussion of the matter. Now that Richard had a new watch that never ran down, our times were always in perfect synchrony. Yet he no longer felt that he was running on my time, nor I on his time. There was his time and my time, which somehow "interdigitated," and the exceptions, such as holidays, illnesses, and so forth, no longer greatly disturbed the overall continuity. And then there was free time or playtime, which "belonged" to neither of us and was inviolable, but gave us time for relaxation, a suspension from the pressure of time. In this time he worked out the conclusions for his book and turned it in on time for the newly arranged deadline. The analysis also finished "on time," bringing with it a very real change in his daily experience of self constancy. In one of his many attempts to summarize what had occurred, Richard said, "I am who I am from day to day . . . it's not always who I would like to be but it's there . . . it's solid. At the beginning I never even dreamed that it would be possible, and probably I never even wanted it. . . . I was afraid that change would be even more disorienting. . . . I never understood you could have change and continuity also. . . ."

I believe that in one sense what Richard was trying to describe was the development of a new state of everyday consciousness, existing on a higher level of abstraction. I have suggested elsewhere that the normal adult waking state of consciousness is a developmental achievement (Bach, 1977), and that the inability to freely alternate between states of subjective and objective self-awareness may implicate both developmental deficits and defensive functions, such that the conflict maintains the disability and the disability supports the conflict. In the working through of archaic transferences, the patient, through a laborious process of differentiation and reintegration, gradually becomes able to form and hold more abstract conceptualizations not only of self and object, but of time, place, person, causality, and so on. The individual moves from concrete imagery to abstract conception, analogous to Piaget's description of the development of "concrete" and "formal" operations in latency and adolescence (Bach, 1977; Piaget & Inhelder, 1969). In this sense Richard could now locate himself on an abstract time continuum that had become internalized; the analog clock was no longer necessary as a concrete perceptual experience, and the digital clock could function simply as a "signal" of internalized time. In a poetic way his dream had come true: he now had "an old-fashioned alarm clock with bells" inside of him.

DISCUSSION

I have tried in this chapter to supplement the usual categories of bodily constancy and emotional constancy with the idea of ego state constancy. While all these concepts are intricately connected and perhaps derivable from one another, the idea of state constancy seems to have some heuristic value in predicting reactions to the analytic regression, understanding their genesis, and perhaps also in suggesting technical interventions.

The refusal to entertain a regressed state of consciousness, like Mrs. Smith's refusal "to fall in love," can prevent a treatment from beginning or can impede the progress of one already under way. On the other hand difficulties with halting a regression can lead to addictive states, interminable analyses, malignant regressions, and psychotic episodes.

The patient's fear of regression in analysis seems to relate in part to anxiety at being confronted with major contradictions in the ego, contradictory states which the ego might be incapable of encompassing and synthesizing, and which might leave the patient in a state of helplessness, confusion, and fragmentation. It is a fear specifically of regression to an ego state that would permit: (1) a loss of volition, that is, a change from activity to passivity, which is nonreversible without help and which places the ego at the mercy of the object or at the mercy of the drives; and (2) a loss of reflective awareness or perspective on the self that would affect reality testing and allow the person to "drown" in subjective experience from which he could not extricate himself unaided. The regression would then not be in the service of *his* ego, but would require the help of another ego to save him.

We may at this point wonder what might be the childhood circumstances that would produce such a possibility, or even the fear of such a possibility. The history of the development of states of consciousness is yet to be written and is indeed scarcely begun. It probably awaits not only new theoretical formulations but also new methods of investigation as, for example, rapid-eye-movement (REM) studies have enlarged our knowledge of sleep states. We know that at 4–5 months the infant appears to be developing nuanced states of the sensorium, which have been described by Wolff (1959), Escalona (1962), Mahler (1968), and others. There can be little doubt that environmental response to these alterations of state, even at an early age, plays an important role in their further development. Likewise, it seems reasonable to suppose that children who have been helped through overwhelming traumatic states such as hunger, illness, and tantrums by appropriate parental responses will develop a different attitude toward these states than will children who have been left to "drown" in them. In a less obvious but no less important way, the mother influences the growing child's attitude toward multiple states of consciousness and indicates their acceptability or unacceptability.

It was clear, for example, that my first patient, Mrs. Smith, had rarely engaged in pleasantly shared regressive experiences with her mother, whether of mutual bodily contact, mutual fantasies, songs, games, fairy-tales or, even later, mutual shopping expeditions, or simply gossiping together. Her experiences with her mother were constantly pulling toward a clear and alert state of consciousness, in part self-induced to control her overwhelming anger, but also partially because the mother herself was incapable of pleasurable regressive experiences and regarded them with horror.

There are parents who treat their child in one stable way so that the child learns a particular way of dealing with the parent but does *not* learn other affective and cognitive states. Such parents do not allow themselves to be utilized *by* the child; the child never gets the sense of exploring aspects of himself by utilizing the parent for different purposes. On the contrary, it is the child who is being utilized by the parent, being manipulated, being seen in some particular way as an extension of some parental fantasy. Such children may develop stable ego structures, but the structures are fragile and limited. As adults, they may find a particular niche in reality to accommodate their stabilized position, but they are unable to view the world from multiple perspectives; and to interpret to them from outside their stabilized position arouses great anxiety.

Thus Mrs. Smith grew up to be a woman who, though highly cultured, was terrified of creativity. Her reality testing was impeccable but state specific, and her capacity for "playing," in Winnicott's (1971) sense, was pathologically deficient. Altered states were a source of terror rather than joy, for she had little confidence in her ability to use them and recover from them. She clung desperately, single-mindedly, and concretely to the secondary process sphere in which she could operate, because she felt incapable of trusting her capacity for state constancy.

We have seen, for example, that she was terrified of "falling in love" because this meant complete emotional surrender to an object who would mistreat her (A. Freud, 1952). Such patients fear the oscillations between states of negativism and being autonomous at the same time. Thus they hesitate to surrender themselves not only to love objects, but to intense emotional experiences of any kind, for fear that they will "lose themselves" in emotional quicksand and be "drowned" in their deep longings for passivity.

I have mentioned earlier that one of the central problems of self constancy is to account not only for the sense that one remains the same person through multitudinous transformations, but also to account for the sense that one is alive and can change, to account for the possibility of emergent growth. In these patients with structural defects, one frequently notes some problem in experiencing their life as an ongoing *process* with an internally guaranteed continuity. On the contrary, they tend to experience both their life and the analysis as an additive cumulation of successive *moments,* each one separate and without any necessary connection between the preceding moment or session and the following moment or session (Bach, 1975, 1977). The causal connection between moments of life, which if internally guaranteed, gives one the feeling of a reliable *process,* is lacking in these patients to a greater or lesser degree. By contrast, their experience is of a succession of *moments* whose continuity can only be guaranteed by the stability and goodwill of the object. In the transference regression this object becomes the very source of life, the guarantee of the continuity of the self, and to aggress against it becomes the equivalent of self-annihilation. Ultimately, Mrs. Smith despaired of change because she felt she had bought self-continuity at the price of abject surrender to her objects. By reconstructing me as a good object at a distance and without engagement, she could maintain both her sense of aliveness and also her independence.

Had she once more permitted herself to "fall in love" or to engage the transference regression, it is likely that her sense of volition would have become attenuated and that she would have experienced life changes as "miracles," that is, as externally caused by my (divine) intervention. I call them "miracles" by analogy with Schreber (Freud, 1911) in order to underline their essential resemblance to the more extreme psychotic forms of this phenomenon. But in fact these externalizations also resemble the artist's self-created muse or narcissistic double, whether actual figures like Dante's Beatrice or Freud's Fliess, or mere figments of the poetic imagination. The primary difference is not one of function, since all of these figures serve to displace responsibility and guilt as well as to provide externalized structure, but rather one of volition and terminability. The great artist voluntarily creates his muse, endows it with power and, indeed, may struggle violently against it, but ultimately can release himself from bondage when his purpose has been served. At the very least, the artist's cognitive functions are not paralyzed. Both Mrs. Smith and Schreber feared their bondage and, like a hypnotic spell, were unable to terminate it by themselves unaided.

Finally, a word about the reversibility of figure and ground. It may have seemed to the reader who has followed me thus far that I am making overly much of an insignificant and perhaps even accidental perceptual phenomenon. I have used the capacity to allow figure–ground alternations as a metaphor of the capacity to allow for alterations in states of consciousness. We have seen that Mrs. Smith was strongly defended against both possibilities and that this was no mere coincidence. Indeed, I believe that the analogy carries further and that Piaget's fundamental processes of assimilation and accommodation, like introjection and projection, are to be found in the archaic mirroring and idealizing transferences. From this perspective, the self in the grandiose mirroring transference is figure, while in the idealizing transference the self forms the ground for the idealized object. Thus, Mrs. Smith's refusal to engage a transference process, which she both wished and feared might swallow her up, was a refusal to engage the projective–introjective processes that would lead to psychic growth, and was symbolized by her refusal to allow the normal perceptual phenomenon of figure–ground reversal.

In contrast, my second patient, Richard, had much easier access to his altered states, although diagnostically he appeared far more disturbed than did Mrs. Smith. In the course of the treatment he developed a playful relationship to regressive alterations of consciousness, but even at the beginning, when he feared "going crazy," he was willing to try the couch if I would be there for him.

Although the basic wishes and fears of both patients were similar and Richard's pathology considerably greater, he proved to be more amenable to analysis and, in the long run, healthier and more creative. An important factor in this outcome seemed to be his capacity to engage and eventually to integrate a variety of ego states, that is, to develop the function of state constancy. This capacity seems related to early maternal experiences, as well as to ongoing positive regressive experiences with parents, lovers, friends, and with oneself.

By positive regressive experience I refer to the playful creative experience. Whether the model is mutual gazing or peek-a-boo, creative sexuality, or the artistic experience, it need not be without anxiety—indeed, it hardly ever is. But like the tightrope walker, the return to safe landing must be negotiable; at first a safety net is required, which can later be dispensed with. The provision of this safety net is inherent in the psychoanalytic situation, which with "good-enough" matching between patient and analyst, induces a creative regression that can be mutually terminated.

Originally, the child learns to manage alternate ego states with the help of the parent, thus internalizing a reliable function of state constancy. When this help is not reliably forthcoming from the parent, an attempt is made at self-regulation, using modalities appropriate to the particular stage of development where the derailment occurs. Attempts at homeostatic self-regulation have protean manifestations that can range anywhere from rocking and head banging in infancy to masturbation and many of the addictions and perversions. A common example currently is the class of eating disorders in which foods are used, like sedating or stimulating drugs, to regulate states of excitation. These disorders may be classified as being "on the way toward self constancy."

Self constancy, as we have seen, has at least three major components that appear to form a developmental sequence:

1. A reliable sense of one's bodily continuity in space and time
2. A reliable sense of emotional homeostasis (self-esteem regulation)
3. A reliable sense of self-continuity across alternate states of consciousness.

When we examine the constituents of these alternate states, namely, alterations in thought processes, in reflective awareness, and in voluntary effort and spontaneity, it appears in the light of our clinical material that the crucial factor is the experienced sense of volition or intentionality. Thus, I agree with both Gill and Brenman (1959), as well as Balint (1968), that the difference between a "benign" or workable transference regression and a malignant or unworkable regression is not in the degree to which thought processes are primitivized or self-observation and reality testing are lacking, but essentially in the degree to which all of these are seen by the patient as actively sought or passively suffered. I believe the crucial dimension to be the *experience* or activity of passivity, and that this determines not only the patient's ability to lend himself to a therapeutic regression, but also the extent to which the regression will prove to be benign or malignant. Ultimately, the developmental line of self constancy should lead to a reliably constant sense of the self as an active, choice-making agent. This view has broad implications for the therapeutic stance one must assume with the more disturbed patient; however, it is beyond the scope of this chapter to discuss these implications specifically.

When Chuang Tzu questions whether he is a butterfly dreaming he is a man, or a man dreaming he is a butterfly, we may view this ultimately as a question about activity and passivity. Whether one chooses to remain asleep or to pursue the difficult task of being alive is less relevant than whether or not one experiences the possibility of choice. For it is this possibility of choice, of internalized self-volition, that binds the multiplicity of ego states into a reliable sense of self constancy.

REFERENCES

Bach, S. (1975). Narcissism, continuity and the uncanny. *International Journal of Psycho-Analysis, 56,* 77–86.

Bach, S. (1977). On the narcissistic state of consciousness. *International Journal of Psycho-Analysis, 58,* 209–233.

Bach, S. (1980). Self-love and object-love. In R. Lax, S. Bach, & J. A. Burland (Eds.), *Rapprochement* (pp. 171–197). New York: Jason Aronson.

Balint, M. (1968). *The basic fault.* London: Tavistock.

Escalona, S. K. (1962). The study of individual differences and the problem of state. *Child Psychiatry, 1*(1).

Freud, A. (1952). Studies in passivity. In *The writings of Anna Freud* (Vol. IV, pp. 245–259). New York: International Universities Press, 1968.

Freud, S. (1911). Psychoanalytic notes on an autobiographical account of a case of paranoia. *Standard Edition, 12,* 9–82. London: Hogarth Press, 1958.

Freud, S. (1915a). Observations on transference-love. *Standard Edition, 12,* 157–171. London: Hogarth Press, 1958.

Freud, S. (1915b). Thoughts for the times on war and death. *Standard Edition, 14,* 273–300. London: Hogarth Press, 1958.

Freud, S. (1940). Splitting of the ego in the process of defense. *Standard Edition, 23,* 273–278. London: Hogarth Press, 1958.

Gill, M., & Brenman, M. (1959). *Hypnosis and related states.* New York: International Universities Press.

Khan, M. (1972). Dread of surrender to resourceless dependence in the analytic situation. In *The privacy of the self* (pp. 270–279). New York: International Universities Press, 1974.

Kohut, H. (1971). *The analysis of the self.* New York: International Universities Press.

Mahler, M. (1968). *On human symbiosis and the vicissitudes of individuation.* New York: International Universities Press.

Mahler, M. (1972). Rapprochement subphase of the separation–individuation phase. *Psychoanalytic Quarterly, 41,* 487–506.

Piaget, J., & Inhelder, B. (1969). *The psychology of the child.* New York: Basic Books.

Rapaport, D. (1967). *The collected papers of David Rapaport* (M. Gill, Ed.). New York: Basic Books.

Steingart, I. (1984). *Cognition as pathological play in borderline–narcissistic personalities.* New York: S. P. Medical and Scientific Books.

Winnicott, D. W. (1971). *Playing and reality.* New York: Basic Books.

Wolff, P. H. (1959). Observations on newborn infants. *Psychosomatic Medicine, 21,* 110–118.

CHAPTER SEVEN

Self and Object Differentiation

BERNARD BRANDCHAFT

Analysts have increasingly recognized the importance of self and object differentiation, as regressions within the psychoanalytic process revealed deeply lying psychological configurations in which the demarcation of boundaries remained stubbornly obscure. Alerted by problems encountered clinically in this area, psychoanalytically trained observers of infant and child development generally came to agree that the recognition of "I" from "not-I" is a unique measure of the progress of the entire developmental process. Stolorow and Lachmann (1980), summarizing this point of view, state that "The first developmental task to face the infant, central to the beginning articulation and structuralization of his representational world, is the differentiation of subjective separation of self representations from representations of his primary objects . . . and the rudimentary establishment of self–object boundaries" (p. 3).

Psychoanalytic investigators have described this area of development and its vicissitudes from differing perspectives. In Melanie Klein's metapsychology the point at which such differentiation is established is the achievement of the depressive position—for her, the decisive precondition for normal development. Kernberg (1975) places the accomplishment by the early ego of the differentiation of self-images from object images, and the integration of libidinally and aggressively determined self and object images in the same preeminent position. Mahler has isolated separation–individuation as the phase in which the child gradually separates out and differentiates his self-representations from "the hitherto fused symbiotic self-plus-object representations." She sees this as the central task of childhood upon which further development hinges.

Despite general agreement of the importance of the differentiation of self and object, many questions arise. How does the process occur? If it be true that "no man is an island," and if we are not to ask "for whom the bell tolls," to what extent and in what areas does a commonality of boundary continue? To what extent does the blurring of commonality or its absence constitute a miscarriage of the "hatching process"? What factors in the developing infant and in its surroundings facilitate normal individuating processes, and what factors impede and stunt these processes? How can we distinguish between: (1) a "delusion" of common boundary maintained defensively, and (2) the persistence of a subjective experience of commonality because those developments that lead naturally to gradual demarcation of self and object boundaries have been arrested? The answers to these questions are not merely of academic interest, for upon them will depend our clinical approach to persisting problems in this area; so also will the contributions of psychoanalysis to child-rearing practices be determined.

In this chapter I propose to examine briefly the findings of some influential investigators. I will attempt to clarify some assumptions that underlie their observations. Finally I shall attempt to apply the findings of self psychology to the questions I have raised and to illustrate the importance of these findings with clinical material.

KLEINIAN VIEWS

The matter of self and object differentiation was first addressed in depth in the work of Melanie Klein and her co-workers. The infant's development from the beginning, they proposed, is influenced by the necessity of its immature ego to deal with the death instinct and with the intolerable anxiety of annihilation stemming from it. This first developmental task is accomplished by the deflection of the death instinct, partly by its projection into the primal object and partly by conversion of the death instinct into aggression. At the same time a relationship is established with an ideal breast in a similar manner. Part of the self, containing libido, is projected outward and the rest is used to establish a libidinal relationship with this ideal object, which is created in order to satisfy the ego's instinctive striving for the preservation of life. The infant's wishes are for unlimited gratification, and he experiences frustration as "an attack by hostile forces" that is also immediately projected to the outside. Experiences of gratification and frustration become the basis of the infant's organization of experience into libidinal and destructive ("good" and "bad") parts of the self and object. The perception of the ideal breast is reinforced by gratifying experiences of love and feeding by the real external mother, and the perception of an "all-bad" breast is reinforced by experiences of deprivation and pain.

In this view homeostatic equilibrium is maintained optimally in periods of freedom from hunger and tension when there is an optimal balance between libidinal and aggressive impulses. "This equilibrium is disturbed whenever, owing to privations from internal or external sources, aggressive impulses are reinforced" (Klein, 1945, p. 198). The internal sources that disrupt homeostasis are oral instinctual—greed and envy.

The primary task after survival in this earliest phase of development is to acquire, to keep inside, and to identify with the ideal object seen as life giving and protective, and to keep outside the bad object and those parts of the self harboring the destructive instincts. Thus, defensive operations of the ego, splitting and projective identification mounted against instinctual forces (and parts of the self and internalized objects containing them), characteristically dominate early development. Archaic ego defenses persist, in this view, owing to constitutionally pathological destructiveness and are intensified by an insufficiency of gratifying part–object experiences. The dominating anxiety is paranoid. Differentiation of self and object are continuously interfered with or nullified by these archaic defensive measures of the infantile ego. The further development of the differentiation process takes place under the influence of the inherent integrative tendencies of the ego. The infant's capacity increases to bring ideal and all bad parts of the self and internalized object closer togther by reducing splitting and projection. In this way, with the infant's increasing acceptance of the ownership of his destructiveness, recognition of his feelings of guilt, and reinforcement of the capacity to repair his damage to his objects, a relationship is established between a whole, realistically perceived object and an integrated, differentiated, and realistically perceived self.

The role of objects in this developmental process is threefold. First, they are required to provide a preponderance of "good," gratifying experiences as against "bad," frustrating experiences. Second, objects are required to fulfill their "holding function," that is to "contain" the infant's projections of destructive parts of the self—his bad internal objects and his anxiety—and to modify them internally so that they are transmitted back to the infant in less virulent form. And third, objects are required to possess inherent characteristics for purposes of the infant's identificatory needs, which will not be so far distant from the idealized qualities that the infant seeks so as to do violence to his growing sense of reality. Failures in any of these spheres will affect the outcome of the differentiating and integrating processes by increasing the intensity of the instinctual conflict and by reenforcing the primitive defenses and so imperil the successful resolution of the "depressive position."

Two further additions to this brief summary are relevant to this discussion. On the matter of disintegration anxiety, Klein attributed its first appearance to the workings of the death instinct. Subsequently, when she observed disintegration anxiety within the analytic process, she continued to explain it as evidence of pathologically destructive instincts, now deliberately employed. Segal speaks of disintegration as "a defensive measure . . . the ego fragments and splits itself into little bits in order to avoid the experience of anxiety" (1964, p. 17).

The clinical significance I attach to these and alternative concepts of disintegration (fragmentation) and the anxieties associated with them will become clearer shortly.

A second matter of interest is contained in the following passage:

The essential difference between infantile and mature object relations is that whereas the adult conceives of the object existing independently of himself for the infant it always refers in some way to himself. It exists only by virtue of its function for the infant and only in the world bounded by his own experiences. Whilst in reality the infant is utterly helpless and depends for the maintenance of his life completely on the mother (or her substitute) in phantasy he assumes an omnipotent position to his objects—they belong to him, are part of him, live only through and for him—he confirms his prenatal oneness with his mother. (Heimann, 1952, p. 142)

Klein's was the first systematic attempt to study development in the preoedipal period by actually observing children from the age of 2½ years closely and continuously in an analytic setting. Her observations opened the possibility of more accurate inferences on early development, for her subjects reduced the distance in age from these formative developmental processes, compared to the former field of analytic investigation. It is now clear that Klein's work has had a major influence on subsequent investigators, clinically and theoretically. For example, consider the following passages in light of contemporary theories of development elaborated by Kernberg (1975) and Mahler (1971).

My experience has led me to believe that from the very beginning of life, libido is fused with aggressiveness, and that the development of libido is at every stage vitally affected by anxiety derived from aggressiveness. Anxiety, guilt and depressive feelings at times drive the libido forward to new sources of gratification, at times they check the libido by re-enforcing the fixation to an earlier object and aim.

. . . It seems that the search for new sources of gratification is inherent in the forward movement of the libido. The gratification experienced at the mother's breast enables the infant to turn his desires towards hew objects, first of all towards his father's penis. Particular impetus, however, is given to the new desire by frustration in the breast relation. It is important to remember that frustration depends upon internal factors as well as on actual experiences. Some measure of frustration at the breast is inevitable, even under the most favorable conditions, for what the infant actually desires is unlimited gratification. Frustration and gratification from the outset moulds the infant's relations to a loved good and bad breast and to a hated bad breast. The need to cope with frustration and the ensuing aggression is one of the factors which lead to idealizing the good breast and good mother and correspondingly to intensifying the hatred and fears of the bad breast and bad mother which becomes the prototype of all persecuting and frightening objects." (Klein, 1945, pp. 378–379)

The developments that Klein observed in her young patients were influenced by her attempt to maintain a "neutral, nongratifying" setting, relying only on transference interpretation. The question inevitably arises as to whether the developments she described were analogous to those in a child experiencing "normal" frustration. (See Kohut, 1971, for a discussion of optimal vs. traumatic frustration and their consequences.) Mahler has shown convincingly that there is a different qualitative developmental outcome in a child reacting to tolerable as against excessive frustration, and this holds true in every developmental phase. Brandchaft and Stolorow (1984) have described borderline symptomatology as arising "within an intersubjective field consisting of a weak and vulnerable self and a failing, archaic selfobject" (p. 356). From the perspective of psychoanalytic self psychology, it is not primarily Klein's determination to adhere strictly to the analytic procedure that is at issue. It is rather that, in accordance with the dominant theories of the time, her observations failed to take into sufficient account the factor of inadequately cohesive and vulnerable self structures that lay behind the defensive and aggressive behavior she observed. In my own work I have seen repeatedly that in similar analytic situations, interpretations of defenses or of instinctual forces can have a fragmenting effect. On the other hand recognition and investigation of the selfobject failures being subjectively reexperienced and of the events that precipitate them, of their specific hierarchies of meanings, and of their impact upon the psychological organization of the patient, as well as the developmental traumata that they revive, can have reparative effects.

MARGARET S. MAHLER

Mahler's view of the differentiation process is contained in her description of the maturational phase of separation–individuation, occurring from about 4–5 months of age until the beginning of the 4th year of life. In this phase and its processes, the psychological birth of the individual is described as taking place.

The normal passage through this phase is determined by the events of the preceding developmental phases, the early autistic and especially the symbiotic phase. Success or failure in the symbiotic phase promotes or impedes the subsequent individuation process. The main task of the autistic phase, the first weeks of life, is to establish and maintain physiologic homeostatic equilibrium under the changed postpartum conditions. Mahler notes, "The newborn's waking life centers around his continuous attempts to achieve homeostasis" (1967, p. 741). This is accomplished by the mother's ministrations as a need-satisfying object and the infant's attempts to rid himself, by his own means, of unpleasurable tension. However, from the 2nd month on, dim awareness of the need-satisfying objects marks the beginning of the phase of normal symbiosis. Symbiosis

. . . describes that state of undifferentiation, of fusion with mother, in which the "I" is not yet differentiated from the "not-I." . . . The essential feature of symbiosis is hallucinatory or delusional somatopsychic, omnipotent fusion with the representation of the mother and in particular delusion of common boundary of the two actually and physically separate individuals. (This is the mechanism to which the ego regresses in the most severe disturbance of individuation and psychotic disorganization which I have described as "symbiotic child psychosis.) (Mahler, 1967, p. 742)

Within the symbiotic matrix the rudimentary ego of the newborn infant is complemented by the emotional rapport of the mother's nursing care. This permits the structural differentiation that leads to the individual's "organization for adaptation: the ego" (Mahler, 1967, p. 742). In this phase, dawning and recurrent awareness of separateness are denied and the delusion of fusion maintained because, as Klein also theorized, awareness of separateness threatens to unleash destructive unneutralized aggression beyond the infant's capability to rid himself of it and thus to overtax the stimulus barrier (Mahler, Pine, & Bergman, 1975, pp. 225–226).

Whereas in the earliest states of development, the breast or bottle belongs to the self, toward the 3rd month, the object begins to be perceived as an unspecific need-satisfying part-object. The infant begins to be able to hold tension in abeyance, to wait for and confidently expect satisfaction, and only then is it possible to speak of the beginning of an ego and of a symbiotic object as well. This is brought about by persisting memory traces of the pleasures of gratification. By the 6th month the smiling response indicates that the infant's symbiotic partner is no longer interchangeable and that there is now in operation a specific symbiotic relationship with the mother.

An important aspect of the symbiotic phase is that the immature infant cannot achieve homeostasis on his own and requires the mother for this purpose. If the mother fails beyond a certain degree, neurobiologic patterning processes are thrown out of kilter and somatic memory traces are set, which are vulnerable to later reactivation.

Mahler describes how at 4–5 months, the infant reflects alterations of states of mind—"ego states," "states of the sensorium." These are, in general, related to the oscillation of attention investment between inner sensations and symbiotic libidinal attractions. States of "alert inactivity" begin to be recognized in which the infant scans the outside world, then checks back with the mother's face. This now signals the beginning of the hatching process, and "expansion beyond the symbiotic orbit." This pattern is repeated in an expanded and more complex way in the "practicing" subphase of the separation–individuation process, and later in the rapprochement subphase in still more complex patterns.

The more nearly optimal the symbiosis, the mother's "holding behavior,"

. . . the more equipped has the child become to separate out and differentiate his self representations from the hitherto fused symbiotic self plus object representations. Especially impressive is the mutual cuing which takes place. Infants present a wide variety of cues; the mother responds selectively to only certain of these cues. The infant alters his behavior and, we may suppose, his development in relation to the selective response. From this circular interaction emerge patterns of behavior that are to become part of the child's future personality. In this way each infant becomes the child of his own particular mother. (Mahler, 1967, pp. 749–540)[1]

---

1. This observation provides an illuminating background for understanding how and how much each patient also becomes the analyzand of his own particular analyst, reflecting both the strengths and limitations of that analyst, as well as the patient's own. Observations of a similar kind in selfobject transference have led to the formulation that development occurs within and is the product of a field of intersecting subjectivities, and of psychoanalysis as a study of that field (Stolorow, Brandchaft, & Atwood, 1983).

The differentiation process occupies the subsequent period from 6 months to 3 years and is the main task of that period. It occurs along two intertwined tracks. The process of individuation consists of those achievements that mark the assumption of the child's own individuality. The process of separation consists of the child's emergence from symbiotic fusion with the mother.

Mahler's research into the separation–individuation phase consists of a systematic study of average mothers with their normal babies from 6 months through the 2nd and 3rd year of life. Although the individuating process in which the differentiation of self and object normally occurs confronts the child with (minimal) threats of object loss, which the maturationally predetermined ascendance of autonomous functioning inevitably entails, this is countered by the child's pleasure in independent functioning in the "libidinal presence of the mother." In this phase the infant becomes a toddler and "his hitherto symbiotic level of need satisfaction is gradually transformed into object relationship" (Mahler, 1962, pp. 308–309). The conceptions that here translate observable data into psychological terms are thus compatible with Freud's concepts of narcissism as a way station to the development of object love.

In Mahler's view the endstage of this process through its subphases results in a "sense of identity" and in internal "object constancy." She stresses again and again observations that demonstrate that optimal evolution of the child's innate potential "is either facilitated or hindered by the conscious and, more particularly, the unconscious attitudes of the mother. . . . Striking a balance between mothering without undue frustration, on the one hand, and without intrusion or stifling of the infant's individual, inborn rhythm of needs on the other hand, is a task not easily achieved by the average mother in our culture" (Mahler, 1962, p. 310).[2]

For a description of the psychological processes by which the result of a cohesive "sense of identity" and internal "object constancy" are achieved, Mahler leans heavily on Klein's formulations, if not on her time schedule:

We may assume that the confluence and primitive integration of the scattered "good" and "bad" memory islands into two large, good and bad part images of the mother, do not occur before the second year of life. . . . Only now, from twelve–eighteen months on, in the subsequent eighteen month period of separation–individuation, are the rapidly alternating primitive identification mechanisms possible and dominant. We

---

2. It is clear that "average expectable environment" (or "good-enough mothering") are radically different concepts when viewed from the subjective experience and structuralization of the developing child or from that of the mother or other outside observer. Failure to take this difference into account causes the observer to shift conceptual focus to "constitutional factors" and to formulating concepts of endopsychic pathology (see, e.g., Klein, 1945).

owe their description to Melanie Klein (1932). . . . Solid integration, in which there is a blending and synthesis of "good" and "bad" mother images, even in normal development . . . [is not achieved until three and a half years on. Then] the child should increasingly be able to respond to the "whole mother," to realize that one and the same person is able to gratify and disturb him. (Mahler, 1979, p. 114)

THE PERSPECTIVE OF SELF PSYCHOLOGY

The observational studies of Mahler have added enormous richness and depth to the data of early development. They have emphasized the importance of interplay between developing infant and child and his objects and have confirmed beyond question the contribution to impaired development of failures in the object in response to the child's developing, changing, and expanding needs.

The introduction of self psychology by Kohut and its gradual refinement and elaboration, with accumulated experience by him and his co-workers (Kohut, 1971, 1977; Tolpin & Kohut, 1980; Stolorow, Brandchaft, & Atwood, 1983; Stolorow & Brandchaft, 1984; Wolf, 1980) over the past dozen years, lends substance to that emphasis, while providing a sometimes different perspective on the developmental process. Its data are derived from observation of the analysis of self disorders as they appear in the selfobject transference.

A note is in order concerning this source of data. Originally, the analysis of narcissistic disorders as outlined by Kohut (1971) was confined to a relatively small group of patients, later to be recognized as comprising the group of severe self disorders (on a continuum from severe to mild) (see Stolorow & Lachmann, 1980). Two factors operating in concert have contributed to an increasing awareness of a far wider spectrum of self disorders, and to the concept of the self, the organization of experience, as the supraordinate configuration in development and in psychopathology (Kohut, 1977). The first is increased recognition with revivals of selfobject needs in analytic transferences concealed behind so-called "positive" and "negative" instinctual or differentiated object transferences. In these the analyst is experienced subjectively as indistinguishable from, as an extension of or in the functional service of, an inadequately demarcated self. These needs and the underlying primal configurations have been massively unrecognized because they may be heavily defended against or they may be discouraged by analytic nonrecognition or interpretation as "outmoded" or "defensive." A typical instance is one in which, whatever the verbal interchange, the patient has a constant preconscious or conscious concern over the analyst's regard, and in which this background concern is never made the focus of systematic investigations or is bypassed by considering it to be the consequence of projective mechanisms. The second factor involves new insights obtainable from a consistent shift in focus to one within the "contextual unit" (Schwaber, 1981) or "intersubjective field" (Stolorow *et al.*, 1983). In the latter conceptualization

... psychoanalysis seeks to illuminate phenomena that emerge within a specific psychological field constituted by the intersection of two subjectivities—that of the patient and that of the analyst . . . [as differentiated from] psychoanalysis as a science of the intrapsychic focussed on events presumed to occur within one isolated mental apparatus and from a science of the interpersonal, investigating the "behavioural facts" of the therapeutic interaction as seen from a point of observation outside the field under study. (Stolorow *et al.*, 1983, pp. 117–118)

The unique value of this source of data, with its focus at the interface of intersecting, differently organized subjectivities, is that it makes possible the exploration of an individual's subjective experience directly and in depth and thereby establishes direct links between the organization and structuralization of self- and object representations and the particular subjectivity with which that individual is interacting. No claims can be made that this source of data, and therefore the concept formation that follow from it, are superior, only different. Nonetheless, it is a direct application and extension of Mahler's critical *observations*, while omitting theory-derived *inferences* of the role of instincts in development. "The infant gradually alters his behavior in relation to [the mother's] selective response. . . . It is the unconscious need of the mother that activates out of the infant's infinite potentialities, those in particular that create for each mother the child who reflects her own unique and individual needs" (Mahler, 1967, pp. 749–750). As with any theory, its value can only be established by its utility.

Most analysts who are familiar with this process and the data it yields will, I believe, be struck as I have been by the similarity between these data and many of the observations of Mahler and her co-workers on developing children. This similarity has undoubtedly stimulated analysts, Shane and Shane (1980) as examples, to attempt to reconcile the findings from the two sources within an expanded conceptual framework. Tolpin (1980) and Kohut (1980) in numerous publications have indicated their objections, insisting on the demarcation of self psychology from the developmental psychology of Margaret Mahler.

The clinical findings of the analysis of selfobject transferences indicate that differentiation of self and object demarcation and delineation of their boundaries and individuated self-expansion occur in two overlapping stages. The stage of development of nuclear cohesion involves the consolidation of a stable cohesive self and the acquisition of those internal regulatory structures that maintain and recover self-esteem and psychological equilibrium. The stage of self-expansion is marked by the gradual demarcation and consolidation of self and object boundaries and the gradual development of an individualized array of goals and ambitions. In both stages the individual's organization of experience and its developmental impetus and direction are influenced to a great extent by the field within which it operates, the self-selfobject unit. I have referred previously to our characterization of this unit as an "intersubjective field," as it is clear to me that the infant reacts subjectively (and structuralizes his subjective world) to reflections of the way he impinges upon the subjectively organized psychological structure of his parents with their specific conscious and unconscious self and object configurations.

THE FIRST DEVELOPMENTAL TASK: STAGE OF DEVELOPING COHESION

Clinical experience with severe self disorders, where the blurring of self and object boundaries is especially marked, yields important data about differentiating processes and interferences in the first stage, that of developing cohesion. These patients correspond to the group observed and described by Mahler as "borderline." Their symptomatology is similar to that which Klein described earlier as belonging to the paranoid–schizoid position. These patients show a persistently negatively colored self-regard, a marked degree of temporal and spatial instability, and a marked vulnerability to fragmentation anxiety and disintegration symptomatology (Stolorow & Lachmann, 1980). They suffer protracted states of disequilibrium and dysfunction, severe disruptive states. These states appear to be analogous to some of the "ego states" of altered sensorium observed by Mahler. This multifaceted clinical syndrome generally occupies the first and sometimes prolonged period of analysis of severe self disorders. The patient in this stage attempts to form a bond with the analyst within which he can maintain and recover basic psychological equilibrium and continuity of function. In such cases the individual has manifestly failed to have taken over intrapsychically central regulatory functions. On this basis it has therefore been conceptualized that such patients suffer from a structural deficiency disorder—referring to structural in a broader sense than the narrower definition of tripartite structure. In the face of such inability to maintain or readily recover psychological equilibrium (and with it a reliable sense of reality and continuity of their own existence), these patients seem to have two general courses open to them. On the one hand they are thrown back upon a variety of self-soothing efforts—drugs, alcohol, and food especially—to reduce tension and/or a variety of self-stimulating efforts. On the other hand they turn to objects, termed "selfobjects," as a substitute for a variety of equilibrium-maintaining and restoring functions and structure they lack. When this turning coalesces around the person, or more properly, around the functions and qualities of the analyst, a developmental process has been reinstated that was interrupted at specific points in childhood (Kohut, 1971).

CLINICAL ILLUSTRATION OF STRUCTURAL DEFICIT: MS. B

Ms. B, 35 years old, entered analysis following a divorce from the father of her three children. Shy and timid, she spoke in a voice barely above a whisper. In spite of her evident high intelligence, her life was one of substantial hardship and deprivation, contributed to by a paralysis against acting in her own behalf. She received only the barest financial support from her ex-husband, and was underpaid in her employment. Her demeanor, her posture, and her words, while retaining a modicum of pride, nonetheless conveyed an attitude of shattered confidence in herself and a low-keyed and bleak expectation of what life held in store for her. This became more glaring when, as the analysis unfolded, broadly diverse and striking talents and accomplishments emerged from beneath her self-disparagement.

Her outstanding complaints at first centered around the persistence of a pervasive contentless depression with painful feelings of exhaustion. As the analysis proceeded these states of mind were relieved during the analytic week. When the week drew to a close, and on weekends, she would regularly experience periods of increased tension, apprehension about her future, and a marked inability to think, concentrate, or organize herself around her tasks. Sometimes she would lose her sense of direction and spatial continuity, start toward a destination and find herself off course, having failed to take a turn with which in other states of mind she was thoroughly familiar. In more severe states she would feel herself floating in space without any attachment, and at such times also experienced herself as shrinking smaller and smaller in a terrifying way. Sometimes she sought relief from those states and the threatening loss of the reality of her existence through sexual relationships, clearly in desperate attempts to halt the fragmenting and depleting processes she so graphically described. Such states were reminiscent of those of Mahler's patient A (1971, p. 417). Ms. B, as had patient A, wanted to sit up. Loss of visual contact with the analyst would regularly produce this symptomatology while reestablishment of visual contact would terminate it.

From many observations I find myself in agreement with the inference that "the earliest waking life of the infant centers around his continuous attempts to achieve homeostasis" (Mahler, 1975, p. 43). In the neonatal state these center around physiologic homeostasis in order to ensure physical survival. In this process the mother, in complementing and completing the functional unit, has had to undergo a transformation for which the antenatal period has prepared her, as the infant has been prepared for his own part. The father is also involved from the first through interaction with his wife and the effects upon her of his own subjectivity in relation to her and the infant. This preparation of both parties in one phase for the changed role of a succeeding phase proceeds from the infant's birth to the parents' death. Perhaps this period of postpartum establishment of a physiologic homeostatic unit corresponds in time to the period described as autism by Mahler.

Autism sometimes carries the implication of absorption in need-satisfying or wish-fulfilling fantasy as a denial of reality (Mahler *et al.*, 1975, p. 6). These inferences are drawn in part from the observations of "borderline" and psychotic states. My own observations lead me to infer that these reflect a subjective view of the world in which no solid boundaries have as yet come into existence. The adult observer's view of this state as delusional or involving denial of reality seems to me an example of the subjectivity of the observer.[3]

I believe that from the first the primary relationship is dictated by the functional position the mother occupies in the child's biologic system and in his rudimentary psychological field. Clinical material indicates that first vectors that operate in the transference are needs to maintain within initially small and later expanding limits and to recover psychological homeostasis. This view of an archaic bond in the service of an emerging nuclear self questions the accepted view that the earliest psychological tie is instinctual, unless the concept of need-satisfying is broadened significantly. The drive relationship appears to accompany and be secondary to the functional, regulation-maintaining tie within the self and (self)object contextual unit. Equally, when these primitive states are reenacted in the analytic transference, it is not my impression that our patients seek unlimited gratification. Rather, I observe that having reestablished a functional unit, they seek to maintain both the unit and the temporal stability and spatial cohesiveness of the self, which depend upon that tie and which protect against disintegration. When these needs are inadequately met (insufficiently to avert throwing the neurobiologic processes out of kilter), or when ensuing states of disruption are insufficiently responded to, the stage is set for that hypercathexis of behavior that will later appear to the observer as "clinging" and "coercive" (Mahler, 1971, p. 413). It seems to me also that the infant begins his existence with a "confident expectation" that his basic needs will be met. When the infant's expectations are responded to optimally, he gradually accomplishes his first developmental task. The infant retains a basic sense of supported self-confidence, an essentially positive outlook, and the foundational elements of a "basic trust." The basic trust, which will later develop, is dependent not only on memory traces of positive, confidence-imbuing selfobject experiences; it also will be based on a subjective sense of the growing strength of the infant's own psychological structure, on the increasing ability to trust his own perceptions, and upon the experience of having been able to influence significantly the conditions that affect the infant in his own milieu. I find that "basic trust" and

---

3. The clinical significance of this theoretical difference cannot be overestimated. When a patient with a severe self disorder attempts to reestablish an archaic bond in which self and object boundaries are fluid, ill defined, or nonexistent, interpretations of such states as defensive will regularly be experienced as severe narcissistic traumata and result in borderline symptomatology (Brandchaft & Stolorow, 1984).

psychic object constancy are dependent upon the prior achievement of a firm nuclear self, not the reverse. These crucial psychological developments are always co-determined by the adequacy of archaic selfobject experiences in relation to the particular child and his needs. This view profoundly influences the focus of analytic interest, the observations that are made, and the nature of interpretations, which in this phase concentrate on investigating and attempting to explain in dynamic and genetic terms the complex psychological states and changes in these states that are reactive to changes and dysynchronies in the analytic (selfobject) milieu.

Such findings support Kohut's view that the central task and accomplishment of childhood is the attainment of a nuclear cohesive self. Progress in this primary area brings with it gradual differentiation of self from within the initially poorly differentiated self–selfobject matrix, together with a gradual demarcation of self and object boundaries. The self–selfobject unit undergoes various progressive and regressive transformations but persists throughout life. It appears that the "shadowing," "refueling," and "rapprochement" Mahler describes are indications of the persistence of this basic tie in successive stages.

Clinical findings support Mahler's theory that this unit persists throughout life. However, this persistence is accounted for by the changing, maturing, and expanding selfobject needs of the growing individual. Equally, the maturation of selfobject needs requires phase-specific changes in the child's selfobjects to enable caretakers to assimilate the child's changes into their own subjectively structured preexisting self and object representations. The persistence throughout the entire life cycle of the archaic need for the "all-good" symbiotic mother of infancy is an indication of a partial phase-specific failure. "Independence," in contrast to the transformation and maturation of selfobject ties, marks a breakdown of the unit, even though that may be necessary for further development if the unit fails to subserve its essential purpose in the maturational transformation of experience.

The needs for responses that will result in a consolidation of the nuclear cohesive self, as well as the distress of mounting tension when this consolidation is impaired, are communicated by various cues. As previously mentioned, Mahler emphasizes this cuing (Mahler et al., 1975). The mother also transmits cues to which the baby responds so that the baby adapts his own requirements to the conditions established by the mother's cues. However, the mother may not make the necessary "recentering" changes and may be grossly unresponsive to the infant's expanding and diversifying cues. Instead she may need the baby to be exquisitely responsive to her cues in order to maintain her sense of self. The infant will adapt to the mother's cues if that is necessary to maintain his ties, and permanent developmental arrest or derailment may occur. The child may then, for example, hide his own needs and become a "good baby," develop a false self and a premature "self-reliance," articulate his own distancing devices, and/or develop his own means of soothing or protest.

All these component and hypertrophied functions will remain unintegrated into the internal regulating structure of the personality.

Affect ties are established on the basis of primary selfobject needs: loving, when these needs are responded to and thus contribute to the cohesion of the self; aggressive–assertive or imperatively raging or erotogenic, when there is a breakdown of the functioning of the unit. When drive derivatives, sexual or aggressive, then appear as subsequent organizing configurational units, we have come to recognize these as urgent attempts at restoration. A derailment has occurred in the normal progression toward nuclear self-cohesion. In either instance long-term and repeated experience has shown us that if we interpret the erotic or destructive manifestations as primary when they appear in the transference (e.g., the desire to possess and control the oedipal or preoedipal mother, or the recurrence of primary destructive drive derivatives in negative transferences), the disruption regularly increases and conflict symptomatology appears. Alternatively, there may be a compliance and constriction of the reactivated selfobject needs and a repetition of the limitation of transformational, structure-building, and repairing potential. Similar consequences follow interpretations of these events as defensive—against the conflicts of ambivalence—or as persistence of archaic splitting mechanisms evidencing a failure to have synthesized good and bad object representations. However, when we understand the underlying vulnerability of an insufficiently integrated self, interpret the underlying disruptive state, and relate it to breakup of the equilibrium and function maintaining self–selfobject unit, equilibrium is restored, self-cohesiveness is reestablished, and the unit recovers its functional integrity. Such interpretations, which take note of the specific fragmentation–depletion experiences, affects, and sequelae of each individual patient, reenact and replicate in the analytic setting the idealized maternal function, which regularly integrates asynchronous experiences and affects within a larger continuous organizing process.

I find that gradually, through the repeated analyses of these disruptive states, the cohesiveness of the self increases, and a floor appears, which maintains and recovers the patient's self-esteem. The intrapsychic assumption of regulatory functions then follows. In my observation each step in this interaction promotes the differentiating process, both the temporary breakup and the way in which reestablishment occurs. A cohesive self forms and with it a recognizable continuous, definable, subjective "I." Put in reverse, differentiation of self and object are interfered with in direct proportion to the extent to which more archaic functions continue to be vested in the selfobject so that self differentiation and maturation, progressive demarcation of self and object boundaries, and progressive expansion and broadening of the self–selfobject unit are frozen. I find that gradually increasing self-cohesion precedes and enhances the ability to maintain intrapsychic connection with the object through positively toned memory traces.

Before the infant has succeeded in establishing a durably cohesive nuclear self and thus has to rely upon the mother for the achievement and recovery of homeostasis, failure beyond a certain degree results in "neurobiological patterning processes being thrown out of kilter and somatic memory traces being set which are vulnerable to later reactivation" (Mahler, 1967, p. 745). I find evidence of this in severe disruptive states and that the specific vulnerabilities, that is, the failures of idealized or firming function to which the patient is reacting, are explained in that they contain the encapsulated and encoded memory traces of such out-of-kilter early experiences. These can be recovered to certain depth (Brandchaft, 1983). My technique, especially in severe disorders of the self, accommodates to the principle that failures in the analytic surround should be kept to a realistic minimum in order for structuralization to replace out-of-kilter fragmentation. However, experiences of selfobject failure are inevitable and predetermined, and these should be investigated carefully from within the patient's subjective frame of reference.

I have observed that behind mental states, which are frequently described as negative transference or resistances, are severe disruptive states. I thus find myself in disagreement with Kernberg's (1975) conclusion that these so-called negative transferences or resistances are reactions of frustration that indicate defensive splitting and a primary failure of synthesis of good and bad internal objects, and with Mahler's (1971) conclusion that they are the ejection of bad objects in order to keep internal all-good objects intact. I also find myself in disagreement with those who maintain that homeostatic equilibrium, from which differentiating and integrating processes emerge, is dependent upon the balance between libidinal and destructive instincts, or instinctual investments, or the relation between internalized good and bad objects.

To sum up, my clinical findings lead me to postulate that early development is centered around attempts to maintain and recover self-cohesion within the self–selfobject functional unit. The central threat to the developing infant and child is that of disintegration. This may be severe or mild, may be experienced or countered in a large variety of ways, but it now dominates development until nuclear cohesion is firmly established. I specifically differ with the assumptions of Klein that the primary threat arises originally from the operation of a death instinct. I do not believe from my clinical evidence that disintegration is defensively employed as described by Segal (1964), but rather that it is passively and helplessly experienced. That is why, in my view, patients cling with such desperation—why they employ such desperately coersive efforts to stay the threat of fragmentation. It seems to me that the inference of an ego actively fragmenting itself was made in order to fit unmistakable observational data (fragmentation) into a preexisting theory (the infant's supposed persecution anxiety arising from death or destructive instincts).

My differences extend also to Mahler's view of disintegration in the symbiotic phase, and are not altered by her rejection of the concept of the death instinct. She retains the essential features of the importance of drive derivatives to equilibrium maintenance and subsequent intrapsychic processes. She and her co-workers conceptualize this as follows:

Dawning and recurrent awareness of separateness are denied because such awarenesses threaten to unleash destructive un-neutralized aggression beyond the infant's capability to rid himself of it. . . . The concept of narcissism remains rather obscure in both psychoanalytic theory and usage unless we place sufficient emphasis on the vicissitudes of the aggressive drive. During the course of normal development protective systems safeguard the infant's body from oral sadistic pressures which begin to constitute a threat to his body integrity from the fourth month on. (Mahler *et al.*, 1975, p. 47)

In other words, our divergences are not related to the narrow consideration of death versus aggressive instinct, or of earlier or later postulation of complex psychological processes, but the broader question of centrality (cohesiveness and integration of total nuclear self vs. integration of drive derivatives or internal object representations) to the discrimination between primary and secondary factors in the developmental process.

The requirements for analytic interpretation are different when the analyst believes the patient clings because that patient considers his destructiveness a threat than when the analyst is aware that the loss of (self)object threatens the continuity and vitality of the patient's self-experience, and the dissolution of structural boundaries of the self and so undermines the continuity of awareness that he exists at all. In the first instance, the pathogenic factor that occupies the therapeutic focus is fear of instinct; in the second, it is the fragility of organization which is necessitating the urgent restoration of the selfobject tie.

In my findings "separation anxiety" and "anxiety of the loss of love," describe the precipitating factors but fail to take account of the subjective depth experience. This seems to be one or another degree and form of fragmentation or depletion anxiety induced by physical or psychological separations of the pair, which constitute the functional intersubjective unit. Severe and repeated fragmentation experiences interfere with and derail differentiating self and object processes; they bring it about that archaic selfobject needs remain unmodified. The structure whereby regulatory functions might be carried on internally remains unacquired. Untransformed, these selfobject needs continue in a now out-of-phase distorted and imperative form. The splitting, which Klein, Mahler, and Kernberg note, is not a defensive measure of an immature ego but a product of recurrent fragmentation that does not permit normal differentiation and integration to occur. I find my evidence fully supports the observations of the early Kleinians with regard to the child's subjective experience of his objects (see above quotation from Heimann, 1952). I disagree that the infant maintains this subjective view of his objects defensively, but find rather that the infant's experiences of a poorly differentiated object is characteristic of the earliest period of life before differentiating processes have become consolidated developmentally in the form of a cohesive self and stable object representations.

The establishment of a nuclear cohesive self marks the completion of the first major stage of the differentiating process. It is accompanied by a cognitive, experiential, and functional demarcation of self and object boundaries. It sets the stage for the beginnings of individualized self-directed goals and ambitions, the further differentiation of self and object, and the emergence of a new set of maturing and syntonic expectations of each toward the other. The self–selfobject milieu, relieved of its more archaic functions, is thus transformed into a more complex unit, employed in the service of backing up, buttressing, inspiring, encouraging, guiding, and shaping the further development of an individualizing self toward the living-out of its basic design, the fulfillment of its own destiny.

CLINICAL CASE: MR. J

Mr. J was a 40-year-old professional man who entered treatment with intense hypochondriacal fears. Tall, dark, enormously engaging and appealing when not wracked with fear, he nonetheless considered himself small and unattractive. He was aware that although he enjoyed some aspects of his professional life, it left him with a feeling of a lack of fulfillment. He sought relief from these feelings, as well as from more acutely distressing states, by an ingenious variety of sexual activities with a number of women with whom he maintained connections for such occasions and purposes. His hypochondriacal fears centered around the threat of cancer in various parts of his body. The specific predisposition may have been created by his relation to his overanxious mother, who appears to have been hypochondriacally concerned with any indication of the onset of a childhood illness or injury. She would attempt to dress him and to prepare him in such a way as to ensure that he would go through his childhood without colds or other illness and without incurring setbacks or reversals. Each day, for example, until he was 10 years old, she would stand him naked on the toilet seat while she scrubbed him before he went off to school, carefully retracting his foreskin to make certain no debris remained hidden to do its unseen damage and to be discovered too late. Whenever in spite of her precautions he hurt himself or caught a cold, she always conveyed the impression to him that he had done something wrong.

His attacks of hypochondriasis always followed some disappointment or rejection by a person of importance to him, an older professional associate in whose practice he had joined, or a woman friend who deserted him. On such occasions he would panic, inspect himself obsessively, and be unable to concentrate on anything but the impending doom.

On one occasion following a 3-week break in the analysis, he had a very severe reaction. As in previous episodes, he demanded absolute reassurance that nothing was wrong with him. When I failed to provide the powerful response he needed, he went to a succession of oncologists. Any hesitation in their manner or voice filled him with renewed terror. He finally sought out the specialist whom most other specialists agreed was the most authoritative specialist in the field. He described how the physician appeared in his white coat—tall, stately, and absolutely assured, "like Moses coming down from Mt. Sinai with the word of God." "Moses" inspected him carefully then told him in unequivocal tones, "Now listen! You do not have cancer! There is nothing wrong with you! I want you to stop looking at that pimple—it will go away! And I don't want you to come back for this ever again, do you understand?" The patient described how his anxiety disappeared like snow melting in the warm sun!

He subsequently described how disappointed he had been that I wasn't more concerned. He felt he was dying, that he couldn't stand the pain anymore, and that I had acted as if nothing serious was happening to him! He revealed that then he had turned to God and had pleaded with God to give him just one more chance. He confessed that he hadn't done with himself what God would have liked him to for having been created; he hadn't realized the enormous potential that God had granted him. He had not studied in school, he had caroused around, drinking and overeating. He pleaded with the deity, "Won't you give me one more chance to realize my potential; to fulfill my destiny!"

This patient's case demonstrates the beginning engagement of an archaic idealizing transference toward the analyst, whose unavailability to him brought about a severe disruptive state with deeply frightening fragmentation anxiety. The patient was unable to maintain a sense of structural continuity of his body self. In this state a more archaic regressive form of idealized selfobject emerged in the form of a relationship to God and to the materialized god in the white coat. Impressive is the patient's awareness of his need to acquire the structure that he so desperately lacked through a link with an omniscient source of comfort and strength. Implicit also is the recognition that the belated achievement of a firm self has the precondition of Mr. J's ability to realize his own as yet unlimited potential.

The achievement of a nuclear cohesive self is marked clinically by a marked decrease in the intensity and duration of disruptive states experienced on separations from the analyst, together with an abatement of measures such as drugs, overeating, and compulsive sexuality or masturbation that were formerly employed in maintaining the structural integrity of the self. It ushers in a new stage with new selfobject needs and thus requires new understandings and analytic responses. Very frequently, the situation seems to resemble that described by Mahler in relation to the ascendancy of free locomotor capacity and the child's ability to stand upright (1971, pp. 409–410). This nodal achievement in childhood, accompanied by a cognitive development of the beginning of representational intelligence, probably marks the phase of nuclear cohesion. The child proudly displays each accomplishment and proclaims joyfully "look at me everybody!" In analysis, very frequently, the achievement of psychological balance, the ability to stand more firmly on one's own psychological structure, introduces, sometimes hesitantly and tentatively, sometimes effusively, the stage of the grandiose self. With it are activated intense yearnings for mirroring responses needed to firm and confirm the reality of a differentiating self-representation. "Mirroring" needs refer to the experience of the patient and not necessarily to the actual responses of the analyst. We would presume that these mirroring needs reactivate the most basic configurations of the rapprochement phase together with the developmental deficits stemming from selfobject limitations and failures in that period.

In this and subsequent phases of development and throughout life, the self–selfobject unit is no less necessary than in the earlier stages although its functions and qualities keep changing. "As seen by the psychoanalytic self psychologist, normal development . . . does not rest on a 'separation of self and object.' . . . the essential therapeutic task is not the achievement of self–object separation but the re-entering into the course of the line of self–selfobject relationships, at the point where it had been traumatically interrupted in early life" (Kohut, 1980, p. 453).

The responses of selfobjects to the needs of the developing child are determined by a host of factors. Although it is self-evident that the infant interacts at every phase with the personality structures of the parents, it is no less true that the parents are interacting with their own more complex, rigidified, and highly organized personality structures with the germinal structures of the infant–child. If the subjectively organized psychological structures of the parents, with their conscious and unconscious self and object configurations, are not able to adapt themselves sufficiently to the changing, individual, phase-specific needs of the developing child, the stage is set for developmental arrest, derailment, and pathological symptom and character formation. Numerous factors determine insufficient adaptations in the parents and prevent the recentering that is necessary at successive developmental phases. One crucial factor, which is pertinent to this discussion, is the extent to which parents have failed to establish firm and stable self and object boundaries. Such boundaries are necessary if the parents are to be able to participate in the child's subjective experience, to reinvoke the necessary communality of boundary, without the threat of losing their own. It is this capability that enables the child similarly to develop the ability to share in the parents' subjective experience without losing his own, with all the momentous implications of socialization as enhancement or as self-obliterative. In a previous paper I wrote:

In childhood and in analysis, the conflict situation was produced by the same forces; not the intrinsic intrapsychic energies and agencies, but the insistent supra-ordination of the pathological selfobject needs of his objects, including me in the transference, to the legitimate selfobject needs which remained from his childhood—to define an authentic self and to initiate its own intrinsic pattern of development within a (responsive) setting. (Brandchaft, 1983, p. 352)

Increased experience with the analysis of selfobject transferences leads me to emphasize and expand this point. Conflict situations and resultant structuralized intrapsychic conflict seem to accompany both phases of self-development. Mahler (1975, p. 80) has described the child's fear of the mother's engulfment during the rapprochement phase. She has described how the mother's need to maintain symbiotic fusion interferes with the normal development of individuation. Analyses of self disorders reveal a wider area in which the mother's archaic narcissistic needs and self structural deficiencies forcefully occupy the center of the child–mother unit and thus can impair the child's development in every phase. The child adapts to the mother's cues if the mother cannot adapt to those of the child. If, in addition, the child cannot find a satisfactory route to differentiated growth in turning to the father, the conditions have been created for structuralized conflict. When the child adapts to the condition dictated by the imperative of maintaining a tie to its faulty selfobject, the child restricts his own differentiating and individuating growth. These conditions may include the wholesale inclusion or exclusion of perceptions, because such perceptions threaten the parents' own perceptions of themselves. These conditions also include the child centering himself around the expectations of the parents and organizing himself around the avoidance of injury to their narcissistic vulnerabilities. This process can begin early and tends, with repetition, to become automatic. The resulting conflict is not the conflict of preoedipal instinctuality or of the defensive persistence of primitive object relations; it is the conflict between stunted and deformed germinal nuclei containing (now out-of-phase) selfobject strivings for a pathway toward maturation and transformation of selfhood on the one side and, on the other, the restrictive and defensive structure that has been laid down.

We find that a similar process occurs frequently in the oedipal period in relation to the father. A spurt in development, and specifically toward consolidation and expansion of the gender self, occurs where its appearance is greeted and responded to enthusiastically by parental selfobjects. However, the spurt can meet with a wide variety of faulty selfobject responses. The films *The Great Santini* and *Amadeus* currently depict this situation in artistic form. In *The Great Santini* it is the father whose narcissistic integration is threatened by the growing manhood of his son. In *Amadeus* it is Salieri, the greatest court composer of the day, who is the twilight of his career realizes his own mediocrity when the young Mozart appears and performs, and who subsequently disintegrates and descends into an interminable narcissistic rage against Mozart and God. Hostility and resentment toward a parent, and later an analyst, who blocks the yearning to complete the self and enlarge its horizons, are certain to exist in conscious, preconscious, and unconscious form and to break out sometimes violently. However, it is a grievous error to consider, as it is frequently considered, that the normal vigorous strivings of a child to realize his maximum potential are indications of patricidal (or matricidal) wishes—even if the parent reacts in a manner to give credence to such a view.

CLINICAL CASE: MR. K

Mr. K was a 52-year-old man who had had a prolonged analysis. He was a composer of unquestioned talent, though he questioned it many times. He began to play the piano at the relatively late age of 11 years, and at 16 years of age performed solo in concert. At the age of 21 years, he was commissioned by his country's leading music foundation, at the recommendation of its outstanding conductor, to write an opera. From the drabbest and dreariest of childhoods, the world opened up before him. If his childhood fantasies of being remembered with Mozart, Beethoven, Schönberg, and Stravinsky were not then realized, still, a sizeable opportunity lay ahead and excited him—and he fled. He fled to obscurity, across the country to Hollywood, where his talents found increasing recognition, though they now were patterned to someone else's story and concealed in the background behind visual images—stopped, started, and cut into at the whim of the director or the editor.

After some years of analysis his old yearnings returned. But composing was excruciating. He would start, tear up what he had written, start again, and repeat the same process a thousand, tormented times. He would go to his desk, be seized with paralyzing anxiety, and flee. And berate himself. What lunacy had him in its grip that he continued to pretend that he was a composer. A composer without a note! Even if he could complete a piece now, he would be laughed at. All the others who had started with him had folios of solid work—many pieces—while he had been busy stepping on his feet and making money. His contempt for himself was boundless! Again and again he determined to burn his music, every page, and himself together with it—or again flee to some small town in exile and live out his days in invisible obscurity.

Some progress in his analysis, some strength borrowed, some understanding of his fear of annihilating criticism and his consequent need for perfection to avoid it, enabled him to begin and complete several pieces. Again an important commission was offered him and again the terror. Deadlines! He would never finish. It was no use! No one would be surprised when he failed to deliver; everyone would know that he was a fraud, as indeed he himself had always known in his deepest of hearts.

But in the analysis a pattern began to emerge more clearly, and I noted it to him. Every time he seemed to feel more expansive, more optimistic, and more confident in himself, it was immediately followed by a constraining reaction. He confirmed this and noted that it also applied to his work. That is, he recognized that his work was not characterized by unyielding and unremitting obstacles. Rather, he would think about some part of it, begin to feel alive and enthusiastic, and then become anxious and the process would stop. This succession repeated itself over and over again. Subsequently he would approach his desk, begin, and then become anxious. He would have to eat, walk around his garden, talk to his wife, water the plants. He had the whole composition worked out in his head, could see it and hear it from start to finish—yet he could not commit it to paper. He was thus repeating endlessly in miniature the pattern of his young manhood when opportunity opened its door and he fled. It became clear that the expansion of his self, its growth, signal demarcation, and creative progress had come to be experienced as a threat to him. Now important pieces of his history emerged.

In one session Mr. K was describing the home of his childhood. He had had a room until his brother was born when Mr. K was 4 years old. After that he shared his room. But he recalled that the room had nothing to mark it as his. Not a book, not a picture, not a favorite toy could he recall. He remembered that he did manage to save money laboriously over a long period of time until he had enough to buy a bicycle, which he had long yearned for and was told he could have if he saved his money. But when he asked his mother to buy him the bicycle, she said she needed the money for something very important and would he mind if she borrowed it. He had agreed, but he now recognized that she would have been devastated if he had not given it to her. He recalled how many times when he had said no, she had turned from him saying, "Well maybe you'll do it for your stepmother," and how frequently she would cry, "You're killing your mother!" He thought about the bicycle and he thought now that she didn't need the money! She was afraid he would get hurt on the bicycle. We came to see how much she regarded any excursions he could make into the outside world as threats to her security. How often was repeated the sequence of his world opening up and hers closing down, and how gradually he adapted to her needs and became more and more constricted. He stayed very close to home!

One session saw him again talking about his lonely adolescence. "What did you do during all that time," I asked, as he told how he had been unable to concentrate in school and frequently had been truant. "Nothing," he replied, "absolutely nothing!" But we both simultaneously then recognized that in fact he had been practicing on the instrument a relative had given him, and that he spent many hours a day with his music. We also became aware of the origin of the feeling that he was doing nothing. His parents responded to his interest with evident anxiety. On the one hand they were proud of his early accomplishments, which were truly unique, of prizes he won and of praise that was repeated to them. On the other hand they would remind him that such an interest could not enable him to earn a livelihood, that he should develop an interest in business or something else that was substantial. Playing piano was OK in a finishing school for girls . . . or perhaps as a hobby of the son of a rich man! He would try to tell his father of his dreams and of his longings to write great music, to be sought out and sought after and listened to by audiences who would appreciate how beautiful his music was and who would recognize and confirm that he had a contribution to make. His father would become taut and invariably respond, "Right! Big shot! They're waiting for you! How come you're wasting your life!"

An additional factor emerged. Mr. K had always felt that his father was a sweet, if distant, man who was and remained a junior partner in a small grocery store—the object of continuous caustic scorn and abuse by his wife who blamed him daily for her lost opportunities and the emptiness of her life. He recalled how he felt sorry for his father, and he remembered especially how bored and irritated his father was when someone praised Mr. K. Memories returned of his father's frequent denigrating comments, his father's readiness to believe anything bad that anyone reported to him about his son, "Yes," he would say, "That's how he is. His mother can't do anything with him!"

I have come to recognize this situation as prototypical. The child's world opens up and that of the parent closes down. A threat is posed by the child's growth, expansion, or spontaneity. The mother reacts to the threat and the child's expansion is suppressed. A father's narcissism is threatened by the son's achievements as they make him more aware of his own missed opportunities. Such experiences have come to be familiar to self psychologists. They indicate a need for a reconsideration of the metapsychological assumptions regarding the constituents of the oedipal conflict as described by Freud and with its centrality for development of psychopathology. My findings indicate that these failures in a unit that the expanding child continues to need are a major obstacle in the crucial phase of individuated striving and achievement. One might regard them as failures in the transformation potentialities of the self–selfobject functional unit, a reversal of the normal intersubjective field.

SUMMARY

Various views of the psychological differentiation of self and object have been presented and contrasted in this chapter. Clinical material has been presented to illustrate how the concepts of self psychology in this area have been derived. It is the author's belief that the reconstructions permitted by the analysis of selfobject transferences, together with the perspective of development occurring within a field of interacting subjectivities, afford the possibility of confirming, extending, and amending the historic contributions of Mahler to the further understanding of human psychological development.

REFERENCES

Brandchaft, B. (1983). Negativism, negative therapeutic reaction and self psychology. In A. Goldberg (Ed.), *Future of psychoanalysis* (pp 327-362). New York: International Universities Press.

Brandchaft, B., & Stolorow, R. (1984). *The borderline concept: Pathological character and iatrogenic myth?* In J. Lichtenberg *et al.* (Eds.), *Empathy II* (pp. 333-358). Hillsdale, NJ: The Analytic Press.

Heimann, P. (1952). Certain functions of introjection and projection in early infancy. In *Developments in psychoanalysis* (pp. 122-168). London: Hogarth Press.

Kernberg, O. (1975). *Borderline conditions and pathological narcissism.* New York: Jason Aronson.

Klein, M. (1932). *The psychoanalysis of children.* London: Hogarth Press.

Klein, M. (1945). The oedipus complex in the light of anxities. In *Contributions to psychoanalysis* (pp. 339-390). London: Hogarth Press, 1952.

Kohut, H. (1971). *The psychoanalysis of the self.* New York: International Universities Press.

Kohut, H. (1977). *The restoration of the self.* New York: International Universities Press.

Kohut, H. (1978). *The search for the self* (Vol. 2) (P. Ornstein, Ed.). New York: International Universities Press.

Kohut, H. (1980). Summarizing reflections. In A. Goldberg (Ed.), *Advances in self psychology* (pp. 473-554). New York: International Universities Press.

Mahler, M. (1962). Thoughts about development and individuation. *The Psychoanalytic Study of the Child, 18,* 307-325.

Mahler, M. (1967). On human symbiosis and the vicissitudes of individuation, *Journal of the American Psychoanalytic Association, 15,* 740-763.

Mahler, M. (1971). A study of the separation-individuation process. *The Psychoanalytic Study of the Child, 26,* 403-422.

Mahler, M. (1979). *The selected papers of Margaret S. Mahler, M.D.* New York: Jason Aronson.

Mahler, M., Pine, F., & Bergman, A. (1975). *The psychological birth of the human infant,* New York: Basic Books.

Schwaber, E. (1981). Narcissism, self psychology, and the listening perspective. *Annal of Psychoanalysis, 9,* 115-132.

Segal, H. (1964). *Introduction to the work of Melanie Klein.* New York: Basic Books.

Shane, M., & Shane, E. (1980). Introduction and psychoanalytic developmental theories of the self. In A. Goldberg (Ed.), *Advances in self psychology* (pp. 19-46). New York: International Universities Press.

Stolorow, R., & Brandchaft, B. (1984). Intersubjectivity II: Development and pathogenesis. In G. Atwood & R. Stolorow (Eds.), *Structures of subjectivity* (pp. 65-84). Hillsdale, NJ: The Analytic Press.

Stolorow, R., Brandchaft, B., & Atwood, G. (1983). Intersubjectivity in psychoanalytic treatment: With special reference to archaic states. *Bulletin of the Menninger Clinic, 47,* 117-128.

Stolorow, R., & Lachmann, F. (1980). *Psychoanalysis of developmental arrests.* New York: International Universities Press.

Tolpin, M. (1980). Discussion of Shane's paper. In A. Goldberg (Ed.), *Advances in self psychology* (pp. 47-68). New York: International Universities Press.

Tolpin, M., & Kohut, H. (1980). The psychopathology of the first years of life: Disorders of the self. In S. Greenspan & G. Pollock (Eds.), *The course of life.* Washington, DC: U.S. Government Printing Office.

Wolf, E. (1980). On the developmental line of selfobject relations. In A. Goldberg (Ed.), *Advances in self psychology* (pp. 117-135). New York: International Universities Press.

CHAPTER EIGHT

Early Determinants of Self and Object Constancy

RENATA GADDINI

The concept of object constancy implies the capacity to internalize an object representation in a stable way. In order to be able to do so, a basic core of mental organization must have arisen so as to include an inner space into which to internalize. This basic core, which is bodily and mental at the same time, originates in the very first months of life from mother's holding; it has been indicated by Winnicott by the term "self."

DEVELOPMENT OF THE CONCEPT OF SELF

As we know, Freud did not use the term "self." In his 1915 paper he refers to love–hate relationships as an attitude of the ego. In fact, in the papers of that period, prior to the introduction of the structural theory, Freud uses the term "ego" most often to mean what we now call self. He mentions, for instance, the relation of the total ego to objects. As I see it, "total ego" is close to what Winnicott has referred to as the self. In Winnicott's 1971 letter to his French translator, who had questioned him about the word "self," he wrote:

For me the self, which is not the ego, is the person who is me, who is only me, who has a totality based on the operation of the maturational process. At the same time the self has parts, and in fact is constituted by these parts. These parts agglutinate from a direction interior–exterior in the course of the operation of the maturational process, aided as it must be (maximally at the beginning) by the human environment which holds and handles and in a live way facilitates. The self finds itself naturally placed in the body, but may in certain circumstances become dissociated from the body and the body from it. The self essentially recognizes itself in the eyes and facial expression of the mother and in the mirror which can come to represent the mother's face. Eventually the self arrives at a significant relationship between the child and the sum of the identifications which (after enough of incorporation and introjection of mental representations) become organized in the shape of an internal psychic living reality. The relationship between the boy or girl with his or her own internal psychic organization becomes reinforced or modified according to the expectations that are displayed by the father and mother and those who have become significant in the external life of the individual. It is the self and the life of the self that alone make sense of action or of living from the point of view of the individual who has grown so far and who is continuing to grow from dependence and immaturity towards independence and the capacity to identify with mature love objects without loss of individual identity.

THE SELF AND THE OUTSIDE WORLD

The theoretical frame of reference for understanding how the infant moves from the organization of a self to a relationship with the outside world—a move requiring the previous achievement of a sense of self constancy—is rather basic. We assume that self constancy will link up with object constancy to construct a sense of reality. Greenacre's (1968) speculations on this point are most apt. "Has the latter [sense of reality] reached an equilibrium permitting a base of ordinary expectation from the surroundings, or is it at a stage when only the very familiar is to be relied upon?"

What does the "very familiar" mean? To me, it means the continuity with mother for which the neonate searches, to make up for his loss and incompletion. It means reunion with the mother after separation at birth.[1]

Mahler refers to this stage as the "symbiotic phase." In my view the psychological birth of the individual with an initial sense of self might be usefully differentiated from an earlier stage (first 3 months?), which is the stage of the organization of the self. As described by Winnicott it is formed on the basis of bodily experiences and is therefore concrete. Escalona (1963) has come close to this idea. In her discussion of the determinants of individual development, she writes that early learning takes place through an area of concrete experiences, including olfactory, tactile, and coenesthetic contacts with the mother. With increasing neurophysiologic maturation, these bodily experiences undergo a process of mentalization. From 3 months on, perceptual skills as well as fine motor skills (prehension, reaching out, etc.) mature rapidly. Consequently the infant, initially capable only of visually tracking for fleeting moments, now can look and see distinctly. Distant senses (sight, vocal communication, etc.) acquire continuously increasing value in respect to the "close" senses (touch and smell) in this stage of development. All these events contribute to the mentalization of the self and to the organization of the "vicissitudes of pleasure," which W. Clifford Scott (1981) refers to as

---

1. Bion's (1965) idea of "catastrophe" as connected to a "change," for example, to the introduction of the different at a time when psychological birth with a sense of self has not yet taken place, comes to mind in this connection.

"positive affects." In this developmental view, feeling and thinking are based on sense data, a concept similar to Piaget's view that cognitive development can be traced to its origins in early sensorimotor activities.

THE SPACE BETWEEN SELF AND MOTHER: PREOBJECTS

What is essential for all this to take place is the mother's consistent and "good-enough" care of the individual child, allowing basic trust to develop with mutuality as its natural expression. Only if there is a self can an ego develop, with a variety of identifications; a self is a necessary but not sufficient condition for relating to the outside world without loss of identity. In order to develop his own ego, the infant has to untie himself from the primary union with his mother and must have been given a potential space for growth. It is in this potential space (between self and mother), which develops out of separation and loss and includes concern and mourning, that a transitional object (or area) will take place. It will be used by the child to cope with loss, holding on to a part of the daytime world even as he or she leaves it.

The libido theory allows us to understand some aspects of the mother's investment in the infant's body and body functions and, reciprocally, of the infant's investment in the mother's body and her surroundings; it also helps us understand aspects of the nature of what I call (Gaddini, 1978) the "precursor" of a transitional object (TO) and of what has been called the fetish-object. Both the precursor and the fetish are distortions in the formation of an object-representation. In contrast to what the transitional object will eventually become, the mother's holding surrounding is not represented in either the fetish or in the "precursor." Neither provides for total loss. The precursor is used at a time when subject and object are not as yet distinct (stage of the subjective object), and it provides for the continuity and the completion that was lost with birth. That is why I referred to them as "precursors," no matter whether they are part of the mother's body, like a hand, a wrist, a nevus, or hair, or part of the infant's body, like a thumb, a lip, the tongue, a specific cutaneous area, or a pacifier shoved into the mouth of a needy baby to "passify" him (Winnicott, personal communication, 1968). Very little introjection or elaboration takes place in relation to these precursors, as they all belong to the stage of the preobject.[2]

Fetishes also belong to the stage of the preobject, and they also compensate the child in terms of completion and continuity. They differ greatly, however, in the time of their appearance—early infancy in the case of the precursors, the second part of the 2nd year in the case of the infantile

---

2. Through the years, I came to see the nipple, rather than the breast as a whole, as the infant's privileged element in terms of completion and sense of being a unit. The breast, in this view, is the whole for a part, the massive for the specific, a phenomenon not unusual in early life, a time when sensorial differentiation is not yet achieved.

fetish. The latter is a time, as Greenacre (1969) points out, when the child is acquiring cognitive awareness of his genitals. Further, the outside world, at this time, is full of threats, from the child's point of view. Drives are no longer contained by the mother's holding. Urges from within, instinctual arousal, contribute aggressive connotations to the outside world by projection, particularly when specific events occur in *reality*, such as the birth of a sibling, illnesses or hospitalization, sadistic events, changes of locale, and the like.

THE NONACHIEVEMENT OF IDENTITY

The following clinical vignette illustrates the consequences of cumulative traumata occurring in critical stages of individuation and of identity achievement in a vulnerable 16-month-old child.

F was 6 years old when he came to see me because "he was withdrawn and no longer talked."

He was the first of three children, born into an aristocratic family. His birth was kept secret for 2 months, as he was conceived before the wedding. During these 2 months mother and baby lived as a self-contained unit, isolated and hidden from strangers' eyes. The baby was breast-fed for nearly 6 months, with a certain flexibility and "carelessness," according to his guilt-prone mother (mother regrets that she used to read at feeding time).

Though his father was a cadet, his grandfather's first name was given to him, because the firstborn son had not yet had a male offspring. The firstborn son later had one, however, when F was 21 months old, and *this* baby became the heir. F *had* to give up *his* name to the new baby, and be given a new name, to which he had to learn to reply. F's developmental milestones had been within normal range, and at 21 months of age, therefore, he was able to express himself verbally, with a large and appropriate vocabulary (as is often the case with the mothers of autistic children, his mother used to write a lot, including a diary of her child's achievements). The change of name, underlined by the environmental embarrassment every time the new name was pronounced, was perceived as a *total* attack on his identity. At the time he also had a bad spell of whooping cough, which made him most miserable.

Meanwhile, a baby sister was born when he was 16 months old. F was taken to see her in the hospital. While there he was subjected to a cystoscopy, remembered by his mother as "a very traumatic one because of the child's rebellion." The reason for the cystoscopy, which took place shortly after he had seen his naked new sister being dressed, and in the same room, were frequent bouts of "cystitis." Circumcision was also performed on that occasion.

When F was 2 years and 4 months old, the family moved to another house in the same country village where the family castle was. At the time he was not eating or sleeping well. It was around this time that he was taken to watch the killing of a pig. Words reminiscent of the bloody episode were mumbled by him for a long time, while he was gradually losing the communicative sense of speech. By 3 years he was, in fact, talking in a manneristic way, and he no longer interacted verbally with people. He became more and more withdrawn, talking only to himself. A question that he was heard to repeat obsessively at the time was, "To whom does it belong?" He would ask this about a variety of things, such as the sun, the birds, the road, and so on. When he was 4 years and 6 months old, he once asked his mother "to get some milk into her breasts and to let him suck them, the way he did as a baby." Mother notes that "she used to be quite liberal in terms of nudity," particularly in summer, which is when the episode took place. He said to his mother that one breast had "belonged" to him, and the other had been sucked by his sister.

By the age of 5 he was entirely mute, and wore a blank expression when asked, "What is your name?" Parents remember with visible guilt the embarrassment of people who were around. When F had reached the age of 6 years, they came for help.

The child I saw was very attractive, although completely withdrawn, a well-developed boy for his age, restrained in movements and voice tones. He did not take initiatives, except for drawing figures, which he did in a very casual and slow way. These figures were mostly horses, sometimes donkeys or bulls. They were stylized, like graffiti, at times stereotyped, and they all had large, visible genitals. He also drew some human figures; great attention was given to the mouth and teeth. His gross motor abilities were poor; he was slow and clumsy. His fine movements were coordinated though rather rigid. In treatment he developed his language to a point, and grew into a passive and poorly engaged adolescent, with a limited capacity for learning from experience, who went from one fear to another, from one compulsion to another in his usual frozen, unrelated way.

SELF CONSTANCY AND SELF-REPRESENTATION: THE INFANTILE FETISH

I cannot but wonder whether F's capacity for internalization and for maintaining representations, necessary for achieving object constancy, were unable to develop because some basic organization was lacking, a self in which to internalize relationships, events, experiences, object-representations. The pathological self–object relationship with his mother did not give him an opportunity for self–object negotiation and took him gradually into pathological self-contained narcissism, as is typical of psychotic formations.

At times it is the precursor plus something else, usually mother's clothing or a foot or a shoe, which are combined in the child's attempt to restore a sense of completion of the self and of his threatened sexual identity; this gives birth to a fetish.

The following observational vignettes are examples of how castration (in terms of anxiety of self-loss) is basic to the structure of the infantile fetish. The infantile fetish may be the (transitory) temporary filling of a void caused by a sudden loss. This loss has to do with the primary object, and specifically, with the nipple. We may, therefore, in the case of the infantile fetish, paraphrase Freud's statement that "the foot represents a woman's penis, the absence of which is deeply felt" in young children, the foot or a piece of maternal clothing may come to represent the breast's nipple, the absence of which is deeply felt. The infantile fetish represents a part-object and not a function in relationship to a person; therefore, it is not like a TO, which serves as a symbol. The property of representing a function in relationship to a person, and to develop it in the ambience of this total person, is in fact typical of the TO, with which the child evokes the lost union with mother. While the TO has no erotic connotations, these are always present in the case of the fetish. As I have indicated previously (Gaddini, 1975):

I believe that the fetish reduces anxiety, but it seems to me that it does so through the creation of a different kind of tension, an excitation of a libidinal character. The T.O., on the other hand, actually reduces the anxiety directly. This is the basic factor that differentiates the two states, that of the normal child who has a T.O. and the deviant child who has the fetish. Both children turn to their "objects" in an attempt to reduce painful anxiety, but only the first succeeds in doing so. (p. 73)

C was 3 years old when he began to make use of his mother's stockings at times of depression and in going to sleep; while doing so, he got excited and had an erection. From the early months of life he had sucked two fingers of his left hand while going to sleep. Later, he also began to rhythmically tickle the right hand thumb, to the point of bleeding. His mother intervened, bandaging the thumb with the idea of protecting it from deformities. The moment the thumb was bandaged, C stopped scratching it, and he also stopped sucking the two fingers. It was at this time that he began using his mother's stockings.

E, the only child of young parents, was fed on a rigid schedule (briefly at breast) and had a pacifier, to which he was greatly attached, since his first weeks of life. When he was nearly 3 years old, his mother, who was preoccupied about the possible consequences for his teeth, removed the pacifier and told him that "it had been thrown into the sea." He cried a great deal and for days had difficulty going to sleep. Finally he seemed to resign. In those days when he was trying to adapt to the loss, it was noted that he got interested in women's feet, which he touched and held eagerly, getting excited and having an erection. It was the mother who called my attention to the close connection in time between the removal of the pacifier and his searching for women's (never men's) feet.

The observation of a number of cases like the two just mentioned, in which the removal of a nipple substitute (what I have called [Gaddini, 1978] the "into-the-mouth precursor") has been followed by an attachment to an infantile fetish, has suggested the idea to me that the fetish, in certain circumstances, is a direct derivation of the loss of the nipple. Greenacre (1968) comes close to this idea when she writes: "While the fetish function is limited to concern about the genitals, it too has a relation to the mother and sometimes there are indications of memories of her breast. But these seem to have been *derived mostly from an early period of confusion between breast and penis*., From this it derives that while the fetish is necessary to the adult fetishist to complete the sexual act, it is often the narcissistic need rather than the expression of tender love which is satisfied.

INFANTILE CONFUSION BETWEEN BREAST AND PENIS

I would like to underline the term *confusion* and to elaborate upon it. How does the penis relate to the breast in the child's unconscious fantasy? How does the child come to search for a penis, the moment he loses the breast? It seems to me that when the child loses the breast (or that which stands for it, such as a pacifier), he displaces onto his own penis the investment that was originally in the breast. He then compulsively searches for women's penises, mother's breast displaced onto the penis. In this operation of displacement, in fact, the penis, for the child, is the breast.

But then, if the child's penis is the breast, the penis is omnipotent. If, however, the breast is lost, the child feels impotent.

All these events may occur in a close sequence, and may give way to infantile fetishism, long lasting or transitory. Will the child's penis, however, ever be a genital penis again? Or will it keep on being a breast, or something close to it?

A woman's foot seems to be, in this context, the searched-for feminine penis. In the child's fantasy, it is the breast which has become the penis, in his own body. We came to understand the genetic problem of the infantile fetish as stemming from breast and penis confusion a long time ago. What are the dynamic steps involved? Denial is the child's defense against breast loss. In denial there is an implication that women have a penis which is, in fact, a breast. The breast is, for him, a breast–penis. But the child wants a penis–breast. In the child's conscious mind, denial is at the same time denial of a feminine penis, as though stating: "Women do not have a penis" and discovering that they have a penis–breast. But what he has lost is a breast–penis. The child fetishist is searching for it.

Greenacre (1968) writes: "The appearance of an infantile fetish under the stress of incipient awareness of the anatomical genital differences between boys and girls is suggestive of regression to the feeling-thought of the mother's breast not only as a direct comfort but as a substitute to offset the seemingly castrated state of the mother".

I do not have entirely clear yet, *what* is the outcome of the infantile fetish, and *how* the infantile fetish relates to the fetish of the adult fetishist. I recently had occasion to see a slow-maturing male child aged 6 years, with some autistic traits, who used to seek for women's feet, getting an erection. He had this fetish from the ages of 3–5 years, having begun to depend on it at the time of his pacifier's removal at the age of 2½ years. By the age of 5 years, he had begun kindergarten, and women's feet did not seem to interest him nearly as much as they had previously, although he remained slightly attracted to them when in motion or "erect."

In conclusion, I feel that the infantile fetish has a more direct derivation from the "into-the-mouth precursor," which primarily is the breast nipple or a substitute. The latter's removal, or loss, seems to serve as the origin of the fetish. It is likely that for both—the transitional object and the fetish—"the mouth–breast axis is the focus for the early object" (Greenacre, 1969). In the case of the transitional object, it seems to be the skin contact and the softness that matter, whereas these kinds of sensuous "externals" are much less significant in the genesis of the fetish.

Roiphe and Galenson's (1973) interesting cases, significant as they are for the hypothesis the authors propose, do not provide clinical material through which to trace back the way the infants related to their early objects and their substitutes, nor to the way they lost them. These authors' hypothesis is that symptomatic castration reactions, extremely violent at the time, will develop when there is a confluence of the following three conditions: (1) indications of the normal sexual arousal have already appeared, usually between 16 and 24 months; (2) the child, in the context of this sexual arousal, has had the opportunity to observe the anatomic difference between the sexes; (3) the child has had earlier experiences, such as birth defect, severe illness, surgical intervention, loss of a parent, or, in general, not good-enough mothering, which have resulted in an instability in the self and object representations.

The description of one of Roiphe and Galenson's (1973) three cases — Suzy, with her intense, frightened crying when her walking–talking doll's battery fell out, and her subsequent massive rejection of the beloved doll ("Suzy would have nothing to do with it anymore")—is reminiscent of the type of reaction young children have when their "precursor" is mischievously manipulated or altered. I have seen a number of children appearing terrified when a breast nipple was painted black or covered with a bitter substance, or a pacifier was altered in some manner to discourage sucking on it. The sequence seemed to be: fright, then rejection of the breast, then denial. Entirely different is the repression that the TO undergoes when the child has separated and is progressing in his individuation; the TO simply ceases to occupy the child's attention and drops out of sight.

The concept of intermediary states between the TO and the fetish, which I came to recognize after Greenacre's (personal communication, 1969) suggestion, is very illuminating, in my view. The element that differentiates the transitional object from the fetish in these intermediary states is that "the latter contains anger, born in castration panic." Whichever the castration is—whether it is a castration of a genital phallus or of a breast phallus—it is experienced by the child as a threat of disintegration. Sadomasochistic fantasies are quite commonly associated with fetishism. As Greenacre (1969) writes:

Even when no clear overt sadomasochistic rituals or activities have appeared, such feelings were implicitly . . . expressed in the magic killings, of not looking, silence, and similar attacks by denial or deprivation. . . . In some instances [sadomasochistic tendencies] are clearly traceable to derivative repetitions of the original actual traumata which have contributed to the intensification of the castration panic.[3]

In conclusion, I agree with the previous researchers on the point that the fetish serves to define and supplement the body schema, and that "this . . . reparative construct is the result of the undermining of the sense of body integrity," and that the fetish originates out of what may be referred to as a separation–individuation distortion. I find myself diverging when we come to the genesis of it.

The dynamic of fetishism, writes Greenacre (1968), is a consequence of the discovery of the anatomic differences between the sexes. As such, "it requires some degree of predisposition to give it much force." However, "this stern obligatory need to believe in the phallic mother must be preceded by disturbances in the first two years of life which drastically affect the progress of separation and individuation (Mahler, 1968), and in consequence interfere with the developing object relationship and the orderly progress of the libidinal phases." In my experience it is not so much the *observation* of the anatomic difference that matters, as much as the *sensation* of having lost the primary completion of early body self, as it is built at the breast.

LIBIDO DIFFERENTIATION

One may wonder how much the libido theory contributes to our understanding of the developmental movement from the self to the outside world. On the basis of libido we can understand investments and disinvestments, differentiation and dedifferentiation in the course of the maturational process. We may also understand defenses and massive

---

3. Greenacre (1981) underlines how important the patterned sucking reaction of the lips and mouth, present at birth, is, followed soon by hand-to-mouth movements. "Here it seems probable that the baby is using his fist or finger for gratification before the centrally organized representation of his own body is well enough assembled and put together for him to distinguish whether they belong to him or are a gift from the outside."

regressions on the part of an already self-sufficient normally aggressive toddler, who resumes thumb sucking as an aspect of regressive behavior.

The way libido differentiates takes us back to the fact—as Freud has repeatedly stated—that mental processes originate from drives; that is, mental processes originate from the body. They are part of the self, the primary core of which is physical but also mental since it is upon this bodily base that mental organization takes place. This primary core results, as previously mentioned, from the reestablished union of the mother with baby after separation at birth. From the body, development proceeds toward the mind and toward mental operations. The term "basic mental organization" is an equivalent of the term "self" in this view.

Freud wrote concerning the libido theory:

From the vantage point of psychoanalysis we can look across a frontier which we may not pass, at the activity of narcissistic libido, and may form some idea of the relation between it and object libido. Narcissistic or ego libido seems to be the great reservoir from which the object cathexes are sent out and into which they are withdrawn once more; the narcissistic libidinal cathexis of the ego (self) is the original state of things realized in earliest childhood, and is merely covered by the later extrusion of libido, but, in essential, persists behind them. (Freud, 1905, p. 218)

The following is a statement that I find myself reading as a sort of prophetic anticipation and that I somehow connect with the self's organization as I now see it taking place. It reads:

It is easy to guess that the vicissitudes of the ego libido will have the major part to play in this connection, especially when it is a question of explaining the deeper psychotic disturbances. . . . We are then faced by the difficulties that our method of research, psychoanalysis, for the moment affords us assured information only on the transformations that take place in object libido, but it is unable to make any immediate distinction between ego libido and the other forms of energies. (Freud, 1905, p. 218)

All this takes us to a point: Where does narcissistic libido end and object libido start, and how does this relate to the sense of self and of identity?

Greenacre (1958) is careful on the point of identity. She notes that the term "identity" has two important aspects: one internal and the other external. An internal sense of self is not sufficient to produce a sense of identity.

In my experience almost everything young infants do in the absence of the mother is a way of evoking her, an attempt at reestablishing union with her (after having lost it). In these attempts the infant has no means other than his own body. The infant's body in these cases is invested in, as the mother's body would be were she available, libido and aggression, both at the same time. Spitz's (Spitz & Wolf, 1949) concept of autoerotism implies positive charges, as does MacDougall's (personal communication, 1980). On the contrary, libido is used by the infant, in my view, to counteract aggressive charges. In our study on rumination (Gaddini & Gaddini, 1959) we have learned that the infant begins to ruminate only when the libido becomes involved: We have never seen a case of rumination among infants in institutions since birth. In a way, libido is used to mentalize. This is the reason why rumination is now rightly grouped among early developmental disorders, such as psychosomatic pathology. There is an instinctual implication in the way Spitz used the term autoerotic that is alien to the clinical picture of rumination. The term, in fact, in the way it is used by Spitz, has a purely descriptive connotation and tells little about the direction in which drives move and very little about the individual's economic characteristics and resources. The fact that in rumination, just as in self-rocking, it is the body rather than the mother-outside world that is invested, gives some clues as to the specific organization of the protective maneuvers against anxiety utilized by the infant who is unable to use his libido in mental operations. Both self-rocking and rumination are, in this view, primitive defenses that protect survival, but at the same time interfere with the child's separation–individuation process.

AUTOEROTISM AND SOMATIZATION

"Autoerotic" is one way of saying that instead of turning toward the outside world, the infant turns to his own body, that is, somatizes, which to me means the infant's being incarcerated in his own body. In somatic symptoms or illnesses there is no self-creation (self-representation) nor individuation, because there has not yet been separation. The body is the primary object, the mother oriented to illness instead of to total health. There is no creation at all. Creation presupposes having lost. It is, in fact, to re-create in a space that has been left empty by loss, and implies concern and mourning; Winnicott has called this space *"potential space."* Only after a loss, in the absence of the primary object and in the space left empty by it, may creation take place. It implies that neurophysiologic structures have matured enough to allow elaboration and symbolization of the primary sensorial experience and that there has been an environment catalyzing this elaboration, to allow the child the introjection of a good primary surrounding.

In somatic symptom formation as well as in self-rocking and in rumination, the maturational element implied in self-representation and in symbolic creation (such as transitional objects) is missing. As we know, to build defenses in the soma is a primitive sort of protection, and very little fantasy is involved. Because of the deficiency of the mental element, such as we find in primary experiences, we should refer to them as protective maneuvers, similar to those we find in autistic children; these take place in the undifferentiated phase of the subjective object (preobject) at a time when subject and object are not representationally differentiated. Little use is made of the outside world on the part of the subject during this phase of development. Besides psychosomatic pathology, there are also other developmental failures based on the pathology of the self.

THE IMPAIRED SELF

An impaired self is not able to survive in itself and does not relate to an object. No mutuality can grow. It may use the object in a variety of distorted ways, which all have a failure of mutuality in common. *Pseudo*-object-constancy may be viewed as one of these ways of not relating. It is like a dependent mother–child relationship, with an occasional role inversion—at times one is the mother, at other times one is the child. From the "outside" we see a couple, two people who may have married and who may even have children, have apparently good jobs, which they manage to hold, and they seem to have a "good life." On the "inside," however, it is a mother–infant relationship. No separation–individuation took place for either of them, no potential space for growth, no authentic self with which to contribute to the outside world, no capacity to have one's own point of view. They keep depending on one another, never having reached self constancy, nor therefore, object constancy. The psychological birth of the human being and the initial steps toward autonomy develop when the individual child is capable of internalization, and depend upon the quality of the inner world that is built out of these introjects. The primary core, which Winnicott has defined as "the self," where the basic mental organization takes place, is fundamental both in assuring an inner space for internalization as well as in determining the quality of the introjects. A complex image of humans derives from this source, where the genetic and the early environment join, striving for mutuality and, so often, failing in this primary aim.

When, due to early disturbances in the mother–infant relationship, there is a severe impairment of object relationships, and this impairment combines with weaknesses of the body- and self-images, distortion and arrest of development are the consequence. Perversions, particularly, are more likely to result when "specifically determined weakness of the body and self images . . . involve especially the genitals" (Greenacre, 1968), or, I would add, a breast equivalent of them (of the phallus).

THE REPARATIVE FUNCTION OF PSYCHOANALYSIS

Psychoanalysis is not only a psychological theory, in the established sense of the term. It is also a conception of the person in depth, not just as the pawn of circumstance, nor just as the victim of his past history and its conscious and unconscious residues, but as both, plus an ego engaged in the business of living with whatever degree of harmony can be achieved between the individual's desires and the real world. Furthermore, psychoanalysis is not a philosophical system; it is a science based on facts. These facts are not always observable; most are discovered in reconstruction, or through their symbolic expression. Unveiling these facts—for example, traumata occurring at a time when the child has not yet a self, nor a "memory," nor even a reasonably secure sense of reality—in a transference relationship (the missed mutuality with mother) brings internal changes. The real nature of the basic transference relationship is a complex one, and I am not sure that I want to get into the topic; I only want to mention, in closing, the *reverie* function of the analyst who is dealing with impairments of the type mentioned, where the sense of reality, as well as body- and self-images, have been altered by fear. This function is not only a holding function, like that of a good-enough parent, but also contains an element of "mentalizing" for the patient, in due time.

Perhaps as in reverie, it may be beneficial for the patient that, in his holding function, at times the analyst limits himself to cues, which imply mutuality and facilitate the patient's basic organization and psychological birth.

REFERENCES

Bion, W. R. (1965). *Transformations: change from learning to growth.* London: Heinemann.

Clifford, Scott W. M. (1981). On the positive affects. *Psychological Journal of the University of Ottawa, 6,* 79–81.

Escalona, S. K. (1963). Patterns of infantile experience and the developmental process. *The Psychoanalytic Study of the Child, 18,* 197–265.

Freud, S. (1905). Three essays on the theory of sexuality. *Standard Edition, 7,* 135–243.

Freud, S. (1915). Instincts and their vicissitudes. *Standard Edition, 14.*

Freud, S. (1920). Beyond the pleasure principle. *Standard Edition, 18.*

Gaddini, R. (1975). The concept of transitional object. *Journal of the American Academy of Child Psychiatry, 14,* 731–736.

Gaddini, R. (1978). Transitional object origin and the psychosomatic symptom. In S. Grolnick & L. Barkin (Eds.), *Between reality and fantasy.* New York: Jason Aronson.

Gaddini, R., & Gaddini, E. (1959). Rumination in infancy. In L. Jessner & E. Pavenstedt (Eds.), *Dynamic psychopathology in childhood.* New York: Grune & Stratton.

Greenacre, P. (1958). Early physical determinants in the development of the sense of identity. In *Emotional growth* (Vol. 1). New York: International Universities Press.

Greenacre, P. (1968). Perversions: General considerations regarding their genetic and dynamic background. *The Psychoanalytic Study of the Child, 23,* 47–62.

Greenacre, P. (1969). The fetish and the transitional object. *The Psychoanalytic Study of the Child, 24,* 144–166.

Greenacre, P. (1981). Reconstruction: Its nature and therapeutic value. *Journal of the American Psychoanalytic Association, 29,* 27–47.

Mahler, M. (1968). *On human symbiosis and the vicissitudes of individuation: Infantile psychosis* (Vol. 1). New York: International Universities Press.

Roiphe, H., & Galenson, E. (1973). The infantile fetish. *The Psychoanalytic Study of the Child, 23,* 147–166.

Spitz, R., & Wolf, K. M. (1949). Autoerotism. Some empirical findings and hypothesis on three of its manifestations in the first year of life. *The Psychoanalytic Study of the Child, 3*(4), 85–120.

Winnicott, D. W. (1971). Letter to J. Kalmanovitch in Paris, January 19. "Introduction," *Fragment d'une analyse.* Paris: Payot, 1975.

Self and Object

CHAPTER NINE

Object Constancy, Object Permanency, and Personality Disorders

DONALD B. RINSLEY

Object constancy may be defined in terms of cognitive–perceptual (mnemonic) and affective (emotional) parameters (Fraiberg, 1969) and is correctly understood to encompass both (A. Freud, 1960, 1968). The mnemonic component has to do with the capacity to summon up a consistent inner image or representation, that is, to have evolved from reliance on recognitory memory to the capacity for evocative memory (Beres, 1968; Hartmann, 1952, 1956), a transformation that likely begins during the last trimester of the 1st postnatal year (Spitz, 1957), is well on the way toward the end of the 2nd year (Metcalf & Spitz, 1978), and is completed toward the latter half of the 3rd year (Mahler, 1965, 1968; Mahler, Pine, & Bergman, 1975). The affective or emotional component is expressed in the growing child's libidinal tie to or emotional bonding with the mother, which has its inception in the symbiotic phase (1–6 months), is marked by the normal 8th-month (stranger) anxiety (Spitz, 1957), and is well developed by the middle of the 2nd year, roughly by 18 months (Nagera, 1966).

Object constancy is not to be confused with *object permanency*, a term originating with Piaget (1937). Object permanency has to do with the growing infant's ability to perceptually differentiate "external" objects from his manipulation of them, to perceive them as existing independent of him per se. In accordance with the results of Piaget's two-barrier-displacement procedure, object permanency ordinarily develops by about 18 months postnatally. The evolution of the infant's emotional (libidinal) tie to the mother and his achievement of object permanency cannot, of course, be regarded as fortuitous, and failure of the former is doubtless related to failure of the latter (Pine, 1974; Schafer, 1968). The implication is that failure to generate the maternal libidinal bond could be expected to result in the developing infant's failure to traverse appropriately the later stages of sensorimotor cognition, with all that this further implies for the later achievement of preoperational, concrete operational, and circular operational (abstract–categorical) thought. It further puts to rest the criticism of Piaget's barrier-displacement procedure that it deals with the infant's responses to manipulable inanimate objects with which there is no libidinal–affective tie, in contrast to the infant's responses to the maternal object, with whom there is.

It is not superfluous to point out that there exists a significant correspondence between the infant's buildup of object representations and self-representations; that the infant is able to perceive objects, including animate and human ones, as apart from his infantile-grandiose construction of them requires the presence of a self, however primitive, that generates such a perception. Proper note is thus taken of the infant's passage, as it were, from the monadic, autoerotic, and primarily narcissistic position to and into the sphere of two-person (better, two-object) psychology, the arena of Balint's (1968) "basic fault."

MEMORY TRACES AND OBJECTS

The following discussion will be addressed to the vicissitudes and effects of the infant's primitive perceptual experiences during the first 6 postnatal months; this period comprises Mahler's phases of absolute autism (0–1 month) and symbiosis (1–6 months) and corresponds with the classical early oral (oral–receptive, oral–incorporative) stage of psychosexual development.

During this period the infant's world is, of course, organized in accordance with the pleasure principle (Freud, 1911), a prototypically all-good–all-bad surround, as well as in accordance with pristine part-object percepts in terms of which the primary feeding part-object (breast) is apprehended as "good" if it feeds and satisfies and "bad" if it does not. The infant already possesses the capacity to differentiate presented food items in terms of whether they taste "good" (e.g., a dilute sugar solution placed on the infant's tongue), hence are swallowed or whether they taste "bad" (e.g., a dilute hydrochloric acid solution placed on the infant's tongue), hence are spit out. It is assumed that the "good" food item, the so-called good breast (part-object) and the mother's positive (i.e., libidinalized) attitude toward the feeding experience, as reflected in the subtle cues associated with her neuromuscular state at the time, together comprise a manifold of perceptual experiences that catalyze mother–infant bonding and proceed concomitantly to lay down positive (libidinal) memory traces in the infant. Conversely, the "bad" food item, the so-called bad breast (part-object) and a maternal attitude of perplexity, undue anxiety, depression, and hence of rejection comprise a manifold of perceptual experiences that either inhibit or distort normal mother–infant bonding and proceed concomitantly to lay down negative (aggression-laden) memory traces in the infant. Highly significant is the fact that the former, positive feeding experience, including its components of holding and cuddling, puts temporarily to rest the infant's visceral-autonomic affectomotor storms, is conducive to healthy digestive-assimilative functioning and leads to repose. By the same token, the latter, negative feeding experience maintains the infant's state of heightened inner tension, including visceral-autonomic lability that disrupts the bonding relationship, resulting in an angry, overirritable, and suboptimally nourished infant (Rinsley, 1979).

It follows that predominantly negative feeding-bonding experiences during the phase of absolute autism, that is during the autoerotic period, may be expected adversely to affect the generation and quality of the infantile selfobject as this proceeds to condense with the inception of the symbiotic phase at approximately 1 month postnatally. A buildup of predominantly negative memory traces thus yields a predominantly negative selfobject that has a number of pejorative effects upon the infant's ensuing development.

If unmodified as a result of later restitutive mothering or therapeutic intervention, the negative selfobject evolves into the growing child's predominant self-percept. Its persistence overdetermines the continued assimilation to it of predominantly negative (aggressively valent) sensory-perceptual experiences, thereby consolidating the accretion of early memory traces, hence of selfobject experiences and representations that will ultimately emerge in the form of a diffuse or "negative" identity (Erikson, 1956, 1963).

The persistent, negative selfobject has the further effect of arresting or fixating the developing infant's early object relations at the symbiotic phase, thereby inhibiting his progress through the subsequent differentiation, practicing, and rapprochement subphases of separation-individuation, hence thwarting the process of desymbiotization (Mahler *et al.*, 1975). The process is complex, involving repetitive, regressive selfobject refusion in the wake of efforts toward desymbiotization (Jacobson, 1954a, 1954b, 1954c, 1957, 1964, 1971). It is as if the otherwise healthy increment of exploratory motility that accompanies the infant's entrance into the separation-individuation phase threatens to loose the powerful "raw" aggression associated with the negative selfobject, an occurrence that must be inhibited lest what there is of the positive selfobject ("good breast") be annihilated.

Although only larvally within the sphere of two-person psychology, the persistent, negative selfobject forms the basis for the ensuing development of the *basic fault* (Balint, 1968) that is derived from a failure of "good-enough mothering" or of adequate "holding" (Khan, 1963; Modell, 1963, 1968, 1975; Winnicott, 1950-1955, 1951, 1960), representative of an essential failure of goodness of fit, mutual cuing, or communicative matching between mother and infant. As a consequence, the infant's entrance into and developmental use of the sphere of transitional experience (Winnicott, 1951) are inhibited and transitional objects assume the features of fetishes (Dickes, 1978).

The persistent, negative selfobject has the further effect of overdetermining the primitive splitting defense as a result of arresting or fixating the infant's development at the level of magic–hallucination, a state of affairs that augurs balefully for the child's later transition from reliance on splitting to the onset of normal repression, the generation of whole-object relations and the eventual working through of the depressive position with resultant acquisition of the capacity to mourn. Persistent magic–hallucination within the context of a predominantly negative selfobject, with its compensatory function of creating a longed-for, need-satisfying feeding object, that is, a good-enough maternal part-object, fixates the infant at the point at which differentiation of the self-created and objectively reappearing maternal figures (object permanency) fails adequately to develop, with resultant inhibition of the later development of reality testing.[1] An additional, related effect is protracted infantile megalomania, expressed in part through feelings of entitlement, that is, that one may indeed command need-satisfaction by means of the motoric expression of magic–hallucination (magic gestures).

The reverberations of these early infantile experiences find evident expression in the history and presenting symptomatology of, for example, the adult who suffers from borderline personality disorder, not to mention the adult psychotic. He experiences relationships in terms of whether they provide and gratify or whether they withhold and deny. His ideation is often or consistently characterized by "soft" or "hard" thought disorder, basic to which is the everpresent pull toward either–or, black-and-white, autistic-preoperational thinking. He feels he is "bad," that something is vaguely or indefinably wrong with him, that he does not really know who or even what he is. His grandiosity leads him into positions that reflect a pervasive sense of entitlement, that all he should have to do to command an otherwise hostile, ungratifying environment to provide for his needs is to signal their presence by means of a repertoire of quasicommunicative metaphors and magic gestural actions. His combination of egoism and readily frustrated dependency leads him into a seemingly endless array of short-lived or unstable relationships, from each of which he passes to the next as if changing tires on his automobile. His sexual relations are more often characterized by deviation as to aim (e.g., sadomasochism) and as to object (anomalous sexual object "choice") and are at basis polymorphous-perverse. His personality generally reflects an addiction proneness, whether in respect

---

1. The relationship among fetishism, splitting and impaired reality testing was originally perceived by Freud (1905, 1927, 1940). In ambivalently attributing a penis to a woman, the male fetishist, deviant as to both aim and object, confounds the penis and the breast much as does the "hysterical" female for whom a penis in the vagina is psychically equivalent to a nipple in the baby's mouth (cf. Fairbairn's [1941] *hysterical transitional mechanism*).

to illicit or abusive drug usage or in relating to others much as if they represent pharmacologic agents capable of easing tension, providing "highs," and the like.

FIXATION AT THE LEVEL OF THE DYAD

Psychoanalytic stage theory has taught us that the developing infant and child traverses three major sphincter-related periods during the preschool years; and further that these sphincters serve as developmental anchor points, as it were, in relation to which are wider and deeper aspects of nascent object relations (Erikson, 1963; Rinsley, 1981). No later than the first trimester of the 1st postnatal year, two-person (dyadic) psychology has its inception within the context of the mother–infant symbiosis. By the end of the classical oral–incorporative (oral–dependent) stage, the infant has already begun the process of separation–individuation from the "symbiotic dual unity" that will result in progressive self and object differentiation and will lead to the later "rapprochement crisis" (16–26 months) that heralds the inception of true object constancy at about 3 years of age. The inception of triadic, oedipal (three-person) psychology now awaits the child's entrance into the on-the-way-to-object-constancy phase at roughly 30 months postnatally. To Spitz's (1957) original three "organizers of the psyche," namely, the 3rd-month smiling response, the 8th-month stranger anxiety, and the acquisition of communicative speech (the "No!" response) is now added a fourth, the oedipal constellation (Kaplan, 1980).

Developmental arrest (or, as some prefer, developmental deviation) at the level of the dyad thus signifies the persistence of the negative selfobject. In "oral" terms it signifies a preponderance of negative feeding and bonding experiences. In "anal" terms it signifies impairment of the capacity for mastery and for exercising impact upon others and the surround. In "phallic" (oedipal) terms it signifies failure to have adequately achieved triadic object relations, that is the father–mother–child complex of differentiated representations, hence failure to differentiate the male object from the female object; and inasmuch as impaired gender-related object differentiation has its counterpart in gender-related self-differentiation, the latter remains essentially unclear.

As noted, the borderline individual complains, not only that he does not really know who he is but in addition that he is not clear whether he is male or female. Again, the result is persistent, partialistic, polymorphous-perverse sexuality, in some cases conveyed by gender-appropriate but excessive sexuality that serves as a defense against the underlying confusion of self- and gender identity and role.

The infusion of triadic–oedipal object relations with dyadic, predominantly anal-stage object relations in these cases thus severely contaminates the gender-related issues common to the former with issues of impact, control, and mastery common to the latter.[2] One major effect of this contamination (the so-called preoedipal Oedipus) finds expression in the strongly sadomasochistic features that typify the individual's later emergent sexuality, in which issues of dominance and submission override and ultimately vitiate the capacity for intimacy or, in more classical terms, the achievement of genitality. Evident in such cases is the deployment of defenses against the unrequited and fearsome wish for symbiotic reunion and refusion, conveyed in both the regressive polymorphous-perversity that signifies a return to pristine sphincter equipotentiality and the reliance upon obsessional, affect-isolative, primarily cognitive defenses, including ritualisms and undoing, directed toward scotomatizing or disavowing that wish.

Thus is defined the husband who abuses his wife, whether by physical or verbal assault, when she does not keep the house "just so," keep the children quiet, and so on. Analysis of such a case generally reveals several "levels" of pathological interaction: sexual intimacy with the wife signifies incestuous relations with the mother; the "mother–wife" is, however, a (breast) part-object toward which primitive rage is directed when it is perceived as a split-off, "bad," ungratifying part-object that fails to relieve tension, preclude annoyances, and the like; again, at an even deeper level, intimacy threatens the terrifying yet ardently wished-for symbiotic reunion against which the rage serves as a defense. In such cases, the sadomasochistic components are not difficult to perceive.

Kohut's (1971, 1977) contributions to the psychology of the self and to the psychology of narcissism are grounded on a larval two-person psychology (the selfobject). Kohut applies his views and his psychoanalytic technique to that group of patients he considers to be suffering from narcissistic personality disorder, characterized by the persistence of what he terms *stable, cohesive selfobjects*; these individuals maintain a sundered self (or, better, self–object representation) comprising a *grandiose self* and an *idealized parental image,* both of which become evident in the so-called mirroring transference during the course of treatment. In such cases the selfobject may be viewed as a manifestation of a pathologically persistent maternal introject (Rinsley, 1980a) in relation to which the individual may indeed achieve occupationally and intellectually but at the expense of seriously impaired object relationships. By contrast, individuals suffering from borderline and psychotic disorders suffer from the persistence of what are termed *fragmented, unstable selfobjects*, that is, by endopsychic selfobject representations that are prone to regressive reanimation or revivification (Jacobson, 1954a, 1954b, 1954c, 1964; Kernberg, 1966) and to willy-nilly reliance upon introjective–projective defenses (Rinsley, 1980a). In such cases, the individual's everreadiness to

---

2. Ovesey's (1969) cogent distinction between homosexuality and pseudohomosexuality comes to mind in this connection.

experience the disruptive effects of *abandonment depression* is easily observed, whether in general behavior or within the context of the therapeutic transference (Masterson, 1974, 1975, 1976; Masterson & Rinsley, 1975; Rinsley, 1977, 1978, 1979).

OBJECT INCONSTANCY AND OBJECT IMPERMANENCY: CLINICAL EXPRESSION

The inability to consistently summon up internal representations or images of others, whether eidetic or not, comprises the clinical expression of *object impermanency*, reflective of failure to have progressed beyond reliance on recognitory memory; at best, it signifies the persistence of fragmented, unstable selfobjects that typify the psychotic and the borderline personality, the latter in particular when approaching psychotic levels of experience. If such summoning up is indeed possible but the representations or images so generated prove to be essentially devoid of libidinal affect or ungratifying, then one speaks of *object inconstancy*, reflective of the persistence of stable cohesive selfobjects that typify the narcissistic personality. In keeping with the view of Anna Freud (1960, 1968), object constancy implies an affective (libidinal) investment in the object that reinforces the evocative recall of the object representation or object image; by the same token, without such affective reinforcement, extinguishment of the object representation could be expected or, in the alternative, its evocative recall would represent little more than a regressive revivification of the sought-for inanimate object as in the case of the 18-month-old infant.

Clinical experience with both borderline personalities and narcissistic personalities leads to the conclusion that the borderline individual suffers the symptomatic ravages of object impermanency, whereas the more purely narcissistic personality suffers from the effects of object inconstancy. Both share a common impairment of internalized object relations, reflected in the so-called *split object relations unit*, rendering both subject to *abandonment depression* (Rinsley, 1980a, 1981, 1984, 1985).

The borderline individual's "all-good–all-bad" self and world view, grounded on the persistent, pristine splitting defense, is further reflected in a pattern of shifting, unstable affective and interpersonal relationships that in turn convey the persistence of fragmented, unstable selfobjects. As noted, the hallmark of these selfobjects (really part-selfobjects) is the individual's reliance on primitive projective and introjective defenses by means of which the archaic revivified ("demetabolized," Kernberg, 1966), self and object representations, with their charges of unneutralized ("raw") instinct, readily traverse the porous ego boundary, thereby passing "in and out," as it were. Associated with the untrammeled operation of these defenses is the individual's episodic descent into frankly psychotic experience ("micropsychosis") with its accompaniments of dysphoria (mood disorder) and impaired abstract–categorical ideation (thought disorder) that typify the more regression-prone borderline personality. Significant impairment or failure of evocative recall in these cases signals the frightening extinguishment of stable, reliable, "good-enough" mental representations accompanied by the resurgence of the aforementioned, frighteningly revivified "bad" mental representations. The inability to summon up or evoke "good" mental representations further results in what might be termed *fantasy deficiency* with its associated inability to anticipate and foreplan, hence the impaired frustration tolerance that leads to the impulsivity that characterizes much of the behavior of borderline individuals. Related also is the phenomenon termed *alexithymia*, comprising both fantasy deficiency and the inability to describe or discuss one's feelings, a symptom that is frequent among patients who suffer from psychosomatic disorders (Nemiah & Sifneos, 1970; Sifneos, 1973, 1975).

The developmental pathogenesis of borderline disorder has been traced to a particular form of mother–infant interaction, specifically a depersonifying "push–pull" relationship within which the growing infant, later child, receives libidinal reinforcement for passive-dependent, anaclitic behavior, that is, for remaining symbiotic, and is threatened with the loss of libidinal supplies, hence with rejection or abandonment in the wake of efforts toward separation–individuation (Masterson, 1974, 1975, 1976; Masterson & Rinsley, 1975; Rinsley, 1977, 1978, 1979, 1980a, 1980b). This pathogenetic pattern has its inception during the differentiation and practicing subphases of separation–individuation (6–15 months) and reaches its peak during the rapprochement subphase (16–26 months), thereby arresting the child's development at the level of partial self–object differentiation that underlies and typifies borderline psychopathology.

In accordance with the concept of the diagnostic–developmental spectrum or continuum (Rinsley, 1980a, 1981), the narcissistic personality is considered to represent a "higher level" borderline personality. Additionally, the narcissitic personality is viewed as closer to the "neurotic border" (Grinker & Werble, 1977; Grinker, Werble, & Drye, 1968; Ornstein, 1974). As noted, the pathological selfobject (pathogenic maternal introject) of the narcissistic personality is subject to the vicissitudes of projective–introjective defenses to a much lesser degree than in the case of the borderline personality, and then usually or only under conditions of major stress that signifies abandonment. It is as if the mother had sanctioned what must be regarded as a spurious separation–individuation in these cases such that *the narcissistic individual appears to have desymbiotized* while clinging, as it were, to the idealized maternal part-object representation that, in association with the corresponding part-self representation, proceeds to generate what Kohut has termed the *grandiose self*. Metaphorically, the maternal message has been, "You may go through the motions of separation–individuation, hence you may achieve, but only if everything you accomplish is in relation to me." The effects of this injunction upon the narcissistic individual's interpersonal relationships are evident in the complementary maternal injunction that amounts to a preclusion of whole-object relations; thus, although the narcissist's interpersonal relationships are ordinarily not as unstable as are those of the borderline, they pervasively suffer from failure of empathy, exploitiveness, and emotional aloofness (Rinsley, 1985).

Kernberg's (1980) paper "Regression in Leaders" in particular describes these and related characteristics in the talented, ambitious, narcissistic personality who rises to leadership responsibilities with devastating effects on others and on the organization for which he or she works in a supervisory or executive position.

The object inconstancy from which the narcissistic personality is noted to suffer signifies failure or deficiency of affective–libidinal cathexis of otherwise mnemonically evocable object representations or object images, with relative preservation of the capacity for evocative recall per se, which is seriously deficient in the borderline individual. Again, in contrast to the borderline personality, the narcissistic personality suffers no deficiency of preparatory or even creative fantasy except that such fantasy is essentially devoid of affective–libidinal investment, hence ultimately of humaneness.

The Nazi holocaust brought to public view a host of basically emotionally aloof (schizoid), unspeakably sadistic persons such as Josef Goebbels and Adolf Eichmann, architects of the Jewish "final solution," who were otherwise intelligent or even gifted and who, in true as-if fashion, could be engaging and even charming when their ends suited such behavior. And until his latter-day deterioration, Hitler himself, an organizational and charismatic genius, was one of the world's greatest and most evil leaders. The files of history are replete with a host of essentially narcissistic personalities, ranging from such outstanding personages as Alexander the Great to such lesser ones as the American mobster, Alphonse Capone, both gifted and both immeasurably egomaniacal.

Again, there is the immensely successful, affluent captain of industry or leading intellectual whose relationships are shrewdly and skillfully exploitive, who views his family as a coterie of indentured servants, for whose greater glory they exist and serve. Depressed wives of such narcissists complain that they rarely see, much less are intimate with, their husbands, and the children of such unions display a high incidence of emotional disorder, including delinquency.

A COMMENT ON PATHOGENESIS

The criterion here set forth that is assumed to distinguish the borderline personality from the narcissistic personality, namely the capacity for evocative memory in the latter and its impairment or deficiency in the former, deserves further comment. It should be noted that Spitz (1957) relates the infant's 8th-month (stranger) anxiety to at least a larval capacity for evocative recall at that time (Fraiberg, 1969) and that some 10 months later the infant has achieved object permanency (Piaget, 1937). Again, full object constancy, developed toward the latter half of the 3rd postnatal year (Mahler, 1965, 1968; Mahler *et al.*, 1975), signifies the child's capacity to evoke a stable, reliable inner representation or image of the absent mother.

It is necessary, therefore, to attempt to account for the apparent dissociation of affective–libidinal cathexis from the evocable mental representation or image in the case of the narcissistic personality. An important clue is provided in the narcissistic personality's notable degree of obsessional character organization, with its abundant reliance on affect-isolative defenses to which reference has already been made (Rinsley, 1985). Thus, if ideas and images are essentially bereft of affective investment in such cases, where, in effect, has the affect gone, to be replaced by the pseudo-affect that typifies the external object relationships of many narcissistic individuals? The answer in part appears to lie in different depersonifying or appersonative mother–infant interactional patterns that respectively characterize emergent borderline and narcissistic personalities (Rinsley, 1980b). Whereas the future borderline personality is threatened with a cut-off of essential libidinal supplies, that is, with abandonment should he pursue separation–individuation, the future narcissistic personality is so threatened only if separation–individuation compromises the integrity of the symbiotic selfobject or, in other words, the tenaciously introjected pathogenic maternal part–object. In this latter case an obsessional character organization is now seen to develop as a defense against the regressive wish for symbiotic reunion or refusion, basic to which is the prematurely evolving capacity for evocative image recall that is dissociated from the affect linked to the pathogenic maternal introject. The result is an apparently coherent, "adultomorphic" *false self* (Winnicott, 1960). Such internalized object relations may additionally be understood in terms of Fairbairn's (1941) obsessional transitional mechanism, by means of which both the "good object" and the "bad object" are introjected (Rinsley, 1968). In terms of the sort of depersonification (appersonation) that typifies the mother–infant relationship in these cases, one may conceive of a process of generation of a false self by means of a premature, idealizing introjective generation of a spurious whole object ("good" plus "bad") that remains essentially undifferentiated from its correspondingly spurious whole self ("good" plus "bad").

THE TRANSITION FROM MAGIC TO FANTASY: A FURTHER COMMENT ON ENTITLEMENT

Magic hallucination and magic gestures characterize the world of the primarily narcissistic infant; their original function is to command the flow of need-satisfying supplies from the pristine part-object (breast); hence, they reflect the very earliest part-object relations. As the infant enters the 2nd postnatal year, the function of language will come to serve the same magical purpose as the expanding vocabulary at the infant's narcissistic disposal comes to be invested with magical significance (word magic) with the propensity for the overvaluation of words and thought that characterizes the classical obsessional personality and the narcissistic personality, and finds more primitive expression in the symptomatology and utterances of psychotics and borderline personalities.

The achievement of object permanency at approximately 18 months of age represents the result of what the psychoanalyst terms *internalization*. As McDevitt (1980) points out,

At the end of the practicing subphase and the beginning of the rapprochement subphase (between 12 and 18 months) we see a more active type of imitation in which the child takes more initiative. . . . The model now used by the junior toddler for his imitations and beginning identifications consists of mental representations of the behavior patterns of the love object. As Piaget . . . has pointed out, deferred imitations and symbolic play, as well as verbal evocation of the mother in her absence, indicate that behavior has become detached from its previous motoric context and now rests on representation in thought. (pp. 137–138)

The term *transitional* aptly applies to this momentous shift from purely sensorimotor to early preoperational functioning. In Winnicott's sense it signifies the generation of that creative "space" in which representational manipulation of self and "outside" may occur within the realm of pure fantasy while, at the same time, the reality of both is preserved. In Fairbairn's sense, it signifies the "dichotomy and exteriorization of the object" by means of which the "external object" is progressively endowed with the characteristics of reality and self and object, as it were, come to be differentiated.

The individual possessed of average or rather better intellectual endowment expresses the result of the transition from magic to fantasy in terms of preparatory or anticipatory fantasy that signifies the capacity for delay of drive discharge (frustration tolerance) that is basic to appropriate foreplanning. The gifted individual comes additionally to express it through fantasy-generated creative play, from which emerge the scientific and artistic achievements of culture. The borderline individual never adequately manages the transition, while the narcissistic personality does so only in a context of emotional asepsis and at a fearful price in terms of impaired internal and external object relations.

A most significant symptomatic manifestation of failed or impaired transition from magic to fantasy among borderline and narcissistic personalities is their sense of entitlement, the conviction that "the world owes me a living." Entitlement is described in the DSM-III (American Psychiatric Association, 1980), under narcissistic personality disorder, as follows:

"... expectation of special favors without assuming reciprocal responsibilities, e.g., surprise and anger that people will not do what is wanted." Frustration of the sense of entitlement among borderline personalities is prone to provoke them to reactive rage, abject despair, or retaliatory aggression, whether verbal (devaluation) or physical; among narcissistic personalities it evokes rather lesser degrees of chagrin, depression, and often milder varieties of retaliation; common to both are feelings of rejection (abandonment).

Gestural and word magic lie at the basis of the sense of entitlement, specifically the infantile wish that others should intuit the unexpressed or metaphorical meaning behind one's words or acts or should divine one's needs without having to be told.

Among the more severe schizotypal borderline personalities, the sense of entitlement merges into "... magical thinking, e.g., superstitiousness, clairvoyance, telepathy, '6th sense,' 'others can feel my feelings'" and "ideas of reference" (American Psychiatric Association, 1980). Among those deteriorating toward psychosis, the next regressive step is characterized by the appearance of frank delusions, both nihilistic and persecutory, and of illusory, hallucinatory, and somatic delusional experiences.

SUMMARY

The foregoing discussion has addressed the interrelated phenomena of object permanency and object constancy with particular attention to the impact of their impairment upon the development of internal object relations, and specifically as conducive to the persistence of the primitive selfobject.

In keeping with the concept of the developmental spectrum or continuum, as elsewhere set forth (Rinsley, 1980a, 1981, 1984), the narcissistic personality is considered a less primitively organized variety of the borderline personality in view of their common, disordered internal object relations, based in turn upon the pathogenetic push–pull mother–infant relationship.

REFERENCES

American Psychiatric Association (1980). *Diagnostic and statistical manual of mental disorders* (3rd ed.). Washington, DC: Author.

Balint, M. (1968). *The basic fault: Therapeutic aspects of regression.* London: Tavistock.

Beres, D. (1968). The humanness of human beings: Psychoanalytic considerations. *Psychoanalytic Quarterly, 37,* 487–522.

Dickes, R. (1978). Parents, transitional objects, and childhood fetishes. In S. A. Grolnick *et al.* (Eds.), *Between reality and fantasy: Transitional objects and phenomena* (pp. 307–319). New York: Jason Aronson.

Erikson, E. H. (1956). The problem of ego identity. *Journal of the American Psychiatric Association, 4,* 56–121.

Erikson, E. H. (1963). *Childhood and society* (rev. ed.). New York: W. W. Norton.

Fairbairn, W. R. D. (1941). A revised psychopathology of the psychoses and the psychoneuroses. In *An object-relations theory of the personality* (pp. 28–58). New York: Basic Books, 1954.

Fraiberg, S. (1969). Libidinal object constancy and mental representation. *The Psychoanalytic Study of the Child, 24,* 9–47.

Freud, A. (1960). Discussion of Dr. John Bowlby's paper. *The Psychoanalytic Study of the Child, 15,* 53–62.

Freud, A. (1968). Panel discussion held at the 25th Congress of the International Psycho-Analytical Association, Copenhagen, July 1967. *International Journal of Psycho-Analysis, 49,* 506–512.

Freud, S. (1905). Three essays on the theory of sexuality. *Standard Edition, 7,* 135–243. London: Hogarth Press.

Freud, S. (1911). Formulations on the two principles of mental functioning. *Standard Edition, 12,* 218–226. London: Hogarth Press.

Freud, S. (1927). Fetishism. *Standard Edition, 21,* 152–157. London: Hogarth Press.

Freud, S. (1940). Splitting of the ego in the process of defence. *Standard Edition, 23,* 275–278. London: Hogarth Press.

Grinker, R. R., & Werble, B. (1977). *The borderline patient.* New York: Jason Aronson.

Grinker, R. R., Werble, B., & Drye, R. (1968). *The borderline syndrome: A behavioral study of ego functions.* New York: Basic Books.

Hartmann, H. (1952). The mutual influences in the development of ego and id. In *Essays on ego psychology* (pp. 155–182). New York: International Universities Press, 1964.

Hartmann, H. (1956). Notes on the reality principle. In *Essays on ego psychology* (pp. 241–267). New York: International Universities Press, 1964.

Jacobson, E. (1954a). Contributions to the metapsychology of psychotic identifications. *Journal of the American Psychoanalytic Association, 2,* 239–262.

Jacobson, E. (1954b). On psychotic identifications. *International Journal of Psycho-Analysis, 35,* 102–108.

Jacobson, E. (1954c). The self and the object world: Vicissitudes of their infantile cathexes and their influence on ideational and affective development. *The Psychoanalytic Study of the Child, 9,* 75–127.

Jacobson, E. (1957). Denial and repression. *Journal of the American Psychoanalytic Association, 5,* 61–92.

Jacobson, E. (1964). *The self and the object world.* New York: International Universities Press.

Jacobson, E. (1971). *Depression.* New York: International Universities Press.

Kaplan, L. J. (1980). Rapprochement and oedipal organization: Effects on borderline phenomena. In R. F. Lax, S. Bach, & J. A. Burland (Eds.), *Rapprochement: The critical subphase of separation-individuation.* New York: Jason Aronson.

Kernberg, O. F. (1966). Structural derivatives of object relationships. *International Journal of Psycho-Analysis, 47,* 236–253.

Kernberg, O. F. (1980). Regression in leaders. In *Internal world and external reality: Object relations theory applied.* New York: Jason Aronson.

Khan, M. M. R. (1963). The concept of cumulative trauma. *The Psychoanalytic Study of the Child, 18,* 286–306.

Kohut, H. (1971). *The analysis of the self.* New York: International Universities Press.

Kohut, H. (1977). *The restoration of the self.* New York: International Universities Press.

Mahler, M. S. (1965). On the significance of the normal separation-individuation phase with reference to research in symbiotic child psychosis. In M. Schur (Ed.), *Drives, affects, behavior* (Vol. 2, pp. 161–169). New York: International Universities Press. (Reprinted in *The selected papers of Margaret S. Mahler* (Vol. 2, pp. 49–57). New York: Jason Aronson, 1979.)

Mahler, M. S. (1968). *On human symbiosis and the vicissitudes of individuation: Infantile psychosis* (Vol. 1). New York: International Universities Press.

Mahler, M. S., Pine, F., & Bergman, A. (1975). *The psychological birth of the human infant: Symbiosis and individuation*. New York: Basic Books.

Masterson, J. F. (1974). Intensive psychotherapy of the adolescent with a borderline syndrome. In S. Arieti (Ed.), *American handbook of psychiatry* (2nd rev. ed., Vol. 2, pp. 250-263). New York: Basic Books.

Masterson, J. F. (1975). The splitting defense mechanism of the borderline adolescent: Developmental and clinical aspects. In J. E. Mack (Ed.), *Borderline states in psychiatry* (pp. 93-101). New York: Grune & Stratton.

Masterson, J. F. (1976). *Psychotherapy of the borderline adult: A developmental approach*. New York: Brunner/Mazel.

Masterson, J. F., & Rinsley, D. B. (1975). The borderline syndrome: The role of the mother in the genesis and psychic structure of the borderline personality. *International Journal of Psycho-Analysis, 56*, 163-177. (Reprinted as The etiology of borderline personality. In D. B. Rinsley *Treatment of the severely disturbed adolescent* (pp. 241-270). (Revised and reprinted in R. F. Lax, S. Bach, & J. A. Burland (Eds.), *Rapprochement: The critical subphase of separation-individuation* (pp. 299-329). New York: Jason Aronson, 1980.)

McDevitt, J. B. (1980). The role of internalization in the development of object relations during the separation-individuation phase. In R. F. Lax, S. Bach, & J. A. Burland (Eds.), *Rapprochement: The critical subphase of separation-individuation* (pp. 135-149). New York: Jason Aronson.

Metcalf, D. R., & Spitz, R. A. (1978). The transitional object: Critical developmental period and organizer of the psyche. In S. A. Grolnick *et al.* (Eds.), *Between reality and fantasy: Transitional objects and phenomena* (pp. 99-108). New York: Jason Aronson.

Modell, A. H. (1963). Primitive object relationships and the predisposition to schizopohrenia. *International Journal of Psycho-Analysis, 44*, 282-292.

Modell, A. H. (1968). *Object love and reality: An introduction to a psychoanalytic theory of object relations*. New York: International Universities Press.

Modell, A. H. (1975). The ego and the id fifty years later. *International Journal of Psycho-Analysis, 56*, 57-68.

Nagera, H. (1966). Sleep and its disturbances approached developmentally. *The Psychoanalytic Study of the Child, 21*, 393-447.

Nemiah, J., & Sifneos, P. (1970). Affect and fantasy in patients with psychosomatic disorders. In D. W. Hill (Ed.), *Modern trends in psychosomatic medicine* (Vol. 2, pp. 26-35). London: Butterworths.

Ornstein, P. H. (1974). On narcissism: Beyond the Introduction, highlights of Heinz Kohut's contributions to the psychoanalytic treatment of narcissistic personality disorders. *Annals of Psychoanalysis, 2*, 127-149.

Ovesey, L. (1969). *Homosexuality and pseudohomosexuality*. New York: Science House.

Piaget, J. (1937). *The construction of reality in the child*. New York: Basic Books, 1954.

Pine, F. (1974). Libidinal object constancy: A theoretical note. *Psychoanalysis and Contemporary Science, 3*, 307-313.

Rinsley, D. B. (1968). Economic aspects of object relations. *International Journal of Psycho-Analysis, 49*, 38-48.

Rinsley, D. B. (1977). An object relations view of borderline personality. In P. Hartocollis (Ed.), *Borderline personality disorders: The concept, the syndrome, the patient* (pp. 47-70). New York: International Universities Press.

Rinsley, D. B. (1978). Borderline psychopathology: A review of aetiology, dynamics and treatment. *International Review of Psycho-Analysis, 5*, 45-54.

Rinsley, D. B. (1979). Fairbairn's object-relations theory: A reconsideration in terms of newer knowledge. *Bulletin of the Menninger Clinic, 43*, 489-514.

Rinsley, D. B. (1980a). The developmental etiology of borderline and narcissistic disorders. *Bulletin of the Menninger Clinic, 44,* 127–134.

Rinsley, D. B. (1980b). Diagnosis and treatment of borderline and narcissistic children and adolescents. *Bulletin of the Menninger Clinic, 44,* 147–170.

Rinsley, D. B. (1981). Dynamic and developmental issues in borderline and related "spectrum" disorders. *The Psychiatric Clinics of North America.*

Rinsley, D. B. (1984). A comparison of borderline and narcissistic personality disorders. *Bulletin of the Menniger Clinic, 48,* 1–9.

Rinsley, D. B. (1985). Notes on the pathogenesis and nosology of borderline and narcissistic personality disorders. *Journal of the American Academy of Psychoanalysis, 13,* 317-328.

Schafer, R. (1968). Aspects of internalization. New York: International Universities Press.

Sifneos, P. (1973). The presence of "alexithymic" characteristics in psychosomatic patients. *Psychotherapy and Psychosomatics, 22,* 255–262.

Sifneos, P. (1975). Problems of psychotherapy of patients with alexithymic characteristics and physical disease. *Psychotherapy and Psychosomatics, 26,* 65–70.

Spitz, R. A. (1957). *No and yes: On the genesis of human communication.* New York: International Universities Press.

Winnicott, D. W. (1950-1955). Aggression in relation to emotional development. In *Collected papers: Through paediatrics to psycho-analysis* (pp. 204–218). London: Tavistock, 1958.

Winnicott, D. W. (1951). Transitional objects and transitional phenomena. In *Collected papers: Through paediatrics to psycho-analysis* (pp. 229–242). London: Tavistock, 1958.

Winnicott, D. W. (1960). Ego distortion in terms of true and false self. In *The maturational processes and the facilitating environment: Studies in the theory of emotional development* (pp. 140–152). New York: International Universities Press, 1965.

CHAPTER TEN

Psychic Integration and Object Constancy

PETER L. GIOVACCHINI

INTRODUCTION

Psychoanalytic theory and practice, when viewed over the span of the existence of psychoanalysis, have followed a definite sequence that is determined by the types of psychopathology confronting clinicians. I need not belabor whether psychopathology has changed throughout the years; Reichard (1956), among others, has already explored this question. Rather, I emphasize how psychodynamic formulations based upon id–ego conflicts have been supplemented by theoretical constructions that elaborate structural deficits.

In this chapter I wish to extend the structural viewpoint and investigate how attributes of the external world become part of the psyche. This is an object relations focus that highlights interactions with external objects and the acquisition of developmentally higher levels of psychic integration. The acquisition of psychic structure is a reciprocal process; that is, as helpful experiences with the surrounding world lead to the endopsychic registrations and structuralization of function units that later coalesce into adaptive ego executive mechanisms, the ego's expanded capacities enable the psyche to seek out and profit from further potentially beneficial segments of reality.

The current focus on character structure relies heavily upon the investigation of cognitive factors. The exploration of cognition once again stresses the importance of object relationships, both as to their role in psychic development—the progression from early amorphous prementational states (Giovacchini, 1979) to cohesive ego organizations capable of tripartite modalities of relating—and the ego's ability to carry on various psychic functions relative to the inner and outer world, functions that are characteristic of particular developmental levels.

Psychodynamic formulations have not become useless as we move into structural and cognitive areas. The patient will determine which frame of reference is appropriate. Rather than leading to the replacement or condemnation of certain clinical concepts as erroneous or anachronistic, these additional viewpoints should enrich our perspectives about the variability and range of the human mind (see Wallerstein, 1981).

Recently there has been considerable discussion and controversy regarding whether various theoretical positions that involve a structural rather than a psychodynamic drive focus are clinically useful and to whether these conceptual models even belong in the psychoanalytic frame of reference. Many of these articles take Kohut's works (Kohut, 1971, 1977) as a point of departure and illuminate various facets of his ideas, often supporting them and occasionally modifying or cricitizing them. I have criticized most of his basic new formulations and definitions (Giovacchini, 1977, 1979) and do not wish to belabor them further. Instead I propose to refer briefly to areas that other authors have elaborated on and that are pertinent to our further understanding of structural and cognitive elements as they permit us to apply our psychoanalytic insights and techniques to the treatment of patients suffering from primitive mental states as well as patients who have achieved relatively high degrees of ego organization and developmental advancement but who are also capable of deep regression in which many sophisticated structure and functions are for the moment lost. Indeed, such a regression represents the essence of their psychopathology.

Dorpat (1976), for example, distinguishes between structural conflicts and object relations conflict. He attempts to create a dichotomy that reflects differences in explanations based upon conflicting drives and those that point to defects in psychic structure that cause impaired psychic functioning and are manifested in disturbed behavior and adaptations. He is, however, introducing a somewhat different perspective in that he is subdividing structural problems into two types: The first involves intrapsychic *structural* conflicts rather than clashes between opposing drives, and in the second the primary difficulty concerns faulty relationships with external objects. I find it difficult to maintain such a dichotomy because, as I am certain Dorpat would agree, the intrapsychic always affects the quality of object relationships. It is simply a question of emphasis. Freud (1924a, 1924b) had something similar in mind, in terms of drives however, when he contrasted the neuroses with the psychoses, asserting that the former were the outcome of intrapsychic conflict, a conflict between the ego and the id, and the latter resulted from rifts between the ego and the outer world, from our contemporary vista, the outer world of external objects.

Coen (1981) reviews the concepts of selfobject and preoedipal objects. He does not find it "useful to differentiate selfobjects from a more general class of preoedipal objects." Apparently, when dealing with preoedipal objects, the psyche is not operating on the basis of mature whole-object relations. Freud (1914) postulated that the earliest object relationships were narcissistic attachments (secondary narcissism), which define the selfobject (see Boyer & Giovacchini, 1967, p. 269) and these, of course, are pregenital (Freud, 1905) or preoedipal in nature. Consequently selfobjects and preoedipal object relationships, inasmuch as they are formed on the basis of secondary narcissism, are identical. Much discussion would prove to be superfluous if we remind ourselves of various features of the developmental hierarchy Freud had outlined, particularly his progression from autoerotism to primary narcissism, to the beginning of object relationships with secondary narcissism, and finally to relatively nonnarcissistic whole-object relationships, which are the outcome of the resolution of the Oedipus complex.

Returning to early developmental phases and their correspondent psychopathology, Levine (1979) reminds us of the importance and structure promoting qualities of sustaining object relationships. The barometer by which to gauge psychic structure is, according to Eisnitz (1981), the self-representation. He believes it offers us a framework by which we may view clinical phenomena. It is a final pathway evolving from the id, ego, and superego and "provides the 'set' that organizes and gives a special quality to ego functions and object relations under pressure of unconscious wishes" (Eisnitz, 1981). Wallerstein (1981) recognizes the importance of all aspects of the psychic apparatus, the self as well as the drives. He believes we should not unnecessarily subordinate or diminish the traditional focus on the vicissitudes of sexual and aggressive drives.

Many clinicians would agree with Eisnitz about the importance of the self-representation, particularly when dealing with borderline patients (Kernberg, 1975) and other patients suffering from character disorders (Giovacchini, 1975b). Sandler and Rosenblatt (1962) were among the first to conceive of the psyche in terms of self and object representations and the representational world. Hartmann (1950) first mentioned the concept of "self," which he introduced into the psychoanalytic literature. He distinguished the self from the ego, the former being connected with a subjective sense of being and the latter referring to an abstract concept of a particular functional unit of the mind.

I agree with those clinicians who prefer to use the term "self-representation" to designate an ego subsystem that incorporates various aspects of a person's identity and can be contrasted with other intraego formations that are depictions of external objects but are preserved internally as object representations. This is in accord with Jacobson's (1964) orientation. The term "self" has a much looser connotation and can be thought of as a general reflection of the psyche in its totality. Federn's (1952) attitudes about self-feeling are similar to this viewpoint about the self and highlight the contrast between the self, a supraordinate structure, and the self-representation.

SELF-REPRESENTATION AND OBJECT CONSTANCY

Fraiberg (1969) approached the establishment of object constancy from the viewpoint of the clinician. Noy (1979) more recently and also from a clinical viewpoint discussed cognition in a wider context and distinguished primary and secondary process cognitive elements and whether the perceptual apparatus is focused primarily on the inner or the outer world.

Fraiberg discussed two different types of memory: recall and evocative memory. The sensory apparatus, when functioning at the level of recall memory, recognizes an object when it appears in the perceptual field without retaining a reproducible memory trace of that object. There must be some mental representation but it is not sufficiently structured that it can be evoked without the presence of the external object; that is, if it is not sufficiently cathected so that it can be consciously experienced. This occurs with evocative memory, the same capacity Piaget (1954) discovered in his experiments, the capacity which enables the psyche to "remember" an external object even when it is not actually present.

These distinctions are significant because they have implications about emotional development and the achievement of psychic structure. Spitz (1957) believes that object constancy occurs considerably earlier than is believed by other psychoanalysts such as Fraiberg and Anna Freud (1951), who place its beginning at 18 months. Spitz postulates that it begins at 8 months, when stranger anxiety is first manifest. However, he links the ability to maintain a mental representation of the mother to a "special stress situation" (Fraiberg, 1969, p. 17), whereas Anna Freud writes about libidinal object constancy as a stable inner object representation even when there is no need, even when the object is experienced as unsatisfactory.

Piaget (1954) concentrated upon cognitive rather than libidinal factors and worked with three interrelated concepts: object permanency, object constancy, and evocative memory. Permanency refers to the inherent stability of the object, its independent status in time and space. He viewed object constancy as the stabilized (permanent) intrapsychic representation of an object regardless of its actual presence or absence, a structural achievement that occurs with the capacity for evocative memory. He agrees with many analysts, placing these developmental events around the age of 18 months.

Piaget's experiments were with inanimate objects, but he believed that the structuralizing processes responsible for animate and inanimate object constancy are the same. In fact, according to Piaget, animate object constancy occurs slightly before inanimate object constancy. His experiments established a hierarchy that is important to both the study of normal development and psychopathology.

The ego progressively structuralizes and acquires a multifaceted internal object representation, which is retained despite large libidinal fluctuations. As these cognitive functions are established, there is a corresponding formation of the identity sense. Along with the refinement of the object concept, as Piaget called it, there is a parallel structuring of the self-representation. The qualities of both self and object representations are the outcome of the ego's integrity or its psychopathological defects.

As object representations become more cohesive, integrated, and sophisticated, boundaries between self and object representations become increasingly distinct. This causes a further consolidation of the self-representation, which is experienced as an enhancement of the identity sense.

In essence, there is a parallel development between object constancy and the constancy of the self-representation. The failure to reach such levels of integration has many psychopathological consequences. The inability to attain *self-representational constancy*, or its loss through regression, is the basis of much of the psychopathology that patients currently present to us.

Our patients often confront us with overwhelming amounts of data that clearly demonstrate the lack of constancy of self and object representations. Frequently, they suffer from intense anxiety because they cannot maintain a cohesive identity sense when there are changes in their familiar environment. They have little or no flexibility. They require an absolutely constant environment in order to support the shaky integration of the self-representation and to be able to preserve the boundaries of object representations. If they can no longer continue in their usual minimal construction of boundaries of self and object representations, there is the danger of destructive fusion when circumstances upset their usual equilibrium. Such problems present special technical difficulties and often complications in the psychoanalytic situation, which I will discuss in the following pages.

Another frequently encountered clinical phenomenon concerns the loss of self-esteem. Most borderline patients who suffer from structural defects uniformly demonstrate a profound sense of worthlessness and a lack of purpose and definition of values, all associated with the amorphous qualities of the self-representation. In treatment this negative self-appraisal may prove to be especially impervious to analytic resolution, because neither the patient nor the analyst is able to relate it to any focal internal conflicts, external precipitants, or etiologic infantile traumas. There is nothing in the patient's background that is sufficiently specific to account for the looseness of integration and the rigidity of the self-representation.

The patient has learned how to adapt to the infantile world, and within such a context he is able to avail himself of adequate amounts of self-esteem and keep self and object representations somewhat differentiated. When he moves outside the confines of this ambience, as is inevitable, his usual equilibrium is drastically upset and self-esteeming adaptations become ineffective. The analytic setting itself also represents an ambience that is different from the infantile environment and is intrinsically threatening to some patients suffering from particular types of psychopathology, because within such a context infantile defenses cannot continue functioning. This creates intense problems for the analytic relationship, but they are not always insurmountable.

From this discussion we can infer that the integration of self and object representations and their internal consistency or constancy can be conceptualized from the vantage point of different levels of psychic structuralization. For example, the self-representation can be well organized and cohesive but at a primitive level. Kernberg (1975) believes this is typical of the borderline personality organization.

Organization of the self-representation within a primitive context is now familiar to most analysts as we come to understand our borderline patients better and as our clinical experience broadens. Object constancy, however, has been considered an attribute of a relatively advanced developmental stage and has not been viewed as belonging to earlier phases. This made sense because we have assumed that emotional development proceeds from states of lesser structure to states of greater structure. The study of cognition has, to a large measure, supported the viewpoint that psychic development proceeds in an additive fashion.

This developmental progression, in view of our clinical experience, requires reconsideration. Our patients provide us with data that require that we carefully think out how what might be an ordinary developmental sequence becomes distorted by psychopathology and contributes to the final pathologically constructed ego organization. The borderline patient is a case in point if we accept that he has a relatively stable integrated self-representation although it is primitively organized. In other words, this emphasizes that a *primitive state need not be equated with a lack of structural organization*. Perhaps such an equation is valid for the neonate but not necessarily for the adult, who is the product of a developmental sequence.

What can be said for the self-representation also applies to object representations and object constancy. Some primitive ego states, the outcome of psychopathology, can relate to the external world on the basis of object constancy. The ego is able to maintain a mental representation of an external object without its actual presence. Still, the psyche, by and large, has achieved only a minimum of differentiation with poorly established boundaries between the inner and outer world. This particular situation is characteristic of specific types of psychopathology and modes of relating.

For example, certain patients relate to the analyst and people in general only on the basis of their needs. This would be expected of patients who are experiencing an analytic regression, but this orientation is not limited to the treatment setting. The analyst learns that the exclusion of the recognition of external objects as persons and the total lack of mutuality and reciprocity is characteristic of all their relationships. Nevertheless, they do not lose mental representations when the external object is absent, a situation I will describe in the next section.

In analysis these patients are often intense and obviously needy. As a rule, they are humorless and their viewpoint about themselves, their friends, and the world is constricted. They may be vociferously demanding and can have a tremendous impact on the analyst because of the immediacy of their needs. However, it also happens that because of being treated only as an object and as a nonperson, the therapist defensively reacts with analytic neutrality.

Some clinicians, Modell (1968) in particular, consider this type of relating, which in treatment leads to specific disruptive countertransference responses, to be typical of narcissistic patients. Undoubtedly this is true, but it also includes patients who phenomenologically display no signs of a narcissistic orientation. Their object relations, as discussed in the previous section, are preoedipal and narcissistic, but their ego structure is characterized by a lack of, rather than an apparent surplus of, ego–libido, which usually represents an overcompensatory defense to bolster a self-representation plagued with a profound sense of inadequacy and worthlessness. These patients are totally preoccupied with themselves, but they also reveal, sometimes parade, their feelings of worthlessness. There is a diversity to their underlying character structure, ranging from borderline states to depressive and even obsessive–compulsive organizations.

PSYCHOPATHOLOGY

Developmentally, it is possible to trace a continuum from an amorphous ego state in which intraego structures are unformed and precede object relationships to one that contains well-differentiated self and object representations and operates on the basis of object constancy and mature whole-object relationships. With psychopathology there are varying degrees of regression and fixation, which were first described in terms of drives (Breuer & Freud, 1895). Here, I will discuss how the mechanisms of regression and fixation affect the structure of self and object representations, and I will begin by describing patients who exhibit very primitive fixations.

These patients have fairly amorphous self-representations and have not yet achieved object constancy. As is generally true, absolute distinctions are difficult to make when dealing with emotional states. The type of patient I am about to describe demonstrates a relative absence of object constancy, and in some very primitively fixated patients it can approach total absence.

Loss of Mental Representation

A married woman in her late 30s demanded daily appointments. She told me during her first session that she could not tolerate my being away. She realized that I would occasionally take a vacation or otherwise leave the city, but she found this extremely upsetting. She knew she had to accept the fact that from time to time I would leave, but she demanded that I would let her know about it well ahead of time. I let her know immediately about my next trip, which was almost 6 months away. This did not particularly help inasmuch as she spent most of her time reviling me for planning to go away, which she at first presented to me as desertion and abandonment.

I learned that the patient felt she needed me to be constantly present, 7 days a week, 24 hours a day. Knowing that this was impossible, she had to at least know where I would always be. She revealed that without knowing my location her mental image of me would fade away. She had to have some communication with a person in order to be able to hold a mental representation of that person. In addition to her demands regarding my presence, she had the itinerary of all of her friends, and she kept daily telephone contact with about a dozen of them.

Her life had a frenetic quality to it. Everything she did was done with intense excitement or, more accurately, considerable agitation. She suffused the consultation room with all-pervasive tension, which she generally felt as painful. Although the patient was clever and sometimes witty, her excitement was usually grim and humorless.

She complained that she knew very little about pleasure, but she was not particularly depressed. She described a stae of anhedonia. Her general attitude seemed pathetic, but it was difficult to classify it definitely.

I learned that she was, for all ostensible purposes, incapable of feeling. For example, she literally did not know if she were hungry, thirsty, sexually aroused, or had to defecate or urinate. All she felt was an amorphous type of inner tension, and she relied mainly on its predominant anatomic location to determine which organ system was primarily involved.

She perceived herself in the same amorphous fashion as she experienced feelings. She had no sense of who she was, where she fit in the world, or the purpose of her life. She had been unable to continue college in another city because she apparently suffered from a severe emotional decompensation that necessitated hospitalization. She had all the signs and symptoms Erikson (1959) placed under the rubric of the identity diffusion syndrome.

She had a poorly defined identity sense, which could be accounted for by early life experiences, especially the fact that she was the neglected younger child of an identical twin sibship. The diffuseness of her self-representation reached such intense proportions that she sometimes wondered whether she were alive. She was in constant terror about "dissolving into nothing."

Returning to the discussion of amorphous feelings, she reported always feeling anxious, but was not better able to define what she meant. She had not been able to connect her anxiety, if that is what it was, to any situations that might either precipitate or terminate it. Nor did her associations (she did not report many dreams) supply clues as to unconscious conflicts that would account for her diffuse feeling or its intensity. I could not understand its source.

In one session she surprised me when she said she was the source of her anxiety. She told me she could turn it on and off as one turns a faucet on and off. Then she proceeded to demonstrate what she meant. She had been relatively calm and composed at the beginning of the session, a state that soon changed as she decided to demonstrate how she could create anxiety. She said, "Now I will feel anxious," and as if she commanded her autonomic nervous system to respond, she showed all the visible signs of anxiety. Her pupils dilated, she developed "goose bumps" and I could see small trickles of perspiration on her brow. She then stated she would no longer feel anxious and just as suddenly all of the autonomic signs of anxiety vanished.

Although her affective tone was, according to her, poorly discriminated, she was, nevertheless, able to generate feelings. She had a modicum of conscious control as she so dramatically illustrated. Still she was far from being completely in control, since she was driven to produce anxiety. Otherwise, she experienced what she called "apathetic terror," which was associated with a fear of dissolution. Clearly she was describing an existential crisis.

Federn (1952) used the same words, "apathetic terror," as the patient to describe an ego that is losing its cohesiveness and integration. Byschowski (1952) also described similar subjective states in schizophrenic patients who were not only withdrawing from the external world as Freud (1911) discussed, but whose identity sense was crumbling. That is the way my patient viewed herself. She was terrified that if she did not create anxiety she would cease to exist. She compared her situation to a person pinching himself to determine that he is awake. To feel nothing meant she was dead. To feel something, although it was painful, reassured her that she was alive. Without anxiety she perceived herself as a vacuum, as an empty terrifying void. She produced an affect that was phenomenologically similar to anxiety to protect against a more fundamental anxiety, the fear of annihilation.

To summarize briefly, this woman is representative of a class of patients who have practically no capacity for object constancy. This is evidenced by an inability to form and hold a mental representation of an external object without the presence of that object. This does not mean, as it did with Piaget's (1954) children, that the person has to be within the subject's visual field. With adult patients the knowledge of a person's whereabouts—if the person is not too far away and is immediately available, at least by telephone—suffices to maintain an internal object representation.

Correspondingly, the self-representation is tenuously constructed, and these patients suffer from severe identity problems.

Fear of Fusion and Loss of Self-Esteem

Analysts are becoming increasingly familiar with patients who vigorously resist beginning treatment or who later in treatment create an impasse that threatens to disrupt therapy (see Giovacchini & Boyer, 1975). I am referring to a group of patients who also suffer from character defects but who have a greater, although still minimal, degree of object constancy than the patient described in the previous section. There is a quantitative continuum between these two groups, and the tenuous nature of self and object representations account for the difficulties in constructing and maintaining an analytic setting.

I will describe a patient, a successful, very bright young man in his early 30s, who was extremely conflicted about starting analysis. On the surface, this was odd because he had tried for many months to get me to see him for analysis. Since my schedule was full, I had tried to refer him to various colleagues, but he adamantly refused to see them because he was afraid they would not want to analyze him because he was "too sick." Thus, it was particularly surprising when he tried to manipulate me into not analyzing him.

He spontaneously gave me a long detailed history, obsessionally filling in every detail of past development. It is not necessary here for my purpose to summarize his history. I will just mention that he had a successful but passively uninvolved father and a beautiful, apparently narcissistic mother who doted on him. He was an only child, who attracted considerable attention because of his innate talents and intellectual precocity.

At the beginning of the third session, I briefly instructed him about free association and the use of the couch. I knew this was an interruption of his intention to further information concerning his past, but I saw no purpose in letting him continue as he had been. I often do not tell patients anything, usually asking them to lie on the couch and letting them decide what they wish to talk about or in some instances simply letting them remain silent. With this patient, although he had initially confronted me as someone eager for analysis, I believed he would have gone on indefinitely sitting up and continuing with his narrative and avoiding the couch.

He politely listened to me but seemed bewildered. However, he approached the couch but moved the pillow to the other end and proceeded to lie down, a position in which he would be facing me. I corrected him immediately and he turned himself around. He started speaking in a less organized, preplanned fashion, often hesitating and indicating a modicum of anxiety. Five minutes before the end of the session, he sat up and said, "I've had enough." He did not leave, however; he continued talking until the end of the session.

The patient cancelled the next four sessions, each time having what appeared to be "legitimate" reasons. For example, he cancelled his next appointment because he had the flu with a fever of 103°F. He recovered rather quickly but not until he missed the second session. After that he was unexpectedly sent out of town by his firm, which caused him to miss the last two sessions.

When he returned he walked toward the chair, but I motioned him to the couch. Again he reluctantly walked toward it but he did not lie down. Sitting up, he told me that his problems were current and immediate and he did not want to get lost in the morass of his past. This seemed bizarre, since he had gone into such extensive details of his early childhood and development.

I had some vivid feelings that I will discuss in the section dealing with technical factors and countertransference. For the moment, I will reveal that I had to resist the impulse to tell him angrily that he should stop wasting my time. Either he would let me analyze him or he could go elsewhere. I restrained myself by remembering the simple principle of psychic determinism. The patient had to be reacting to some profound anxiety that prevented him from relaxing and regressing in an analytic context. So I explained to him he could determine whether he talked about the past or the present. In this regard he had complete autonomy. However, for technical reasons as well as my personal comfort, I required that he use the couch. If I felt that treatment could progress in any other fashion, one in which he would be more comfortable, I would be glad to conduct therapy on that basis. However, I and the psychoanalytic method had limitations and I knew no other way in which I could comfortably proceed. I also felt that by letting him sit up we might be evading some fundamental problems. He did not seem happy about what I said but he acquiesced. I somehow felt we had avoided a power struggle.

I learned later that the patient's initial reluctance to begin analysis was the outcome of his ambivalence. He desperately wanted analysis but he was frightened. He understood that the aim of analysis is to foster autonomy but he was afraid of losing control. To lie on the couch and not be able to look at me signified that he was helpless and vulnerable. Looking at me meant that he was in control as he maintained his vigilance. His dreams and associations indicated that basically he was afraid that I would engulf him, making him part of me, and he would dissolve into nothing. He was terrified that he would become my "handmaiden."

Apart from obvious masochistic, homosexual transference elements, he was dominated by the fear of fusion, which recapitulated the infantile symbiotic fusion with his mother. The fear of symbiotic merger made it difficult to begin analysis, and during treatment he experienced transference regression in a frightened painful fashion, but he had considerable resiliency and integration and had developed sufficient trust in the analytic setting that he was able to move in and out of regressed states that corresponded to the symbiotic stage. It was interesting to note how he came out of the regression; that is, how he used certain adaptations to protect himself from fusion.

As he usually conducted himself in daily life, he would become rigid and concrete in his observations and attitudes when regaining his composure after a period when he felt that I was "swallowing" him to make him part of myself. He recognized how this fear stemmed from his infantile past, but he still experienced it intensely and painfully. In the regressed state he perceived me in a vague, blurred, indefinite way and had extreme difficulty in maintaining a coherent image of both me and himself. As he emerged from such a state, we both became very distinct in his mind, distinct and sharply separated.

At these moments he seemed to have lost his ability to free associate and was outwardly directed. He no longer had any capacity for introspection. He would ask me innumerable questions, the types of questions that are usually directed toward physicians, such as "Are we making progress? What is my prognosis? Can we summarize what we have accomplished?" and similar queries which I had no inclination to answer. During these periods he had assigned us specific roles. He was the patient and I was the doctor. However, he also viewed himself in terms of his work and various social roles, but his concepts about himself, me, and the world in general were stilted and mechanical.

His memory was unusually good when he exhibited these concrete qualities. He could retain a mental representation of me with unusual clarity and could recall in details my mannerisms, the inflections of my voice, and accurately remember exactly what I had said. This was in sharp contrast to his orientation during regressed states in which self and object representations lost their distinct qualities and became fused.

Clearly, his concrete state was a defensive adaptation to protect him from the dissolution of his self-representation that he feared would occur with symbiotic fusion. He had defensively achieved object constancy, but it was not entirely a developmental achievement. Object constancy was part of a defensively constructed ego state that did not permit him any access to the deeper layers of his personality. This was reflected in his behavior and general functioning in that he was inflexible, unfeeling, and inhibited in working creatively, a severe handicap in view of his professional position.

Still, in contrast to the previously mentioned patient who had problems in forming and maintaining mental representations, who in essence had achieved only a minimal, almost nonexistent object constancy, this patient had traversed a considerable distance on the developmental scale. The fact that he could construct an ego state based upon object constancy, even though defensively motivated, is indicative of basic integrative capacities.

Much more can be written about the disruptive nature of symbiotic fusion or lack of a harmonious fusion. There are various psychopathological constellations of the mother–infant merger, which include an inability to merge, ranging from the mother who totally abandons her infant to mothers who sadistically attack their children either symbolically or actually. I believe that patients suffering from severe structural psychopathology have not been able to fuse with the internalized representations of their mothers, and their mothers, in turn, are unable to relate intuitively to their children because of structural defects of their own which interfere with their maternal capacities.

Lack of fusion or defective fusion is the outcome of psychopathology. My patient—and there are many patients who are characterologically similar—organized himself around the axis of what we might call a pathological object constancy to defend himself against the threat of being fused to a mother who would stamp out his individuality in order to enhance herself. From one viewpoint he was using elements of a later developmental phase to protect himself from an earlier one. He was paradoxically regressing in a forward direction.

Still, the stage that defensively included object constancy was primitive in many respects, as evidenced by its concreteness, rigidity, and insular isolation from other developmental phases. Its narrow, constricted view of the world and limited responses are indicative of an infantile, vulnerable orientation rather than the maturity associated with nondefensive object constancy.

Such a defensive ego state is characterized by strict definitions of values. These patients, as occasionally did my patient, deal mainly in polarities. Everything is good or bad, true or false, and based on the strict dichotomies of love and hate. There is no in-between room for illusion.

Winnicott (1953) wrote about the development of the capacity for illusion while describing the formation of the transitional object in the context of the mother–infant symbiosis. The mother and the infant are psychically fused, and the mother's optimal nurturing ministrations cause the infant to believe that the source of nurture resides within the self. This is, of course, an illusion but one that the mother supports rather than challenges. The child develops the security that he will always have his needs satisfied and that he is in control of his destiny. I realize that these formulations involve considerable adultomorphosizing but a harmonious symbiotic phase, such as Winnicott described, is instrumental for the establishment of self-confidence, flexibility, and the capacity for pleasurable illusion, which can lead to playful activities and exploration and in later phases to creative accomplishment. The perception of external objects is based upon a multifaceted object constancy. The defensive object constancy I have described is almost the total antithesis of the above.

Constricted View of External Objects

This final group of patients I am about to discuss have progressed further on the developmental scale than those just described. They have emerged from the symbiotic phase and have achieved object constancy. However, these patients' view of external objects, although stable, is inflexible and constricted. In some respects their outlook is similar to the patients described in the previous section, but there are significant differences in psychic structure. The construction of object constancy is not particularly a defensive adaptation, a protection against fusion, for this group. Instead, object constancy is the outcome of defective development, and the resultant ego organization causes specific orientations toward the outer world and behavioral patterns, that is, unique ways to relate to external objects. In treatment, their modes of relating create characteristic transference reactions and countertransference difficulties.

Although the type of psychopathology that patients in this group present is not, relatively speaking, particularly severe or bizarre in its manifestations, their treatment is often experienced as tedious. For example, I found myself reacting to a 35-year-old married man with annoyance, although there were no obvious reasons why I should have had such a feeling.

The patient was a highly successful professional who was quite articulate and had an excellent command of the language. He had considerable wit and his descriptions of inner feelings and outer events were picturesque and entertaining. My feelings puzzled me.

Perhaps I had anticipated what would happen. He continued in the same clever style, but he turned from description of the inner world of his psyche and of his environment to nagging and complaining about treatment. He had a rigid obsessive character configuration, and similar to the patient I discussed in the previous section, he became demanding in a concrete fashion. However, unlike that patient, his concreteness was not as pervasive. He could easily become psychologically minded and make use of free association, fantasies, and dreams for introspective purposes. Even his nagging and complaining were transient. He periodically became concrete, rigid, and demanding, but this orientation was punctuated with other attitudes that are more propitious for analysis. Most of the time he presented material that was helpful in maintaining an intrapsychic focus. Paradoxically, his preoccupation with himself, rather than being favorable for analysis, struck me as being a deterrent for treatment and was disturbing me.

Although I wish to defer the discussion of countertransference to the next section, in which I intend discussing technical factors, I still have to include countertransference factors briefly here because they are indicators in a general sense of the particular type of psychopathology that was confronting me. Unlike other superficially similar clinical situations, I did not believe the patient was withdrawing from me, shutting me out, or even diminishing my worth by projecting feelings of inadequacy into me. There were some such projections, but they did not dominate the transference, and even if they had, there was no reason why they should have interfered with the course of the analysis or have upset me. In fact, none of the defensive adaptations I have mentioned should have been reason for concern. They are common enough defensive stances for patients suffering from structural problems and intrapsychic conflicts.

My description of my patient's mode of relating, which I found disturbing, requires amplification. I had the impression that he was not aware of me as a person. He made me feel as if I were unidimensional and lacked depth. I was only a vehicle for his needs, and the external world was simply revolving around him, having no other focus. This sounds to be the orientation of narcissistic patients, who deal with external objects as if they were selfobjects. Their analyses often cause the analyst to feel that he does not exist in his own right and apart from the patient. The therapist may even feel the type of anxiety that is characteristic of an existential crisis (Giovacchini, 1972, 1979). This was not the situation with my patient. He did recognize me as separate and apart from himself but in a limited way.

At the beginning and end of sessions, he was always courteous and respectful, a contrast to his occasional outbursts of recrimination and sarcasm during the session. However, when feeling especially mellow, he might spend all of his time discussing topics he knew I found exciting and sharing intellectual interests with me. He seemed to be relating to me as a person;

nevertheless, I did not feel as if he were. I still reacted as if I were being excluded although clearly this was not so.

I then realized that I was responding to his emotional tone rather than the content of what he said. Although his material was interesting, the way he presented it was tedious and dull. He never smiled and was totally devoid of humor as an affect although, as stated, he could be witty. He often looked depressed, confused, and perplexed but never animated, enthusiastic or happy. At his best he would be calm and mellow. The combination of directing everything back to himself even when he began by focusing on something that interested me and his humorless mode of presentation made me uncomfortable. I was able to relax when I understood our relationship in terms of his infantile past.

As long as the patient could remember, his mother had been in treatment with a prominent analyst because of a chronic depression. When the patient was 6 months old, his mother had been hospitalized for several months. In spite of her severe emotional difficulties, he was told that she was a good and devoted mother. He remembered being well taken care of as a child but he could not recall ever chatting or playing games with her. Apparently, she was constantly depressed and never smiled.

She related to his immediate needs with a sense of immediacy but she could not go beyond the need-gratification level. I was able partially to reconstruct and speculate about the early maternal interaction from the way he related to me and from my countertransference responses. I also had the opportunity to gather information about the mother from her analyst, who emphasized that she had not been able to recognize her son as a person, but simply as a baby who had to be fed and changed. He confirmed that she never sang or cooed to him. In fact, since the analyst had been interested in her mothering behavior, he had asked her about the various developmental milestones of her son's life. When questioned, she did not recognize that her child had a smiling response or felt stranger anxiety. Certainly, she had not tried to evoke a smile from him, and as far as her analyst could tell, she had not smiled in his presence. She did not seem to get any pleasure from her son. He was a chore that she conscientiously took care of but not a person whose presence would fill her with pride and a sense of accomplishment.

I felt exactly the same way. I also felt no pride or sense of accomplishment about the treatment relationship. We did not smile at each other and I took it to mean that he was not pleased to see me. To him, it meant nothing because, like his mother, smiling was a foreign habit.

I have emphasized that I was not being ignored in the same manner that some narcissistic patients totally exclude external objects and concentrate only on themselves. The mother's analyst was again helpful. He did not classify his patient's relationship with her son as being primarily narcissistic or engulfingly symbiotic. He believed that because of her depression she could only relate to external objects in a constricted fashion, which in regard to her son meant she could only relate to the immediacy of his needs. She could not deal with him as a person in his own right who was emerging and developing as an autonomous human being. She had no intuition or empathy; she could not establish emotional resonance with him. She simply looked after him in terms of physical needs, which permitted him to reach a developmental level that includes object constancy but a constricted view of external objects based upon his needs. He neither received nor gave emotional sustenance.

Of course, he had received some emotional sustenance; otherwise, he would not have been able to achieve even a constricted form of object constancy and levels of psychic development that led to a fairly successful career and moderately adequate social relationships. He was much further advanced emotionally than the children Spitz (1945) described, whose physical needs were taken care of but who were kept isolated in cubicles. This patient could relate fairly well to the external world, but he was considered selfish, eccentric, and rigid.

Many patients suffering from characterologic problems have similar backgrounds and evoke disruptive countertransference reactions during treatment. The analyst has to understand the patient's structural defects and constrictions in order to overcome his reluctance to continue analysis.

TECHNICAL FACTORS AND COUNTERTRANSFERENCE PROBLEMS

Each category of patients presents unique problems in the treatment relationship, based upon particular facets of their psychopathology. The psychoanalytic method as well as some of the formal elements of the psychoanalytic setting may reinforce the patient's resistance or be experienced as a repetition of the traumatic past, causing intensification of problems rather than providing relief from inner disruptive feelings. This imbrication of treatment method and psychopathology, a situation I have called the *psychoanalytic paradox* (Giovacchini, 1975a, 1979), leads to special technical problems.

Obviously, the patient who insists that the analyst always be available and in extreme cases refuses to leave at the end of a session is unreasonable to the point of being intolerable. Such demands are the outcome of an inability to maintain a mental representation of the analyst between sessions, a lack of evocative memory as Fraiberg (1969) would conclude. Nevertheless, there are limits to the manifestations of psychopathology the analyst can tolerate and at the same time maintain an analytic setting. Some of these patients cannot be treated in a conventional fashion.

There are no specific recommendations or techniques that make such patients analyzable. If the therapist is highly motivated to treat patients who cannot maintain mental representations without external reinforcement, he might have to alter drastically his work style. I supervised a younger colleague who saw his patient early in the morning in the restaurant of his office building so that he could control the end of the session by leaving when the time was up. After approximately 6 months of treatment in this unconventional manner, he was able to return to his office and the patient has been able to control her need to remain there forever. Another colleague insisted on the patient's hospitalization so that he did not have to be anxious about the patient not leaving at the end of the session. Some patients cannot be treated on an outpatient basis.

Another colleague had to terminate treatment with the ultimatum that he did not want to see or hear from the patient for the next 6 months. He insisted on a vacation from the treatment; he needed to declare a moratorium so that he could feel comfortable about resuming treatment, and the patient had to realize that she also had certain obligations as a patient. She slept on the floor of his waiting room, called him all hours of the day and night, and even rented an apartment in the same building so that she could keep account of his movements. When she realized her analyst was adamant and serious, she moved away, abided by his terms, and returned to treatment in 6 months.

These patients have serious ego defects and behave in an irrational, unpredictable fashion. Their infantile world was irrational and unpredictable in that their early object relationships were inconsistent, and frequently the mother was totally absent. Their unreasonable demands often represent an attempt to establish a sense of continuity, to create a world in which they will not feel abandoned or vulnerable. However, because they are recapitulaing the traumatic, unreasonable elements of their traumatic infantile environment, they repeat childhood frustrations that disrupt the analytic setting.

The second group of patients described in the previous section have a much lesser impact on the therapeutic action than the patients just described. Nevertheless, they may be very difficult to treat inasmuch as they confront us with another aspect of the psychoanalytic paradox. They often cannot accept certain formal elements of the analytic process such as lying on the couch and free associating. The treatment impasse usually occurs at the beginning of treatment, and if the analyst is not willing to modify his approach by, for example, letting the patient sit up, the patient may abruptly terminate.

The young man I described used the couch at my insistence, although he protested vehemently. In two other instances the patients terminated. A middle-aged woman did not return for her next appointment after her 1st hour on the couch. Another patient, after 3 months of treatment, moved out of the city to join her mother in another city, claiming that she had received sufficient benefit from analysis that she could now continue on her own. These patients had intense resistance to analysis.

For this group of patients, the inner conflicts are reinforced by the "rules" of analysis. Throughout their lives they have erected defensive adaptations to deny their basic feelings of vulnerability and helplessness. Inasmuch as their self-representations are perceived as tenuous and object constancy is not firmly established, they fear analytic regression. They are terrified of fusing with the analyst and have to be constantly vigilant in order to maintain control. Consequently, lying on the couch and free associating are especially threatening.

The analyst has to decide whether he wants to modify his therapeutic stance, perhaps by permitting the introduction of parameters, as Eissler (1953) described. If the analyst strictly maintains the analytic setting he runs the risk of losing the patient early in treatment. I have tried both approaches.

The analyst's personal orientation is especially important in choosing an effective method of treatment, analysis or modified analysis, for this group of patients. When I have tried to treat them on their own terms, so to speak, I have not been particularly successful. On several occasions the patients were pleased and felt they had benefited from treatment, but other than some rearrangements of life circumstances, in one instance a divorce, I did not feel that much had been accomplished in terms of acquiring further psychic structure and resolution of intrapsychic conflict.

Undoubtedly, idiosyncratic elements of my character contribute heavily to my evaluation of these treatment situations. Countertransference is an important determinant as to how we wish to treat these patients. I found myself reluctant to relinquish my analytic identity, which is part of my professional ego-ideal, by offering these patients something other than analysis. Inasmuch as their self-representations are tenuously constructed and they have achieved only a precarious type of object constancy, I feel more secure if I hold firmly to my analytic orientation in terms of my identity and continue to view external objects (patients) from that perspective. These attitudes, which some may consider to be rigid, may very well influence what I evaluate to be a lack of therapeutic accomplishment when I have tried to practice nonanalytic therapy.

Still, the number of patients who fled from analysis is comparatively small. By far the larger majority have been able to begin treatment by tolerating analysis, and as they understood their vulnerability in terms of fear of fusion, they have adjusted well to the analytic setting. Some of the patients who left returned later, and I was glad that I had not jeopardized my potential for conducting analysis with them by attempting another form of treatment.

To summarize briefly, the treatment of the group of patients who fear fusion and relinquishing control may become complicated because of certain formal elements of the analytic setting and untoward countertransference reactions. The analyst may feel his professional ego ideal threatened when the patient refuses to accept basic analytic procedures such as the fundamental rule and the use of the couch. This is in contrast to the first group of patients who are unable to hold mental representations without external reinforcement in that they threaten a general disruption of the analytic setting by destroying its temporal boundaries. The patients I have just discussed are much more circumspect; they reject very specific factors to defend themselves against a basic vulnerability, which is the outcome of tenuous object constancy and a blurring of boundaries between self and object representations.

The third group of patients present treatment difficulties because elements of analytic technique bear some similarity to the nuances and modes of relating that are characteristic of early object relationships. The patient's reactions to these similarities lead to specific countertransference problems.

These patients relate to objects in a constricted manner, a reflection of the way their mothers related to them. They have attained a constricted form of object constancy. As discussed, this meant that the mother related to the infant in terms of the immediacy of his needs but not as a potentially autonomous evolving human being. She related to her child in a unidimensional fashion, only in one frame of reference.

As a patient, the individual may perceive the analytic relationship as being identical to the early interaction with his mother. He may view analysis as unidimensional and confined to only a single frame of reference. Indeed, the analyst wants to restrict himself only to an intrapsychic focus and not enter into the patient's external world. For many such patients the intrapsychic focus is expressed by urgent needs, and living in the outside world is equated to being accepted as a person in their own right. They want the analyst to relate to them in both frames of reference.

However, under the pressure of the repetition compulsion, they also try to create a situation in treatment that repeats the early mother–infant relationship in the transference. Usually the reverse of that relationship is recapitulated in that the patient treats the analyst the same way his mother treated him, and this creates the countertransference problems I have briefly mentioned. The problem is intensified because the analyst, or rather, the analytic method aggravates potential problems, and the repetition compulsion is reinforced by the analytic approach. The transference may be impossible to analyze.

Specifically, restricting the interaction with the patient to interpretations and the maintenance of a neutral stance is reminiscent of the constricted relationship with the mother, who could allow herself no emotional involvement with her child. The analyst is equated with the unavailable mother. The patient suffers the same infantile deprivation in the current treatment setting. This ordinarily happens in the transference relationship, but usually the analyst's neutrality creates a backdrop that causes infantile transference elements to stand out, whereas with these patients, infantile reactions blend with the analyst's operational mode. Consequently, their transference implications are obscured, and the patient believes he is confronting a reality similar to the one he knew in infancy.

The patient needs to repeat infantile deprivations, but he also wants to be gratified, to make up what he lacked in his early object relationships. This is a compensatory attempt characteristic of the patient who has achieved a degree of psychic structure that supports object constancy and allows the patient to seek segments of the external world that lead to gratification. The patient tries to obtain this compensatory gratification from the analyst. In adult life the patient is able to make demands he could not make in infancy because then he did not have sufficient ego structure to assert himself; he also felt too vulnerable and helpless. Patients suffering from primitive mental states do not have the resources to reach out toward external objects.

There are many countertransference responses to the patient's mode of relating, which are generally shared by analysts. On many occasions I have heard analysts in workshops and seminars discuss their treatment relationships with undisguised irritation. Our reactions are often subtle and elusive. Most of them are the outcome of the patient's combination of attempts to reproduce constricted infantile object relationships in the transference and to seek from the analyst what he could not get from his mother, but in these interactions there are different facets that create specific reactions.

The resolution of transference depends upon the patient recognizing that his feelings are, for the most part, based upon infantile projections and his ability simultaneously to view the analyst as analyst. If these two frames of reference cannot be kept separate, then the therapist is confronted with the difficult clinical complication of a psychotic transference. If the analyst, by responding to the patient's manipulations, assumes, in part, the role of an infantile object, the treatment impasse becomes compounded. The analyst often becomes angry and confused and feels threatened in his analytic identity. The patient has put the therapist in the untenable position of failing him. This may create havoc, especially if the analyst does not recognize that it is inevitable, as the consequence of the repetition compulsion, that the patient experiences the analyst as not relating to him, as withdrawing from him and being constricted and unempathic. The analyst, because of his professional ego ideal, finds it difficult to accept such a nonanalytic evaluation and may resist it.

The analyst feels the patient's nagging complaints as painful. Whatever the therapist gives the patient by way of interpretation is off the mark. The analyst is not in tune, locked in, with the patient's feelings. Insights do not help, meaning that the analyst does not understand the patient nor does he want to. If the therapist does not maintain his analytic focus, that is, view these complaints as material, he may feel discouraged, frustrated, and guilty. The analyst is faced with the problem of determining how much of what the patient says is, in fact, a correct appraisal as the analyst becomes increasingly confused. The analyst may even attempt to compensate for what he begins to feel as his uselessness by becoming more interpretatively active, but the patient continues to feel misunderstood.

Recently I saw a hospitalized adolescent schizophrenic patient who demonstrated some of these issues more clearly than patients who have not regressed to such a primitive level. This young man felt that no one cared for him and he described himself as "emotionally isolated," although the hospital personnel did everything possible to relate to him and they catered to his physical needs as quickly as possible. They even tried to anticipate his needs, but they were remarkably unsuccessful. Consequently the patient would frequently experience mounting agitation often culminating in a physical attack on some staff member and necessitating that he be put in restraints. After such an episode the patient became paranoid, feeling that people did not like him and attacked him because they felt he was unlovable. However, this paranoid orientation was not fixed and would soon dissipate as he started again to participate in ward activities.

When I saw him in consultation, he was relatively calm at the beginning of the interview. Since he was not particularly spontaneous, I asked him some questions concerning the reason for hospitalization and how he was getting along on the ward. He gradually began to volunteer information, so instead of continuing with my questions I just listened and occasionally made a comment about what he had said. For a while we seemed to be chatting amiably and fully at ease. Then the mood seemed to change. He found some fault with every comment I made. Somehow I had missed the point. I had misunderstood him or I had misplaced his emphasis. He communicated these reactions in a covert fashion but his disagreement with the direct statements I made was explicit. He also became increasingly agitated. He leaned forward on the edge of the chair and looked as if he were about to spring. He appeared conflicted as he was struggling to control himself.

I saw him as a hurt, confused child, feeling ashamed and humiliated as if he were overcome by his feelings and had a tantrum. He appeared as if he had been badly hurt, and without knowing how, I felt responsible. I remained silent for a few minutes and let him talk without interruptions. He became a little calmer and then I said that apparently I had not been in tune with his feelings and had not really understood what he was trying to tell me. He smiled and visibly relaxed and described in considerable detail some of his paranoid preoccupations. However, he was discussing situations from the remote past and far removed from the current setting.

My comment about not having been in tune with his feelings, that I had not been in emotional resonance with him, established a bond between us. He was then able to focalize his rage on specific external situations and objects in order to maintain our relationship on an empathic level. His paranoid ideation was both temporally and geographically distant.

In the analysis of nonpsychotic patients such as those I have just discussed, the recognition that the analyst has to be experienced as nonempathic helps establish a bond, a relationship based upon the premise of being understood and recognized as a person, a situation favorable for analysis. To achieve such an optimal relationship may require some suspension of analytic neutrality and objective interpretation, objective in that it lacks subjective elements and is experienced as impersonal.

Circumstances frequently mitigate against the establishment of a bond between patient and therapist, emanating from the analyst as well as the analysand. Because of the repetition compulsion, as I have discussed, the patient needs to have the analyst relate to him in a constricted unfeeling fashion. The patient behaves in such a manner that causes the analyst to despair and reactively, perhaps even with revenge in mind, to not want to relate to the patient's emotional needs. Martin (1975) described a class of patients he called "obnoxious patients," who are intrusive and make demands that are designed to pull the therapist out of the psychoanalytic frame of reference. The patients I am discussing are more subtly disturbing.

A 40-year-old married woman kept emphasizing how much she needed me to tell her things about the external world because she was too inept and helpless to be able to make critical judgments that would enable her to cope with the exigencies of her daily life. This meant that I was to evaluate everyday events and relationships so that she would know how to respond judiciously. If I did not grant her what she required she would alienate her husband and children and generally create chaos. She acknowledged that she was asking me to breathe for her. She dependently clung to other persons as well, who eventually distanced themselves from her because of her intense neediness. Her self-centeredness finally antagonized her family and friends, and I began to feel the same resentment. This patient did not recognize anyone except in terms of her needs, an example of the constricted object constancy I have been discussing.

She quietly attacked me for not giving her what she needed. These were not vociferous attacks. On the contrary, she would revile herself for her weakness but, nevertheless, she was adept at quiet reproach. She indicated that I was being remiss in my role as therapist by never talking to her and she would ask me numerous questions which admittedly I usually did not answer. In many instances I did not know the answer, but I was also aware of a resistance within me that made me reluctant to respond.

Still, I was far from entirely silent. I answered some of her questions and often made interpretations, sometimes spontaneously and not just as a response to a question. Whatever I said did not seem to count. She did not recognize my interpretations as interpretations or as answers. She viewed them as criticisms and either started arguing with me or attempted to justify herself, although I had been extremely careful to be nonjudgmental. I could feel her reaching out to me, and then when I responded she ignored the fact that I was trying to reciprocate. If she acknowledged my attempt to impart some understanding, she would follow what I said with another question demanding further clarification. If I fell into her trap she would continue questioning every one of my responses. She reminded me of a child who endlessly asks, "why?" She was insatiable.

Her reactions made me feel that I was simply a tool of her needs without any human qualities. I felt frustrated and had to view my countertransference in terms of the immediacy of her needs and her constricted maternal relationship in which the patient felt constantly frustrated, a frustration she now provoked in her external world.

She related the following material, which clearly illustrates how irritating she could be. While having her hair done, she was chatting with her female hairdresser. She told the hairdresser about some of her problems with her children, especially with a son who was having difficulties during his freshman year in college. The hairdresser would respond to her request for advice by making some sensible suggestion. The patient would then object and reveal another aspect of the problem. Again the hairdresser would offer her a solution and again the patient would argue that it would not work. At the end of the appointment, the patient was astounded when the hairdresser had an outburst of anger and told her that she did not want to see her in her shop again.

SUMMARY

The development of object constancy is parallel to the formation of the self-representation. It is a characteristic achievement of a postsymbiotic phase in which the child is able to maintain a mental representation without the reinforcement of the external object's presence in the sensory field, in which the child has acquired the capacity for evocative memory.

The vicissitudes of object constancy become clear in a psychopathological context, as character abnormalities and defective maternal care lead to faulty integration of self and object representations. I have traced a continuum with which I can describe patients suffering from varying degrees of disturbance in maintaining object constancy. This implies object constancy is not simply the end product of a progressively structuralizing developmental process. The traumatic infantile environment causes a type of object constancy that is to some extent adaptive in preserving a psychopathological equilibrium. I have described three types of psychopathology that lead to specific treatment problems and disruptive countertransference reactions.

The first group of patients suffers from what is close to a complete lack of object constancy. They have only recall memory and are relatively unable to hold a mental representation without the actual presence of the external object somewhere in their familiar environment. The second group has a tenuous type of object constancy and a precariously held-together self-representation. These patients need to have control over their feelings and the external world to protect themselves from fusion, which is experienced as total annihilation. The third group has a constricted form of object constancy that causes these patients to relate to external objects only in terms of the immediacy of needs. The external object is not recognized as a person with feelings and a potential for growth.

In treatment all three groups present problems that are the outcome of their structural defects. These types of technical difficulties are created by what I call the psychoanalytic paradox, which represents a situation in which psychopathology becomes imbricated into the analytic setting and leads to treatment impasses and upsetting countertransference responses. The first group of patients disrupts the general setting, the second group affects specific elements of the treatment procedure, and the third group reacts adversely to the analytic stance of neutrality, the technique of interpretation, and a strict adherence to an intrapsychic focus.

I have discussed the impact of these types of structural psychopathology upon the analyst's equanimity and the countertransference reactions they are likely to evoke. This can lead to trying situations in treatment, and sometimes it becomes impossible to conduct analysis, but an understanding of infantile trauma and the resultant maldevelopment of self and object representations often makes it possible to overcome our countertransference disturbances and continue analyzing.

REFERENCES

Boyer, B., & Giovacchini, P. L. (1967). *Psychoanalytic treatment of schizophrenic and characterological disorders.* New York: Jason Aronson.

Breuer, J., & Freud, S. (1895). Studies on hysteria. *Standard Edition, 2,* 1–252. London: Hogarth Press, 1955.

Byschowski, G. (1952). *Psychotherapy of psychosis.* New York: Grune & Stratton.

Coen, S. J. (1981). Notes on the concept of selfobject and pre-Oedipal object. *Journal of the American Psychoanalytic Association, 29,* 395–413.

Dorpat, T. L. (1976). Structural conflict and object relations conflict. *Journal of the American Psychoanalytic Association, 24,* 855–874.

Eissler, K. (1953). The effect of the structure of the ego on psychoanalytic technique. *Journal of the American Psychoanalytic Association, 1,* 104–143.

Eisnitz, A. J. (1981). The perspective of the self-representation, *Journal of the American Psychoanalytic Association, 29,* 309–337.

Erikson, E. H. (1959). *Identity and the life cycle.* New York: International Universities Press.

Federn, P. (1952). *Ego psychology and the psychoses.* New York: Basic Books.

Fraiberg, S. (1969). Libidinal object constancy and mental representation. *The Psychoanalytic Study of the Child, 24,* 48–70.

Freud, A. (1951). Observations on child development. *The Psychoanalytic Study of the Child, 6,* 18–30.

Freud, S. (1905). Three essays on the theory of sexuality. *Standard Edition, 7,* 122–243. London: Hogarth Press, 1953.

Freud, S. (1911). Psychoanalytic notes on an autobiographical account of a case of paranoia (dementia paranoides). *Standard Edition, 12,* 1–82. London: Hogarth Press, 1958.

Freud, S. (1914). On narcissism: An introduction. *Standard Edition, 19,* 67–102. London: Hogarth Press, 1957.

Freud, S. (1924a). Neurosis and psychosis. *Standard Edition, 19,* 147–153. London: Hogarth Press, 1961.

Freud, S. (1924b). The loss of reality in neurosis and psychosis. *Standard Edition, 19,* 183–190. London: Hogarth Press, 1961.

Giovacchini, P. L. (1972). Countertransference problems. *International Journal of Psychoanalytic Psychotherapy, 1,* 112–127.

Giovacchini, P. L. (1975a). Various aspects of the psychoanalytic process. In *Tactics and techniques in psychoanalytic treatment: Countertransference* (Vol. 2, pp. 1–95). New York: Jason Aronson.

Giovacchini, P. L. (1975b). *Psychoanalysis of character disorders.* New York: Jason Aronson.

Giovacchini, P. L. (1977). A critique of Kohut's theory of narcissism. *Adolescent Psychiatry, 5,* 213–235.

Giovacchini, P. L. (1979). *The treatment of primitive mental states.* New York: Jason Aronson.

Giovacchini, P. L., & Boyer, L. B. (1975). The psychoanalytic impasse. *International Journal of Psychoanalytic Psychotherapy, 4,* 25–47.

Hartmann, H. (1950). Comments on the psychoanalytic theory of the ego. *The Psychoanalytic Study of the Child, 5,* 74–96.

Jacobson, E. (1964). *The self and the object world.* New York: International Universities Press.

Kernberg, O. (1975). *Borderline conditions and pathological narcissism.* New York: International Universities Press.

Kohut, H. (1971). *The analysis of the self.* New York: International Universities Press.

Kohut, H. (1977). *The restoration of the self.* New York: International Universities Press.

Levine, H. B. (1979). The sustaining object relationship. *Annual of Psychoanalysis, 7,* 203–231.

Martin, P. A. (1975). The obnoxious patient. In *Tactics and techniques in psychoanalytic therapy: Countertransference* (Vol. 2, pp. 196–205). New York: Jason Aronson.

Modell, A. H. (1968). *Object love and reality.* New York: International Universities Press.

Noy, P. (1979). The psychoanalytic theory of cognitive development. *The Psychoanalytic Study of the Child, 34.* 169–217.

Piaget, J. (1954). *Les relations entre l'affectivité et l'intelligence dans le développment mental de l'enfant.* Paris: Centre de Documentation Universitaire.

Reichard, S. (1956). A re-examination of "Studies on Hysteria." *Psychoanalytic Quarterly, 25,* 155–177.

Sandler, J., & Rosenblatt, B. (1962). The concept of the representational world. *The Psychoanalytic Study of the Child, 17,* 128–145.

Spitz, R. (1945). On hospitalism. *The Psychoanalytic Study of the Child, 1,* 53–74.

Spitz, R. (1957). *No and yes: On the genesis of human communication.* New York: International Universities Press.

Wallerstein, R. S. (1981). The bipolar self: discussion of alternative perspectives. *Journal of the American Psychoanalytic Association, 29,* 377–394.

Winnicott, D. W. (1953). Transitional objects and transitional phenomena. In *Collected papers, through paediatrics to psycho-analysis* (pp. 229–242). New York: Basic Books.

CHAPTER ELEVEN

Phenomenology of Failed Object Constancy

MARGARET HAMEL RAY

Writing of failed object constancy and its consequences requires first a definition that is consonant with some, if not most, of the varied uses to which it has been put in the literature and in discussions among clinicians and theoreticians. From the various (Angel, 1972; Arlow, Freud, Lampl de Groot, & Beres, 1968; Fraiberg, 1969) interpretations one may bring together at least five major aspects frequently encountered in the literature. Each is related to the other but independent consideration is possible to a degree. They are as follows:

1. Perceptual constancy of the object; that is, there is established evocative memory for the object.
2. Maintenance of drive investment in a specific object notwithstanding its presence or absence.
3. Capacity to recognize and tolerate loving and hostile feelings toward the same object.
4. Capacity to keep feelings centered on a specific object.
5. Capacity to value objects for attributes in addition to that of its function of satisfying needs.

The above attributes combine and interact to form the internal representations of (1) the self, the self relating to an object, and (2) the object relating to the self. These representations evolve into increasingly complex internal interactions as the individual's drive pressures, ego requirements, defense structures, fantasies, and so on develop. The aspect of object constancy most often emphasized is that of the maintenance of drive investment, be that drive investment libidinal or aggressive in nature and/or feeling tone. It also is generally agreed, however, that the establishment of evocative memory is an essential precursor for the development of object constancy. It would seem from some of Spitz's (1945, 1946b) observations, however, that the establishment of evocative memory itself is in some way contingent upon investment of drive energy in the process of perception.

These aspects can be distinguished and examined somewhat independently; all are essential to the mature relationship marked by firmly established object constancy, and equally, each contributes to the establishment of the other. It would also appear likely that one component may be more strongly developed than another—that one might develop at the expense of some later developing aspect when there is an interruption in development. For example, an insufficiency of the capacity to maintain drive cathexis could interfere with the development of the capacity to tolerate loving and hostile feelings toward the same object. Also, the capacity to integrate good and bad "images" into a whole object would be dependent to a degree upon the firm establishment of the prior or concurrent development of the other two. In other words, while sequences may be relatively fixed, timing may well vary and thereby influence establishment of later maturing elements. Since it is established that there are critical periods (Scott, 1962) for development in other systems, it seems likely that there are critical periods for the ontogeny of object constancy. One purpose of this chapter is to consider some of the possible consequences of disruptions in the development of these different aspects and to place them within the context of the separation-individuation process (Mahler, 1963, 1965; Mahler, Pine, & Bergman, 1975).

It will be immediately apparent that this chapter is to be narrowed in its focus to a restricted segment of the highly complex subject of object constancy. Many areas will of necessity remain untouched. Background, nuances of individuality, chance factors, and the myriad permutations of interactions within the developing child and between him and others in the external world must be neglected in order to highlight some of the factors resulting from failed object constancy. Failed, in this instance, must be understood to refer to relative failure in the move toward object constancy; it is to be understood as disruptions in sequences and timings that may have a greater effect on one or another of the different components of object constancy. It is to be acknowledged that total failure would mean that the child probably would not survive. This restriction of focus invites the criticism of reductionism, linearity of thought, and overschematization. However, bringing in all of the factors of individual differences in temperament, chance factors of idiosyncratic response, and the like would present such a "busy" picture that clarity would be sacrificed.

One aspect of object constancy to be considered is that of mental representation of self and object; another is the closely related but nevertheless distinctive capacity to integrate the "good" (satisfying) with the "bad" (frustrating) qualities in the mental representation of self and object; a third is that which gives stable and enduring representation of external reality, of the nonhuman elements of space, time, form, and content of the intact universe; and a fourth, which is of marked significance in that it is central to the concept and integral to the development of the other aspects, is the enduring emotional relationship to self, object, and external world. It is the capacity to retain attachment even though the object is no longer satisfactory or apparent. This latter equality is the one that is most frequently referred to as *the* definitive element. These aspects are interdependent, and deficiencies in development can be found in any one or more of these components, while others may be relatively intact. It is reasonable to assume that each contributes a distinctive quality to the personality and nuances to moods and affects of the individual. These assumptions and hypotheses are to be illustrated by clinical observations in this chapter.

I'll begin with the component of mental representation of self and others, the aspect related to that of image constancy and evocative memory. It is featured in the capacity to recognize others and to discriminate among people. The knowledge in this instance is in the sense of emotional conviction regarding cognition and recognition. It gives the sense of conviction regarding one's own and others' boundaries. There is a sense of definition and completeness in outline and in detail. One knows what one looks like and what the world and the people in it look like. There is a sense of confidence in this recognition, which contributes to overall security and ease. The identifying features of this component of "image" of self and object representation include the knowledge of the mental qualities of self and others. The inner representation includes characteristic personality traits, attitudes, opinions, and emotional and mood qualities of the person. Having attained a relatively advanced stage of object constancy, one has the capacity to "understand" others; there is a sense of ease in relating to others. This development would appear to be an important foundation of the capacity for empathy. Furthermore, in those circumstances that are relatively new, and where prediction is uncertain, there is a tolerance for a degree of uncertainty. The "stranger reaction" is not overburdened with anxiety.

Faulty development in this component leaves the person with feelings of uncertainty accompanied by anxiety. One person wanted her picture painted so that she would know what she looked like. There had been times when she looked in the mirror with a sense of disquiet. She "recognized" herself but the feeling of uncertainty persisted. She sought an external stable objectivation of herself to provide a sense of conviction and reassurance that she would always recognize herself. Another patient expressed the worry that he would not recognize his wife or that he might inadvertently snub somebody by not recognizing the person if met in an unfamiliar place or in strange circumstances. Still another, while waiting for her lover at an appointed place and time, experienced a momentary anxiety that she would not recognize him, that she might select some stranger who happened to be there. Analysis of the ambivalences and defensiveness in these relationships and incidents is necessary but proves insufficient for a full understanding of the anxiety. Closer inquiry reveals that there is a pervasive anxiety of this nature throughout interactions that are not fraught with ambivalence. It is the anxiety characteristic of instability of the constancy of mental representation.

The lack of conviction in regard to recognition of oneself in the mirror or of significant others is also evident in regard to personal talents, education, knowledge, opinions, and attitudes. This "readiness for anxiety" seems related to Angel's (1972) description of "symbiotic panic."

One person expressed this anxiety by considering himself to be vacillating with continually changing opinions. He was not in actuality so easily influenced to change his opinions; but his feeling was that he lacked true opinions of his own and that he "borrowed" them. While acknowledging the objective evidence of his accomplishments, he was, nevertheless, not sure that he was who he was. He complained about a feeling of unreality in regard to himself. It was as if his accomplishments belonged to another. This was variously expressed, but the most common was that someone would find out that he was a fraud and imposter and that his accomplishments were the result of some "fluke." These people need visible, external evidence to support them. It is quite possible that this is one strong contributor to the agoraphobic's "fear of being afraid" and need to have a constant companion or to remain in familiar surroundings.

Mahler (1965) and McDevitt (1975) noted that there is a period in normal development during which youthful subjects have not yet attained stable object constancy such that they will momentarily "forget" the mother is in the room or in the adjoining room and begin a somewhat anxious searching. This usually happens after a period of absorbed activity. There is a ready reinstatement of the image upon visual contact with the mother. Previous equanimity is soon restored, and the child once again can be "alone" in the mother's presence and free to become absorbed in his own activities. The analogous situation is when the analysand asks, "Are you there?," following a period of free association and regression. The anxiety that prompts the question seems in part to be related to the temporary diminution of object and self constancy in the analytically induced regression.

Insufficiency of "image" constancy gives rise to feelings of bewilderment, confusion, and isolation. There is frequently a feeling of not belonging anywhere and of not sharing standards, social, and cultural values with one's associates. It also happens that the individual can feel disconnected and estranged from whole periods in his past life and from aspects of his present life. There may be memory for events, places, and periods, but the person views them as though they were experienced by a different person with whom he has little in common.

The second broad category—the integration of the good but also bad self and object representations—is characterized by what is frequently termed "objectivity." Neither aggrandizement nor denigration of self and/or others marks the attitude when this is firmly established. This component contributes to the subjective experience of wholeness and/or completeness. This sense of completeness or wholeness contributes not only to awareness of limitations as well as assets, goals attained, and goals yet to be attained, but also to freedom for aspiration without cramping inhibition or overcompensatory grandiosity and to the capacity for dealing with failure without despair. In terms of the object representation, again there is what is named objectivity. Of significance for the individual's comfort is the acceptance of limitation of the object without experiencing overwhelming disappointment or disillusionment. There is a feeling of ease in that people are "understandable" and that their varying moods and behaviors do not disrupt the sense of continuity and therefore of the recognizability of the person.

Varying degrees of insufficiency in this component are experienced as feeling disjunctive and fragmented. The individual feels undecided about the "truth" about himself and others. There are instances when the person is aware of having two contradictory self-images and images of others. Both are equally true—but the difficulty is in getting them together. Each image separately leaves the individual feeling vaguely dissatisfied that the image is "untrue" even though the individual observations are valid. Oscillation between the disparate views is frequently accompanied by mood swings (Mahler, 1966). Associated is the fluctuating self-esteem (Kohut, 1971, 1972). In the attempt to maintain a stable self-representation, it sometimes happens that individuals will attempt to be entirely one or the other of the part-images. One person remarked, "I only want to be good—I only want to feel loving. I can't stand to dislike anyone." She was not unaware of—did not repress or deny—her negative feelings toward people, but she could not integrate them into the total experience. Another chose to be all negative and to maintain that she disliked everybody and that she was unable to love. "Consistency" was a quality she valued above all else. She felt she was not herself when she experienced friendly feelings. When these nuances are experienced as separate "entities," the individual often complains that he cannot "understand" himself or others.

The third aspect of object constancy to be developed and stabilized and of significance is what has been termed as "reality constancy" (Frosch, 1966). Mental representation of the nonhuman space–time elements of external reality is the aspect that many theoreticians warn against confusing with the "perceptual constancy" of experimental psychology. However, I submit that this element of object constancy is essential to the establishment of the "stable object," which is the referent in studies of perception. It is the drive cathexes of these "percepts" that give the "sense of reality" to the perception of things and places. This component of object constancy gives the feeling of confidence in one's spatial orientation, in one's time sense as well as in the recognition of places and things. There are those who have achieved the cognitive development where objects in the sense of "things" are recognizable regardless of perspective, distance, and other stimulus qualities. People with unreliable object constancy, however, experience a feeling of spatial ignorance. This is the person who fears that he will forget where he lives, go to the wrong house, or not recognize his home. He experiences feelings of bewilderment and continual apprehension, feelings frequently expressed by the agoraphobic. He "knows" where he lives, where his friends and other intimates live, but he cannot shake the apprehensive feeling of not knowing for certain. A comment frequently heard is, "I know, but it doesn't change my feeling. I'm always a little afraid." One young woman described the "cause" of her anxiety as follows: "It's as if I were looking at things through glass. I can't make real contact with what I see." The subjective experience of loose ties to reality, remarked as feeling "unreal" refers to the unreliability of the mental representation of the external world.

The fourth component to be discussed is, of course, primary and crucial to the others. Its full development guarantees sufficient cathexis of representation of all aspects of self, object, and external world. This is the element of the maintenance of an enduring emotional relationship with all aspects of life. Cathexis of inner representations is maintained in the face of deprivation, frustration, and loss. Characteristically, the relationship to objects is primarily positive, but transient ambivalences and negative responses can be tolerated. The relationship to love objects can be maintained even in periods of hostility engendered by the inevitable frustrations from conflicts of interest. Mental representations of external reality—of the nonhuman environment—can retain their cathexis also. The integration of good and bad qualities can be maintained with the establishment of the capacity to maintain these emotional investments.

With the attainment of object constancy, there is no need for compulsive love nor is there need to maintain a persistently hostile attitude. Furthermore, the emotional relationship can be maintained in all its complexity. One feature that distinguishes the mature relationship from all of its precursors is this complexity. The full relationship of attained object constancy retains some of the elements from earlier periods. There is a capacity for transient symbiotic union, tolerance for reciprocal dependency, and the capacity to assimilate both admiration and disapproval. While there is pleasure in pleasing others, the attainment of object constancy helps to free the individual from excessive need to please. The capacity to love and to believe one is loved is assured. In his paper on the capacity to love, Bergmann (1971) noted that the capacity to love could be developed while the capacity to believe that one is loved could be defective. These do not necessarily develop simultaneously. Thus it is apparent that in each aspect deficiencies that interfere in varying degrees with full relationship to self, others, and material reality can occur.

It is of interest to consider ways in which the attainment of object constancy can be related to the developmental phases of the separation-individuation process. Of concern also is to determine whether different kinds of anxieties are associated with these phases correlated with different aspects of object constancy.

It is generally accepted that Mahler's (1968) observations of earliest infancy indicate that there is an objectless state that predates all that may legitimately be called "relationship." It is of relatively short duration, and until about the 2nd month of life, there appears to be only comfort–discomfort responses on the part of the developing individual. During this period of "normal autism," physiological normalizing activities such as temperature orientation, expulsive phenomena, and ingestion and discharge activities are the primary functions. While it may appear to be a psychologically closed system on the part of the infant, there is nevertheless some response to the ministrations of the caretaker. The beginnings of bonding seem to be laid down even in this supposedly "nonrelating" phase. The mothering person is auxiliary to all of these physiological functions, and her presence and contact contributes to this transformation into an emotional relationship. It is the mother at this early phase who does the relating. She interprets and satisfies needs, acts as a barrier to excess stimuli, and by her own emotional contribution fosters the development of the psychological relationship, and this interactive process releases the nascent growth toward object constancy. From a purely physiological point of view, the necessary handling alone contributes significantly to the cathexis of sensory systems. A cautious generalization from animal studies (Harlow, Glueck, & Suomi, 1972) suggests that physical handling supports not only rapid growth of subhuman mammals but also their alertness and responsivity. The Wisconsin primate studies (Harlow, 1962; Harlow & Harlow, 1962; Harlow, Harlow, & Suomi, 1971) experimentally demonstrate that while surrogate mothers can contribute to what Erikson (1950) refers to as basic trust, its establishment is more firmly fixed in the presence of the "live" mother—her activity in responding supports development of confidence. Even the "poor" mother contributed to early development of an interactive mode. Mahler's (Mahler & McDevitt, 1968) observations of the symbiotic stage of development also strongly support the contention that the beginnings of object constancy can be documented as occurring in this very early phase and that this early relationship will have a profound effect upon utilization of purely biologic satisfactions. The Wisconsin studies indicate that the preference for lactating versus nonlactating surrogates was of significance during only the first 90 days of life, with its "drawing power" diminishing over time. Rocking surrogates remained a significant variable for a still longer period. In monkeys contact comfort was of most significance not only for the alleviation of anxiety but primarily for the development of normal relationships. Monkeys reared only with surrogates not only did not develop normal peer relationships when exposed to peers following what amounted to "isolation" rearing, but such "instinctual" behaviors as sexuality also were disordered. In the human mammal it is clearly demonstrated (Spitz, 1945, 1946a) that contact also contributes strongly to bonding and thus to the separation–individuation process and to the gradual attainment of object constancy.

There are indications that ambivalence, anxiety, and/or rejection on the part of the mother gives tension to her handling, which might interfere with the efficacy of that handling. During this early phase of "normal autism," the emotional involvement of the mother seems to be of paramount significance to the early cathexis of primary structures and physiological mechanisms that appear to be fundamental to the transition to the phase of symbiosis. While the infant's activities are primarily physiological in nature, they are endowed with a "signaling" function that interacts with the mother's ministrations. It seems reasonable to hypothesize that signaling–response interactions act as releasers to the innate "bonding" potentials and thus usher in the other psychological components and give impetus to the unfolding of the separation–individuation process. Gradual attainment of object constancy in its varied aspects would thus be tied in with the different substages of the separation–individuation process. It seems reasonable to assume that the attainment of object constancy proceeds in stages similar to and correlated with the stages of separation–individuation.

Insufficiency of response to these tension states would appear to contribute to the readiness to fall into anxiety states of a specific nature. These anxiety states are diffuse, objectless, and primarily physiological in expression and experience. Schur (1955) remarked on these "anxiety equivalents," wherein the anxiety is not experienced as such but is expressed as itching, skin eruptions, asthmatic attacks, and the like. He related these to interferences in temperature orientation associated with insufficient experiences of contact. Tentativeness of handling frequently characteristic of anxious and/or emotionally unavailable mothers can contribute to the physiological reactions to loss of physical support. Some patients do not report the usual physiological accompaniments of anxiety, such as rapid heart beat, sweating, and the like, but are more aware of a sensation of "falling" and a reflexive sharp intake of breath and grasping reflexes that are sometimes accompanied by feelings of loss of orientation and of giddiness. This reaction seems similar to that reported by Angel (1972), which he names "symbiotic panic."

In the earliest part of the next phase, that of symbiosis, there is as yet no differentiation between self and object. So long as the object is available and the symbiotic unity is preserved, the experience is one of being intact. It is during this phase that the component of object constancy, which gives definition and stability to inner representation of self and object, is laid down. Via the emotional involvement of the mother associated with her ministrations, the body surfaces become yet more strongly cathected. In the later periods of the symbiotic phase, there is the emergence of the representation of body–self, which is the foundation for the formation of mental representation of the self–object unity.

Disturbances in this phase leave the individual subject to excessive anxiety that differs from that of the prior stage in that it is experienced as such. Winnicott (1962) terms it "unthinkable." He distinguishes four forms of this primitive anxiety: (1) going to pieces, (2) falling forever, (3) having no relationship to the body, and (4) having no orientation. Angel (1972) details some of the associated defenses and characterologic developments attendant upon this "symbiotic panic." Attenuated forms of this kind of anxiety can be recognized in vague feelings of apprehension about getting lost. A frequent complaint is of a faulty sense of direction, of being easily "turned around" on emerging from a theater, leaving a building by an exit different from the entry point, or of losing direction in a new city as a result of using a different approach to a familiar area.

At this very early stage the sense of being intact and of being oriented in space depend upon confidence in the continuity of self–object unity. A behavior modification technique in the treatment of minor addictions (cigarette smoking particularly) and of agoraphobia is the use of subliminal exposures to stimuli, such as "my mother and I are one." Psychoanalytic insights, interestingly, are being introduced into the traditionally antipathetic psychology of behaviorism! To say that a disruption of a relationship can occur at this stage is really to speak by analogy, since the usual definition of relationship at least implies distinct and separate people. Nevertheless, it is permissible to refer to this stage of development relationship as of "symbiotic relationship." Disruption at this stage, then, results in experiences of threats of disorganization rather than in a sense of loss. Grief, experiences of longing or loss are not yet fully developed capacities. The "unthinkable" anxiety and readiness to panic can well remain as a substratum even after further development has resulted in the development of the capacity for grief and mourning.

It is during the differentiation subphase of the separation–individuation process that there is the burgeoning of the structuring of the inner world. With the diminution of symbiosis, there is the beginning of the formation of self and object representation as distinct from each other. The object relationship begins to be more in the nature of reciprocity, more distinctly one "object," the child, relates and responds to another "object," the mother or another person. The relationship rests upon need satisfaction primarily, but there are changes in the nature of need from purely nutritional and physiological to an increase in need for interactive and affectional gratification. Mutual vocal signaling and facial and gestural communications begin to outstrip the potency of the nutritive needs. There is a beginning of the response to satisfaction of these various and increasingly complex needs as coming from an object outside the self and beginning of a dim sense of needs arising from within the self.

At this time, while the sense of self begins to emerge in mental representation, the mother and the universe tend to remain as continuous with each other in the mental representation. Furthermore, self and object are only partially and unstably differentiated. The gestalt of self and object as separate is unstable in organization and the emergence of figure is easily reversible, with consequent threat of blurring of boundaries. The anxiety in this instance begins as "signal" but still has the quality of primal anxiety. Its signal function is of threat of dissolution of newly formed boundaries of both self and other, and of falling into the primitive anxiety of the symbiotic panic. A danger specific to the early phase of the differentiation subphase is loss of object–universe blend and of loss of newly developed self boundaries. When there is disruption of the relationship in this phase, a premature "stranger reaction" can be precipitated with accompanying anxiety, which further disrupts the newly emerged organization.

A hiatus in the development of object constancy occurs here when there is premature or abrupt reversal of the emotional climate. This situation tends to bring about a premature and traumatically sharp awareness of separateness, and is accompanied by feelings of helplessness. The sharpened sense of separateness that occurs prematurely can disturb the smooth completion of object–universe differentiation. There is a regression in the object constancy line, so that any loss or separation experience can then reactivate the earlier feelings of loss of all support and landmarks. Reality and space–time, form and content are threatened with being swept away with the loss of the object when there is an arrest or regression to this stage in the development of object constancy. During an LSD trip, for example, the threat to be avoided according to one patient, was that associated with looking at what he called "the split." This was where "things parted" and his feeling was of "falling through a hole in the universe." A young woman said, "I have to know you're there or where you are. I have to put you in a *place*. That's what keeps things from flying off in all directions." She felt anxious when she watched a TV commercial in which the world rapidly receded into the distance. Another patient remarked: "I don't dare get mad at you . . . if I do, it's like I throw you out, you won't exist any more—and then there'll be a big empty void. There's nothing to hang onto, and I'm just out in endlessness." Another said, about the necessity for structure, "I have to write myself a tight script so I won't feel all at sea . . . I can't stand the feeling of loss of bearings." These examples illustrate how loss of the object did not result in loss of self—as it does in an earlier stage; the loss in these instances is not limited to the loss of the object—as it will be in a later stage—but in a loss of the universe or of its intactness. During this stage of differentiation, the self is separate but the object is still continuous and, metaphorically, identical with the world.

During the second subphase of the separation–individuation process, the period of "practicing," the representation of self and object are further differentiated. Secure in the reliable relationship with the mother, the child can differentiate further, making more complex discriminations that are libidinally cathected. The important contributions of the father and siblings and an expanded libidinized circle deserves more attention but must be left to an already extending literature. It is recognized, however, that emotional relationships with the human environment expand to include others besides the mother; even strangers can not only be tolerated, but at times, even be met with interest. Despite these advances, libidinal cathexes of mental representations fluctuates at times during this period. Even in the presence of the mother, a novel situation can give rise to anxiety depending upon the state of the child. Fatigue, illness, or an upsurge of aggression contributes to these fluctuations and the manner in which novel situations are met. Also during this period, if the mother herself or some other significant person in the child's world appears in a novel situation, the child may show signs of distress. A radical change in the mother's mood or mode of expression can be disruptive. Because the differentiation of the mother and the libidinization of the mental representation of the child's universe does fluctuate, recognition may fail, and the child is subject to loss with concurrent regression and disruption of his universe. Anxiety, at this stage, has already taken some of the quality of signal anxiety and as such is more manageable and reduced by a return to familiarity. Extremely sensitive children apparently pick up nuances in emotional climate more readily than others and are more prone to the disruption of the figure–ground configurations. A change in the child's own mood or orientation can also disrupt the organization and leave the child threatened with loss of self boundaries and loss of external world. This period, however, is not so critical in its long-term repercussions as the earlier periods. There has been the development of other ego structures that contribute to the stability of the established self–object differentiations and of the stability of the configurations of the universe and people in it. Partial development of the different aspects of object constancy, which bind self, objects, and universe into more stable configurations, lessen the impact of disruption in that its effects are more readily reversible.

Those whose development remains at this level frequently are continually hurried in their activities. They seem apprehensive about giving full attention to ongoing activities and often they will express anxiety about this feeling of being hurried. The "hurry up" pressure is not only related to the anxieties from anal problems; not infrequently, it is also related to an anxiety that absorption in ongoing activities will bring about a feeling of loneliness—a sense that the surroundings will disappear. Preservation of the intactness of the surrounding universe takes precedence over both expansion of interest and absorption. Impetus toward further growth and expansion of competence and interests are hampered by this kind of anxiety. This conflict over expansion and growth versus the "status quo" frequently finds expression in dreams of being held back or delayed.

In preserving the sense of intactness, some people show a precocious independence and competence. One person's friends and family could not understand why a particular young woman sought treatment. She appeared to be the epitome of competence, independence, self-assurance, and industry. She was agreeable, helpful, and even-tempered. Yet one of her first statements when she entered treatment was, "I need someone to share my head." Another with a similar outward demeanor spoke of "missing identity," of fears of getting lost and remarked about using the telephone, "There's something about the disembodied voice—it gives me an all-gone feeling—as if I'd been dropped."

When the disturbance occurs in this phase of development, anxiety is much more contained than in those with earlier disruptions. These people are frequently anxious about "becoming anxious." Anxiety itself is felt as threatening to disrupt a subjectively experienced tenuousness of organization of the inner world. In spite of apparent self-sufficiency, there is expressed a need for guidance and instruction. Guidance and instruction are in point of fact dispensable. The need is related to the brittleness of the sense of adequacy, which is a self-directed distortion of the friability of the intactness of the external world—the world of mother–world continuity. The sense of inadequacy is in the sense that loss of the object or connection with it means also the loss of the reliability of the universe. Basic trust has not expanded to include the trust in the reliability of the nonhuman environment. As such, it rebounds to a feeling of helplessness translated as lack of trust in one's own capacities to deal with the external world.

That subphase referred to as "rapprochement" is of exceptional significance in the ultimate transition to mature object constancy. It is during this period that the attachment to love objects becomes firm so that it is retained under stress. It is also during this period that the self-representation is more firmly established. In some ways it is a recapitulation of the other phases of the separation–individuation process. Expansion and autonomy with independent and separate activities alternates with increased clinging and shadowing behavior. These oscillations serve the purpose of strengthening the representation of self and object. In a sense it is a practicing of the attainment of object constancy. These oscillations contribute to the filling in of the mental representations of skills, attitudes, and emotional qualities that give the sense of uniqueness and individuality to the sense of self. Discrimination of objects as well as strengthening of the cathexes of mental representations of the nonhuman sector of experience are increased with the continuous "checking back" so much engaged in by the rapprochement child. These oscillations help to fix—in the sense of permanence and reliability—attributes of the self, objects, and universe so that self-sufficiency, competence, and self-regulation, and sense of confidence in self are supported by the sense of expanded confidence in the universe of others.

In terms of the capacity to form enduring and meaningful relationships with a wider world, rapprochement and refueling also serve to solidify the emotional confidence in the reliability of emotional bonds and in the capacity of the self to preserve emotional bonds and the cathexes of the representational world. It is in this phase that constancy of self and object representation makes possible momentary regressions, fantasy, creativity, and endurance of uncertainty without excessive anxiety or fear of anxiety. Anxiety itself can be tolerated without its sliding into panic states.

Many of those who have had a limitation in the opportunity for smooth progress during this phase seem to have an apprehensive attitude toward play, fantasy, and creativity. They seem to have a more than expectable anxiety about regression or about the possibility of regression. In addition, there may be a reluctance to move on to new attitudes or to a modification of existing attitudes. The "negative therapeutic reaction," transiently in evidence with some patients, seems related to this apprehension. These are not the intractable reactions but rather those that require a continued working through of the anxiety about change. In these instances insight is not readily followed by change. In addition to the apprehension, there is, of course, an underlying anger at the deprivation of an adequate rapprochement period, which must be worked through before insights will be acted upon outside the analytic situation. One patient remarked, "Whenever I developed a new skill or showed independence, I wasn't allowed to backslide. It's just too much to always keep going forward."

It is during this developmental period, of course, that fear of loss becomes fear of loss of love as distinguished from fear of loss of the object. Prior to this time, the intactness of the object was necessary for a secure orientation in time and space. At this phase of development, however, there is the introduction of the fear of loss of love and an increasing capacity for loving for the object. Without solidifying of self and object representation, with the increased capacity for relationships, the object and the external world do not disappear under stress of frustration or deprivation. With the concern over loss of love, the capacity for mourning the lost object and the lost relationship proceeds in development. It is of particular importance that the self-representation is now clearly distinguished. For the stable self-representation makes it possible for the individual to be free from dissolution anxiety and therefore to become capable of mourning. It is the self which mourns, it is the self which "knows" that it is the love object or the love from the object that it lost . . . not the self. The person who cannot mourn cannot love, and this is primarily related to inconstancy of self-representation. Self, object, and universe disappear (or threaten to) for the person whose development of object constancy is faulty. One should say that the person dares not love, for loss of another under such conditions quickly becomes loss of the object, loss of the universe, and loss of self.

Subsequently, there is further development toward stable object constancy. It is during later stages in development that object relationships can be maintained regardless of the absence of satisfaction. It is also the result of this later development that lost objects can be mourned and abandoned. The abandonment of lost objects and the capacity to seek new objects is closely tied to stability of the differentiation of the loved object and the universe. The universe remains intact even while mourning is intense. Thus it is that new and important relationships are possible. This stage is frequently referred to as the "final" stage in the attainment of object constancy.

Greenacre noted (1971) that object constancy was hardly used in reference to adults. Nevertheless, she seems to concur that the process of the attainment of object constancy may well be a lifelong matter. It is true that at the end of the 3rd year, the different elements of object constancy become sufficiently well established that a blow does not destroy the totality of development. Reversibility of effect is relatively guaranteed. Thus, loss of object, either in terms of actual physical separation or in terms of the relationship, does not result necessarily in regression to loss of self nor does it result in loss of external reality. Other love objects remain, the capacity for relationship remains, and the "knowledge" of objects remains. While loss of parent of either sex during the later periods of childhood is traumatic, surrogate objects can be introduced and development can proceed.

Internal representations are relatively stable. Both self and object are differentiated from each other and from the "universe." Object representations are integrated, and there is a minimum of "splitting" of good from bad qualities. During this later period anxiety associated with grief and mourning is subordinate to the affect of grief. Mahler (Mahler *et al.*, 1975) repeated what she had emphasized earlier, that at the end of the 3rd year the child is "on the way to object constancy" and to a sense of identity. The different elements of object constancy have made their appearance.

It is recognized, however, that object constancy is not finally established by the end of the 3rd year. Indeed, it is questionable whether it can be said ever to be "finally" attained. Its establishment is such that subsequent loosening does not result in irreversible arrests. It is loosened with each new separation whether it is brought about by loss, disappointment, and/or hostility. While the predominant affect at separation is that of grief, there is also some anxiety. It is anxiety, however, that seems to be related to the loosening of object constancy with its consequent threat of regression with loss of integrity of self and universe.

Once this degree of object constancy has been attained, change of mood, activity, or surrounds no longer threatens the object, self, or universe with destruction. There is a proliferating of interests, affects, values, and sentiments. The universe remains intact and is a stable foundation that supports new endeavors. While a novel situation has its accompaniment of anxiety, this can be tolerated and even in some instances enjoyed as enhancing the excitement of challenges. It is possible that the person who welcomes change and novelty and is an innovator is one in whom object constancy is firmly established. This facilitates further development of ego functions in all of their variety and complexity. This is not to be understood as denying that some of these qualities cannot be developed without the attainment of full object constancy, but the distinguishing characteristic is that of basic mood and ease in these developments.

Interference during this latter phase has its effect upon the strengthening of object constancy and on the basic mood of the individual. Interference at this time leads to lessened constancy in each of the sectors, each being established but somewhat unstable, with associated anxieties from each stage of development still in operation. Ambivalence remains a recurring discomfiting experience, self-esteem is too readily shaken, and there is self-consciousness and reluctance to differentiate further by way of learning new skills and exposing oneself to a variety of experiences. Feelings of inferiority frequently disrupt functioning, and shame reactions can become pronounced. These people function best in situations that are conservative and predictable and where change is slow-paced. They are sensitive to what has been named "future shock." Object constancy is maintained but with an underlying tension. The ordinary exigencies of life and change impinge somewhat more painfully upon them than upon their more fortunate peers.

When object constancy is minimally, or rather, less than optimally established, one effect can be compulsive love. There is a need to maintain a relationship beyond its natural ending. This clinging to outmoded relationships is variously rationalized and can appear as loyalty. Compulsive love can be expressed also as a need to be constantly "in love." "I'm a love junkie" one person said, remarking that he needed to be in love to feel alive and functional. There are also some who upon "falling in love" lose or have lessened their ability to be interested in other aspects of life. In other people a defensiveness about close relationships is in evidence. Relationships may be cool and distant, and there may be in some cases a marked avoidance of differences or conflict of interest. Relationships may be kept at a minimum. There is a need to emphasize one's individuality; there may be a need to avoid change in values, attitudes, or behavior. Group activity may be avoided or engaged in with more than moderate tension. There can be an aura of apprehension that the marginally attained and maintained sense of separateness and relatedness will be lost. An experience of "everything is too much and too complicated" is sometimes reported. Others retain a sense of childlike awe, together with a feeling of being unable to "figure things out." At this stage of development, then, it appears that many defenses and compensatory behaviors are possible.

Once established, object constancy can be further strengthened by repeated separations with consequent regressions and recapitulation of development with each subsequent regaining of object constancy. Each new activity or role in life can be treated as a separation process in the sense that one leaves the familiar for the new. The 3-year-old who goes to nursery school recapitulates the separation–individuation process through its various subphases and particularly the fourth subphase. With the subsequent regaining of object constancy, total development is enhanced. The child's adjustment and activity become more "mature." These results have been documented by the study reported by Speers, McFarland, Arnaud, and Curry (1971), who also found that those 3-year-olds who did not go through the regression–recapitulation process evidenced disturbance in their development and showed marginal or insufficient object constancy. Not only was there marginal object constancy but it was not enhanced by the nursery school experience. These children not only showed little advance in the variety of activities, formation of new relationships, and growth in affective repertoire, but on follow-up several years later, there was in some instances an actual diminution in tested ability. Some of these children upon entering nursery school appeared much more "mature" than those who showed the characteristic regression and recapitulation. Their mature seeming behavior covered an underlying fear of abandonment and apparently fear of loss of mental representation of the object world. Thus, it seems clear that the attainment of object constancy is more than a "once-and-for-all" phenomenon. Object constancy, loosened but not destroyed, by repeated "tolerable" separations and by changes in function and role, is strengthened by these repeated recapitulations of the separation–individuation process and in regaining object constancy.

Object constancy of sufficient firmness makes possible the abandonment of lost objects and the continuous change and redefinition of self through new experiences and through the development of new skills, activities, and interests. The development of object constancy, once it has been attained, is a continuous process. Its further development relies upon revision of self and object representations and upon the capacity to form new relationships. It is also basic to the capacity not only to endure the accelerating changes in knowledge, values, and attitudes but also basic to the capacity to be innovative. Object constancy includes confidence in the continuity of the self through change.

As Greenacre (1971) has suggested, the unique relationship with the analyst provides an opportunity to repair the capacity to form relationships and to strenghten object constancy. The reliability of the analytic relationship facilitates the regression that makes possible the recapitulation of the separation–individuation process with its attendant reworking of the anxieties and defenses associated with relative failure during the different stages on the way toward object constancy.

In summary, the attainment of object constancy is conceptualized as a developmental process which is, in effect, continuous throughout the life cycle. Correlated with the separation–individuation process, it has identifiable stages, each with its typical anxiety. While each stage rests upon preceding stages and is influenced by the separation–individuation process, each also has its own impetus contributed to by cognitive development, motor development, and the like. Difficulty at earlier stages—while having influence upon later stages by reason of the residual anxieties and defenses developed to cope with them—does not halt passage through these subsequent stages. Emphasis in this chapter has been upon the influence of mothering through each stage. However, it is to be understood that other experiences are also influential. In each stage as one follows another, these other experiences have increasing impact upon development. Developmental "failure" is viewed as relative. The effects of such "failure" differ from stage to stage. The significance of recapitulation–regression in life experiences for further development of object constancy was touched upon. The capacity for regression–recapitulation was noted as a significant variable that can be facilitated by the reliability of the therapeutic relationship in psychoanalysis. These many factors make the effects of "failure" of object constancy at its different stages, if not reversible, at least modifiable throughout life, particularly when psychoanalysis intervenes.

REFERENCES

Angel, K. (1972). The role of the internal and external object in object relationships, separation anxiety, object constancy and symbiosis. *International Journal of Psycho-Analysis, 53*(4), 541–546.

Arlow, J., Freud, A., Lampl de Groot, J., & Beres, D. (1968). Panel discussion on object constancy read at the 25th International Psychoanalytic Congress, Copenhagen, July 1967. *International Journal of Psycho-Analysis, 49* (2–3), 506–512.

Bergmann, M. (1971). The capacity to love. In J. B. McDevitt & C. F. Settlage (Eds.), *Separation–individuation: Essays in honor of Margaret S. Mahler*. New York: International Universities Press.

Erikson, E. (1950). *Childhood and society*. New York: Norton.

Fraiberg, S. (1969). Libidinal object constancy and mental representation. *The Psychoanalytic Study of the Child, 24*, 9–47.

Frosch, J. (1966). A note on reality constancy. In R. M. Loewenstein, L. M. Newman, M. Schur, & A. Solnit (Eds.), *Psychoanalysis: A general psychology*. New York: International Universities Press.

Greenacre, P. (1971). Notes on the influence and contribution of ego psychology to the practice of psychoanalysis. In J. B. McDevitt & C. F. Settlage (Eds.), *Separation–individuation: Essays in honor of Margaret S. Mahler*. New York: International Universities Press.

Harlow, H. F. (1962). The heterosexual affectional system in monkeys. *American Psychologist, 17* (1).

Harlow, H., Glueck, J., & Suomi, S. (1972). Generalization of behavioral data between non-human and human animals. *American Psychologist, 27* (8), 709–716.

Harlow, H. F., & Harlow, M. (1962). Social deprivation in monkeys. *Scientific American*, November, 136–146.

Harlow, H. F., Harlow, M., & Suomi, S. (1971). From thought to therapy: Lessons from a primate laboratory. *American Scientist, 59*, 538–549.

Kohut, H. (1971). *The analysis of the self*. New York: International Universities Press.

Kohut, H. (1972). Thoughts on narcissism and narcissistic rage. *The Psychoanalytic Study of the Child, 27*, 360–400.

Mahler, M. (1963). Thoughts about development and individuation. *The Psychoanalytic Study of the Child, 18*, 304–324.

Mahler, M. (1965). On the significance of the normal separation–individuation phase. In M. Schur (Ed.), *Drives, affects, behavior* (Vol. 2). New York: International Universities Press.

Mahler, M. (1966). Notes on the development of basic moods. In R. M. Loewenstein, L. M. Newman, M. Schur, & A. Solnit (Eds.), *Psychoanalysis: A general psychology*. New York: International Universities Press.

Mahler, M. (1968). *On human symbiosis and the vicissitudes of individuation* (Vol. I: *Infantile psychosis*). New York: International Universities Press.

Mahler, M., & McDevitt, J. (1968). Observations on adaptation and defense *in statu nascendi*: Developmental precursors in the first two years of life. *Psychoanalytic Quarterly, 37*, 1–21.

Mahler, M., Pine, F., & Bergman, A. (1975). *The psychological birth of the human infant.* New York: Basic Books.

McDevitt, J. (1975). Separation–individuation and object constancy. *Journal of the American Psychoanalytic Association, 23*, 713–742.

Scott, J. (1962). Critical periods in behavioral development. *Science, 138*, 949–958.

Speers, R., McFarland, M., Arnaud, S., & Curry, N. (1971). Recapitulation of separation-individuation processes when the normal 3-year-old enters nursery school. In J. B. McDevitt & C. F. Settlage (Eds.), *Separation–individuation: Essays in honor of Margaret S. Mahler.* New York: International Universities Press.

Spitz, R. (1945). Hospitalism: An inquiry into the genesis of psychiatric conditions in early childhood. *The Psychoanalytic Study of the Child, 1*, 53–74.

Spitz, R. (1946a). Anaclitic depression. *The Psychoanalytic Study of the Child, 2*, 313–342.

Spitz, R. (1946b). Hospitalism: A follow-up report. *The Psychoanalytic Study of the Child, 2*, 113–117.

Winnicott, D. (1962). Ego integration in child development. In *Maturational processes and the facilitating environment.* New York: International Universities Press.

Clinical Theory and Application

CHAPTER TWELVE

Object Inconstancy and Paranoid Conspiracy

HAROLD P. BLUM

There are still many enigmas concerning the pathogenesis and structure of paranoia and the different forms of paranoid psychopathology. This chapter continues my investigation and reconsideration of the psychoanalytic theory of paranoia (Blum, 1980). My emphasis here will be on the mental representation of the persecutor and certain features of the paranoid persecutory system as viewed in a contemporary theoretical framework.

The paranoid personality tends to misperceive and distort reality in selected areas. Persistent fantasies of outer or inner danger coexist with unreasonable expectation and exaggeration of hostile threat and exquisite sensitivity to minor mishaps and injuries. Affection and commitment are unreliable, and disappointments in relationships are regarded as potentially menacing or malevolent.

Expectations or conviction of infidelity, betrayal, and conspiracy appear, with rage and hate directed at "disappointing" love objects or their disguised, symbolic representations. With paranoia, there is always a potential for conspiracy in which the patient will be victimized, and there is associated suspicion, distrust, and a readiness to accuse others of malice and to defend oneself. The conspiracy may be localized or general and may involve quite imaginary, composite, or fragmented figures. The therapist may be maintained outside the conspiratorial system as a protective object. However, the ambivalent paranoid patient is likely to become the fantasied hapless victim of the therapist, and with paranoid transference, the treatment itself may be regarded as a conspiracy. Narcissistic, negativistic, and aggressively disposed, the transference of the paranoid patient is then manifestly an embattled, omnipotent struggle with persecutory fantasy that is at least partially confused with current reality.

This chapter is an updated and revised version of an earlier paper on the same subject which appeared in the *Journal of the American Psychoanalytic Association,* 1981, *29,* 789–814.

There are transitional paranoid states with varying degrees and reversibility of distrust, suspicion, and projected hostility, as can be seen clinically and in forms of prejudice and social apprehension. Paranoid personality is compatible with advanced personality development in many other areas and with the maintenance of intact language, logic, sublimations, and so on (Freud, 1911). Encapsulation of the paranoia protects the rest of the personality and the rest of the patient's interests and object relationships from regressive invasion.

The disposition for the use of projection, particularly projection of aggression, criticism, and reproach is potentially present in everyone. Others may be blamed for any disappointment, injury, or transgression, and unacceptable impulses are externalized. Frustrations, misfortunes, psychological and physical injuries occur throughout life, and in childhood are often blamed on the parents. In infancy, if aggression is not tamed or internalized, it is particularly directed and projected onto the mother and her surrogates. After ego–id and self–object differentiation and the later persistence of fantasy, affective reactions, and ego attitudes (McDevitt, 1980), some degree and focus of hate is ubiquitous, and a "safe" target for hatred is often needed for psychic equilibrium. With secondary defenses, irrational hatred may be rationalized and justified. Transient, regressive paranoid reactions, therefore, may occur in almost any patient, but this is a situation quite different from the fixity of paranoid ideation, projected hostility, and the malignant distrust of the paranoid personality.

In earlier centuries the terror of persecution by perfidious witches or those possessed by the devil are historical analogues of individual paranoia. There may be, however, significant differences between the individual paranoid personality and group paranoia. While the particular individuals may be attracted to certain groups because of similar underlying paranoid psychopathology, the persecutory reactions of large groups dominated by a paranoid personality are not identical with individual paranoid dynamics. Furthermore, there is a certain variability in the personality structure of paranoid patients, and there are certainly differences from transient paranoid regression to paranoid states, to the fixed paranoid personalities referred to in this chapter. Paranoid schizophrenia, though related to the paranoid personality, may be a different illness, classified as one of the schizophrenias.

Problems of fragmentation and fusion of intrapsychic representations, of unresolved and regressive symbiosis are more characteristic of paranoid psychosis. The paranoid personality usually displays greater differentiation and intact structure, but distortions of an incompletely negotiated separation–individuation with precarious stability in some areas of ego function, intrapsychic self and object representations, and self-esteem regulation. Engulfment–enslavement conflicts here are not so much related to issues of fusion as to omnipotent demands concerning control, domination, intrusion, and possession of or by a narcissistic object endowed with overwhelming aggression. In the paranoid personality, fantasies of fusion or annihilation may be concurrent with maintenance of ego boundaries and organization. That boundaries and representations are unstable is related to aggressive defense of and continuing definition of boundaries. The patient may imagine that thoughts and feelings are deviously communicated to or from others and secrets stolen and betrayed. Paranoid fears of invasion and engulfment are paired with paradoxical fears of desertion and disloyal rejection so that neither intimacy nor separation are acceptable. There is no comfortable distance or position, and if the subject is not being watched and controlled, then the narcissistic object must be jealously guarded with monitoring of movement and direction. The use of projection may blur fragile ego boundaries, but may also be part of an enfeebled effort to master internal danger through externalization and external control.

Adult paranoid personalities have attained oedipal and further development. The quality and importance of the Oedipus complex and of postoedipal phases varies in different cases. Special forms of paraonia, such as those following massive adult trauma (e.g., paranoia following a severe physical illness or in a holocaust survivor), may not be identical in etiology and underlying structure with other cases. In such survivors later damage and regression may be more significant than infantile developmental deviation and deficit. In the more usual type of paranoid personality discussed here, the infantile features and determinants are likely to be predominant.

The final structure of the personality has features from all phases of development, all of which have contributed to the normal personality as well as the pathological paranoid deformations. However, infantile narcissism and preoedipal impairment of self and object constancy (Jacobson, 1964; Mahler, Pine, & Bergman, 1975) may dominate the clinical picture. Oedipal regression in the transference and in external life is shaped and colored by preoedipal fixation and arrest. The Oedipus complex has set its own stamp on the personality, but has been reciprocally determined by unresolved antecedent developmental problems.

The paranoid's pathological object relations and the nature of the intrapsychic representations are related to difficulties in the process of separation–individuation as well as in later development. The preoedipal predisposition and determinants are very important in paranoia and are responsible for severe narcissistic and sadomasochistic distortion and vulnerability to oedipal disappointments and castration threats that interfere with successful resolution of the Oedipus complex.[1]

---

1. Freud (1922) cites a case of jealous paranoia reported by Mack-Brunswick "which went back to a fixation in the preoedipus stage and had never reached the Oedipus situation at all" (p. 130). Freud's acceptance of the importance of preoedipal determinants is consonant with his evolving views of paranoia (cf. p. 120), although the problems then discussed would today extend to both sexes and to issues of developmental arrest and oedipal regression and distortion.

Oedipal conflicts, for example those connected with jealousy and envy, death wishes, and castration, will be expectable but should be understood as rife with narcissism, preoedipal aggression, and annihilation anxieties. Oedipal transference and particularly defenses against murderous and homosexual wishes may be in the foreground, but the latent core of the paranoid personality usually involves preoedipal problems that have led to the arrest and to the distortion of later development. The dangers of object loss and loss of the object's love, and later castration anxiety in all its forms, become for the paranoid personality overwhelming persecutory threats. The ego disturbance and the lack of object and self constancy leave the patient prone to multiple conflicts and problems. Given that development involves interweaving and interpenetrating influences, the impaired object relations are also associated with disorders of narcissism, identity, and sexual identity.

These remarks may seem to be superfluous, but they may also be worth stating at a time of analytic controversy concerning structural deficit and development deviation and arrest, preoedipal determinants, and a nuclear Oedipus complex. Theories of paranoia have variously emphasized primary deficits, core conflicts, and defensive impairments. An example of deficit would be in primary process regulation and reality testing; core conflict involving homosexuality and masochism; defenses of projection with denial and regression also leading to ego dysfunction. The narcissistic disturbance now represents both developmental deviation and regression. Different cases may present varying admixtures of core conflicts and developmental failure. The problems are very complicated, and research has been restricted by the lack of current, reliable, analytic data. Most paranoid personalities are borderline or near-psychotic characters, and the majority of these cases are probably not analyzable, but may be treated by analytic psychotherapy.

Newer psychoanalytic developmental knowledge will be highlighted with clinical application toward enlarged understanding of preoedipal transference determinants and derivatives. Just as we know that id derivatives emerge only through the ego, so the preoedipal influences are filtered through oedipal and later developmental phases with accretions, overlay and overlap, reorganization, and transformations. This complicates transference analysis, but our appreciation of subtle dyadic transference issues where the analyst represents the preoedipal mother and a narcissistic object has greatly increased (Loewald, 1979). In addition, it is important to try to disentangle areas of developmental arrest from fixation and regression. The arrest and pathological distortion (Kernberg, 1975) of narcissism in paranoia, with "homosexual" self-love, can now be distinguished from the negative Oedipus complex, although there are usually intense interrelated problems of phallic narcissism. Additionally, "homosexual panic" may represent fear of fusion with loss of boundaries.

Freud (1937) noted that persecutory delusions are rationalized with ego alteration, but that the delusions are also compensatory efforts at cure through restitution of the patient's relationship to the object world and to reality. Freud offered a number of explanations for the fixity and rigidity of paranoid ideation. Freud called attention to the element of historic truth and to the kernel of truth that also appeared to be confirmed by current experience (Freud, 1922, 1937). The paranoid may have actually had infantile experiences of threat to survival, of fragmented and disorganized ego states, and of primitive modes of experiencing and perceiving reality (Frosch, 1967; Niederland, 1974). Anna Freud (1952), referring to the negativism in certain types of borderline patients, which would certainly apply to paranoid personalities, noted that the dread of passive surrender to the love object implied a threat of a primary identification with the loss of identity because of merger with the love object. The negativism was understood as a defense against the regressive disintegration or disorganization of the personality. A precarious self-definition was also maintained by opposition to objects and by defining the self by what one is *not* or by what one opposes (Wangh, 1964). The paranoid personality also demonstrates other problems with respect to the self-image and the experiencing self, for example, problems in regulation of self-esteem and self-respect and exquisite sensitivity to narcissistic injuries and frustrations, with concomitant affective states of humiliation, shame, disgrace, and narcissistic rage (Kohut, 1972). Problems in object relationship are parallel to these problems, and the lack of object constancy, so frequently encountered in the paranoid personality, is often partially represented and replaced by the constantly negative object relationship with the persecutory object.

In considering the inner representational world of the paranoid, it is important to keep in mind the degrees of differentiation of self and object, of new object and primary object, and of the libidinal and aggressive balance in the personality. Lack of consolidation of the highly aggressivized psychic representations is associated with the persistent tendency to split representations into idealized and devalued, good and bad, persecutory and protective object. This type of splitting, in conjunction with projection and denial, are all indications of defensive impairment of ego development and object relations.

To avoid becoming confused by dealing with these problems as intellectual abstractions, let us confront some of these issues as they become manifest in clinical material.[2]

The patient was a married female in her late 20s who was treated in psychotherapy for 1 year, during the last several months twice a week. Her past history included a period of hospitalization for psychological disturbance at the age of 19 years and psychotherapy as well as pharmacotherapy for her

---

2. I am indebeted to Dr. Rick Linchitz for permission to use this case material. Analytic data would greatly benefit research, but is scarce or unavailable for the reasons Freud (1911) described in the Schreber Case.

anxiety and tension. She warned her therapist of a terribly complex and difficult past treatment experience, but she was also able to function in her external life and maintain her job as well as attempting to advance herself in graduate education.

As her present psychotherapy progressed, the patient had become more and more preoccupied with thoughts about her therapist: What was he doing, where, and with whom? She spent her waking hours brooding and scheming, and hired a detective to follow the therapist. She learned where he lived and entered his home without his permission or knowledge. There were incessant phone calls to the therapist and other phone calls to his home and to his wife at which the caller immediately hung up. The therapist correctly assumed this was part of the patient's telephone activity. If she didn't telephone and didn't have him followed with her agent or herself chasing closely behind, she was afraid she might become incontinent. She derived a sense of power over the therapist and thought she avoided the humiliation of incontinence and a sense of helplessness. One month before, he had been away on vacation, and she had been afraid that he died. That, she thought, was the beginning of murderous thinking on her part, with the fear that she might lose control and kill him if he wasn't already dead. He could leave her, betray her, but she at the same time would not allow it. She not only called him at all hours, but there were days when she spent many hours in the waiting room, watching him and other patients come and go, and not incidentally, instilling anxiety in the other patients as well as the therapist. Sometimes she was confused between herself and the therapist. If they had shared thoughts and feelings, did they have an independent existence as different persons? She assured him that he didn't really have to worry, that she would never kill him, but if she was going to act destructively, she would kill herself first, equivalent to killing the poorly undifferentiated therapist as well.

At the same time that she was having these thoughts of suicide and homicide, she also thought that hiring a detective was a form of protection, not only for herself but for the therapist. She was protecting him through following and constantly watching over him. Her mother had died of a neoplastic illness when the patient was in her teens, and she felt that because she didn't exert precaution and watch her mother, she was then destined to find her mother dead. Now she would protect and watch over the therapist whom she also loved. She thought of him erotically when she was having sexual relations with her husband. Having found out that the therapist's wife was pregnant, she wanted to have something growing inside of her, just as she wanted to be mother, to be with or become like her mother, in order to keep her mother alive. When confronted with the many intrusions into the therapist's setting and relationship, she realized that she was making the treatment impossible, but also indicated that she lacked the inner resources to restrain her need to possess and control the therapist.

It would be remiss in this case not to cite the patient's incomplete differentiation, yet with some preservation of ego boundaries. The patient demonstrates structural achievements, albeit with poor structural consolidation and concomitant with arrests and impaired ego functions. It is certainly possible to infer identification with the lost maternal object, the replacement of the mother with oedipal guilt, the intrusion into the house as into the forbidden primal scene, and the preoccupation with the therapist's infidelity with another woman who would unconsciously represent the homosexually loved partner. She had the therapist followed the way a jealous lover or spouse might hire a detective to check on the fidelity of the partner. It is well to keep in mind that this patient has an Oedipus complex, with oedipal conflicts and passions. However, I do not think that that is where the patient is fundamentally "understood," and that the central treatment issues and transference paradigms were primarily at an oedipal level. It is possible to infer some of the patient's adolescent and oedipal conflicts in the material, but it is not difficult to understand that the patient had not surmounted many preoedipal problems, and that she had not successfully negotiated separation-individuation (Mahler *et al.*, 1975).

Her oedipal organization was infiltrated by these distorting preoedipal influences. Oedipal jealousy continued and condensed her preoedipal possessiveness and envy, and oedipal disappointment and loss also represented her preoedipal separation conflicts and her injured, precarious self-esteem. Oedipal attachment and passion masked her symbiotic dependence, her longings for the omnipotent object and external nurturance. There was little affect modulation or capacity for delay and a propensity for rage when narcissistic and oral demands were thwarted.

Based upon additional psychoanalytic knowledge of paranoia, of early development and structure formation, and more data from this patient and similar patients, the transference here to the therapist appears to be that of a transference to the preoedipal mother who was also a narcissistic object. The patient's behavior and transference attitudes are strongly suggestive of a toddler who is clinging to the mother, shadowing the mother, occasionally, ambivalently darting away, and whose basic mood is not one of established trust (Erikson, 1963) but a negative basic mood of distrust and lack of confidence (Mahler, 1971). Her infantile reactions are derivative of a need to keep the mother constantly within reach or within sight and hearing range—to dominate, control, and entirely possess the mother's interest and attention. Any move on the mother's part outside this narcissistic and omnipotent object orbit meets with increased negativism, opposition, and anger. To not have the organizing, omnipotent object within reach at her beck and call would be to confront the danger of not only separation anxiety, but also disintegration, panic, and the fear of overwhelming and disorganizing regression and aggression.

On the one hand the patient is all powerful, consuming, and controlling, with numerous conspiratorial agents such as detectives at her command. The detective is an extension of her body ego, her perceptual and contact apparatus, her hand and eye. The detective is thus a narcissistic object and extension of herself. The patient is the omnipotent mother who will watch and protect the infant–therapist. The therapist must be protected from her own destructiveness and consuming desires. On the other hand she is the helpless, separated infant who has not yet achieved object constancy and who must have the presence of the object to maintain ego integration. Her fear of losing sphincter control without the presence of the object is not only that she will become extremely apprehensive and enraged, but that she will regressively lose ego control and orientation without the presence of the organizing object. The patient demonstrates features that have been well described in the older literature in terms of the ambivalent conflict between retention and expulsion of the object, Mahler's (Mahler *et al.*, 1975) delineation of the rapprochement crisis, and more general problems of development and structural consolidation in the 2nd year of life. However, no specific locus of developmental failure is assumed or inferred here in the pathogenesis of paranoia.

In this case the mother blamed the patient for the mother's malignancy. The mother herself, therefore, was regressively lacking in empathy, used projection, and might have tended to see the patient as a real or potential persecutor. The daughter, who was blamed in later life, possibly also was regarded ambivalently as a threat to the mother's vitality during the patient's infancy. We may infer here that the patient was repeating in the transference a markedly disturbed infantile relationship. There were overt separation conflicts, severe regressive and panic potential, an inability to be comforted or to find self-comfort, and little experience of self-reliance in the mother's absence.

The patient's behavior with the therapist is reminiscent of those children who do not permit the mother to leave the room, who demand constant attention and find reasons to be with the mother, to insist that the mother be with her, to feed, read, play, go to the bathroom, and so on. This patient may be compared to the child who is exquisitely sensitive to the mother's whereabouts at all times, who shadows the mother, and who displays the separation, sleep, and mood disturbance that may be precursors of serious developmental conflicts. Here are antecedents of later ideas of reference and delusions of being watched, which are also explained and determined by primal scene exposure, superego pressures, and so on. The darting away from the mother (that may alternate with coercive clinging) protects the patient not only against the revived threat of symbiotic engulfment, but may invite the mother to give chase (Mahler *et al.*, 1975, pp. 82–89). Some infantile mothers may reciprocally cling to and shadow the child. Overly demanding infants may deplete the reserves of maternal nurturance. The mother may resent the infant's dependency (or autonomy), and the mother may demand that the infant function as a narcissistic extension of herself, while the infant may demand that the mother and later objects function as an auxiliary ego and as a narcissistic omnipotent extension of himself. Various forms of aggressive, coercive, or negativistic behavior in the toddler may be followed by narcissistic withdrawal or other personality transformations that impede developmental potential.

With respect to the clinging, coercive children who will not leave their mother or let her leave, who keep her within reach and sight, it is not possible to predict which of these children will later develop ideas of reference. There are many possible outcomes, and much depends upon the capacity for developmental mastery and later beneficial influences and transformations.

These struggles for omnipotent control and possession have their analogues in conflicts in later development and adult life. Florid fantasies of oedipal infidelity may persist with oedipal disappointment, jealousy, and rage. In treatment a transference–countertransference bind may develop in which the patient's jealous and tenacious watchful shadowing and clinging arouses anxiety and anger in the therapist. The patient then not only fears the therapist's rejection and desertion, but also may sense the therapist's actual anxiety and aggression toward the patient. With the interweaving of this type of transference and countertransference reactions, one may get escalating regression in both patient and therapist with paralysis or disruption of the therapeutic process. This type of escalating struggle may revive and recapitulate similar struggles between parent and child, sometimes with pathogenic developmental consequences. Areas of developmental failure or deficit and tendencies toward regression may be related to such pathogenic patterns and converging infantile traumata.

The infantile omnipotence and narcissistic vulnerability to which I have referred is often partly due to narcissistic and ego arrest, and partly due to defense and the severe regression accompanying the precipitation or exacerbation of the patient's illness. The patient is often afraid of being engulfed and enslaved with loss of autonomy and identity. The patient is afraid of his own tyrannical demands and may project his infantile attitudes and narcissistic wishes onto the therapist. The patient, as in the case just noted, may attempt in behavior (as well as fantasy) to engulf and enslave the therapist, trying to regain the lost narcissistic omnipotence and reunion with the narcissistic object, who is regarded as essential for psychic survival. Such patients are abjectly dependent and want the omnipotent object, the early narcissistic preoedipal mother, to be a hovering guardian angel, ever nurturant, approving, and protective. Yet closeness or intimacy engenders the danger of invasion of ego boundaries and autonomy. The paranoid is guarded and distant, yet chronically resentful of narcissistic frustration.

The lack of internalization of the comforting, constant mother is associated with a lack of ego integration. Poor frustration tolerance and impulse control, fragile self-esteem, and unneutralized aggression leave the patient predisposed to severe sadomasochistic dispositions and rage reactions. When object constancy is not fully attained, there is also narcissistic arrest with untamed infantile omnipotence.

In more regressive states these patients refuse to recognize that the analyst or therapist is an independent object, just as it was difficult to accept their own mother as an independent object with her own needs and attitudes. (There may be greater or lesser degrees of boundary formation and differentiation or merger.) Simultaneously, the threat to the patient's sense of coping and the danger either of narcissistic fusion or of separateness and helplessness may mobilize various forms of intrapsychic defense and of regressive–adaptive behavior designed to ward off the catastrophe of loss of ego integration and dedifferentiation (or in the most regressed patients, structural fragmentation). In the therapeutic situation, separations or silence, questions, or intrusiveness may be experienced by the patient as a major assault.

The murderous fantasies that so often appear at the juncture of object loss and narcissistic injury are indicative of the patient's inner lack of resources and the feeling that the therapist does not or should not exist without the patient and affectively belongs to the patient; the patient cannot exist without the ego support and synthesis of the therapist, who is a dyadic partner. The exquisite vulnerability of the patient may be compensated by fantasies of grandiosity, by ruthless exploitation of the object or substitute objects designed to demonstrate power and control over the object world and punishment of the disappointment object. To preserve the good object, the patient may split the object world and the self-representation into "good and bad" (Klein, 1932; Mahler et al., 1975). The splitting of representations may be viewed either as an ego defect, as a defense, or both. What begins as a failure to achieve integration, possibly based upon a constitutional deficit, may be utilized by the ego for defensive purposes (Kernberg, 1975). At the same time, the excessive utilization of such defenses as projection and denial severely interfere with both ego integration and reality testing.

While transference, idealizations, and hostile devaluations typically are linked to the family romance of the oedipal phase of development, in more narcissistically disturbed patients and those with more severe arrest and regression, the idealizations and devaluations are extreme, take on fantastic distortions, and are poorly differentiated from each other. Aggressor and victim, tyrant and slave, sadist and masochist, may be globally identified with each other or even fused as in the identification of the masochist with the sadist. This is usually unconscious, so that the conscious persecuted position is a defense against the opposite paired tendency (Kanzer, 1952).

From the point of view of the genetics and dynamics presented, the paranoid personality maintains a tenuous and highly ambivalent relationship with the persecutory, narcissistic object, and in fact, cannot give up the manifestly narcissistic and hostile, sadomasochistic relationship. The paranoid unconsciously creates this relationship in fantasy, and may seek to be persecuted and to persecute in reality. The paranoid patient evokes hostility and may provoke the "persecution" that is consciously feared.

In emphasizing the complexity of these types of reactions in later life and other associated paranoid phenomena, I also want to insert a cautionary note about reconstruction. The transference patterns in cases of very severe developmental arrest and distortions and in cases of severe ego regression do not revive actual infantile relationships in their original form. It is important for the therapist to reconstruct in his own mind the general outlines of the infantile patterning of the patient's psychological function. The reconstruction is based upon the transference repetition, the life history, and so on. This is not to say, however, that the transference repeats the real infantile object relationships, so that analytic reconstruction in these cases is a very complicated effort. Because of projection, denial, splitting, and other infantile defenses, and because of the general invasion of the cognitive process with the primary process, self and object representations are distorted, not only by the patient's specific psychological disturbance, but by the general characteristics of unconscious transformations. The persecutor, as is well known, may have the attributes of the repressed unconscious—sinister, evil, smelly, devouring, destructive, and the like. The object will not correspond to the real mother or for that matter, to any of the caretaking objects of infancy, nor to the patient's own infantile self.

It is well to be reminded here of Abraham's (1924) and Klein's (1932) formulations of paranoia in terms of fixation to the sadism of the late oral and anal phases of development. The child's own sadism and aggression are projected, with fantasies of destroying the object. Murderous paranoid fantasy may take the form of insatiable cannabilism or anal aggressive elimination of the fecal object. The child is also threatened from within, Klein proposed, by reintrojected objects and part-objects endowed with destructive attributes. Paranoid patients are preoccupied with all manner of sexual and aggressive assault. However, what I want to emphasize is not the instinctual drive fixation so much as the related distortions of object and self-representations. This complicates the laborious process that is necessarily involved in reconstruction of the patient's actual development, experience, and object relationships.

The pathogenesis of paranoia is not any simple failure of endowment, the environment, the mother's ministrations or empathy, or of the child's response. The child has not been persecuted necessarily by a malevolent mother, nor has the mother simply been unable to adapt to an "impossible" child. Many different congenital, constitutional, and experiential factors contribute to the etiology of such serious conditions as paranoia. The complemental series and multiple factors Freud described still hold (Niederland, 1974).

Even where there has been a history of continued ambivalent struggles and embattled relationships, the child's distortions of the parent into the equivalent of monsters are distorted exaggerations and elaborations of the parents' and the child's own unacceptable instinctual and exploitative impulses. The disturbed toddler may not be able to utilize affectionate interest, may have temper tantrums and physically and verbally abuse any caretaker, and may fretfully and negatively oppose every caretaking action. The extremely infantile adult patient may engage in similar behavior while attempting to preserve some relationship with the nurturant, concerned object.

At an earlier phase of life, the patient may have been actually exposed to severe traumata and threats to psychic survival (Bak, 1946; Frosch, 1967). Patients with a history of paranoia have often had childhood paranoid episodes, and the adult paranoid reactions are recapitulations or derivatives of the earlier childhood paranoid episodes and paranoid trends that were present in childhood and in a borderline adolescence (Blum, 1974, 1980). Actual persecution and identification with paranoid or with persecuted objects may be important issues in some cases, but are not essential etiologic factors.

I shall now return to the paranoid's peculiar relationship with the "inconstant object," the ambivalently loved object who seems to be both persecutory and needed. The "constant" persecution is also a substitute deviant need-satisfaction from a narcissistic object in whom there is "no confidence." I refer to paranoid suspicion, jealousy, and accusations of disloyalty, paranoid scheming, vindictive exploitation, and actual betrayal of individuals, groups, and causes to which they claimed allegiance and fidelity. As Jacobson (1971) noted, these patients might feel an irresistible urge to look for an opposite group while complaining and bearing grudges about their supposedly unjust experiences with their former friends and allies. The urge to betray, and actual acts of betrayal, are often rationalized upon the basis of just punishment and revenge. Because of the blurring of boundaries and the lack of object and self constancy, the wish for independence and/or autonomy will be experienced as the betrayal of the deserting object who wants to be separate with his own attitudes and interests.

Children are egocentric, "solipsistic," and infantile omnipotence only gradually yields to increasingly realistic appreciation of the object world, with "decentering" of the way the child thinks. Infantile experience is interpreted in terms of psychic reality, a reality transfigured by ego immaturity and defense. The lack of object constancy is an important factor in infantile attitudes of coercion, desertion, rejection, and chronic resentment. A. Freud's (1965) general observations in this area are pertinent to paranoid pathogenesis:

Before the phase of object constancy has been reached, the object, i.e., the mothering person, is not perceived by the child as having an existence of her own; she is perceived only in terms of a role assigned to her within the framework of the child's needs and wishes. Accordingly, whatever happens in or to the object is understood from the aspect of satisfaction or frustration of these wishes. Every preoccupation of the mother, her concerns with other members of the family, with work or outside interests, her depressions, illnesses, absences, even her death, are transformed thereby into experiences of rejection and desertion. On the same basis the birth of a sibling is understood as unfaithfulness of the parents, as dissatisfaction with and criticism of the child's own person—in short, as a hostile act to which the child in his turn answers with hostility and disappointment expressed either in excessive demandingness or in emotional withdrawal with its adverse consequences. (pp. 58–59)

The inconstant object does not or cannot be allowed to have an independent existence, the threat of betrayal and desertion is everpresent, and the problem is not simply the closeness of the external object but intrapsychic separation and the attainment of object constancy. In this sense, the constant, hostile persecution is the reciprocal of libidinal object constancy and may be regarded as a desperate effort to preserve an illusory constant object while constantly fearing betrayal and loss. Once the capacity for fantasy repetition of hostility is obtained after 18 months of age, there can be a constancy of hatred originally toward the preoedipal mother (Blum, 1980; Sandler, 1972). Some capacity for libidinal attachment persists if object ties are at all maintained. The "all-bad" persecutory object is not recognized as the same caretaking object that nurtures and is simultaneously the mirror image of the projected all-bad despised self. In paranoia the hated object and hateful self are linked in projective–introjective processes and incomplete separation-individuation. The manifest persecutory object may be heterosexual or homosexual or may be a group representing the implacable family members, who are seen as allied against the patient in a projection of his hostility to his family (Bak, 1946).

Fantasied, or real, and inevitable disappointments in the self and infantile objects are distorted and used to justify and rationalize the feelings of persecution. As in the secondary elaboration of a dream, the conspiracy is made coherent and given a pseudoplausible construction. The manifest change from friend to enemy, love to hate, is the culmination of the paranoid predisposition to narcissistic rage, hostility, and splitting of representations. Dr. Jekyll becomes Mr. Hyde with the onset of paranoid regression and persecutory transference. Jekyll and Hyde may not consciously recognize their original or their reciprocal relationship, or their "interidentification" and potential refusion. The split may be in the object or self-representation.

Freud (1923) first noted this type of split representation and antithetical affective states of good and evil, "God and Devil." "It does not need much analytic perspicacity to guess that God and the Devil were originally identical—were a single figure which was later split into two figures with opposite attributes. In the earliest ages of religion God himself still possessed all the terrifying features which were afterwards combined to form a counterpart of him" (p. 86).

The negative Oedipus complex, because of its avoidance of rivalry and challenge, is particularly linked to paranoid fears of castration, passivity, and weakness. Homosexuality may mean masochistic submission and victimization (Meissner, 1978), just as masochism may disguise castration and homosexuality. Manifest issues of phallic narcissistic dominance are suffused with preoedipal influences centering around the patient's need to coerce and control, devour and dominate the ambivalently loved and hated, needed and despised narcissistic object. Oedipal homosexuality may be modeled on earlier passive oral and narcissistic object relations; both oedipal defeat and the betrayal of the child by the parents in the child's primal scene may be linked to the paranoid patient's preoedipal inconstancy and narcissistic injury. A dyadic transference may be inferred with the preoedipal issues coexisting with, within, and behind manifest oedipal transference.

The patient may be as confused in his identity as in his object ties, but the need for the object is apparent, a relationship that has to be maintained even at the possible cost of mutual destruction. Since the psychic survival of the self and of the object is not possible in the absence of the relationship, the persecutory object is sought or shadows the paranoiac. The shadowing of the omnipotent preoedipal mother imago, via projection, becomes the patient's being followed, ensnared, and struggling with separation. The split dyadic object representation still represents the projections and primary identifications of the simultaneous vulnerable and aggrandized self. The persecutory object, whose presence in all-or-none infantile terms, indicates the absence of the love object, paradoxically also represents that object to whom there has to be some positive attachment. The paranoid is desperately attached and coercively clings to his persecutor and to the constancy of conspiracy.

Beating fantasies, organized as development proceeds, may be conscious in many of these patients in childhood and adolescence and form the core of the later adult paranoid fantasy. Later systems of persecution and attack include regressive derivatives and transformations of the childhood beating fantasy (Bak, 1946; Freud, 1919). The persecution and victimization are eroticized in degree and sometimes idealized, as in martyrdom. However, paranoid fantasy tends to be less erotic than aggressive and less representative of internalized conflict than masochistic fantasy. In the paranoid patient the beating fantasy may be confused with reality or regressively experienced and enacted in terms of primitive narcissistic and sadomasochistic selfobject relationship. Paranoid regression will selectively involve personality structure and the beating fantasy. The structure of the personality and of the beating fantasy in paranoia is more primitive and more narcissistic than in the masochistic character (Blum, 1980). The patient identifies with and often colludes to form alliances within the family while engaging in a conspiracy against others, so that the underlying fantasies of conspiracy, espionage, and betrayal may have been enacted in various disguised forms during childhood. This becomes part of the kernel of truth in the later fantastic paranoid conspiracies, which also condense actual experiences of collusion, mistreatment, and narcissistic injury, trauma, and the hostility engendered by their own suspicion, provocation, exploitation, and disloyalty. The paranoid's role of victim is itself exploited.

Because of the structural regression, arrests, and deficits, the projected superego discerned in paranoia is not that of mature superego structure and function. The watching, accusing object has regressive overtones of the preoedipal precursors of the superego. It is no simple matter to differentiate projection of aggression and externalization of superego elements. The superego of the paranoid is poorly internalized and remains prone to regression; it is then archaic, punitive, and unable to assert effective control and regulation, or to offer self-comfort and tolerance. Lack of superego stability, the continued projective–introjective processes, and poorly integrated, absolute ideals and injunctions leave the paranoid patient prone to acting out and to experiencing humiliation and shame rather than guilt and self-reproach. The persecutory plot is thus also a misguided and disguised effort, not only to protect the good self and object, but to reestablish the watchful, concerned care that is reliably internalized in true object constancy. The quality of superego internalization and integration and capacity for guilt are important prognostic considerations in paranoia, and the patient is also paradoxically in search of the object as auxiliary superego and ego.

It is very difficult for those patients to accept responsibility for their lives, frailties, and feelings. Impulses are temptations to be punished, blame and shame are also projected, and objects of temptation or of anger are transformed into persecutory objects. Acceptance of illness or help itself threatens their narcissistic "invulnerability." Narcissistic injury is denied and undone, and there may be simultaneous mobilization of narcissistic rage and persecutory beating fantasy. The "need" for the persecutory object and persecution may be associated with breakthrough of the wish to persecute. The grievance and grudge of the paranoid toward the "disloyal" inconstant object should not be underestimated in strength or tenacity, and in fantasy further and prior injury may be avoided and avenged by a preemptive strike and counterattack.

The degree of hostility and vindictiveness in the paranoid personality depends upon ego modulation of affect and impulse, the balance between love and hate, and between masochistic attachment and narcissistic rage. Splitting of representations is usually incomplete, and the persecutory object may be eroticized anew. However, in some paranoids, there is a more implacable, "pure" hatred (e.g., Hitler) expressed in the persecutory system, imbricated in what is presumed to be a precarious narcissistic personality organization. Without object constancy, distrust and suspicion of betrayal are associated with the panic hate–rage affects that are so readily mobilized. Love is a condition for the repression and for the taming of hatred. The paranoid's predominant hatred may be associated with ambivalence, but with arrested, deficient, and deviant love. Paranoid hatred is part of the disturbed ego and affective state and is not primarily a reactive disguise for repressed love. The lack of object constancy is related to paranoid suspicion and hostility and may, in itself, be part of a vicious cycle of unneutralized aggression, projected hatred, and failures of internalization, integration, and libidinal investment of self and object representations.

There are many possible outcomes to the instability and regressive loss of object constancy. The clinical picture depends upon many other factors, including the capacity to reverse regression and to maintain ego integration and reality adaptation. The paranoid personality is particularly prone to narcissistic injury and to impaired consolidation of emotional object constancy and individuality. In paranoia there is a proclivity to confuse and fuse the hostile object and self-representations with attempts to project, eject, and externally control and coerce the unreliable, dangerous, narcissistic object. The destructive loss and attempts to regain object constancy are part of the paranoid persecutory struggle. It is a malignant illness when there is an inexorable narcissistic tyranny with constant expectations of malice and betrayal and a constancy of hatred that permeates the personality.

The persecutory object relationship is a central aspect of paranoia and will have features from all developmental phases. In the psychotic forms of paranoia, the object may be incompletely differentiated from the self or may be a fragmented object with condensation of fragments of self and object representation. In the paranoid personality, where many areas of the personality remain intact, object relationships are more cohesive and integrated, although still unstable and lacking in object constancy in the persecutory relationship. The narcissistic system of megalomania and persecutory object relationship attempts to preserve the crucial relationship with the inconstant narcissistic object. The constant persecutory object inconstancy is a distorted malformation and replacement for libidinal object constancy. Expectations or conviction of infidelity, betrayal, and conspiracy are common, with hate and rage directed at the inevitably disappointing, faithless objects or their disguised representations. There is always suspicion and distrust of the object, but a need to search for and be shadowed by the object, to be persecuted and to persecute the betraying narcissistic object who inflicts narcissistic injury. The "constant" persecution displays the hatred and may disguise narcissistic and masochistic gratification in the attachment and bondage to the persecutor. Because of instability of boundaries and the lack of object and self constancy, the wish for autonomy is experienced as betrayal of the deserting object who wants to be separate, and the wish for narcissistic fusion may be defended against and experienced as a dangerous intrusion or invasion and a threat to identity. The "inconstant" object does not and cannot be allowed to have an independent existence, and the threat of betrayal is ever present along with the need to maintain the relationship at all costs. The paranoid appears to flee but is always followed or follows his dyadic persecutory partner.

In paranoid regression the manifest change from friend to enemy, love to hate, is the culmination of the paranoid predisposition to narcissistic injury and rage, narcissistic and sadomasochistic object relationship, and the splitting of self and object representations. Narcissistic, preoedipal issues and unresolved problems of separation–individuation may be discerned within and behind oedipal conflict and distortions. Conflict and deficits are subsumed in a widened contemporary perspective of the development and structure of paranoia. In addition to the pervasive narcissism and use of projection, the ambivalent splitting in which hate overrides love, the failure of self–object constancy, and malignant mistrust are interrelated and, in varying degree, consequent to developmental arrest, fixation, and regression.

REFERENCES

Abraham, K. (1924). A short study of the development of the libido viewed in the light of mental disorders. In *Selected papers on psychoanalysis* (pp. 418–502). New York: Brunner/Mazel.

Bak, R. (1946). Masochism in paranoia. *Psychoanalytic Quarterly, 15,* 285–301.

Blum, H. (1974). The borderline childhood of the Wolf Man. *Journal of the American Psychoanalytic Association, 22,* 721–742.

Blum, H. (1980). Paranoia and beating fantasy: An inquiry into the psychoanalytic theory of paranoia. *Journal of the American Psychoanalytic Association, 28,* 331–362.

Erikson, E. (1963). *Childhood and society.* New York: Norton.

Freud, A. (1952). A connection between the states of negativism and of emotional surrender. *International Journal of Psycho-Analysis, 33,* 265.

Freud, A. (1965). *Normality and pathology in childhood writings* (Vol. 6). New York: International Universities Press. 1966.

Freud, S. (1911). Psychoanalytic notes on an autobiographical account of a case of paranoia. *Standard Edition, 12.*

Freud, S. (1919). A child is being beaten. *Standard Edition, 17.*

Freud, S. (1922). Some neurotic mechanisms in jealousy, paranoia, and homosexuality. *Standard Edition, 18.*

Freud, S. (1923). A seventeenth-century demonological neurosis. *Standard Edition, 19.*

Freud, S. (1937). Constructions in analysis. *Standard Edition, 23.*

Frosch, J. (1967). Delusional fixity, sense of conviction, and the psychotic conflict. *International Journal of Psycho-Analysis, 48,* 475–495.

Jacobson, E. (1964). *The self and the object world.* New York: International Universities Press.

Jacobson, E. (1971). *Depression.* New York: International Universities Press.

Kanzer, M. (1952). Manic depressive psychoses with paranoid trends. *International Journal of Psycho-Analysis, 33,* 34–42.

Kernberg, O. (1975). *Borderline conditions and pathological narcissism.* New York: Jason Aronson.

Klein, M. (1932). *The psychoanalysis of children.* New York: Grove, 1960.

Kohut, H. (1972). Thoughts on narcissism and narcissistic rage. *The Psychoanalytic Study of the Child, 27,* 360–400.

Loewald, H. (1979). The waning of the Oedipus complex. *Journal of the American Psychoanalytic Association, 27,* 751–776.

Mahler, M. (1971). A study of the separation–individuation process: and its possible application to borderline phenomena in the psychoanalytic situation. *The Psychoanalytic Study of the Child, 26,* 403–424.

Mahler, M., Pine F., & Bergman, A. (1975). *The psychological birth of the human infant.* New York: Basic Books.

McDevitt, J. (1980, November 25). Brill lecture. Presented at the New York Psychoanalytic Institute. New York.

Meissner, W. (1978). *The paranoid process.* New York: Jason Aronson.

Niederland, W. (1974). *The Schreber case: Psychoanalytic profile of a paranoid personality.* New York: Quadrangle.

Sandler, J. (1972). In A. Lussier (Reporter), Panel: Aggression. *International Journal of Psycho-Analysis, 53,* 14.

Wangh, M. (1964). National socialism and the genocide of the Jews. *International Journal of Psycho-Analysis, 45,* 386–395.

CHAPTER THIRTEEN

Libidinal Object and Self Constancy Enhanced by the Analytic Process

RUTH F. LAX

The significance that the attainment of libidinal object constancy and self constancy plays in the development of good object relations as well as in the maintenance of healthy narcissism and self-esteem is widely recognized. By presenting relevant details of a patient's analysis in this chapter, I hope to show how the holding environment—an integral part of the analytic situation—and the technique of reconstruction are especially suited to enhance libidinal object and self constancy in a patient suffering from developmental arrests.

Dewald (1976), Gitelson (1962), Khan (1960), Loewald (1960), Modell (1976, 1978), and Winnicott (1963) have all addressed themselves to the significance of the dyadic nature of the psychoanalytic situation and pointed out the extent to which the classic analytic setting contains elements analogous to an ideal mother–infant and/or mother–child relationship. Of particular relevance are the analyst's reliability as an object; his availability during the analytic work, exclusively for the patient's needs; his non-judgmental and noncritical attitude; his empathic concern and responsiveness; and his capacity to comprehend the patient's psychic unconscious reality and to subsequently help the patient understand and cope with it in an adaptive and autonomous manner. The analytic situation also provides safe limits for the patient's expression of libidinal and aggressive fantasies.

The ambience thus created enables the patient to experience the analytic situation as a symbolic "holding environment" (Winnicott, 1960), offering an illusion of protection from both internal and external dangers analogous to the conditions provided during infancy and childhood by "good-enough mothering" (Winnicott, 1956, 1963). Under such circumstances, according to Gitelson (1962), anaclitic dependence becomes reactivated and with it the potential for the development of basic trust. The patient not only utilizes the analyst as a transference object for reexperiencing past fantasies, life events, and significant object relations, but he also makes therapeutic use of what *he* responds to as a *new* experience provided by the analyst within the context of the analytic situation.

All these factors, to the extent to which they correspond to the growth-promoting actuality of a "good-enough" mother–infant and/or mother–child dyad, constitute the embedded "holding environment" potentialities of the analytic situation. These factors have a therapeutic significance for patients suffering from developmental arrests, since they contribute to psychic change (Stone, 1981). To the extent to which this type of patient suffers from amnesia, *reconstruction*, as suggested by Freud (1937), can substitute for missing memories and is a technique of choice because it contributes to the analytic restoration of the continuity and cohesion of the self (Blum, 1980).

THE CASE MATERIAL

As is frequent with children who come to treatment at their parents' behest, Jim, 24 years old, came, docile and submissive, because of his wife's urging. His wife, Theresa, complained about his close attachment to his father and accused him of submitting to his father's exploitation. Jim's father had given him half-ownership of his small engineering shop, which barely "broke even." Jim supplemented his meager salary by cheating his father on business expenses. In contrast to his father, who held advanced degrees and was considered a world expert in his field, Jim had barely managed to graduate from high school.

Jim, dirty, unkempt, affecting the manner of a beatnik, could give no reasons of his own for wanting to be in treatment, although he was unwilling to concede that he was taking this step to please his wife. Jim experienced his father as harsh and demanding, yet felt he could always count on him to "bail him out of trouble." Jim insisted that theirs was the usual father–son relationship: The father gave the commands and Jim "rebelled but in the end did father's bidding." Jim described Theresa as beautiful, intellectually superior, but emotionally inconsistent. In their marital quarrels, Theresa used sex and Jim used money as weapons. Theresa seemingly dominated the relationship and looked down on Jim. Jim spoke of occasionally having violent outbursts of anger at Theresa and of getting stoned and drunk.

It soon became apparent that it was indeed Jim who wanted to come for treatment. He came four times a week, arrived punctually, and paid on time. As the treatment proceeded, I became more and more puzzled by "lacunae" in Jim's stories: namely, the cause for a particular feeling, state, or event was always missing. When I shared my observation with him, Jim began to listen to what he was saying. He recognized that he, too, could not figure out how the events or feelings came about. He subsequently questioned Theresa and his parents. When I shared with him my puzzlement that "they knew and he did not," he grew pensive and then genuinely perplexed. He decided he "would watch and observe." His manner was *not* one of compliance in this self-imposed task, but seemed based on a genuine identification with my therapeutic wish "to find out." We discovered over the next months that he went blank when he felt criticized, anxious, or angry. He was amazed by this discovery, and he became increasingly self-observant.

Toward the end of the 1st year, while in a pensive mood and relating some story, Jim mentioned his stepmother. When I asked whom he meant, he said, "My mother, my stepmother—*what difference does it make?*" Only then did I learn that Jim indeed had a stepmother, whom he called "mother." He was uncertain about the fate of his "real" mother. He thought she had died. Jim had an amnesia for most of his childhood, vague recollections of the latency years, sporadic memories from adolescence, and absolutely no memory of his real mother. When speaking of his earliest years, he repeated over and over, "I remember most of the time being alone in my room, being terribly afraid, often in terror. I wanted to be with father as much as I could." Only father stood out clearly in the chain of continually changing, faceless governesses, maids, and housekeepers.

Jim was amazed that I attached significance to his mother's death and to his ignorance about this event. He asked, giving no reason, whether he could come for treatment five times a week. The transference significance of his request was analyzed much later.

Jim's parapraxis led to my "discovery" that he lost his mother in childhood. The manner in which I learned about the death of Jim's mother suggested that we were beginning to deal with his deepest and most crucial "secret," repressed and rerepressed in the course of his childhood. When Jim was 9 years old, his father married a widow with three daughters. His stepmother adopted Jim. For the emotionally starved youngster in search of a mother, stepmother became mother, ambivalently loved. Wanting to be his stepmother's *real* son, Jim denied his adoption, which simultaneously obliterated the existence of his own mother, of her death, and significantly contributed to making the past an even more deeply buried secret.

The *prescribed* analytic role of concern and empathy provided Jim with a matrix analogous to that of an ideal "holding environment," wherein he felt safe enough *not* to resist the regressive pull inherent in this situation. Such a regression is in the service of the analysis, preliminary to and fostering psychic change (Kris, 1950; Loewald, 1981). Jim felt he could trust me and depend on me. He used me as an auxiliary ego. A strong, childlike transference developed. Because of his infantile "love for me" (Freud, 1923), Jim identified with my attitude of inquiry, which subsequently led to his developing an introspective attitude and to the uncovering of unconscious motives and conflicts. Initially, his wish to please me was the main factor motivating him to combat lapses into blanking out; later, this same wish to please led to his analysis of the causes and the contents of the blanks.

As Jim transferentially obtained the gratifications of early object relatedness and with it a sense of security, he felt confident he would be accepted by me in spite of his shortcomings. His anxiety diminished and with it his characterological defensiveness and rigidity, enabling him to become more introspective. Likewise, his tolerance for psychic distress increased. A modification of certain unconscious defensive patterns occurred. Namely, without specific analysis, the automatic defensive withdrawal—the blanking out, which also affected his thinking and made him appear somewhat stupid and passive—diminished and to some extent even came under conscious control. His submissiveness and wish to ingratiate himself, defenses in response to chronic patterns of narcissistically injurious object relations, also decreased. In this phase of treatment the symbolic "gratifications" derived from the unconscious meaning of the holding-environment aspects of the analytic situation were the most significant factors accounting for psychic change. The modifications in the patient's defensive patterns had an important therapeutic consequence: They "unsettled" the rigid psychic structure without causing intolerable anxiety. Consequently, the psychic apparatus once again became flexible and permeable, suggesting that a limited, therapeutic structural regression took place.

Helping patients who have suffered object loss in their first 5 years to resume their arrested development can be achieved when the analyst is a reliable object, a model for identification, and the therapeutic relationship is strong enough for the patient to tolerate grief (Wolfenstein, 1976). Fleming, on the basis of her extensive experience in this area (1972, 1974, 1975, 1978; Fleming & Altschul, 1963), noted that "the patient comes to the analyst for help as a child comes for refueling" (1972, p. 39). To facilitate the resolution of such developmental arrests, Fleming suggested that the analyst respond to the patient's primitive object needs for affective communication and be available as an auxiliary ego to help the patient develop a capacity for introspection.

The findings of the 1965 panel on "Depression and Object Loss" (Levin, 1966) suggested that object loss in childhood may result in ego arrest at the developmental level at which the loss occurred. Such an arrest may specifically manifest itself in the area of object relations. In such a case the transference relationship to the analyst will be colored by the psychic need for an object necessary for psychic growth and maturity.

A preoedipal idealizing transference dominated the first phase of treatment. Jim "used me" in the transference as a need-gratifying object by interpreting my noncommittal "mhms" as signals of encouragement, as signs that I was empathically available, and also as esteem-regulating devices. Simultaneously, Jim became more and more confident that he could expose his weaknesses and problems in the analytic situation without experiencing narcissistic mortification. He began to reveal more about his current life and about his past. He ended every hour with, "I'll see you . . ." and I would nod. Years later, analysis revealed that the nod gave to him the important reassurance: I will be here, available for him.

The following dream describes Jim's unconscious wish at the time and also the way he experienced the analytic situation: "I had a gold chain with some ornaments and you came over and looked at it, and then I got up and we went out together. The weather was very nice." Associations: "It is like you came over and looked at me with love. Like when I was a baby. The feeling in the dream was very comfortable and natural. You looked at my ornament. It felt like you were playing 'kitchy, kitchy koo' with me, the baby. I felt very secure and warm." I did not analyze, at the time, the symbolically apparent erotic components of the dream and the exhibitionism.

Jim would snuggle into the couch. He was early for his sessions. He greeted me with a smile. It was my impression, based on the transference, his nonverbal behavior, and some dreams, that he was *replicating* in the analytic situation the loving, preloss experiences with his mother (Fleming, 1972). Certain ego strengths and fantasies suggested to me that Jim experienced "good-enough" mothering at least during the first 2 years of his life.

During the 2nd year of analysis, from Jim's rather inarticulate and halting description of events, a picture emerged of a man who felt put-upon by his wife, father, stepmother, and friends. Jim, in a passive–resistive–aggressive fashion, acquiesced to these demands, dreading he would otherwise be abandoned. Seemingly, Theresa, aware of Jim's fear, exploited it and threatened to leave him whenever she was displeased. This would induce Jim to give in. "Blanking out," drinking, using drugs, and occasionally having violent outbursts of rage were his way of dealing with his unhappy marriage and life.

Jim's increasing capacity for self-observation made him more and more aware of his memory blanks. It became apparent that "blanking out" with no subsequent memory of what occurred served a defensive function. It was an unconscious automatic process occurring during an interaction with a significant object that enabled Jim to dissociate and thus avoid becoming aware of an overwhelming painful affect. In later years when he had acquired deeper insight and understanding, Jim described the onset of these states by saying, "I felt as if I became paralyzed by fear and my mind was going blank."

The decrease in Jim's defensiveness and psychic rigidity enabled him to remember dreams and have associations, which evoked hazy memories of childhood experiences. Jim also started to question his father. A bare outline of that period emerged. Jim's mother had died suddenly and unexpectedly following a very brief hospitalization 2 weeks before his third birthday. Associations to a vague visual memory give credence to the probability that Jim watched, paralyzed by fear, as "they were taking her away," apparently on a stretcher. Shortly thereafter, grandmother, who lived with the family and had mothered him during his 2nd year while mother worked, disappeared. Father and son moved from the suburbs to the city. Jim reported the following recurring nightmare: "I find myself in my room as a young boy chased by 'things,'" adding after a long silence, "Things belonging to the past are haunting me. Something terrible happened."

During this phase of treatment, when Jim again described his state of terror following one of his wife's threats to leave him, I finally understood the genetic roots of his panic. Thus, I not only interpreted the unconscious conflict between his dependency needs and anger at Theresa, but could also offer the first of a series of reconstructions designed to help Jim become aware of the psychic causes of his panic states.

Following Freud's (1937) definition of the reconstructive task as a search for "a picture of the patient's forgotten years that shall be alike trustworthy and in all essential respects complete" (p. 253), I connected Jim's hazy memory of the incident when "they took mother away" with as detailed a depiction as possible of his state of helplessness and abandonment experienced at that time. I continued making such reconstructions whenever dynamically appropriate. I stressed not only the fateful events, but also ego attributes and functions characteristic for his age, the nature of his relations to mother, father, and grandmother, the intrapsychic conflicts stirred up by mother's death, and his emotional state following it. I was guided in making these constructions by the work of Mahler (1965, 1972a, 1972b, 1974), Mahler, Pine, and Bergman (1975), the findings of Bowlby (1960), and my own work as a child analyst. I pointed out to Jim repeatedly that the threat of abandonment in the present appeared to him as such a terrible danger because it reevoked the frightening repressed events of the past, namely, being suddenly abandoned (through death) by mother when he was a little boy dependent on her for his basic security. I stressed that mother's death was a catastrophic event of such magnitude that it became overwhelming and paralyzing. He could not comprehend it at the time it occurred. I reconstructed: "When mother did not come back, you probably searched for her, called her, cried for a long time, were even angry with her, and finally filled with despair, may have concluded, 'Mom left me and is not coming back because I am bad.'"

Fleming (1978) refers to such reconstructions as "telling the patient a story about himself." This is indeed the case when memory is completely absent. Kris (1956), Greenacre (1975), and Blum (1980) have said that reconstruction may become an integrative force, a force for subsequent unconscious fantasies and memories. My reconstructions became more precise as the analytic process progressed, and they filled the psychic void subsequent to the total repression caused by Jim's traumatic loss.

This trauma became the predominant organizing factor causing a deformation of Jim's psychic development. It disrupted processes leading to the internalization and unification of the maternal imago, as well as the evolvement of object constancy. Thus the split into the good and bad maternal imago persisted (or recurred due to regression), and object representations remained disjointed. The self-representation likewise remained split, with the helpless, powerless self predominating. The primitive nature of the superego manifested itself by cruelty and corruptibility. Partial ego arrest was also indicated by the incomplete development of the synthetic function and a certain primitive quality of other ego functions. Regression occurred to the developmental level at which fear of libidinal object loss is paramount. Jim experienced and perceived objects primarily as need-gratifying or need-frustrating; ambivalence predominated in all object relations.

My reconstructions did not evoke memories, but did provide Jim with "something to hold onto," an understanding that was helpful because it mitigated his terror when current, dynamically comparable situations reactivated unconscious infantile panic. At such times, like a child, Jim reminded himself of what I had said and this had a soothing effect: "I wasn't quite so scared . . . it was a little as if you were there with me." He thus made use of the reconstructions in a manner analogous to the developing child's internalization of parental instructions, which the child uses to guide himself. The process can be viewed as a step leading to the consolidation of an internalized object representation.

The nature of the transference suggested that the modulating effect of the reconstructions was due in part to the fact that Jim had shifted his dependency needs and was using me as an auxiliary ego. When away on business trips, he would phone at his appointment time, ostensibly "not to miss" his sessions. Years later, analysis of his need to make these telephone calls indicated he could only function when away by making sure that I was still here and available to him. Subsequently, as the fear of abandonment subsided and the nature of the transference changed, Jim not only began to tolerate separations; he initiated them autonomously.

The reconstruction also seemed to enhance Jim's sense of self-continuity. The panic states following threats of abandonment no longer seemed to him so mysterious. He used his understanding of them to mitigate the feeling of dread by reassuring himself he no longer was as helpless as in his childhood.

The gratification stemming from my emotional availability, which Jim transferentially experienced as nurturing, and my consideration for his narcissistic vulnerability decreased his defensiveness. This resulted in some abatement of the childhood amnesia.

Jim, via analysis of the paralyzing fear with which he responded to Theresa's abandonment threats, also came to examine the unconscious rage he experienced at such times. This led to the uncovering of his unconscious fantasy in which mother was not dead but "had left him and gone away." Although Jim's predominant feeling was that "mother's leaving was his own fault," he now recognized he also was angry at mother and thought of her as "bad for having left him." He experienced a sense of perplexity and exclaimed: "How could this be? . . . How could a mother do this? Leave her child? She was not a good mother."

Following mother's death and grandmother's departure, father became Jim's most significant object. In subsequent years, Jim, driven by the fear of abandonment, loneliness, and the need for emotional security, began to spend many hours with his father in the latter's laboratory. He watched his father, sat quietly, grateful his presence was tolerated. Because of his need for contact with his father, Jim submitted to father on father's terms. Reflecting on it now, Jim complained, voicing misery and anger: "There was no other way to be with father. He had no time, he had to make a living. Father did not play with me, though he bought me all the toys a child could wish for. I wanted to be with him . . . who else was there? I loved him even though I hated him." This intense ambivalence to father persisted.

Motivated by his need for love and fear of his father's criticism, Jim learned to perform assigned tasks, first imitating and subsequently identifying with his father. Eventually he became father's apprentice. Father expected Jim to do the assigned jobs perfectly, and Jim complied though he experienced rage and frustration.

Jim's psychic development was profoundly influenced by his father's tyrannical, explosive, and demanding personality. Afraid of being "thrown out," as were maids, governesses, and girlfriends when they displeased father, Jim retreated to docility. He recalls praise for always being a "very good boy." He remembers "feeling stupid" and experiencing "blanks" even in childhood. He also remembered being painfully aware that he never knew exactly "what was going on."

I offered another reconstruction to deal with this state of cognitive confusion. I suggested that it was indeed difficult for a child "whose mother had left and failed to return to know exactly what really happened, especially when no one was available to help the child understand. Probably when mother failed to return and he could no longer tolerate her absence, he must have cried and 'carried on' and called for her and hoped . . . and no one helped him comprehend and cope." Jim then told me he did not recall father *ever* speaking about mother or showing him any memento of her. I must have conveyed my surprise and puzzlement to him, in spite of my silence, for he remarked: "I must find out."

Some time later, Jim reported asking father about mother's death and discovering for the first time that there was a great deal of animosity between the parents during the year preceding this event. Because father withheld money from mother when displeased, mother went back to work and grandmother moved in to care for Jim and the household. The marriage was not only "rocky," but the parents were actually planning to divorce. Mother's death occurred only weeks before the court date for the divorce hearing.

Jim was confused and depressed. He said, "I do not know what happened. I know my mother died, *but I feel she left me.* " In the course of ensuing sessions, I made reconstructions that dealt with Jim's childhood feelings of never "quite knowing what exactly was going on." Indeed, this sense of confusion was understandable. Father, in addition to not helping the child comprehend the reasons for mother's disappearance, also did *not* share in the child's despair *about* mother's disappearance. Whereas mother's death was a boundless catastrophe for the child, it probably offered a convenient solution for father, who not only had *no* emotional need to keep her memory alive, but indeed wanted to obliterate it. Father did so in many ways: by moving to a new house, by removing all traces of mother, and by getting a court order forbidding grandmother any contact with Jim. Father's actions contributed to the child's confusion and helplessness. I emphasized that under such conditions, any child would become extremely uncertain and fearful. These childhood events also accounted for Jim's increasing dependence on father. Further, Jim's hopeless calling for mother, the disappointment of his yearning for mother, evoked despair and, no doubt, also anger. These factors, combined with Jim's fear of losing father and father's love and protection, led to his compliance with what he believed father requested: he "blanked out" the past. Believing he was forbidden to inquire and therefore afraid to find out, Jim relinquished his curiosity. Jim's compliance probably also had the defensive function of strengthening the repression of his conflicted feelings toward mother. Subsequently, the lack of curiosity became generalized to a learning inhibition in all areas other than science and mathematics, the fields of father's endeavor.

Freud (1937) states that, although reconstructions do not always lead to recollection, if the analysis is carried out correctly, "we produce in [the patient] an *assured conviction* of the truth of the construction which achieves *the same therapeutic result* as a recaptured memory" (p. 266, italics mine). Jim absorbed my reconstructions with great voracity. Their "fit" with the emotional actuality of the traumatic period of his childhood was indicated by marked psychic changes, which I inferred from his behavior and emotional attitudes. Hence, although Jim produced no fresh memories, I consider the consequences following my reconstructions analogous (though not identical) with the effects of a good interpretation.

After a partial working through, via reconstructions, of the events surrounding mother's death, which included the exploration of feelings of love, despair, and anger toward mother, Jim's characterologic need to comply and his inhibition of curiosity were considerably alleviated. He could now express to father his curiosity regarding mother, and he also ventilated great anger at father in connection with these childhood events. Thereafter, Jim's learning inhibition lifted sufficiently for him to resume his education. He now found tutors to help him master skills he was lacking. He decided to give up drugs and alcohol completely. He wanted to develop a "new image" but as yet did not know "who and what he wanted to be." He considered becoming a scientist, continuing with his business, leaving the business he co-owned with father and becoming father's competitor.

Jim, in this phase of his analysis, for the first time since he could remember *actively* wanted to find out and know. My reconstructions also led to the uncovering of the family conspiracy of silence. Jim pressed father, who now provided him with all the papers pertaining to his mother's death and the pending divorce. Jim looked up his old house. He found his grandmother, who provided him with movies from his childhood and information about his mother and his early years. Nonetheless, Jim still did not experience the reawakening of any memories. He persisted, when speaking about himself as a child, in the use of the third person. I considered this specific use of language, typical for children who have not yet mastered the use of the pronoun "I," indicative of a transference regression and a further confirmation of the correctness of my reconstructions. Jim repeatedly and with pain uttered the phrase, "Who is taking care of the child?" I suggested that the phrase reflected his sense of abandonment as a child.

Jim continued to be locked in a hostile–rebellious, passive–resistive, seemingly unending power struggle with father. Jim correctly experienced father as "the boss who called the shots" and hated feeling completely dependent on father for his livelihood and welfare. At this time, Jim began telling me about his fantasies of great power, wealth, revenge, and triumph over father, which seemed so at variance with the reality of his angry encounters with father from which he emerged in a state of rage feeling powerless and helpless. However, with increased attunement to reality it became possible for Jim to begin to differentiate his psychic need to oppose father and the appropriateness of father's demands, rules, and guidelines. He recognized in a realistic and emotionally appropriate manner that the business was his also, and that it was in his interest for it to do well. Jim now began to pay attention to what his father was saying, even though he still hated the way father said it. He became keenly aware that father was not the kind of person he, Jim, would like to be.

Jim now showed a capacity for perseverance in spite of difficulties. As the analysis of his fear of curiosity progressed and his learning inhibition diminished, Jim became more and more aware of what went on in the business and recognized his own shortcomings. To correct these, he took special courses and began balancing the ledgers and checking on his accountants and advisors. It now became apparent that Jim not only absorbed the father's technical genius (for which he probably had a genetic endowment), but that he also internalized father's standards of excellence, conscientiousness, and dependability. As these became operative, Jim was able to make them his own and use them autonomously.

In the analysis Jim continued to explore his thoughts and feelings about "what he wanted to be" and "the image he wanted to project." He repeated over and over, with an admixture of grandiosity, despair, fear, and hope: "Will I ever amount to something?" His attempts at mastery likewise frequently were a mixture of reality and grandiosity. He imagined that I wanted him to obtain an advanced academic degree. He thereafter engaged in a transferential power struggle with me, insisting I could not force him to do my bidding. A hostile father transference predominated. Jim was accusatory and insisted that I wanted him to bend his goals to my wishes. Analysis of his distortions and of his anger toward me led to his recognition of the transferential nature of his thoughts and feelings. Further analysis of his relationship with father followed, and new material regarding his schooling emerged. Jim had been a poor student in spite of private tutoring, and had felt overwhelmed and mortified by what went on in the classroom. These feelings were compounded by his father's dissatisfaction. Jim marveled at the contrast between his childhood inability to learn and his current scholastic achievements.

After the hostile transference was worked through, Jim continued to analyze his goals, his feelings of inferiority, as well as his grandiose schemes. He once again felt accepted and therefore safe to exhibit his weaknesses and his wish to conquer.

Four years into the analysis, Jim appeared one day for his session in a business suit, clean shaven, his hair fashionably cut. He asked with glee, "Are you surprised?"—pleased he had kept his plan a secret. Jim then informed me of his decision to become *primarily* a successful manufacturer and business-man since his father had not succeeded as an entrepreneur. Jim's plan was to develop their jointly owned workshop into a multimillion-dollar business. Jim's choice reflected his identification with his father and it also pointed to an individuation: Jim now could contemplate realistically succeeding where father had failed.

The exploration and analysis of Jim's gradiose fantasies and feelings of self-devaluation contributed to the formation of his wishful self-image (Jacobson, 1954, 1964). The analysis of his vacillations, changes, and of his identifications (primarily with his father) led to consolidation and integration of the self. The fusion of various self-image elements contributed to the formation of a cohesive self-representation. The attainment of libidinal self constancy now became possible.

During this phase of the analysis, Jim's emotional preoccupation oscillated between Theresa and his father. His relationship to each of them was extremely ambivalent. It contained elements of dependence, rebellion, hostility, submission, love, and hatred. Frequently, a split would occur. Thus, if he had positive feelings toward one, the other would be the recipient of his negative feelings, and vice versa. It seemed to Jim that Theresa and father were similar in many ways. He complained that Theresa, like father, frequently treated him with contempt, belittling him, and injuring his self-esteem. The quality of Jim's relationship to Theresa had many transference elements. His anger frequently was greater than the provocation merited; likewise, dependency, submission, and belligerent feelings appeared inappropriate to the reality situation. The analysis of the transference aspects of this relationship increased his insight and understanding of unconscious motives and defenses.

Wolfenstein (1976) found that patients who experienced early object loss frequently became enmeshed in relationships in which the loss is once again repeated. She attributed this in part to an unconscious wish to force the dead parent to "return and rescue the child."

As the analysis progressed, Jim realized the extent to which he had been driven to marry Theresa by an unconscious longing for security. However, in spite of increased understanding, Jim nonetheless continued passively to comply with her wishes, lest she leave him. Their son, David, was born during this period. Jim immediately formed an intense attachment to David and felt deeply committed and loving toward the infant. He took care of David, frequently assuming the maternal role. A strong identification with his son characterized this relationship.

Following David's birth, Jim began to assert himself more. The marital relationship deteriorated, and Theresa intensified her threats. Though disturbed and frightened, Jim no longer "panicked." In his analysis Jim expressed increased anger toward Theresa for making such threats. I used this reaction as an opportunity to reiterate part of an earlier reconstruction, "that Jim may have felt angry when Mom left and did not come back" (Bowlby, 1960; Spitz, 1957, 1965).

In the 4th year of treatment, Theresa served Jim with a divorce summons. Jim's initial reaction was of amazement and anger, combined with a sense of betrayal. The analysis of this reaction led to further reconstructions regarding feelings he experienced and could not express following his mother's death. This applied especially to Jim's insistence that Theresa's action was "completely unexpected." Jim said, "She [mother] *just* left, and left the child." He was silent for a while and then added, "Did you notice? I speak as if *she [mother] really did it on purpose*; I guess that is how I felt, I could not imagine anything else, how could a child? I feel terrible anger." He continued to analyze "how he must have felt" and also his impotent anger about being abandoned. He was, however, also concerned with "what made mother leave him." This resulted in the analysis of his unconscious belief that assertiveness and anger are "bad," that he was "bad" because he asserted himself and expressed anger toward mother. Jim was unconsciously convinced that this caused mother to leave him. It thus became evident that the repression of the traumatic experiences connected with his mother's death also contributed to a significant repression of Jim's assertive and aggressive behavior. The conflicts related to aggression became unconscious.

Transference analysis corroborated these findings. Because of Jim's conflicts and needs, I unconsciously represented throughout the major part of his analysis the good mother who had to be preserved at all cost. Jim unconsciously feared expressing anger toward me because he dreaded the possibility that I might abandon him. He also held the unconscious conviction that by being "good" he could ensure that I would always love him and stay with him. Thus, hostile transference feelings pertaining to unconscious angers related to childhood issues and conflicts became deflected onto "suitable real" objects in the environment. Such a split in the transference persisted for long periods of the analysis.

Jim was able to view the dissolution of his marriage realistically. Nonetheless, the conflict between the wish to depend and the fear of doing so became activated. Eventually, Jim moved to his own apartment, even though he still felt anxious, and with difficulty tolerated being alone. Jim now began to view himself with some pride as a successful young executive. Though he still needed to rely on father and though the power struggle with father continued, Jim did become aware that in actuality he indeed managed the business and made the decisions.

Jim, in the 6th year of his analysis, bought out father's share of the business. He was quite aware of having done so very generously. Jim now understood the nature of his relationship with father. He enjoyed feeling magnanimous. In a gesture that combined love with revenge, Jim made father chairman of the board, realizing that now he, Jim, was "calling the shots" as president and chief executive.

In contrast to his father, Jim was overly considerate of others and proud of this, since he hated his father's autocratic and tyrannical manner. His interactions were thus marked by exaggerated "niceness" and "kindness," indicative of their reaction formation component. These character traits, however, fulfilled multiple functions. They helped Jim "differentiate" from father, contributing significantly to the development of his sense of separateness and autonomy. They also helped Jim establish a sense of libidinal self constancy since Jim described himself by referring to those traits. Additionally, Jim's considerateness, generosity, and politeness gave him a sense of self-continuity. Namely, from being "a very good boy, he became a very nice, overgenerous, and considerate young man." Jim identified with and enjoyed the praise he received for being "so very nice." He liked himself for being the kind of person others described as "generous to a fault" and "always considerate," and therefore went out of his way to achieve this response. (Intense analysis in the long termination phase was required to work through and modify these reactive character traits.)

Jim's infantile need to be acclaimed manifested itself during this period of his analysis. He spent many hours describing his achievements, seeking my admiration. It should, however, be noted that for Jim this was necessary to enable him to continue the painful analysis of his narcissistic vulnerability, submissiveness, and rage.

The analysis of the transferential elements of Jim's relationship with Oliver, his plant superintendent, helped in the working through of important facets of his feelings toward father and mother. Jim was extremely dependent on Oliver. He had an unconscious fantasy that Oliver would be "the continuously sustaining good father Jim yearned for" while consciously fearing that a catastrophe would occur if Oliver abandoned him. Analysis revealed that this terror was a derivative stemming from the trauma of mother's death. To forestall the possibility of Oliver's leaving, Jim complied with most of Oliver's self-serving requests. Submitting to Oliver's demands and repressing his anger had the unconscious significance of "being a good boy" and therefore ensuring he would not be abandoned.

Reconstructions related to Jim's feelings that "mother left him because he was bad," and continued analysis of the childhood antecedents of Jim's dependence on father and of his repressed childhood rage at father, eventually made it possible for Jim to understand the transference aspects of his relationship with Oliver and the unconscious meaning of his fear that a catastrophe would follow a separation from Oliver. Consequently, Jim could face the extent to which Oliver exploited his neurotic dependency and was able to terminate his relationship with him.

Working through the psychic components of the interaction with Oliver enabled Jim to assimilate and understand the psychogenetic roots of his submissiveness and need to be "such a good boy." This eventually enabled him to become aware of his wish for autonomy and his need to pursue *his own* interests. Jim's self-confidence increased after he assured himself that he could run his plant and manage his business efficiently by himself.

Jim's strong identification with his son made it possible for him to relive vicariously some of the repressed traumatic experiences of his own childhood. When David was 2½ years old, Theresa suddenly became ill and had to be hospitalized. Though Jim stayed with David, as did David's maternal grandmother, the boy was inconsolable. Jim suffered greatly throughout this period and his analytic hours were spent imagining how he must have felt after his mother died. He reported the following dream: "I came to your office and everything was taken out of this room. The walls were blank. I wondered what to do. I was holding my breath, I was speechless." Silence, then: "The shock was not that I was looking at an empty room. It's that *I expected* to see the room I knew—and now *that* room was no longer there. I can't speak. The shock of not finding *what I expected* makes me so perplexed. I am horrified. I don't know how to express it." Tears were rolling down his cheeks. I connected this dream and his feelings with what he must have experienced when he entered mother's room following her death, after father had dismantled it. He probably entered the room in the hope of finding mother. Instead, he experienced the shock of everything familiar gone. Such an occurrence was too overwhelming and too shocking for a 3-year-old to endure and remember.

The dream may also reflect the inner emptiness that became part of him when he absorbed the desolation following mother's death. Further, though associations did *not* follow this path, the dream possibly expressed unconscious fears that I might become unavailable now that Jim was becoming so much more assertive and autonomous. Analysis along these lines might have led to the uncovering of negative transference feelings toward me. I felt, however, in the context of the analytic situation at the time, that reconstruction would serve the analysis better than "pushing" such an exploration.

Toward the end of the middle phase of his analysis, Jim began to view himself consistently as the kind of person he wanted to be. He associated with a group of friends with whom he had common interests. He felt sought after. His performance in most areas of his life was in accordance with his conscious, wishful self-image (Jacobson, 1954, 1964). On balance, successes outweighed failures. His superego had consolidated and matured. Many unconscious aspects of the ego ideal had become modified into conscious, attainable goals. Jim no longer experienced a sense of painful narcissistic mortification when he did not succeed in some of his plans. Libidinal self constancy had developed sufficiently to sustain him during periods when he struggled to attain his goals. Jim's sense of self-directedness increased. This manifested itself by a growing self-affirmation which he expressed with friends, his sweetheart, in business relationships, and eventually with me, when he announced he thought he was "really better and had profited from his analysis sufficiently for it to come to an end."

The working through of Jim's infantile transference dependency and idealization as well as of his reactive character traits constituted the main aspects of a long termination phase. In this phase of treatment, interpretation of conflict and transference resistance predominated.

DISCUSSION

I have tried to show how the holding aspects of the psychoanalytic situation and the technique of reconstruction can ameliorate arrests in the development of libidinal object and self constancy. I have therefore focused in my presentation predominantly on these aspects of the analytic process. According to Stone (1981), the impact of empathy and the holding attitude, properly administered, is facilitating to the adult patient and "may affect . . . elements in ego structure that represent early deprivations and injuries in . . . ego integration" (p. 114). Stone also says: "The 'love' implicit in empathy, listening and trying to understand, in nonseductive devotion to the task, the sense of full acceptance, respect, and sometimes the homely phenomenon of sheer dependable patience, extending over long periods of time, *may take their place as equal or nearly equal in importance* to sheer interpretive skill" (p. 114, italics mine).

Because of Jim's developmental arrest, the "holding" aspects of the analytic situation were an *indispensable* component of treatment, especially in the first phase of the analysis. The ambience they provided enabled Jim to develop the *illusion* of being nurtured. He felt cared for and secure. Basic trust was rekindled. Jim's belief that I would not abandon him diminished his anxiety sufficiently to allow for a limited therapeutic regression in which a trusting, dependent transference could develop. Since this regression reestablished the flexibility of the psychic apparatus, it can also be viewed as a limited structural regression. This transference climate made it possible to analyze the defensive aspects of Jim's object relations. More specifically, when Jim felt safe to examine the reasons for maintaining his defensive posture, the automatic rigid defensive patterns also became the focus of analysis. Thus began the exploration of his inability to think when feeling threatened, his "blanking out," his excessive submissiveness, and his need to ingratiate himself. The changes in Jim's defensive patterns first occurred primarily in response to the manner in which he experienced the object relation aspects of the holding environment embedded in the analytic situation.

In the beginning and middle phases of treatment, Jim used me to satisfy his infantile needs for object relatedness (Fleming, 1978). This contributed to new internalizations, which, combined with the dynamic effect of the reconstructions, provided a spurt to further psychic development.

Of special significance, in view of Jim's pathology, was the reestablishment of a good internal object, made possible because of the idealizing transference in which the illusion of nurturing remained undisturbed. These psychic changes eventually led to the formation of a consolidated object representation and to the evolvement of libidinal object constancy. Concurrently with these processes, the harshness and corruptibility of the superego decreased.

Stone (1961) suggests that the psychoanalytic situation can be regarded as representing "to the unconscious in its primary and most far-reaching impact, the superimposed series of basic separation experiences in the child's relation to his mother. In this scheme, the analyst would represent the mother-of-separation . . ." (p. 105).

Jim's analysis certainly could be viewed this way. The holding aspects of the analytic situation and my reconstructions made it possible for him to explore and work through both normal and traumatic separations.

The changes in Jim's view and sense of himself clearly indicate that the analytic process not only affected the shape of his self-image (Sandler & Rosenblatt, 1962), but also his self-experience. Throughout the analysis a process of growth occurred, culminating during the termination phase in a blending of his wishful and actual self-images into a self-representation cathected with sufficient narcissistic libido to be sustaining (Jacobson, 1954, 1964). This maturational process led to the evolvement of libidinal self constancy. Superior ego functioning in a wide conflict-free sphere, combined with a superego that matured and consolidated in the course of analysis, made it possible for Jim to maintain self-esteem and a realistic attitude about his goals.

These psychic achievements were paralleled by maturation in the area of object relations. Jim now was able to maintain a loving relationship throughout periods of tension and conflict. Attainment of libidinal object constancy, never fully reached but evolving under optimal conditions to higher levels throughout life (Mahler *et al.*, 1975; Solnit, 1982), became evident after Jim developed stable object representations and mature object relations.

The findings of child analysis, child observation, and the analysis just described suggest that within the matrix of good-enough object relations and under *optimal* conditions the evolvement of libidinal object constancy and libidinal self constancy occurs as a reciprocal and parallel process that takes place throughout life. The prerequisite for this development is the eventual internalization, subsequent to the need-gratifying stage, of a "benign presence" that provides a necessary intrapsychic sustaining quality. The attainment of libidinal self constancy, more so than libidinal object constancy, can be complicated by the relationship of the self-image to the wishful self-image and ego ideal. In this process the judgmental aspect of the superego plays an important role. Namely, a harsh and critical superego may interfere with the integration of the self-representation which is necessary for the development of libidinal self constancy. Under such conditions the required balance of narcissistic and neutralized libido with which the self-representation has to be cathected for the maintenance of libidinal self constancy may be lacking.

The above considerations suggest that the establishment of libidinal object and self constancy has two aspects: It involves changes in the dynamic and economic psychic equilibrium while simultaneously contributing to the process of structuralization. Thus libidinal object and self constancy depends on the integration of the respective psychic representations and contributes to this process. The above remarks are based in part on the findings that object constancy is related to the individual's drive state (Hartmann, 1964) and that it occurs when the "mental representation of the need-satisfying object has been organized in the mind and can be evoked as a memory in the absence of the object" (Mahler, 1965). Fraiberg (1969) includes both aspects in her definition of object constancy, namely the capacity to produce a mental image of the object when it is not present regardless of drive and need state.

I would like to conclude with a few brief remarks on the technique employed in this case. I did not "go after" the negative transference during the long beginning phase and part of the middle phase, even though rage was an important aspect of Jim's psychic make-up. Nor did I interfere with Jim's splitting of the transference and with the development and strengthening of the positive transference, since the latter appeared beneficial for the furthering of the analytic process. I was guided not only by Freud's recommendation (1912), but also by the special features of this case. It appeared that as a consequence of the traumatic maternal loss at the age of 3 years, Jim had a specific need to reconstitute a "benign presence." He did so in the analysis by extracting the holding aspects embedded in the analytic situation and experiencing the transference as an illusory situation of nurturance. In this ambience, analogous to the psychic state of a child who in his mother's loving presence can face and deal with what he perceives as a dangerous situation, Jim was able to analyze his defenses and, via reconstructions, reexperience and explore the psychic meanings of his traumatic past. Because of his pathological regression to the stage of fear of object loss and because of the unconscious rage which was also related to object loss, his transference belief in my constant availability was therapeutically essential. This accords with Spitz's (1956) finding that in the first phase of the analysis an anaclitic regression occurs. Spitz compares the functioning of the analyst during this phase to that of the preoedipal mother who provides secondary process organization for the child. This was provided for Jim by reconstructions. Jim's therapeutic regression was preliminary to and had a restorative function that fostered developmental progression (Loewald, 1981).

ACKNOWLEDGMENTS

I wish to thank Maria and Martin Bergmann and Doctors H. Blum, W. Grossman, O. Kernberg, and M. Zimmerman for their thoughtful suggestions and generous criticism of earlier versions of this chapter.

REFERENCES

Blum, H. P. (1980). The value of reconstruction in adult psycho-analysis. *International Journal of Psycho-Analysis, 61*, 39–52.

Bowlby, J. (1960). Grief and mourning in infancy and early childhood. *The Psychoanalytic Study of the Child, 15*, 9–52. New York: International Universities Press.

Dewald, P. A. (1976). Transference regression and real experience in the psychoanalytic process. *Psychoanalytic Quarterly, 45*, 213–230.

Fleming, J. (1972). Early object deprivation and transference phenomena: The working alliance. *Psychoanalytic Quarterly, 41*, 23–49.

Fleming, J. (1974). The problem of diagnosis in parent-loss cases. *Contemporary Psychoanalysis, 10*, 439–451.

Fleming, J. (1975). Some observations on object constancy in the psychoanalysis of adults. *Journal of the American Psychoanalytic Association, 23*, 743–759.

Fleming, J. (1978). *Early object deprivation and transference phenomena: Preoedipal object need.* Unpublished manuscript.

Fleming, J., & Altschul, S. (1963). Activation of mourning and growth by psychoanalysis. *International Journal of Psycho-Analysis, 44,* 419-431.

Fraiberg, S. (1969). Libidinal object constancy and mental representation. *The Psychoanalytic Study of the Child, 24,* 9-47.

Freud, S. (1912). The dynamics of transference. *Standard Edition, 12.*

Freud, S. (1923). The ego and the id. *Standard Edition, 19.*

Freud, S. (1937). Construction in analysis. *Standard Edition, 23.*

Gitelson, M. (1962). On the curative factors in the first phase of psychoanalysis. In *Psychoanalysis: Science and profession* (pp. 311-341). New York: International Universities Press, 1973.

Greenacre, P. (1975). On reconstruction. *Journal of the American Psychoanalytic Association, 23,* 693-712.

Hartmann, H. (1964). *Essays on ego psychology.* New York: International Universities Press.

Jacobson, E. (1954). The self and the object world. *The Psychoanalytic Study of the Child, 9,* 75-127.

Jacobson, E. (1964). *The self and the object world.* New York: International Universities Press.

Khan, M. (1960). Regression and integration in the analytic setting. *International Journal of Psycho-Analysis, 41,* 130-146.

Kris, E. (1950). Notes on the development and on some current problems of psychoanalytic child psychology. In *Selected papers* (pp. 217-236). New Haven: Yale University Press, 1975.

Kris, E. (1956). The recovery of childhood memories in psychoanalysis. In *Selected papers* (pp. 301-340). New Haven: Yale University Press, 1975.

Levin, S. (Reporter). (1966). Depression and object loss. *Journal of the American Psychoanalytic Association, 4,* 142-153.

Loewald, H. (1960). On the therapeutic action of psychoanalysis. *International Journal of Psycho-Analysis, 41,* 16-33.

Loewald, H. (1981). Regression: Some general considerations. *Psychoanalytic Quarterly, 50,* 22-43.

Mahler, M. S. (1965). On the significance of the normal separation–individuation phase. In M. Schur (Ed.), *Drives, affects, and behavior* (Vol. 2, pp. 161-168). New York: International Universities Press.

Mahler, M. S. (1972a). On the first three subphases of the separation–individuation process. In *The selected papers of Margaret S. Mahler* (Vol. II, pp. 119-130). New York: Jason Aronson, 1979.

Mahler, M. S. (1972b). Rapprochement subphase of the separation–individuation process. In *The selected papers of Margaret S. Mahler* (Vol. II, pp. 131-148). New York: Jason Aronson, 1979.

Mahler, M. S. (1974). Symbiosis and individuation: The psychological birth of the human infant. In *The selected papers of Margaret S. Mahler* (Vol. II, pp. 149-165). New York: Jason Aronson, 1979.

Mahler, M. S., Pine, F., & Bergman, A. (1975). *The psychological birth of the human infant.* New York: Basic Books.

Modell, A. H. (1976). The holding environment and the therapeutic action of psychoanalysis. *Journal of the American Psychoanalytic Association, 24,* 285-307.

Modell, A. H. (1978). The conceptualization of the therapeutic action of psychoanalysis: The action of the holding environment. *Bulletin of the Menninger Clinic, 42,* 493-504.

Sandler, J., & Rosenblatt, B. (1962). The concept of a representational world. *The Psychoanalytic Study of the Child, 17,* 128-145.

Solnit, A. J. (1982). Developmental perspectives on self. *The Psychoanalytic Study of the Child, 37,* 201-218.

Spitz, R. (1956). Transference: The analytic setting and its prototype. *International Journal of Psycho-Analysis, 37,* 380-385.

Spitz, R. (1957). *No and yes: On the genesis of human communication.* New York: International Universities Press.

Spitz, R. (1965). *The first year of life: A psychoanalytic study of normal and deviant development of object relations.* New York: International Universities Press.

Stone, L. (1961). *The psychoanalytic situation: An examination of its development and essential nature.* New York: International Universities Press.

Stone, L. (1981). Notes on the noninterpretive elements in the psychoanalytic situation and process. *Journal of the American Psychoanalytic Association, 29,* 89–118.

Winnicott, D. W. (1956). Primary maternal preoccupation. In *Collected papers* (pp. 300–305). New York: Basic Books, 1958.

Winnicott, D. W. (1960). The theory of the parent–infant relationship. In *The maturational process and the facilitating environment: Studies in the theory of emotional development* (pp. 37–55). New York: International Universities Press, 1963.

Winnicott, D. W. (1963). *The maturational process and the facilitating environment: Studies in the theory of emotional development.* New York: International Universities Press.

Wolfenstein, M. (Reporter). (1976). Effects on adults of object loss in the first five years. *Journal of the American Psychoanalytic Association, 24,* 659–668.

CHAPTER FOURTEEN

Illusion, Reality, and Fantasy

J. ALEXIS BURLAND

One of the differences between the developmental perspective and a perspective from the vantage point of reconstructing the psychodynamics of a symptom complex is that the developmentalist conceptualizes in terms of normalcy whereas the clinician in his reconstructions seeks to clarify the sources of psychopathology. At first the major discoveries in psychoanalysis did indeed come almost exclusively from reconstructive work with symptom complexes, so it is not surprising that a kind of moral imperative insinuated itself to some extent into psychoanalytic thinking, asserting that anything other than the full primacy of the genitals, the reality principle, secondary-process thinking, and object constancy was regressive and therefore pathological. Development was viewed as proceeding only forward, except in instances of defensive pathological operations and in dreams. It is of interest that Freud spoke of the thought processes of dreams as "abnormal" (1900, p. 592).

When developmentalists began to view pregenitality, pleasure principle dominance, primary-process thinking, and part-object relationships, not only as aspects of normal infantile development but also with reverberations throughout the life cycle, it gave them a kind of legitimacy, a place in the psychological scheme of things apart from whatever they might also contribute to later symptom formation. It is possible that the so-called widening scope of psychoanalysis refers as much to a change in psychoanalysts' perspectives as it does to an actual change in patient population. That patients previously diagnosed and treated as neurotic on the basis of the content of their symptom presentation are now known to have been more developmentally interrupted than had been suspected is a commonplace occurrence that speaks to our improved ability to see, acknowledge, and understand the persistence of the infantile (see Blum, 1974; Kohut, 1971).

It is with but one piece of this complicated fabric that this chapter deals, the development of the ego's relationship to external reality as part of the developmental process that culminates in the achievement of object constancy. Part of the stimulus for this chapter comes from work with patients who, in spite of the clearly phallic–oedipal content of their manifest symptom presentation, did not relinquish these infantile strivings in spite of seemingly accurate and validated interpretive work. It became evident that they had a particular attitude toward such strivings, an attitude that became evident in examining the form of their communications; insight into the strivings themselves and the symptoms they generated had little effect upon that attitude. Superficially these patients verbalized a reality relatedness that seemed adequate. But on closer inspection it became evident that they experienced illusory misperceptions of reality, which they insisted were "real" and which therefore determined much of their behavior. Until that view of reality was made dystonic and its history and purpose interpreted, progress on content issues remained halted and the infantile neurosis remained unresolved.

Miss A entered treatment in her mid-20s at her mother's insistence, as she was unmarried, had no prospects, and seemed stalemated in her life. Of significance in her history had been the dissolution of her parents' marriage near Miss A's birth, and her mother's remarriage when Miss A was 5 years old. She had reacted to her parents' honeymoon with severe hysterical gastrointestinal and respiratory symptoms, a surprise to her family, who had viewed her as a happy, symptom-free, "normal" child up until that time, an historical claim that cannot be uncritically accepted but can be interpreted as reflecting less than complete empathic tuning in on her daughter by Miss A's mother. Miss A was at first strikingly and stubbornly amnesic for events in her life prior to and early in her mother's remarriage, but could recall how later, at the age of 9 or 10 years she felt intense anxiety whenever her mother and stepfather went out, even for an hour or so in the evening. She also recalled several episodes in adolescence in which her stepfather made suggestive advances toward her, though she had no recollection of her part in the interactions. Starting in midadolescence a pattern of behavior in her romantic life was identifiable, seemingly related to these childhood events. She would become romantically involved with an unavailable man, that is, one who was married, engaged, or clearly not the marrying kind. She would soon start to spin emotion-filled scenarios of trips to the Caribbean Islands and marriage, even simply of "true" love, although on one level at times she knew these were impossible. Her relationship to the man's wife, or fiancée, or other woman in his life was also intense and in the most revealing of her affairs was characterized by typical oedipal ambivalence; she alternatingly wished to identify with the woman or compete against her and replace her, all the while fearing loss of the relationship should the other woman find out about her intentions. She experienced physical discomfort when, alone in her apartment, she was aware that they—the man and his other woman—were out together. At these times, significantly, she overate and occasionally experienced terrifying images of her mother's illnes and death, the focus being on her mother's death leaving her alone.

That she behaved rather than remembered was striking (see Freud, 1914). Greenacre (1950) has pointed out that this tendency reflects a persistence of infantile states of grandiosity in the implied expectation that reality will conform to one's inner state simply by putting that state into action. I was similarly struck by the form in which Miss A experienced these triangular relationships. Everything was automatically interpreted in terms of her longings. Although the men's words, as reported I believe accurately, were unclear enough to be understood as having several possible meanings, and although it seemed most likely that they did not experience their relationship to Miss A with anywhere near as much emotional investment as she, each word they uttered was heard by her as direct expressions of intense deep love or vengeful anger. Her behavior in relationship to them was based upon this reading of their communications. Often it would then be months after the men had clearly ended the relationship before Miss A could acknowledge it. Miss A's wishes were, in effect, changing her world as she perceived it into what she wished it to be. Insight into the oedipal sources of the content of her scenarios did not alter her belief in them. Her seeming oedipal fantasies were revealed to be in form illusory misperceptions of reality to which she clung and which determined her behavior. She clung to them with a tenacity that made clear her investment in illusion as illusion, that is with a "reality" that took whatever form she dictated. As was uncovered later in treatment, she viewed existence as depending upon the consciousness of others; that is, if another was aware of her existence, she existed, so her inability to acknowledge when others no longer were mindful of her was related to her fear that she would then cease to exist. This was felt most intensely in the relationship with her mother, but also with her men friends. And, as suggested above, the reverse also was true, although she was less aware of it; that is, others' existences depended upon her conscious awareness of them, and this involved not just the fact of their existence but aspects of how they acted and felt as well. External reality was not autonomous, in Miss A's eyes, but part of an undifferentiated selfobject amalgam in which she felt varying degrees of control. It is not surprising then that she would be unable to cope with the challenges of the oedipal stage of development as her failure to achieve object constancy left her unable to cope with its object demands.

Mr. B entered analysis because of episodic depressions related to his failure to achieve the goals he had set for himself in life. He was born of humble but aspiring parents; his family's ambition for him included his becoming the family's first professional. Mr. B's own ambitions, on the surface, were similar, but also, it became clear, had strong phallic narcissistic elements; as he put it, his inability to "get it up," in life and in sex, was his major complaint, and to "have one bigger and harder than anyone else's" was his major goal. His relationship with his father was a central dynamic in what could be called his phallic-oedipal masochism; he loved his warm but ineffectual father too much to allow himself to surpass him, so he mobilized defenses against his hostile competitive wishes in order to preserve his loving dependence upon him. Preoedipal aspects of this dynamic were not invisible; for instance, to again quote this articulate man, his transference belief was that the analysis could not be completed until he had "bitten off" my penis, a phrase that graphically pointed to the combined oral-phallic drive derivative preoccupation. But in keeping with his oedipal ambivalence, he could do so only at his own expense—he would defeat me by "flunking out" of the analysis as he had almost flunked out of high school and as he had indeed flunked out of college. He would defeat me by being "unable to get it up" analytically. This direct expression of the prominent negative oedipal constellation served to create a transference resistance with which we struggled for months. This was played out in part around his demand that I talk to him about his multiple current life crises as his father had talked to him when he was in trouble as a child, in a kind, supportive, advice-giving way—by this means, we uncovered, buttressing his reaction formation against his hostile competitiveness. Yet the latter found expression in that he ended up, of course, ignoring his father's advice, and repeating his counterproductive behavior. Similarly, in the analysis this scenario as replayed served as a blatant resistance against the analytic process, with which this well-read man was familiar prior to starting the analysis; as we came to see, in this means he was "biting off" my analyzing instrument. And he managed to get himself into enough day-to-day trouble to both set the scene for these hoped-for "talks" and to prove that he remained floridly symptomatic in spite of treatment. As in all good neurotic symptoms, this constellation served as defense, gratification, and punishment. But interpretations at an oedipal level of this complex psychodynamic proved insufficient. The ambivalent father transference content reflected only the more superficial layers of his overdetermined symptom picture. We uncovered eventually how at a deeper level I was in the transference a "Nazi," that is, someone coldly and autocratically ignoring his wishes, punitively insisting he "grow up" into adult self-sufficiency and potency before he was ready for it; this was the voice of his mother. At times he saw me as a "Nazi Rabbi," which meant to this Jewish man that my "Nazism" was intended for his own good—again, a claim voiced by his mother. Behind the oedipal transference, then, it was the "good" and "bad" dyadic mother of rapprochement with whom he struggled. Much of the self-defeating behavior in the transference, which could be called acting-out and acting-in, was in keeping with a view of the world as dictated by his dyadic needs that I be the rediscovered, or recaptured, good mother-of-symbiosis (hiding behind the good symbiotic father, in part a regressive defense against the oedipal father) or, failing that, that I then be the bad sadistic mother-of-separation of the masochistic son (again, a precursor for the later negative oedipal constellation). With this transference material he was experiencing illusory distortions of reality; unlike an object-related transference fantasy within a smoothly operating working alliance, subject to mutative interpretation, his distorted perceptions of me were syntonically the totality of his perceived reality. If for a moment he perceived me as a real person, even as his "good-enough" psychoanalyst, he felt hurt and became enraged by the autonomy on my part that that perception of me implied. Another example of his reliance upon illusion, as well as the mixed oedipal and preoedipal factors, was a pattern of behavior related to episodes of depression. At such times he would dress in his flashiest clothes, with what he called "up front" underwear and tight pants, and visit a nearby shopping mall. He would stroll around, his purpose being to get women to look at him, particularly at the bulge in his crotch; success would make him feel once again strong and potent. The phallic–oedipal content of that charade is evident; but in its form, in its confusion between internal and external reality, in its use of the woman lookers as narcissistic part-object extensions, it speaks for a far more immature level of ego functioning in which wishes control reality.

From the course of the treatment process with these patients, it was uncovered that behind the phallic–oedipal content of their presenting symptoms there existed another layer of psychological malfunctioning. In other words, drive derivatives on the surface came from one developmental level whereas ego functioning, as seen in the more formal aspects of their symptomatology, came from an earlier level. The ego immaturity was approached via their need to perceive reality in a particular manner; character analysis of this defense uncovered its content, relating to dyadic rather than triadic issues. They had been less than successful in negotiating the hurdles of the rapprochement discovery of separateness. Further, they resisted individuation to perpetuate the illusion of a persistent selfobject relatedness in which internally generated images of gratification were expected to be synonymous with a therefore compliant external reality. Rather than affording them a welcome opportunity for a mutative internalization, fleeting perceptions of me as "real" were frightening evidence of their separateness. Their transference resistances against individuation (i.e., resistances against symptomatic improvement) served as a major means for exacting revenge against the mother-of-separation. Failing to recover and having therefore to remain in treatment forever served as both a retaliatory threat and an expression of the core dynamic, their deeper reason for entering analysis in the first place. The transference, it will be noted, at this deeper level, existed within and contaminated the therapeutic alliance, acting as a powerful resistance.

For Miss A the world was an oedipal scenario, as that was what she wanted. For that not to be so would have meant she was not omnipotent, that her wishes did not create reality, that her self and the objects around her were indeed separate from one another. That was the realization she was fleeing—that, as it came to her in moments of terror, her dyadic mother was "dead."

Mr. B could acknowledge his phallic competitiveness, even his phallic–oedipal masochism. But behind his dependence upon his father, and despite his raging at the mother-of-separation, was the inability to let go of the illusion of the selfobject partner, the mother-of-symbiosis, who, after all, should see to it that his phallic–narcissistic wishes automatically created their anxiety-free gratification, who with a glance would grant him a super-penis. As his words made clear, phallic competence was achieved by the oral route with its implied blurring of the distinction between his powers and the power of his phallic mother–analyst.

The illusory gratification of these patients' dyadic demands was the major resistance against movement toward the achievement of object constancy, preventing successful confrontation of oedipal challenges. I shall now recount some thoughts concerning the development of reality related-ness.

The perception of reality is a complex developmental task that begins in the first weeks of life as memory traces are laid down of day-to-day frustration–gratification sequences (Glover, 1968; Mahler, Pine, & Bergman, 1975; Spitz, 1965). As cognitive maturation proceeds, in particular of the capacity for memory, the infant starts to collect lasting memory traces of these need-based experiences, organized around an associated affective valence determined according to the pleasure–unpleasure principle. Spitz (1965) has written of psychological development in these early months as reflecting maturation more than experience; observations of minimally to moderately inadequate mothering would tend to confirm this. Whereas there is a certain basic minimum responsiveness needed in maternal care for life to be supported at all, infants do show a remarkable capacity to extract an experience of fully adequate care from situations that upon objective examination would appear to be somewhat less than adequate. Accustomed as we are to conceptualizing the mother–infant interaction as a two-party system, in point of fact as far as we know it is not experienced as such by the infant. The so-called "good mother" mental image that develops in infancy is not an image of mother-as-other-person; it is better understood as an image of the infant's own subjectively experienced pleasurable sensations of gratification, associated as time progresses with certain simultaneous tactile, visual, auditory, and olfactory sensations; the facilitating environment functions at this time to support the infant's egocentric illusions, as Winnicott put it (1960). The infant relates to his own subjectively experienced sensations and perceptions, not to whatever their external source might be. The concept of "out there" does not develop until later. In the latter part of the 1st year of life, there is a gradual differentiation between the mental images of self and mother; but it is not until a year later that the infant develops a capacity to differentiation between internal images and external reality.

Freud wrote in 1900 of what we would now call the infantile ego's response to frustration by means of hallucinatory wish fulfillment, or imaging. To the extent that, in the 1st year of life, the infant's needs continue to be adequately met by a mothering person with a consistent arrangement of tactile, visual, auditory, and olfactory characteristics, the nascent ego will increasingly invest with positive affect this conglomeration of sense impressions. When the infant's needs are not adequately met and he is unable to change the situation, the infant will instead invest his energies in imaging, to gratification at the hands of his own accumulated mental images—something I have elsewhere referred to as "autism built for two," because it looks behaviorally or interactionally autistic but is intrapsychically more symbiotic (Burland, 1978). Reality being what it is, no infant experiences a pure culture of fully adequate or fully inadequate care. A ratio evolves between an investment in current sensations and one in memory images of past sensations, reflecting the ratio between experiences of adequate and inadequate mothering. Both modes of operation, for better or for worse, remain within the individual's repertoire, although, as indicated, the ratio itself is a developmental variable.

As survival needs are the central motivation for wakefulness and attentiveness in infancy, it is not surprising that the more emotionally invested mental images are those associated with need fulfillment. Among other things, this means that these images become associated with the belief that needs create gratification, an illusion of omnipotence that is experienced as part of the infant's primary self-perception. This is the illusion Winnicott (1960) writes the mother must facilitate. To the extent that the infant's external reality does this, he will invest narcissistic libido in the perceptual apparatuses, which explore, experience, and define that good-enough reality, and hatching occurs.

The infant does not hatch out of his autistic shell into reality relatedness. The infant hatches first into an illusory selfobject world whose shape and nature are still largely defined in terms of the infant's subjective state. But once the child has hatched, with increasing investment in maturing perceptual and cognitive function, and with the elaboration of increasingly complex, differentiated, and stable mental images, the process that Winnicott pointedly called disillusionment begins, primarily in response to the noncompliance of reality. This is made tolerable by several factors. Significant among them for the purposes of the train of thought of this chapter is the increasing capacity of the infant for self-reliant behavior. The behaviors that characterize differentiation—the exploration, study, and organization of sense impressions of the surrounding world—indicate increasing cognitive sophistication. The infant can now see and hear the mother from a distance, diacritically, so is less dependent upon coenesthetic physical contact to "feel" her presence (Spitz, 1965). The behaviors that characterize practicing—the hypomanic exercise of new musculoskeletal skills—reflect the shift from a consciousness preoccupied with dependent gratification to a consciousness now also delighted with the new sensations and experiences one can actively create with one's own body. Further, the toddler can also actively go after and find or leave the mother, supporting the sense of control. But the hypomania of practicing remains innocent insofar as the toddler has not yet discovered his separateness, and feels supplied as it were by an invisible umbilical cord connecting the toddler to the mother in the manner that a space walking astronaut remains connected to the mother ship.

The development of self-reliance depends also upon trust and confidence in the availability of mother as a coenesthetic experience when diacritic contact is insufficient; one sees this in the refueling behavior of the practicing toddler. That these experiences are often largely illusory in nature is very evident from the observation that the toddler becomes fully refueled even when the mother is not attentive to his presence at her side and therefore objectively is a nonparticipant in the interaction. But the toddler has not yet discovered the difference between his internal image of the mother he wants at that moment and the autonomous "real" external mother.

With rapprochement all of this is shaken. Maturation of cognition enforces upon the child the painful realization of his separateness from the omnipotent mother-of-symbiosis; the already partially differentiated mental image of mother is now seen as relating to an external object. Pleasurable (and unpleasurable) sensations and experiences take on a new meaning—they are identified now as involving a source or the participation of someone separate and apart, and therefore autonomous. With the newly discovered mother-of-separation, "out there," one must actively work to extract those wished-for complementary behaviors that had seemed previously to automatically follow upon one's need for them. This reveals to the child his dependency upon others, as the rapprochement shadowing expresses; but it also identifies for the child areas for self-reliant and autonomous behavior, opportunities for skill development. The ratio between how intensely the child feels the loss as opposed to how intensely he feels the opportunity is an individual variable with important developmental vicissitudes. The struggle between the two is seen in the ambitendent behaviors typical of this developmental subphase, that is, "help me" alternating with "let me do it," "pick me up" alternating with "put me down."

Groundwork as to coping with rapprochement disappointment had been laid down while coping with earlier disappointments. As is true generally in development, the rich get richer and the poor get poorer; that is, those children whose primary objects had been well cathected, who had hatched well, who had found their primary objects willing and able to behave supportively in compliance with their images, who had a good start on the process of individuation and find self-reliant activity pleasurable—such children have multiple internal and external support systems to see them through the narcissistic mortifications attendant upon the discovery of one's own, and one's mother's (and father's) limitations.

Central to my argument is the role played by the development of the firm sense of inside versus outside in coping with rapprochement challenges. Freud, in his discussion of the reality principle (1911), and Hartmann, in his discussion of that paper (1956), both see the discovery of a frustrating reality as a stimulant to improved reality relatedness. The reality principle is a means therefore by which the child learns to actively arrange for gratifications; this ego development serves the process of individuation and helps compensate for the losses of separateness. At this time infantile dependent narcissistic gratifications begin to become superseded by the narcissistic gratifications of self-reliant skill formation and mastery—cognitive, physical, and social—and the development of a new kind of object relatedness in which mutual autonomy is acknowledged and even encouraged. Dependency is not, of course, abolished (Parens & Saul, 1971). But a clear distinction evolves between dependence and independence. Dependent gratifications, with their infantile narcissistic and magical implications, are relegated to a partially unconscious, partially conscious but tacit role as a meaningful qualifier of interactions on an affective level, silent partners to the increasingly environmentally supported facade of indepedent, mannerly, adaptive, socially aware behaviors. For instance, when a mother states, with feeling, that she is proud of her child's self-reliant accomplishments, the double layering of communications is obvious: her affectual pride in her child's self-reliance communicates the shared infantile narcissism of their still ongoing selfobject relationship even while by the content of her words she is encouraging behaviors of the opposite intent.

Starting prior to rapprochement, but picking up in intensity at that time, is the development of that complex of cognitive and affective ego activities referred to as secondary-process thinking. This is a point Freud made in Chapter 7 of *The Interpretation of Dreams* (1900); adaptive secondary-process thinking, rationality, and reality relatedness are rewarded, encouraged, and sought, while primary-process thinking is discouraged as "babyish" and "silly," although it is tolerated in such "unimportant" or "leisure" activities as play, humor, or esthetic enjoyment.

The appreciation of "reality" as opposed to "fantasy" reflects, I believe, the ego's perception of the distinction between those two modes of thinking. "Reality," psychoanalytically and developmentally speaking, is not a noun but an adjective, qualifying certain ego experiences. A sense of reality, feeling real, and the capacity to exhibit realistically adaptive behavior all accompany self-reliance, secondary-process thinking, object relatedness, social adaptiveness, and a sense of the "out there-ness" of external reality. And, significantly, this developmental accomplishment occurs as part of the conflicted process by which the illusory dyad of infancy dissolves, and is very much effected by how that painful process proceeds.

Fantasy is definable in the context of its difference from reality. It is not surprising that children after rapprochement are particularly fascinated with games that relate to what is real and what is not; both, together, have meaning in the way they contrast with each other.

Illusions clinically are different from fantasies in that illusions are experienced as real whereas fantasies are experienced on some level as the opposite of real. Illusions, as I am using that term, differ from unconscious fantasies insofar as the relative importance of form and content are concerned. That is, for illusions, form is as important as, if not more important than, content. By its very nature an illusion defies the acknowledgment of separateness, which is its greatest asset for the child (of all ages) struggling against that lesson of rapprochement. Unconscious fantasies, on the other hand, are dynamically repressed because of their content, not simply because they are fantastic. Both unconscious fantasies and illusions can operate out of conscious awareness, and certainly prior to the defense analysis necessary to bring them into consciousness, unconscious fantasies can be expressed in distorted perceptions of which one is unaware. In fact, in the case of both Miss A and Mr. B it was the discovery that making conscious the content of their defended-against phallic–oedipal fantasies had as little clinical effect as it did that helped alert me to the more formal aspects of their productions and thereby to their illusory nature.

"Reality–fantasy mindedness," then, is an integral part of the process of individuation. It implies the acknowledgment of self and nonself differentiation, with all that that implies including eventually the achievement of object constancy, and functions as a support structure for the child's evolving identity. Frosch (1966) views what he calls "reality constancy" as an ego function that preserves identity and orientation. A clear sense of inside versus outside is buttressed by the experience of fantasy, or subjectivity, as occurring inside, while reality, or objectivity, occurs "out there" (Bach, 1976). A developmental precursor for this is the subjective distinction between the experience of imaging past gratifications and the coenesthetic and later diacritic sensations of current actual gratification.

It is interesting how often the passage of time is used by patients as the arena in which to play out these issues (see Burland, 1980). Memory, of course, is the crucial ingredient in psychological development, especially to the extent that what we call psychic structure is in essence an organization of memories. There is, therefore, a relationship between the capacity to remember and the unfolding of psychic structure. To remember, and to subjectively experience memories as memories, is an acknowledgment of the passage of time. Acting out—and both of the patients referred to above acted out—implies a denial of the passage of time, a clinging to the timelessness of the unconscious and the primary process (for a similar discussion see Greenacre, 1945, 1950). Both of my patients also had problems with punctuality; that is, they functioned on the basis of their "time," not external reality's.

The stability of the more mature ego functions relies upon a firm sense of reality–fantasy relatedness. Literal mindedness in the anxious compulsive, or turning on the lights in a frightened child's bedroom, are everyday examples of the use of external reality to shore up an ego threatened by a regression in the capacity to differentiate between internal images and external reality. Once what is feared might be true is firmly reestablished in the context of reality versus fantasy, the reintegrated, adaptive self no longer feels as threatened by regressive illusory misperceptions. The use of reality relatedness in maintaining ego autonomy against the pull of the unconscious was discussed at length by Rapaport (1957).

My patients demonstrated how clinging to illusion can serve as a resistance against individuation. For them, illusion was also an adverb, a subjective quality to which they were addicted in their flight from the harshness of reality. Individuation was for them a threat, both because in fact the consquences of individuation, including especially the full confrontation with the infantile neurosis, did seem as a threat, but also because they had been less adequately assisted in their developmental transition out of the dyad. Illusion as a subjective mode of operation gave them a sense of the persistence of a selfobject world whose shape was still determined by their needs. The use of illusion served the purpose of keeping alive the mother-of-symbiosis while fighting off the mother-of-separation. Their repeated conflicts with objective reality did not deter them; if anything, they were only driven back with renewed motivation to seek solace in the comforting lap of the infantile position. That is, until their fear of individuation was analyzed.

The oedipal stage of development is, of course, universal, and with the role it plays in the crystallization of psychic structure, it is not surprising that its stamp is visible in almost all symptom complexes. To the psychoanalyst who sees childhood through the retrospectoscope of reconstruction, the oedipal stage, as the last of the infantile stages, is in the foreground, at least partially blocking the view of earlier developmental stages situated in the background. As in the patients described above, it is often the distortions of the oedipal features that serve as the first clues to unresolved preoedipal issues. After all, as the developmental perspective would hold, one copes with the Oedipus complex with the tools at hand, as determined by prior events. In other words, the mere prominence of phallic–oedipal drive derivative content does not mean that conflicts emanating from earlier stages are not also represented in the symptom picture.

In summary, reality relatedness is a developmental construct, a subjectively experienced mode of perceiving certain sense impressions, evolved by the young child as part of his way of surmounting the narcissistic mortifications of the discovery of inner as opposed to outer reality. It reflects a form of psychological operation that supports individuation, secondary process thinking, and social adaptation, and it is encouraged as part of the process of socialization. It evolves side by side with the achievement of object constancy, and the two in the process influence one another. It defines the difference between reality and its partner fantasy, thereby reflecting a distinction that puts a higher value on reality, at least in our Western culture.

Illusion on the other hand is a mode of function associated with and appropriate to prerapprochement thinking with its lack of self and object differentiation. It remains normally a part of the human repertoire of states of consciousness, and can be activated in among other things certain esthetic experiences. But its symptomatic persistence can also reflect a fearful resistance against individuation.

It is important, then, to identify the subtle characteristics that indicate to what extent a patient lives in a world of reality and fantasy, or how much he feels impelled to remain in the world of illusion. In the latter case, character analysis of that ego trait can be expected to reveal a conflict relating to unresolved rapprochement issues, even when the initial symptom presentation is of a neurotic appearance due to its phallic–oedipal content. Failure to achieve reality relatedness and object constancy, then, reveals itself under character analysis to have a latent content of its own.

ACKNOWLEDGMENT

An earlier version of this chapter was presented in January 1980 at a meeting of the Philadelphia Psychoanalytic Society, Philadelphia, Pennsylvania, as the first Presidential Paper.

REFERENCES

Bach, S. (1976). *Some notes on perspective.* Unpublished manuscript.

Blum, H. (1974). The borderline childhood of the Wolf Man. *Journal of the American Psychoanalytic Association, 22,* 721–742.

Burland, J. A. (1978, May). *Discussion of paper by E. James Anthony, M.D.* Presented at the Margaret S. Mahler Symposium, Philadelphia, PA.

Burland, J. A. (1980). Unresolved rapprochement conflict and the infantile neurosis. In R. F. Lax, S. Bach, & J. A. Burland (Eds.), *Rapprochement: Critical sub-phase of separation-individuation* (pp. 377–416). New York: Jason Aronson.

Freud, S. (1900). The interpretation of dreams. *Standard Edition, 4 & 5.*

Freud, S. (1911). Formulations on the two principles of mental functioning. *Standard Edition, 12,* 215–226.

Freud, S. (1914). Remembering, repeating and working through. *Standard Edition, 24,* 145–156.

Frosch, J. (1966). A note on reality constancy. In R. M. Loewenstein, L. M. Newman, M. Schur, & A. J. Solnit (Eds.), *Psychoanalysis: A general psychology* (pp. 349–376). New York: International Universities Press.

Glover, E. (1968). *The birth of the ego.* New York: International Universities Press.

Greenacre, P. (1945). Conscience in the psychopath. In *Trauma, growth and personality* (pp. 165–187). New York: International Universities Press, 1952.

Greenacre, P. (1950). General problems of acting out. In *Trauma, growth and personality* (pp. 224–236). New York: International Universities Press, 1952.

Hartmann, H. (1956). Notes on the reality principle. In *Essays on ego psychology* (pp. 241–267). New York: International Universities Press, 1964.

Kohut, H. (1977). *The analysis of the self.* New York: International Universities Press.

Mahler, M., Pine, F., & Bergman, A. (1975). *The psychological birth of the human infant.* New York: Basic Books.

Parens, H., & Saul, L. (1971). *Dependence in man.* New York: International Universities Press.

Rapaport, D. (1957). The theory of ego autonomy: A generalization. In M. Gill (Ed.), *The collected papers of David Rapaport* (pp. 722–744). New York: Basic Books, 1967.

Spitz, R. (1965). *The first year of life.* New York: International Universities Press.

Winnicott, D. (1960). Ego distortion in terms of true and false self. In *The maturational process and the facilitating environment* (pp. 140–152). New York: International Universities Press, 1965.

CHAPTER FIFTEEN

Maternal Depression, Separation, and a Failure in the Development of Object Constancy

HERMAN ROIPHE
ELEANOR GALENSON

Object constancy, since the concept was first introduced by Hartmann (1952), has been widely recognized as a major developmental consolidation in the central area of object relatedness. Since there is some ambiguity and considerable variation in its usage, it may be well to clearly define at the outset our use of the term. We understand it to mean that the memory traces of the love object enable the child to remain away from the mother for some length of time and still function with emotional poise provided he is in a relatively familiar environment. Presumably, this is due to inner representations of the mother being available to the child. Normally there is a gradual consolidation of the constancy of the object beginning in the latter part of the 2nd year, coming together certainly during the 3rd, and is a function of drive organization, ego development, and experience. There can be no health in later life without the attainment of object constancy, and it is our understanding that an instability in the object constancy is at the core of all narcissistic disturbances.

In this chapter we shall present in some detail the development of one of our research children in whom there was a major failure in the attainment of object constancy, which was already clearly manifest by the end of the 2nd year. The significant experiences that seemed to provoke this distortion in development were a severe maternal depression in the first 4 months of the infant's life and a series of actual separations spaced regularly throughout the 2nd year. This resulted in a child who, by the time she was 2 years old, was unable to function outside the narrow orbit of her mother and was unable to develop the age-appropriate libidinal investment of her relationship to her father. She manifested a persistent depressive mood, and in spite of extraordinary endowment there was a serious constriction in symbolic play. There was a marked distortion in libidinal and aggressive drive organization as reflected in a profound ambivalence and a precocious sadomasochistic erotization.

Jody was just under 1 year of age when she along with her mother started attending our research nursery four mornings a week for 2-hour periods. She was a chubby, blonde, blue-eyed, pretty little girl whose most remarkable feature was an intent visual alertness. While she showed some moderate reaction, as do all of our babies at first, to the new, strange physical surroundings and the many strange adults and children, none of us felt that her intent gaze was a reflection of a still active stranger anxiety.

Her very attractive mother was a stiff, uneasy, anxious, chronically depressed woman who at the age of 29 years had already been married for 9 years before the birth of this first child. She said that she had been used to care only for herself for so long that she found the demandingness of a new baby much more difficult and disrupting than do most new mothers.

Jody's mother was born during World War II in the Netherlands while it was occupied by the Nazis. This Jewish family lived constantly under the threat of being discovered, and indeed her father was shot in the street when she was 1½ years old. When she was 3 years old, she went to live with an aunt in another town, and rarely saw her mother until the end of the war.

Both Jody's parents were orthodox Jews, and consciously wished for a boy child; indeed, they had selected only a boy's name by the time the mother entered the hospital in labor. She was awake, and at the delivery of the head, in a moment of panic thought she saw exposed brain tissue. She immediately experienced a profound depression with unusual, severe fatigue and frequent, contentless bouts of crying, which raged acutely for the first 4 months of her baby's life.

Breast feeding was started in the hospital and continued for 10 weeks, since the mother believed that this was important in order for her uterus to get back in shape, adding almost as an afterthought that the baby would get all the antibodies from the milk. During the 2nd week of the child's life, the mother had a severe cold with temperature elevation and cough, but nursing was continued with the mother wearing a face mask during the feedings.

At the age of 10 weeks, Jody was abruptly weaned to a bottle in 48 hours, since her mother, overwhelmed by the depression, felt compelled to go south for 2 weeks with her husband to rest. Jody was left in the care of her paternal grandparents.

When Jody was 4 months old, at least the acute aspect of her mother's depression appeared to lift. Stiff, with a rather immobile face, still chronically anxious and depressed, the mother nevertheless seemed to find the care of her infant somewhat easier and experienced increasing pleasure in her pretty little girl child. Up until this time Jody was described as sober with an intent, searching gaze, very rarely smiling or in any other way giving any sign of recognition of her mother, and only by 4 months of age could the mother count on getting a smile every time.

At this same point in time, when she was 4 months of age, Jody developed a distinct stranger reaction. By the unusually early age of 6 months, she spontaneously initiated a peek-a-boo game by covering and uncovering her eyes with a bib. In all its subsequent varieties this game continued to be a favorite of hers. By this same time she already developed a remarkable gestural and facial imitation of her mother and also imitatively reproduced several words. By 9 months she had a spontaneous and appropriately used vocabulary of about 6 words, and her speech continued in all its subsequent evolution to be startlingly precocious so that by the age of 1½ years she had an amazing vocabulary, used phrases and sentences of unusual complexity, and seemed to understand a great deal.

By 9 months of age Jody showed a remarkable interest in her mirror image, and within a month would on being asked by her mother point to her eyes, nose, mouth, hand, feet, fingers, and toes. She displayed an intense fear of inanimate objects that had an independent motion of their own, such as a teddy bear whose eyes rolled with a change in position and a windup toy monkey. By 4 months of age the baby would regularly clutch her mother's long hair when her head was bent over her as in feeding or diapering. The mother already at this early stage felt that this was an aggressive hair pulling. However, by 9 months it clearly was a hostile act; several babies at the beach club they attended were already frightened of her hair-pulling attacks.

By the time that this baby started in the nursery, she had already been confronted with major stresses in her development and had demonstrated remarkable precocious capacities to squeeze out of a rather arid environment whatever nutriment she could. The primary challenge of the emotional staleness in the early months as a consequence of the mother's profound depression resulted in a sober-faced intently watchful infant, in whom there was a marked delay in the primal specific attachment to the maternal object as reflected in the lack of both evident recognition of and consistent smiling social response to the mother until 4 months, whereas normally we would expect that this would emerge by 8–12 weeks at the latest.

At this same time, 4 months, and coincident with the lifting of at least the acute aspect of the mother's depression, Jody precociously developed a distinct stranger reaction, which in the normal course of events emerges between 6 and 8 months. Whether the lifting of the mother's depression facilitated these crucial developments or whether the lifting of the depression of the mother was a consequence of the spontaneous emergence of these significant indicators of the infant's specific attachment to the maternal object is, at least to our mind, one of those chicken and egg paradoxes.

In any case we would follow Spitz (1965):

Like the smiling response of 3 months, the 8 month anxiety marks a distinct stage in the development of psychic organization. In the case of the smiling response the sign—

Gestalt of the face is experienced as the homologue of the human partner. In the case of the 8 month anxiety the percept of the strange face is confronted with the memory of the mother's face. It is found to be different and will therefore be rejected. We assume that this capacity of cathectic displacement on reliably stored memory traces in the 8 month old child reflects the fact that he has now established a true object relation and that the mother has become his libidinal object. (p. 156)

While Jody experienced in her early months a major deprivation of maternal emotional nutriment, such was the fierceness of her developmental rush that she succeeded in forging that major victory of the human spirit, and even precociously, a primary attachment to the other person, the maternal object. (This inference is based on careful history taken from the parents. Developmental information prior to 1 year of age is anamnestic and not by our own observation.) This was undoubtedly accomplished under strain and with some fundamental instability in her basic attachment to the object world. The unusually early emergence of very pronounced imitative behavior bespeaks a marked intensification of normal primary identification mechanisms unquestionably in the service of bolstering the wavering attachment to the maternal object in view of her uncertain availability in reality. The startling precocious development of spontaneously initiated peek-a-boo play further confirms the early structuralization of the ego in its efforts at actively mastering the central object loss concerns with which this infant had to deal (Kleeman, 1967).

The very early mirror image fascination and detailed conscious awareness of body parts well before the end of the 1st year reflect a premature body–self differentiation that complements the previously discussed differentiation of a primal object schema. The emergence of a discreet and far from typical fear of inanimate objects that have an independent movement, such as the windup monkey, points up the emergence of the primal discrimination of animate–inanimate. She would seem to see the monkey as inanimate and the fear arises from her childish equation of the independent motion with living forms. This is a part aspect of the core of the adult narcissistic disorder; the fundamental annihilation fear confronts the individual with the threat that the outside object world is dead and consequently that the self too is dead.

This leads us to consider one last but very important detail in Jody's development in the 1st year, the early emergence of what without much question appears to be hostile aggression. The hair pulling, which first emerged at 3 months when the infant reflexly clutched her mother's hair as she bent over her, is entirely normal and part of the biologic givens such as the sucking reflex and rooting behavior which form the nucleus of attachment behavior. What was perhaps unusual was the mother's perception of this as aggressive behavior, which undoubtedly was a projection of the mother's own aggression toward the child. However, the persistence and expansion of the hair pulling in the latter half of the 1st year, its deliberate quality, and the accompanying smile as she continued to pull her mother's hair and to crawl after other children in order to do the same, did bespeak its emergence as a distinct and directed aggressive act. In the foregoing discussion we have made much of the precocious early differentiation of this child. In the process where the subject places the object outside the area of the subject's omnipotent control, that is, when the object schema is experienced as external to the self, the child experiences this as a loss, which inevitably seems to evoke an upsurge of now object-directed aggression (Roiphe, 1979). Indeed, according to Winnicott (1969) this means that the child destroys the object. "The central postulate of this thesis is that whereas the subject does not destroy the subjective object (the projected object), destruction turns up and becomes a central feature in so far as the object is objectively perceived, has autonomy and belongs to shared reality" (pp. 713–714).

As indicated previously, Jody started the nursery 2 weeks before her first birthday. While she could pull herself to the upright posture and manage to walk with support, her exclusive mode of getting about was an active, rapid crawl. Her vocabulary of single words spontaneously and appropriately used was quite remarkable in one so young. Although we heard quite a number of words while she was in the nursery, her language usage was much more expansive at home. We observed her fascination with her mirror image and the detailed discrimination of body parts both on herself and her dolls. In particular, she was noted frequently to point to her umbilicus with great pleasure and she named her mother's and own nipples "teetse." From early on in the 1st year she was regularly exposed to her parents' nude bodies, bathed once or twice a week with her father, and regularly was in the bathroom while her mother used the toilet, although this was not the case with her father.

At 12 months she was observed for the first time to interrupt her general activity, strain at a bowel movement, and develop an inward gaze, and this continued both at home and in the nursery. Coincident with this newly demonstrated awareness of her bowel movement, she also developed the derivative behavior of picking up small bits of paper and food from the floor and bringing them to her mother. At about the same time she would consistently tug at her diapers. Along with this she became fascinated and played with the incoming stream of bath water. Over this same period she showed no tendency to touch or explore her own genitals.

Jody started to sleep through the night from some time shortly after 1 month, and there was very little disturbance in this regular sleep pattern. The going-to-sleep ritual was of more than passing interest. From the time she was first regularly fed a bottle at 10 weeks, up through the entire time we observed the couple, she was held in her mother's arms as she was feeding. The mother, sitting on a straight-back chair, would rock Jody in her arms for varying periods of time until Jody appeared drowsy and would then put her down in the crib. She was never given the bottle in the crib. There she always had a pacifier, which she would sometimes suck and most often just hold. Other than this pacifier on going to sleep, she would occasionally stroke her own hair or finger the bed sheets, but never developed an attachment to a transitional object. Shortly before Jody was 13 months old, her parents went on a 2-week trip to the West Coast to explore career opportunities for the father. She was left at the paternal grandparents' apartment. She was very familiar with both of them, and had a particularly vivid and warm relationship with her doting grandfather, her "Daydee." She seemed to fare quite well there except for those occasions when she was shown a picture of the mother at which time she would appear sad, burst out crying, and dolefully call, "moma, moma." On her parents' return she smiled, and after a moment's hesitation rushed into her mother's arms. When her mother put on her coat preparatory to taking the child home, Jody burst into tears and was not consoled until she herself was dressed and she and her parents left together. Over the next few weeks she continued to show marked anxiety whenever her mother put on her coat and on several occasions jumped when she heard the door slam.

Beginning the first night that Jody spent at home in her own crib, a major sleep disturbance erupted, and while it improved after some 4 weeks, it persisted to a variable degree over the following 8 months that we continued to observe her. During the 4-week period of acute sleep disturbance, she would awaken, frequently in an apparent state of panic, as many as seven or eight times a night. She was allowed to stay up several hours past her usual bedtime until she was so fatigued that she could hardly resist going to sleep. Fussing extended to the preliminary nighttime routine, and for the 1st week or two she even resisted and often refused her naps. She began to insist that the door to her bedroom, which heretofore had always been closed, be left open.

After close to 3 weeks of this, the mother, frantic with fatigue and worry, asked us what she could do to improve this situation. We suggested that she try putting Jody down in her crib to sleep with her bottle instead of the usual routine of taking the bottle in her mother's arms. That night she tried this altered routine, and the child slept through the night. However, the next night she resumed the usual routine of holding her in her arms with the statement, "If she can go to sleep with the bottle she can go to sleep without it." Although this did not turn out to be the case, she never again attempted the altered routine we suggested.

Almost immediately following her parents' return, Jody developed a cold, temperature elevation, and diarrhea, which lasted for about a week. The alteration in Jody's mood was very dramatic and persisted in an acute form for a month after the separation. She seemed anxious and cranky. The child shadowed her mother and literally clung to her, frequently asking to be picked up. After a few days a rampant aggression seemed to explode. While hugging her mother at bedtime, she would suddenly bite her shoulder. She would suddenly and fiercely pinch, slap, pull hair, and for the first time teasing behavior became prominent. While her mother was the principal target, she was rather evenhanded in attacking her observers, the nursery teachers, other children, and her dolls. All of this seemed very much exaggerated when she was frustrated in anything. There was a very curious inconsistency in her relationship to other children. Although she never made any effort to defend herself against any attack or to retrieve or hold onto a toy that another child took away, she would repeatedly and unprovokedly, clutch a fistful of hair of another child and fiercely pull. Her fingers would have to be pried open forcefully, and if the other child would cry in pain Jody would intently stare and her face would often show empathic sorrow. She would often swallow the fistful of hair that she succeeded in pulling out and her mother said that Jody had a very regular diet of her hair. Apart from this, her food intake was sharply diminished so that her only regular source of nutrition was the milk she took in her bottles. This heretofore neat and dainty little girl would sit in her high chair and mess with the food on her plate instead of eating.

Over this entire period Jody showed reasonably steady balance when standing unsupported, and even managed a few steps, but did not begin to walk regularly until she was close to 16 months old. For what it is worth, a number of observers had the distinct impression that her balance was good enough well before she actually began to walk but that she didn't want to. For a month before she herself walked, she was frequently observed to "walk" her dolls and could be heard to say, "doll, walk."

In the 6-week period following the separation, there was a sharp increase in her specific anal, urinary, and genital awareness and preoccupation, along with a continued and expanding general body exploration. She had an unusual interest in eyes, her own, her parents', and dolls', and not only used the word eye but also named the lashes. She continued to be fascinated with her mirror image, exploring her naked body in the mirror, and rather remarkable in one so young, identified her mirror image as "Jody."

Before the separation Jody had shown some rudimentary awareness of bowel and bladder function, as well as some patterning of her activity by these functions. Beginning immediately after the separation and continuing over the next 3 weeks, she consistently tugged at her diaper after a bowel movement and would verbally signal that she had one by saying "caca." There was a decided increase in her interest in the bathroom and for the first time she intently and interestedly watched her mother's toilet functions. She persistently tried to look into and play in the toilet bowl, particularly after her mother had used the toilet. She would be sharply admonished not to with the word "dirty." She continued to bring tiny bits of paper, lint, or food from the floor to her mother, and now saying "dirty" would throw them into the waste basket. She began to climb into small spaces such as into the toy shelf, under cabinets, and into corners, sometimes while having a bowel movement but often at other times as well. A favorite new activity was an endless stuffing of objects into containers and then emptying them. About 1 month after the separation, her interest in the toilet and, in particular, play in the toilet water had if anything become more intense. Since her mother's verbal admonitions were no longer successful in inhibiting her curiosity, her mother would often sharply slap Jody's hand. At this time she became constipated for a few days and after she finally succeeded in having a bowel movement, Jody said, "caca, dada, bye-bye." After this she began to vigorously resist diaper changes for some time after she had a bowel movement with a very decided "no." She also began frequently to hide objects that belonged to her mother.

Just after her parents returned, Jody found her genitals and over the next several weeks there was a gradual increased frequency with which she touched her genitals. Although she frequently had the opportunity before to see her father's exposed penis, she now for the first time pointed to it and said "teetse," her word for her mother's nipple-breast. She now named her own genitals, "gina." She showed a sharply increased interest in her mother's and father's genitals and pubic hair and began to reach out and touch them. She increasingly began to look and reach into her mother's blouse and say "teetse." On several occasions after this she would questioningly ask, "gina?" She began to laugh now when her mother would playfully blow on her perineum during diaper changes, something which before had not elicited any particular reaction. In the nursery she seemed fascinated with a toy rubber elephant, frequently pulling its trunk. Uncharacteristically she refused to call the elephant by name. Both at home and in the nursery, for the first time and repeatedly over the next several weeks, she would straddle the rocking horse and vigorously rock away, laughing in an elated mood.

It may be worth our while to stop and consider at this point the various currents in Jody's development. We have already pointed out the serious instability in the developing self and object schema of this little girl, as a consequence of the relative emotional unavailability of her depressed mother. This vigorous baby seemed to meet this fundamental challenge to her integrity with a precocious libidinal investment of and differentiation from the maternal object. This appeared to be bolstered by the exaggeration of primary identification mechanisms such as the remarkably precocious and prominent gestural, facial, and verbal imitation and the central importance of the visual mode. This precocious object and body-self schematization was undoubtedly accomplished under considerable strain, with more than the usual complement of hostile aggression.

It was both fascinating and heartrending to observe the interactional details by which this narcissistic, depressed mother communicated her own highly compromised object relatedness to her relatively helpless infant. The characteristic going-to-sleep ritual had a most interesting texture. It will be recalled that this mother invariably held her baby in her arms as she gave her the bottle, rocked her until the baby became drowsy, and then put her down in the crib without the bottle to fall asleep. The reinforcing aspect of this characteristic going-to-sleep ritual will on reflection surely become obvious. In this most intense paradigmatic situation of the mother-child inter-action, the feeding situation, this mother offered her baby the maximum of tactile and kinesthetic closeness before that quintessential situation of object loss, going to sleep. The other face of this maternal behavior was that in that final transition to sleep the baby was entirely alone without even that ordinary indication of the mother's presence, the bottle. Now this baby did develop spontaneously some rudimentary transitional behavior such as holding the pacifier, fingering her hair or the bed sheets but never developed any firm attachment to a specific transitional object. Winnicott may have argued that no transitional object emerged because there was not good-enough mothering, and we certainly would not contest this view. However, from another vantage point, in the circumstance where the mother offers her own body in the transition to sleep, this tends in general even where there is good-enough mothering to militate against the investment of an inanimate object with mother–self significance. In this particular instance where the mother's own capacity for object relatedness was so severely compromised, both the adaptive and the pathological significance of her handling of her baby's falling off to sleep are like two faces of the same coin. In view of her very limited capacity to establish for her baby an emotional climate of strong emotional contact, the maximum tactile and kinesthetic closeness during the feeding situation at least tended to reinforce the sense of her presence in this important dyadic interaction; at the same time this same behavior with its rigid insistence on bodily closeness would seem to follow from her own uncertain sense of separateness and body–self integrity.

For this child, then, with an unstable core of self and object, the 2-week separation at 13 months had a rather catastrophic impact. While the general outline of her responses, sleep and feeding disturbances, and an anxious hostile clinging are what we would expect of a child this age, it is the intensity and the duration of the resonance of the experience that is idiosyncratic and a function of the early strain in her development.

The unusually intense sleep disturbance with the insistence of the open door, the repeated need throughout the night to reestablish contacat with the actual mother, and the clinging insistence on physical closeness with her throughout the day reflect the profound challenge of object loss with which this child had to struggle in the aftermath of the separation experience. The incapacity of the mother to follow through, in spite of the initial success on our suggestion for an alteration in the going-to-sleep routine (i.e., putting the baby down in the crib with the bottle), reflects the mother's own compromised capacity for separate functioning. The underlying rationale in our intervention was our effort to expand for this child that intermediate area between the self and the nonself, the object and what is not the object in the challenging transition to sleep. That is, our expectation was that allowing the child the possession of the bottle when she was put down in the crib alone would facilitate her investment of this inanimate object with mother–me significance and thus ease that chilling transition to sleep, which involves a sense of self-dissolution and object loss.

A related and very significant consequence of the separation was a sharp intensification of object-directed hostile aggression. Even in the early, normal differentiation thrust of the child (Mahler, 1968; Winnicott, 1969), as the object is placed outside the area of omnipotent control, or to put it another way, as the object concept becomes external to the self-concept, there is an upsurge in object-directed aggression (Roiphe, 1979) as a complement of the implicit object loss. In a situation of actual object loss such as a separation experience, this is of course very much exaggerated. This was amply evident not only in Jody's biting, slapping, pinching, hair-pulling attacks on her mother, but also spread to her contacts with other adults, children, and inanimate objects. A particularly ominous aspect of the expansion of her hostile aggression was the early sadomasochistic erotization as reflected in the eruption of a particularly sharp teasing of the mother. An equally disturbing development was the emergence of an unusually intense ambivalence as for example while the child was affectionately hugging her mother, she suddenly bit her mother's shoulder. Or we have the observers' repeated experience while Jody was sitting in their laps; they knew something was coming but could not tell until it actually occurred whether it would be a kiss or an attack.

A further reverberation of the separation experience was expressed in Jody's falling ill with a cold, temperature elevation, and diarrhea immediately after her parents' return. It may seem to stretch the reader's credulity too much to ascribe such a commonplace occurrence as a mild illness to the separation. However, in the almost 60 children we have studied in the past 6 years, virtually every child has been left by the parents for a period of more than several days at sometime during the 2nd year. In an overwhelming number of such instances, the children developed some illness such as a cold, diarrhea, allergy, and so on within the 1st week after the parents' return. It is our understanding that the separation experience evokes a sharp upsurge in aggression, which is particularly disruptive to the major developmental thrust of this stage, that is, to the consolidation of the self and object schema. Under these circumtances a precursor of defense, somatization, or to follow Schur (1955, 1958), resomatization would seem to be mobilized; this may be a crucial mechanism in very young children whose libidinal attachment to the object is still quite fragile and whose egos lack the strength and integrity to interpose less compromising psychological defense mechanisms. In this connection we are impressed by the prominence of the somatization mechanism in borderline states where just such a nuclear situation is extant (see Roiphe, 1973, 1979).

Most of the issues that we have discussed thus far have major reverberation in the highly important area of anal, urinary, and early sexual drive organization. Early in the 1st year the infant tends to have his stool during feeding or shortly thereafter, and usually there is no attention to or behavioral reflection of the bowel movement. Toward the end of the 1st year, and certainly early in the 2nd year, there very commonly is a tendency for a general body ridigity, some straining, and not infrequently a brief stilling of other body activity and a withdrawal of attention from the outside. It is not uncommon with our 14- to 15-month-old children to note a fascination with the toilet and particularly the flush with the highly exciting and absorbing observation of the controlled disappearance of the stool, toilet paper, or toy.

This shift in the child's relationship to his own bowel movement seems to follow the normal and at this age typical emergence of a separation conflict with all that this implies about the inner consolidation of self and object schema. Up until the age of 8 months, the child's self-differentiation is extremely rudimentary, and the relationship to the object is essentially a symbiotic one. With the onset of the differentiation subphase of Mahler, there is a rapid quickening in the whole process of self-schematization and a separation of the infant from his mother (Mahler, 1967, 1968). It is at this stage, with the new level of self and object differentiation, that the bowel movement is singularly situated and suited to express the double-faced developing inner concept; something which is part of the self, can be felt inside, has a movement and yet is not alive, has a climactic expulsive pattern, a texture, a smell, and so on, and very importantly a relationship to the nourishing object, and yet when expelled is neither self nor object. Its movement and consistency are subject to the vicissitudes of health and sickness, loving and hating feelings toward the object, and the ultimate control of the toilet process waits on some partial resolution of the conflicts around self-dissolution and object loss. The whole process of attention to the bowel movement and the new relationship to it follows from and is a reflection of the newly developing self and object relationship and is in this sense quite independent of any demand from the parents, either explicit or implicit, for control of these functions.

Jody had already shown some preliminary evidence of anal awareness when the separation experience served to expand her preoccupation with anal functions, particularly as a channel for expressing concerns about the issues of object loss and self-dissolution. Not only was there an increased curiosity about the mother's toilet functions and an implacable fascination with the toilet bowl and flush, but she now began verbally to regularly signal her bowel movements. Bowel patterning of her general activity was readily observable in the emergence of endlessly repeated sequences in which she would stuff small objects into containers and then empty them and in which she would climb into small spaces either while having a bowel movement or at other times as well.

Perhaps the most dramatic reflection of the anal channeling of object loss and self-dissolution concerns, some 3 weeks after the separation, was the growing anxiety she showed when an effort was made to change her soiled diaper. She would fiercely resist, frequently with the new word "no." Interestingly, in this context, she began to hide objects that belonged to her mother. Along about this time she developed a bout of constipation, and when after a few days she finally had a bowel movement she said, "caca, dada, bye-bye," thus vividly expressing the intimate relation of bowel function with object loss concerns. It is commonplace for children during the 2nd year to show a marked reluctance to have their soiled diapers changed for varying periods after a movement. It would seem that this period of time is required to detach from the stool its emotional significance of self and object. While the general outline of Jody's behavior is entirely within the normal range, it is the intensity of her anxiety and the fierceness of her resistance that underscores the particular and unusual concern about body integrity and the threat of object loss.

It will be recalled that right after the separation, Jody demonstrated the sexual arousal typical of children in the first half of the 2nd year as reflected in her beginning and increasing manipulation of her own genitals and the emerging sharp curiosity about her parents' genitals. Quite early in this we saw the stirrings of her perplexity over her observation of the anatomic difference between the sexes as she referred to her father's penis by the name "teetse," her word for the breast-nipple, thus emphasizing the identity of male and female and denying the difference. It is common for most of the little girls we have studied to displace their attention from where the disturbing difference between the sexes is, the genitals, to other areas such as the umbilicus or the buttocks or anal functions where the similarities are after all more pronounced. Only a few weeks later, she developed an unprecedented bout of constipation, and when she finally had a bowel movement it was accompanied by the curious and evocative verbalization, "caca, dada, bye-bye." It would seem to us that this quite probably points to the stirrings of a castration reaction. While in the foregoing discussion of the constipation we had referred to the general concerns about body integrity and object loss, that is, the stool-self and stool-object equation, the child's verbalization would seem to betray the important further concern about the integrity of the genital outline of the body; that is, the stool had acquired the additional significance of the father's phallus.

It is our impression that by the 2nd year with the awareness of the object concept as external to the self-concept and the gradual consolidation of distinct and separate self and object schema, the two parallel zonal vectors, anal and early sexual, become increasingly important in the whole process. The anal, by virtue of its functional characteristics, fullness and loss, is ideally suited to channel feeling and experience having to do with the mother of separation; and consequently as a channel, at least relatively, for the expression of aggression directed toward the object. The early sexual zone would according to our understanding serve as a channel for the more purely libidinal attachment to the object in that the child through the manipulation of his own genitals now actively produces warm, good feelings on his own body, which earlier the child only passively experienced through maternal handling. The anal and early sexual zones are thus two major highways in the child's tortuous journey toward a basic connection to the object world and the gradual organization and internalization of the inner self- and object schema. These two zones then serve as body nuclei around which coherent islands of good and bad object schema gradually consolidate,

We have described and discussed Jody's development through the age of 15 months. A 2-week separation experience had been extraordinarily disruptive, and she had only later begun to show some signs of containing this experience. Over the next 6 months that we continued to observe the child, either one or both parents were away for about a total of 7 weeks, repeated separations ranging from 1 day to 2 weeks in duration. Although the mother had some awareness of how disruptive these experiences were for her little girl, ultimately both parents allowed themselves to be driven by what they both took to be the realities of their situation. No sooner would this sturdy little girl show some signs of mastering one separation experience, than she would be confronted with another.

While she never again showed the same massive acute sleep disturbance in response to any of the subsequent separations, it was also clear that there was no period of time when her sleep was undisturbed. Almost imperceptibly there was an alteration in the mother's handling of the going-to-sleep routine. While the mother continued to hold and rock Jody, she increasingly would pat her backside and hold her hand through the bars of the crib. Sometime along in all this we learned on speaking with the maternal grandmother that Jody's mother, whose crib had always been in the parental bedroom, had also had a pacifier but no transitional object. The maternal grandmother would sit in a straight-back chair and rock her baby by herself rocking back and forth. After the father was killed the crib was moved closer to the mother's bed, and her mother would hold her hand through the bars of the crib. Jody's mother was visibly startled to hear all this (as were we), which she knew nothing of, since it so closely paralleled her own handling of her baby's going to sleep. The relative shift in the going-to-sleep ritual from the body rocking by the mother to the handholding through the bars of the crib took place when Jody was around 16–17 months, very close to Jody's mother's age when her own father was killed.

After each of the subsequent separations, Jody would rush into her mother's arms in happy reunion, but would invariably tend to ignore her father for varying periods of time. When she was a bit older than 15 months, after a 3-day separation, she was for a 48-hour span quite frightened when she was approached by men, particularly strange men; she would avert her eyes and rush to her mother for comfort. At 17 months, after a 2-week separation, in addition to ignoring her father for 2 days she showed a highly unusual name confusion, calling her father by the name she'd given the paternal grandfather, "daydee," and referring to grandfather as "dada." At the age of 18 months, after a 5-day separation, after initially showing some fear of her father on reunion, there was a 2-week period in which there were shifting fears of noises, rolling balls, and shadows. At 19½ months, after her mother was away for 5 days and her father for 2 weeks, she again seemed frightened of her father for several days. Shortly after this she was heard rather pathetically to repeat to herself, "mama, dada, Jody, family." At 20 months, after an overnight separation, she said to her parents, "Jody has two mommies and two daddies." It had been her mother's custom, in an effort to reassure Jody, either before or after separations to say to Jody, "Mommie sometimes goes away but she always comes back." Just shortly before the nursery discontinued, Jody was heard to utter the heartrending and plaintive reply, "Mommie always goes away."

After each of these many separations, there was a gradually extended period of anxious clinging to her mother. The range of her activity at any distance from her mother growingly diminished. More and more the child would intently watch the activities of other children and adults rather than directly engage in self-initiated activity or social interaction with others. She would repeatedly climb to the platform of the slide and instead of sliding down, unless urged to by her mother, would sit there for long periods looking at everything and everybody. In this connection a very poignant play sequence observed at home was very much to the point. Instead of the playful and pleasurable spoon feeding of her doll's mouth, which she had often engaged in before, she now rather sober-facedly would spoon-feed her doll's eyes. In spite of this child's truly remarkable capacity for symbolic representation and imaginative play earlier, there was a growing and ominous constriction in any self-initiated independent play. This became so extreme that there was no organized activity unless she was at her mother's side and later only when her mother would urge her to feed her dolls, put them to sleep, or bathe them, and so on.

After each separation there was invariably a prominent upsurge in hostile aggression with biting and pinching attacks primarily directed at her mother but also spreading to other adults and children. These blunt attacks would gradually diminish, only to be evoked acutely again with each new separation. Over this whole period Jody's teasing behavior became increasingly prominent, as did the peculiar difficulty in differentiating her love–attack modes of approach. As described, after the first separation when Jody was sitting in the lap of either mother or her observers, it was very difficult to predict whether her approach would result in hugging and kissing or an attack. Very frequently the child's embrace would quite suddenly shift to a bite or vigorous pinching.

From 15 months on, Jody continued to strongly resist diaper changes and had entirely stopped signaling her bowel movement. At 17 months, to our surprise, we learned that Jody had probably never seen her own bowel movement. Her mother would deftly and rapidly remove her soiled diaper and then dispose of it in an incinerator chute in the apartment. After telling us this, although we said nothing, the mother changed her routine and allowed Jody to see her bowel movements. For some few months after this, she showed a renewed interest in her mother's toilet functions and would look in her doll's diaper for bowel movements. She insisted on seeing her own soiled diaper, and from time to time made an effort to touch her movement but was prohibited from doing so by her mother.

From the age of 15 months, Jody made a clear verbal distinction between male and female as she would say, "Jody, Mama, gina; Dada, penis." At this point she was reported to notice her mother's tampons and made an effort to pull on the mother's tampon string. She insisted on having a tampon of her own and made an effort to insert it in her genitals. Mother insisted that Jody had never seen a bloody tampon. At this time her favorite activity was the rocking horse, which she would ride vigorously. At 17 months she clutched at her father's penis and pubic hair in the bathtub and was reported to insist with glee, "I'm a boy." For some time after, she was noted to sit on the floor with her legs apart and place various toys between her legs. Toward the end of her 18th month, there was a sharp falling off of genital manipulation, she no longer named either penis or vagina, and for some time she stopped looking at and touching her father's penis. At about this time there was a concomitant increase in curiosity about her belly-button, which she would occasionally again call by the name "teetse," as she repeatedly and vigorously would rub it for long periods of time. This was so extreme that the whole area became red and abraded so that she had to stop the rubbing, since it hurt. At this same time, right after a separation it will be remembered, for the first time she developed a fear of her father as well as shifting fears of noise, rolling balls, and shadows. She was frequently, at this time, observed to clutch her genital area whenever she was frightened. Shortly after this displaced masturbatory activity stopped, she was repeatedly noted to stuff tissues and objects into her blouse and proudly show her breasts. From this time on, although she no longer showed any interest in her genitals, she continued to stuff her blouse and was increasingly interested in the breasts of her mother and her female observers, frequently suddenly pinching them.

This then brings us to the time when Jody was 21 months old, and the nursery group was discontinued so that we were no longer able to follow her development. She was an extremely well-endowed child, whose cognitive functioning, language, and symbolization were distinctly advanced. Routine infant testing reported, "Most impressive was the degree of internal deliberation, consideration of alternatives, and general internal elaboration that seemed to go on in Jody, evident in much of her behavior and seemingly related not only to her considerable cognitive skills but to a degree of inner conflict already present." She was a sober-faced, subdued, largely joyless child, always hovering close to her mother, looking intently at everything that went on around her, and tending to do very little spontaneously, whose general mood might best be characterized as chronically anxious and somewhat depressed.

Clearly, the central experience with which Jody had to struggle over and over again in her short life was the essential unavailability of her mother. Whether it was the emotional unavailability of her mother in her early months as a consequence of her mother's profound depression, or the actual unavailability in the 2nd year as a consequence of her repeated separations, this sturdy little youngster continually fought with a rare forcefulness of spirit to squeeze whatever nutriment she could out of the arid environment in which she grew.

Jody's mother seemed driven in some frenzy of leaving her daughter throughout the 2nd year. While she was distinctly aware of how disruptive all this was for her little daughter, a quick easy denial would overtake this margin of awareness, as she ascribed her child's disturbance to what seemed like an endless teething, colds, her age, and so on. The more we learned about the mother's early childhood, the general climate of anxiety, the murder of her father in the street when she was 1½ years old, her being sent at the age of 3 years to live with an aunt in a distant town and for 2 years rarely seeing her mother, the subsequent frequent moves to strange and foreign lands, the more we were impressed that the frequent separations reflected a demonic compulsion to repeat with her daughter her own very traumatic past. In an interview with the maternal grandmother, it was almost uncanny to learn not only of Jody's mother's own struggle with object loss throughout her early childhood but also the incredible detail in which she unconsciously utilized her own mother's comforting routines, particularly around going to sleep. It was not only her own mother's usual routine of holding her in her arms and rocking back and forth in a straight-back chair, but at 18 months, after her father's murder, holding her hand through the bars of the crib at night; it was at just this time in Jody's life that her mother similarly began to hold her hand at night, although she could offer no good explanation for this alteration in her handling of the child.

An interesting and highly significant idiosyncratic detail of Jody's behavior on her parents' return after a separation was her immediate and joyous reunion with her mother and her tendency to ignore her father for various spans of time beginning with the third major separation during the 2nd year, when she was 17 months old. Already, after the second separation when she was 15 months, she developed an unusual fear of men, particularly strange men, for a few days. It was after each of the subsequent separations that she either ignored her father or on a few occasions was actually afraid of him. Now, of course, it is much more typical during the 2nd year, after a separation for the child on reunion with the parents to ignore the mother and rush to the father. This seems to follow from the fact that separation mobilizes in the child a sharp upsurge in aggression directed at the mother, whose absence is so threatening to the still so dependent child. Ordinarily, the father is spared all this, since he is increasingly utilized by the child as the supporting separator in the whole separation–individuation thrust away from the mother (Mahler & Gosliner, 1955; Greenacre, 1966). We would suppose that from the earliest time in Jody's life there had been very considerable strain in establishing even that necessary primary attachment to the maternal object as a consequence of her mother's profound depression, and the central imperative in her functioning was to spare and bolster that relationship at whatever cost. So that with Jody, on reunion with her parents, in view of her disruptive rage state, it was toward the father of separation that the rage was directed, albeit this trend would serve to compromise her whole development toward ultimate independence.

Now, of course, these mechanisms could only partially be successful in blunting the rage toward the mother. Only a few days after each separation, her hostility would ultimately find its primary target, her mother, as she would direct toward her mother the raw biting, pinching, and slapping attacks. Over time there was an ominous, ever-increasing sadomasochistic erotization of her relationship to her mother as expressed in the increasingly prominent teasing behavior. The intensely developing ambivalence was reflected in the ever-more present difficulty in differentiating the child's love–attack mode of approach; that is, would she kiss or bite, or would a hug turn into a pinching, slapping attack? All of this did not augur well for the age-appropriate separation–individuation thrust and that central and crucial development toward object constancy.

In the highly important area of drive organization during the 2nd year, the newly mobilized and age-typical anal and early sexual zonal thrusts were concomitantly, almost from the beginning, caught up in pronounced conflict. Instead of these zonal trends serving to support and consolidate Jody's developing self and object schema as it normally would, the considerable conflict in these areas only served to further undermine and deplete these significant developments.

We believe that normally the anal zone is singularly suited by virtue of its functional characteristics, to pick up the age-appropriate concerns of object loss and self-dissolution and as an essentially nondestructive channel for the age-appropriate hostile aggression. The child ordinarily wins his victory over all these problematic areas by the ultimate integration of an active and controlled holding on and letting go of the stool–object (Roiphe, 1973). Unfortunately, in Jody's case, that intermediate area in which the stool has a self and object meaning and yet is not self or object was too narrow, and its loss provoked too much anxiety and too readily mobilized rigid denial mechanisms to allow a normal working through and mastery of the underlying loss conflicts.

In a parallel way at this same stage, the normally occurring, early sexual zonal arousal opens a new channel for the consolidation of the libidinal attachment to the object and of a primary genital outline of the body. It will be recalled that the genital self-touching that began in Jody at 13 months gradually increased in frequency and intensity up to her 18th month before it abruptly dropped out. While Jody's masturbatory arousal had something of a normal outline in its increasing intensity, we were from very early on impressed that unlike most other children, she showed very little pleasure gain from her autoerotic genital self-touching. We are inclined to believe that the virtual absence of masturbatory pleasure was a consequence of the contamination of the purely libidinal stream in Jody by very strong currents of hostile aggression as reflected in the unusually pronounced ambivalence and the early, intense sadomasochistic erotization.

By the age of 15 months, she gave clear verbal evidence of her awareness of the anatomic difference between the sexes. At 17 months, just after a 2-week separation, a sharp penis envy syndrome was much in evidence a she gleefully announced she was a boy and was observed often in the week or so following this to sit with her legs apart, holding phallic shaped objects to her perineal area. At 18½ months, after a 3-day separation, there was a sudden abrupt inhibition of any direct masturbatory activity, a sharp falling off of sexual curiosity, and she would only clutch her genital area when she was frightened. For a week or so after this dramatic masturbatory inhibition, she was frequently observed to vigorously rub her umbilicus until the whole area became red and sore and she could no longer do this, since it hurt.

In summary, as a consequence of the considerable disturbance in the mother–child interaction, Jody had to deal with a much greater than ordinary aggressive contamination of libidinal currents. With the emergence of the normal sexual arousal in the first half of the 2nd year, Jody's masturbatory activity was relatively without masturbatory pleasure in contrast to the normal child, in whom the pleasure gain in his own body handling serves to expand and consolidate his sense of self. The insult to Jody's sense of body integrity as a consequence of her awareness of the anatomic difference between the sexes led to a brief period of denial of the fact that she had no penis. The denial was unsuccessful, and there was a distinct and sharp inhibition in the direct zonal thrust and a displacement to the umbilicus. This fierce masturbatory variant was so contaminated with hostile aggression that it ultimately led to self-injury. With this there seemed to follow at least for the time, a total constriction of the masturbatory current. We then saw the reemergence of a reinforced denial through the fantasy of the displaced breast–phallus and the fetishistic attachment to the menstrual tampon (Roiphe & Galenson, 1973b). With all this we have seen the virtual drying up and depletion of that important libidinal wellspring, the early sexual zonal thrust, and a still further accretion to that defensive bulwark, which served bravely but in pyrrhic fashion to preserve her precarious sense of self and object.

By the end of the 2nd year, Jody, now characteristically anxious and depressed, instead of the normal, expanded capacity for independent functioning bolstered by a more secure inner schema of self and object, showed an increasingly hostile clinging to and dependence on her actual mother. In spite of her truly remarkable capacity for symbolization, there was a growing constriction in the broad range of spontaneous, playful activity. Instead of doing things, exploring things, this watchful youngster would stand and look intently, taking things in visually, something perhaps most pointedly if heartbreakingly expressed in her playful feeding of her doll's eyes rather than her mouth. It seems to us that we have been witness to one variety of early development that must inevitably result in narcissistic depletion and a failure to achieve any substantial object constancy, which is according to our understanding the hallmark of the narcissistic disorder in process of development.

As a result of the widening scope of psychoanalysis, we are increasingly called on to treat a bewildering array of narcissistic disturbances. Unlike the neurotic disorders where our genetic constructions and technical rules afford us a therapeutic instrument of unparalleled power, with the narcissistic disorders our genetic theories are at best uncertain and confusing and our therapeutic efforts faltering. The nosological array of narcissistic disorders— the psychoses, the borderline states, the depressions, the perversions, psychosomatic disorders, and so on—are not firmly rooted in our understanding of a genetic topography.

Our clinical experience has, however, succeeded in securely isolating a major developmental failure that is characteristic of all the narcissistic disorders (in contrast to the neuroses), the failure to establish object constancy. In addition it has served to underscore the central significance of disturbances in the preoedipal era of development.

While the work of Jacobson (1964), Greenacre (1953, 1955, 1960), Kernberg (1967, 1970), and Kohut (1971), to mention only a few, has laid out some landmarks in the geography of this distant and essentially preverbal terrain, the problem with these reconstructive explorations is that we unfortunately are peering through the wrong end of a telescope. We will have to turn increasingly to direct observational studies of early development to fill in the details of this highly important terrain. The separation–individuation studies of Mahler (1968) have been a pioneering effort in this direction. We have in some of our case studies (Galenson & Roiphe, 1971; Roiphe & Galenson, 1972, 1973a, 1973b) begun to explore the detailed developmental outline of some disturbances during this era.

In this chapter we have attempted to muster observational details of the mother–child interaction, early drive, and ego development in a little girl who by the end of the 2nd year had developed a major structural fault, the failure to attain an age-appropriate object constancy, which according to our understanding is at the core of all narcissistic disturbances. While the ongoing force of development may serve to patch this over, we believe that this rift in the ego will, like the San Andreas fault, erupt in later life. The differing narcissistic entities are functions of where, during the various stages of preoedipal development, the specific strain or stress traumas have their impact; now they serve to organize characteristic patterns of defensive organization, such as somatization, introjective–projective and splitting mechanisms, primary identification, denial, and so on, and how they affect libidinal and aggressive drive organization, for example inhibition, accretion or sadomasochistic erotization.

REFERENCES

Galenson, E., & Roiphe, H. (1971). The impact of early sexual discovery on mood, defensive organizaton and symbolization. *The Psychoanalytic Study of the Child, 26,* 195–216.

Greenacre, P. (1953). Certain relationships between fetishism and the faulty development of the body image. *The Psychoanalytic Study of the Child, 8,* 79–98.

Greenacre, P. (1955). Further considerations regarding fetishism. *The Psychoanalytic Study of the Child, 10,* 187–194.

Greenacre, P. (1960). Further notes on fetishism. *The Psychoanalytic Study of the Child, 15,* 191–207.

Greenacre, P. (1966). Problems of overidealization of the analyst and of analysis: Their manifestation in the transference and countertransference. *The Psychoanalytic Study of the Child, 21,* 193–212.

Hartmann, H. (1952). Mutual influences in the development of ego and id. *The Psychoanalytic Study of the Child, 7,* 9–30.

Jacobson, G. (1964). *The self and the object world.* New York: International Universities Press.

Kernberg, O. (1967). Borderline personality organization. *Journal of the American Psychoanalytic Association, 15,* 641–685.

Kernberg, O. (1970). Factors in the psychoanalytic treatment of narcissistic personalities. *Journal of the American Psychoanalytic Association, 18,* 51–85.

Kleeman, J. (1967). The peek-a-boo game. *The Psychoanalytic Study of the Child, 22,* 239–273.

Kohut, H. (1971). *The analysis of the self.* New York: International Universities Press.

Mahler, M. S. (1967). On human symbiosis and the vicissitudes of individuation. *Journal of the American Psychoanalytic Association, 15,* 740–763.

Mahler, M. S. (1968). *On human symbiosis and the vicissitudes of individuation.* New York: International Universities Press.

Mahler, M. S., & Gosliner, B. J. (1955). On symbiotic child psychosis: Genetic, dynamic and restitutive aspects. *The Psychoanalytic Study of the Child, 10,* 195–212.

Roiphe, H. (1973). Some thoughts on childhood psychosis, self and object. *The Psychoanalytic Study of the Child, 28,* 131–145.

Roiphe, H. (1979). A theoretical overview of preoedipal development. In J. D. Noshpitz (Ed.), *Basic handbook of child psychiatry* (pp. 118–127). New York: Basic Books.

Roiphe, H., & Galenson, E. (1972). Early genital activity and the castration complex. *Psychoanalytic Quarterly, 41,* 334–347.

Roiphe, H., & Galenson, E. (1973a). Object loss and early sexual development. *Psychoanalytic Quarterly, 42,* 73–91.

Roiphe, H., & Galenson, E. (1973b). The infantile fetish. *The Psychoanalytic Study of the Child, 28,* 147–166.

Schur, M. (1955). Comments on the metapsychology of somatization. *The Psychoanalytic Study of the Child, 10,* 119–164.

Schur, M. (1958). The ego and the id in anxiety. *The Psychoanalytic Study of the Child, 13,* 190–220.

Spitz, R. (1965). *The first year of life.* New York: International Universities Press.

Winnicott, D. W. (1969). The use of the object. *International Journal of Psycho-Analysis, 50,* 711–716.

CHAPTER SIXTEEN

The Vicissitudes of Maternal Deprivation

J. ALEXIS BURLAND

INTRODUCTION

For over a decade several of my consultative appointments have brought me into professional contact with inner-city children reared in a socioeconomic and cultural setting characterized by varying degrees of maternal deprivation. This work has included consultation to special classes for the emotionally disturbed in inner-city public schools, to a foster care agency, to several residential treatment facilities for children in need of placement but unable to cope with the rigorous demands and expectations of foster care, and to a mental health/mental rehabilitation unit in its children's service center and in its facility for helping young unwed mothers learn better mothering skills. Further, in the fall of 1976 I began the analysis of one of these children, one who was in residential care. This was undertaken in order to collect analytic data to enrich the growing body of data I was collecting concerning the vicissitudes of early maternal deprivation (see Burland, 1980, 1984, for further details).

From this wealth of observational and clinical data, several conclusions emerged: (1) there is a recognizable and definable developmental clinical syndrome that results from chronic severe maternal deprivation during the early years of life; (2) many developmental hypotheses gleaned from studies within a "normal" population are confirmed, especially those relating to the importance of the mother–infant interaction and in particular the symbiotic phase for psychological development; and (3) inferences can be drawn from the data as to the treatment implications of this population.

THE "AUTISTIC CHARACTER DISORDER"

As child after child was seen by me in consultation, it became increasingly evident that there was a regularly recurring constellation of symptoms among those with a history of severe and chronic maternal deprivation.

The four characteristics of this syndrome are (1) unrelatedness associated with failure to achieve self and object differentiation and constancy; (2) pathological narcissism; (3) cognitive delay with incomplete hatching; and (4) higher than normal levels of destructive aggression. This syndrome can be understood as reflecting a multifaceted developmental arrest. Due to inadequate mothering, there is, in Spitz's terms (Spitz, 1965), a failure to establish the libidinal object. As a consequence, the infant does not move adequately out of the normal autistic phase of development into the symbiotic; hence, the rationale for the term I prefer to use for this condition: "autistic character disorder."

Certain advances in psychoanalytic developmental psychology make possible the organization of the clinical data in this study into workable and recognizable explanatory formulations. Beres and Obers (1950) attempted a similar ego developmental explanation of the effects of deprivation, noting the resultant immaturity in ego functions, especially the persistence of the pleasure principle, the cognitive deficits, and the poor quality of object relationships. This chapter attempts to continue that effort but with the aid of concepts many of which have been developed or elaborated since that time. There is also the addition of clinical analytic data.

That the sequence of developmental events that leads to the achievement of object constancy is dependent upon adequate mothering has been proposed by many authors, from Hartmann's concept of the average expectable environment (1937), through Spitz's mother–infant "dialogue" (1965), Winnicott's facilitating environment (1960a, 1960b), and Mahler's mother as beacon of developmental orientation (Mahler, Pine, & Bergman, 1975). The newborn, in the normal autistic phase, appears psychologically oblivious to the person who meets his biophysiological needs even though the infant is fully responsive to the meeting of those needs. Although recent research has indicated an active reflexive participation on the part of the newborn, the term "autistic" here refers to the initial absence of psychological participation on the part of the newborn. With neurologic maturation, memory traces are laid down of hunger–satiation–bliss (and of hunger–frustration–rage) sequences (Glover, 1968; Mahler et al., 1975; Spitz, 1965); these serve as early psychological structures that evolve in response to but also increasingly act as participants in the mother–infant interaction, adding recognition and anticipation and therefore increasing psychological participation on the part of the infant. Further, on the basis of the pleasure principle, there is a positive–negative affective polarity to these memories, adding a certain motivational organization to them. With the pleasurable sequences predominant, as is the case where maternal care is adequate, the newborn is gradually brought into the normal symbiotic phase of development; that is, elementary psychological structures evolve, which make possible now a psychological interaction with and tie to the caretaking person. Spitz's phrase—the establishment of the libidinal object—is an apt one, as it underscores the active participation of the infant, both cognitively and affectively, and explains the basis for the specific smiling response, which visibly heralds the achievement of this developmental accomplishment. One might say, then, that by this time, at about 6 months of age, the infant has developed within his budding psychological structures a rudimentary but functional capacity to recognize, respond to, and seek out loving human relatedness. Mindless hedonistic promiscuity, more characteristic of the newborn limited by the structural immaturities characteristic of normal autism, is now replaced by an elementary form of monogamy. As we will see, observational data on infants inadequately reared reveals quite a different course of events.

At about the same time as the mother–infant symbiosis peaks, another developmental event occurs whose significance was made particularly clear by the course of the analysis of the maternally deprived child I will describe later. I refer to "hatching" (Mahler *et al.*, 1975), that is, the progression from within the autistic "shell" into an early form of attentiveness to sensations emanating from perceptual equipment receiving stimuli from the external environment. Hatching is the shift from coenesthetic to diacritic responsiveness, using Spitz's terminology for this event. The child at this point sits comfortably ensconced in the mother's loving lap, attention directed outward, happily if not excitedly enjoying the sights and sounds of his world.

During this second half of the 1st year of life and into the 2nd year, the observational evidence suggests the child is elaborating his internal images of himself, his mother, his other loved ones, his world animate and inanimate at large. Through the differentiation and practicing subphases of the separation–individuation process, he explores the working of his perceptual, cognitive, and musculoskeletal equipment, integrating his perceptions and hypomanically experimenting with his body's increasing capacity for locomotion and manipulation. These activities, sources of both developmental progress and pleasure, are made possible by the support and encouragement within the continuing maternal bond, and diminish in intensity in the mother's absence.

With rapprochement (Lax, Bach, & Burland, 1980) and the discovery of separateness, the toddler experiences great narcissistic mortification, with rage and conflict within the relationship to the mother, but copes, and makes the transition to self-reliance and object relatedness on the strength of internalized resources and continued external empathic support. Under "average expectable" circumstances, the 3-year-old is "on the road to object constancy" (Mahler *et al.*, 1975), with stable and predominantly positively charged introjects. The 3-year-old's capacity if not preference for loving monogamous relationships now includes separated objects as well as selfobjects. These developmental achievements are fueled by instinctual forces that seek the gratifications that ensue from well-functioning first selfobject and then object relationships; these forces are constitutional and therefore present in all newborns. But the degree to which these instincts are gratified is determined by the ego developmental accomplishments during these years; they are not constitutionally guaranteed as they depend in part upon happenstance and therefore are far from universal. The monogamy of which I write is predicated upon the development of stable internal images, built up out of memories of adequate care, and the affective charge that accompanies them. The psyche develops as part and parcel of the process by which internal and external reality are elaborated, differentiated, and stabilized. That, of course, is why drive frustration and environmental inadequacy in the first years of life leave indelible consequences in the form of ego malformations.

With maternal deprivation the inadequate emotional investment in the newborn by the mother leads to a failure in the establishment of the libidinal object. Those rudimentary ego structures that make the move into the symbiotic phase possible do not adequately develop. In observations of mother–infant pairs of this kind, one sees little in the way of a social smile and no specific smiling response. Eye contact between the two is fleeting at best, if not altogether absent. There is little "dialogue"; the mutual cuing, the sensitivity to each other's rhythms is strikingly absent. In severe instances it is as though the mother does not exist for the infant, who remains promiscuous in his equal responsiveness to anyone who offers to meet his immediate needs. That the infant does not exist for the mother is seen, for instance, in mothers who literally forget their babies, leaving them behind when they leave the room without any awareness of it. The babies show little joy, and little evidence of an early structuralizing polarity based on pleasure versus unpleasure; they are either apathetic and vacant, or in distress, and do not seem to reach out for or seek loving relatedness. In the early months very aggressive stimulation by others, or by a coaxed mother, will lead after a few minutes to some happy responsiveness, but it is fleeting. Failure to thrive is endemic among this population, of course. Hatching is abortive or absent. As crawlers and then toddlers, one sees a driven, frenetic hyperactivity, devoid of the hypomania of normal practicing. There is little evidence that internal images are being elaborated; that is, others are not related to in a recognizably differentiated manner, and self-stimulation lacks the consistent pattern that would speak for some degree of organization of internal experiences. Language development is particularly delayed, and those few words one does hear, and can understand, tend to be negative. Almost all activities are destructive, and the mother's interactions with her toddler are almost exclusively limited to angry recriminations and threats, all of which are seemingly ignored. It is a chilling experience being in a playroom with several of these mother–infant pairs: there is no joy whatsoever; play activity is markedly destructive, the toys and furniture broken and scattered; the only verbalizations are angry, with people screaming past one another, ignoring what others say. It is a Pinteresque scene. One can tune in on such children's perceptions of the world as hostile, uncaring, unsatisfying, and unstable, a world view shared in most instances by their mothers who, of course, had reached such a view in a similar manner. Instant gratification and materialism seem to be the only things that generate some degree of temporary comfort for these children, not tuned in to either development or relatedness, still preoccupied in a desperate struggle to find some degree of psycho-physiological homeostasis and peace.

The psychological challenges of rapprochement are beyond such a child's capacity to cope. These children lack the inner resource of stable positive self and object images, and with continuing if not worsening maternal inadequacy, there are few external resources upon which to rely. The intensifying punitiveness of their environment is chilling as their unrelievable distress is interpreted as badness.

By the age of 2 years, they present a clinical picture characterized by interpersonal isolation. These children are almost mute, play alone except for those times they are fighting, and rest by curling up and sleeping on the floor or in a closet. What relatedness they form are all need fulfilling. They are not on the road toward object constancy. They reveal not only a failure to elaborate complex and meaningful images of themselves or others, but also they reveal also little permanence in those transient images, positive or negative, they do form.

Their narcissistic vulnerability is very evident; instant gratification, supporting the illusion of infantile megalomania, is their only source of self-actualization, and any frustration is therefore instantly mortifying. They reveal no evidence of either an adaptive and functional identity or of the kinds of skill development that lead to individuation and secondary narcissism. Their capacity for mirroring or overidealization is limited; one sees as the most common narcissistic restitutive defense a malevolently tinged evocation of the grandiose self (see Kohut, 1971). In my experience with these children throughout the life cycle, many later throw themselves into phallic narcissism with a vengeance, hoping to find in its drive-based phallic aggressiveness a restitutive compensation for their depressive core. But their macho strutting, or sexual promiscuity, is hollow and friable, and not a reliable source of narcissistic support; castration anxiety so quickly triggers underlying separation and annihilation anxieties it is uncontainable.

Cognitive functioning is severely handicapped in large measure as the perceptual and cognitive apparatuses are never adequately cathected; such children are not at all interested in learning or figuring out anything, and continue to reveal their inadequate hatching (as did my young analysand, as we will see) in their mindless disregard for diacritic data about their world.

The predominance of angry affect and destructive aggressive activity is in keeping with the predominance of negative introjects and the failure to libidinally cathect anyone or anything; in this sense, observational data on this population confirms the hypotheses of recent authors that destructive aggression is largely reactive and developmental rather than an expression of an inherent universal destructivenes (see Parens, 1979, for example). But in addition, regardless of its ultimate source, neutralization of aggression does not occur as these children persist in their reliance upon splitting, failing to bring whatever capacity they might have managed to salvage for positive relatedness into contact with their more negative perceptions.

CLINICAL DATA

For purposes of collecting further data, I saw in psychoanalysis a 7-year-old boy suffering from this syndrome. In this chapter I will focus only on the 1st year and a half of the analysis as it was during these months that the analytic work focused on the issues described above.

Jack arrived in care at the age of 4½ years. He had been left at a baby sitter's by his mother, who then disappeared (we later learned she and her four other children left town). The baby sitter called the department of public welfare (DPW) after several days, in large measure as she was finding Jack's behavior unmanageable. As he arrived in care, then, without a responsible adult family member to give a history, it was Jack's condition that spoke for his past. (Several years later when Jack's family unexpectedly returned on the scene, historical information was obtained—with difficulty, however—confirming the deprivation and chaos to which he had been exposed in his early life.) In their files DPW did find a report of an investigation of Jack's home some 6 months earlier, in response to neighbor's complaints about noises and smells emanating from the house. They found that Jack's home was chaotic and in poor repair. His mother had taken in upwards of a dozen runaway teenagers. There were also several dogs who were kept inside, and it was their excrement that accounted for much of the smell about which the neighbors complained. Jack's mother was uncooperative with the investigation, gave little information, denied what was evident for all to see, but made enough promises to the investigator that no action was taken.

Jack arrived in residential care some 9 months later, having demonstrated an inability to cope with the challenges of foster home care. Short and husky, and darkly biracial, Jack had a certain superficial charm. He walked with a macho swagger, and was quite verbal. But to the clinically sensitive observer, he was in fact quite unrelated. He did not discriminate between others, learning few names, making no friends, and treating children and adults alike. He was asocial rather than antisocial. That is, he mindlessly and frenetically sought self-stimulation and self-gratification; but he was oblivious to the needs or feelings of others, or to the structure of his immediate social setting. In school he ran up and down the aisles, started fights, ignored academics altogether. On the grounds he either played his own seemingly disorganized and destructive games, running around breaking things and hitting others, or he interacted with others primarily to beat them up or take away their things. Any pressure put upon him to comply with the group structure caused him to collapse into desperate tears and rages; he had little frustration tolerance. Psychological testing indicated probably average intellectual potential but such immaturity and scatter that his scores were depressed to around 80. On projectives he drew himself without hands, speaking for his sense of powerlessness, and drew home as a scribble with a blank area in the middle he explained was filled with rats and mice. The psychologist could detect a scavenging quality to Jack. When I first met him, he explained his placement with an endless monologue that recounted a house beset by robbers who took baths, killer dogs, avenging midget angels with huge swords with which they cut off the dogs' legs, midget people hiding under the radiators, and so on. When diplomatically asked if any of the tale might have been imaginary, he insisted angrily it was all real.

His adjustment at the home and in school continued to be marginal at best, and for that reason, and because he seemed a good example of the autistic character disorder, he was selected from several candidates to be seen in analysis. This was in October of 1977, some 2½ years after his arrival in residential care.

THE ANALYSIS

Jack's first three sessions could be viewed as his listing his chief complaints. In the first session he first went to the blackboard and wrote his name, but strikingly in that there were several misspellings and he wrote his middle name first, in big letters, followed then by his first name, in small letters and up in a corner, then followed by his nickname rising up a steep slant. He connected fragments of the letters to try to make a picture of a man, which came out quite crooked and distorted. He next played with some puzzles, but was totally unable to get them solved; he initially resisted my efforts at help even though he had sought that help, but eventually could use it, and solve them. Next, he went to the doll house and, moving some figures around the kitchen, talked of food and claimed his mother was visiting him the next day along with her "friend" (current male friend) and Jack's aunt (with whom he had also not had contact for 3 years). Finally, he found a dart gun, but was unable to get it to work even eventually with my help, which again he had sought but could not readily accept (the dart gun, by the way, was easy to use).

In that first session I could see his confused and fragmented identity, his cognitive impotence, his oral yearnings directed toward his mother (and his use of denial), and finally his more stubborn phallic impotence.

In the second session he focused mainly on his struggles with destructive aggression. With a toy gun he played killing certain animals and dolls, or not killing them but instead rescuing them; at other times he pretended to be killing, but then laughed and said he was really asleep. I asked him if he was telling me about a dream, but he seemed not to know what a dream was. He finally alternated between killing and not killing a baby and its mother. In the transference he alternated between wanting and not wanting to kill me as I was not nice or nice. He seemed more "ambitendent," or split, than ambivalent in this play.

In the third session he presented what I took to be infantile neurosis material. Again playing with the gun, the topic was using it in ways he should not, that is, doing "bad" things like killing; this play was interrupted several times by his wondering if it was time to go yet. He then reacted to noises he claimed to hear from outside the door, or through the wall, and near the end of the session, had to "run" to the bathroom. I took this material to refer to masturbatory fantasies and early precursors of guilt, with primal scene aspects as well.

As so often occurs, these three sessions, more or less, indicated the three "phases" of the analysis, which, unfortunately, was interrupted in the middle of the third phase when the mother reappeared, for unknown reasons, and demanded the instant return of her son. We were able to delay this for some 6 months to try to bring the analysis to a conclusion of sorts and to monitor the reunion. The analysis lasted, then, 2 years and 10 months.

In our first 20 or so sessions I focused upon his sometimes more, sometimes less frenetic activity, which led usually to a collapse of ego function followed then by a reorganization if, and to the extent that, Jack could accept or use my efforts at structuralization via running commentary and confrontation. That is, I hoped that by telling him in words what he was doing, he would gain greater awareness and control, and be brought into a self-observing process. For instance, during the 2nd week there was a session of chaotic and unintelligible "silly" and explosive play with the gun. He seemed to have something in mind that he wanted the gun to do or be, but couldn't succeed, would get angry, and would yell at the gun. But his mood had seemed cranky from the start. I reflected back his blaming the gun for his lack of success, implying that his bad mood seemed more to blame. He said nothing, but the next day he came in almost pointedly in a "good" mood, teasing me with smiles while playing with the gun, alternating between killing and not killing. He finally said into the dictaphone that he wanted to be a cop, to catch robbers, and that he loved me as I was nice and helped him. The next session he came in clearly in a bad mood again, said something unintelligible that I think meant he was angry as he was missing something in school, and proceeded to engage in only more intensely wild, unstructured, violent, often unintelligible play. I referred again to his angry mood, and he responded by dictating into the dictaphone an unintelligible, plotless, fragmented sequence of violent encounters between unknown people or animals. I reflected back to him what we were learning about his bad moods: that is, the anger including the anger at me, the preoccupation with violence, the confusion about relationships. I was struck, though, how in these three sessions it seemed to me that my selective response to certain facets of his activity was matched by an almost equally selective response on his part. This tended to wax and wane, however.

Some 2 weeks later in one session he arrived in a good mood and happily repeated some of the activities from our first session. But this deteriorated, and he was soon again frenetic, chaotic, violent, with malevolent giggling, and much blaming of toys for his failure to achieve what he wished—thought it was totally unclear what that was. But he then went to the phone, and pantomimed trying to call someone but being disconnected. He then claimed I could make the call without its being disconnected, and so insisted I do so, though he could not clarify whom he was trying to reach, or why. I was able then to link up his mood with connection or disconnection, that is with separation issues; I also commented on his hope that I can help him with that. I sensed his reaching out, and felt it important that I acknowledge it.

During the next week an interesting session occurred. Jack came in in a rage, as a game he had been playing with a child-care worker in the cottage had been interrupted for our time together. He screamed in tears of utter desperation, as though the world was ending, and there was no hope. He screamed he hated me, and insisted he be allowed to go at once. I reflected back to him how hard it was for him to deal with interruptions; they seemed to make it hard for him to know if I was a good guy or a bad guy, and that I wondered if that made him ask the same questions about himself. He screamed he knew that he was bad, and that it was my fault as I'd interrupted his game. He drew a picture of me on the chalkboard, with a huge monstrous head, twisted arms and legs, and huge teeth all around and on top of my head. I reflected back that when he gets as angry as this even my face and body change into ugly shapes. He made threatening gestures toward me with the chalkboard eraser, and I continued to reflect back to him, calmly, how frightening his anger must be to him as he fears he can't control it. He got a baby doll and fed it, though angrily and roughly. He then screeched and cursed into the dictaphone, but interrupted himself several times, asking me to speak into it, though in contrast to him, softly, clearly and nicely. I was saying something about how he wasn't sure about who he was, wild or not, good or bad, but as I spoke he leapt into the desk chair—"my" chair—and beamed with pleasure. I said he seemed to feel he'd be a lot better off if he were me. He agreed with delight. And he was most reluctant to end this session that he had refused to begin.

That very rich hour, our 25th, which said so much about the instability of his introjects, his use of splitting, and his reliance upon oral incorporative restitutive maneuvers pretty much recounted the material that was to be our focus over the next months, material first indicated in our first session.

Over the next few weeks a pattern emerged in which Jack would quite literally fall apart when it became time to end our sessions. This was usually expressed in increased impulsive violent play or activity. In one session a large wooden box filled with chalk packed in sawdust flew at my head, to both my and Jack's surprise, requiring I duck to avoid possible serious injury. That session had begun with his expressing anger that I had not shown up, as a substitute parent, on the previous evening's "Parent's Night Dinner." His outburst of violence against me was very upsetting for Jack, who ran screaming to the cottage, claiming that I hated him, was trying to kill him, and was refusing to ever see him again. It was necessary, I felt, after discussion with Jack about it, to give 10- and 5-minute warnings about the end of our sessions. In keeping with this transference–separation material, he was expressing worries in the cottage as to what he would do if I were sick and therefore unable to see him.

This intense separation anxiety material was accompanied by increased references in the play material to (restitutive) largely malevolent grandiosity. He would insist we play games such as monopoly, clearly beyond his ego's ability, but did so by *his* rules, which meant a confused and chaotic activity, impossible to follow, during which he claimed repeated victories of some sort or another. He would climb up on top of furniture and proclaim he was not just taller but was the tallest person in the world. He would "leave" our sessions early, although then returning to make sure I had noticed, or "arrive" late (i.e., hang around outside the door first) to act as though *he* was in charge of comings and goings, as we put it. He would throw his coat or toys on the floor, and with a supercilious look on his face demand that I pick them up.

With my help some of this megalomanic material was identified as angry, destructive, and cruel. He utilized the dictaphone for this; he would record his cursing and screeching, then play it back, calling what he heard "bad," or "garbage," or "craziness." He revealed how structure was dependent upon selfobject togetherness; that is, his "goodness" was dependent upon my (psychological) presence. He would announce he was going to be "good," and then would pantomime a smiling kind of mock goodness; then he'd announce, "Now I'm going to be bad" and act destructively. In one session he inserted, at the good-to-bad transition point, "Is it time to go?" I said "Good-byes bring out the bad Jack in you." He agreed with much emphasis.

Over subsequent weeks we began to explicate the characteristics of "good Jack" as opposed to "bad Jack"; there was also a "6-million-dollar Jack," that is, the omnipotent Jack. We identified what brought out each of the Jacks to the surface. For instance, in one session, he had toy blocks disappear, requiring much in the way of searching to find them; when found, they were first spanked for "badness" but were then beaten and crushed mercilessly as he acted increasingly imperious; it was possible, then, to identify separation issues again at the core of his concerns. "Bad Jack" played "smash–crash games," my term for his unstructured and "mindless" destructive activities. It seemed that physical separation brought out the destructive "bad Jack," and was accompanied by a perception of me as what we called the "bad Dr. Burland" and against whom he raged. Noncompliance with his demands that I be his "slave," in particular who cleans up his messes, gave rise more to the "6-million-dollar Jack" who treated me in an utterly contemptuous and aloof manner. A graphic vignette: In one session he ran in, threw his coat on the floor, and screamed at me to pick it up. I quietly reflected back to him what he was doing, in the terms we had come to use, and he threw himself on the floor in (mock?) tears, screaming I hated him and was trying to kill him. He then got the box of small plastic toy soldiers, put a chair on the desk, sat on it as though on a throne, and "crushed" handfulls of the soldiers, scattering their "dead bodies" about, chortling with malevolent delight.

This material was also expressed about others; for instance, when one day his school teacher was absent because of illness, Jack was quite low-keyed. He tried to "call" her on the phone but couldn't, then handled that frustration by playing school in which he was a most haughty, all-powerful, rejecting, and overcritical teacher. He played Evil Knievel games that began with some reality, related to what Knievel had actually done, but the play soon deteriorated into more and more fantastic and impossible feats that Jack insisted were "for real," or into pantomimed activities in the office, which approached sufficient risk to himself or to toys such that he was clearly asking for limits. This latter felt very much like darting away, that is, an interactional pressure put upon me to be a "better mother," a better and more aggressive selfobject.

In the middle of the 5th month of the analysis, Jack introduced for the first time material directly expressing his painful passive but ambivalent yearnings for his mother. Along with many of the other children he was a fan of the TV actor Freddy Prinz, and was quite visibly depressed when Prinz committed suicide; he was mute almost throughout the session in which he told me of this, staring sadly at the floor. When I reflected back to him how deeply he was lost in thought, and that they seemed like unhappy thoughts, he said he was thinking about his mother, and was afraid she was in trouble; he curled up in his chair, and went, it seemed, to sleep.

He began making references also for the first time to events that allegedly took place at home before his mother deserted him. The session in which this first occurred was of interest in that it opened with his "being me," sitting in my chair, calling himself by my name, and so on, in what seemed to be a happy manner. Positive introjects it seemed were being evoked. He then recalled playing with a brother and sister, fighting in the bathtub, making messes, and infuriating his mother. Finally, he began making "bathroom noises," joking about "BM's," laughing at another child who was a soiler, squatting on the desk, and dropping BM's of clay for me to clean up. His affect changed suddenly and dramatically from wildly silly to utter despair when he noted that some of the clay got stuck to his corduroy pants and he feared the house parents would rage at him; in this we saw the vulnerability of his mental structures. But the earlier material also showed his beginning, and somewhat successful, efforts at constructing a sense of self out of a pastiche of introjects, identifications, and memories.

Let me insert a comment here about how I saw Jack's capacity for object relations at this point. Clearly he was reaching out, but it seemed equally clear that he was limited to selfobject interactions. One could view his aims as narcissistic, that is, a desperate attempt on his part to pull together or create, or better yet, find a self; or, thinking psychogenetically, he was struggling to rouse the illusion of a selfobject mother–infant dyad in which he would experience some measure of narcissistic stability and safety. His perhaps surprising ability to enter into the analytic process came from this, I believe; that is, he would—so to speak—out of that desperation follow me anywhere, even "into analysis." One might be tempted to view some of this activity on his part as identification with the aggressor; that is, out of his selfobject dependency upon me I was, to him, the one with the power, therefore the aggressor. But from Jack's intrapsychic viewpoint I did not think that he had achieved sufficient self and object differentiation to construct mental images of other objects with clear characteristics after which to remodel his mental image of himself, using Sandler's representational world as my conceptual framework (see Sandler, Chapter 4, this volume.). On the other hand, he could elect to include an overidealized perception of me as part of his self-object narcissistic support system, although his ability to do so was quite vulnerable. What he was doing was more like projective identification than identification "proper." He was in this revealing his inability to deal with rapprochement challenges, but due to prerapprochement issues he had failed to resolve adequately.

Over the next few weeks, during approximately the 6th month of the analysis, Jack moved back and forth between presenting himself on the one hand as "good" or "nice," his words for it, almost always in the context of pleasing or going along with certain adults: his teacher, his social worker, the child-care staff, or myself; and, on the other hand, presenting himself as "bad," which meant playing mindless "smash–crash" games, making messes, and refusing to clean up (sometimes with clear anal connotations as indicated by his imitations of loud bathroom sounds). Part of being "bad" was being imperious and cruel toward me, demanding in particular I be his "slave." This material increasingly felt to me much more like communication than acting in; a working alliance was evolving. An example: In our 71st session, he began by making food out of the clay, but it was "yucky" and "droogy" (local word referring to fecal matter), and indeed the clay soon became "BM" dropping from his bottom. He then made faces out of the clay, which he smashed and stabbed, all with malevolent giggling and grandiose disregard for those he was mutilating. With me he was demanding and bossy, ordering me to pick up his mess, or give him treats, or pull him up over the edge of the desk like an amusement park ride. These demands were made impulsively, without follow through, and seemed to be forgotten as soon as they were made. I simply reflected back to him how he seemed to be interested in me only insofar as I gave him treats or obeyed his orders, that I was a candy machine or monkey bars, but nothing else; and I reflected back to him how his view of the world was as a place where food is BM, people get smash-crashed, there are only slaves and slave masters. But he listened to me intently, and nodded in agreement as he spontaneously went about the business of cleaning up in a cooperative way at the end of the session.

The sessions continued their up and down course, however, with scattered and confused ones, filled with mindless smash-crash activities alternating with more organized ones. There was one session throughout which he played the card game Fish, by the rules, and with minimal tension; he even won more games than he lost, announcing when we tabulated the score at the end of the session, "I know my cards, and I know my rights!" This could be viewed as self-assertion, expressing his improving sense of self; and it can be seen as evidence of consolidation of ego strength, especially around identity. In the very next session, for contrast, he came in whining about how hard things were at school—too much work, too many rules; then he made half-hearted stabs at games, falling apart in particular around having to accept the rule structure. He tried to create a shooting match game with a plastic gun, but couldn't come up with a set of rules that would work the way he wished. He seemed to be having trouble integrating his wish for victory and mastery with the need for submission to external structure and demand, the former feeling narcissistically positive, the latter making him feel like a "slave." His view of life seemed to offer but two alternatives: omnipotence or narcissistic mortification; in this we see his continued demand for selfobject relatedness. He was not yet ready for identification with a separate object's skills or values; he was still limited to appropriating a selfobject partner's illusory omnipotence or collapse.

Over the next few weeks the content of his activities included for the first time direct references to good mothering and good mothers; mother dolls would be nice to their babies, he talked of mother snakes protecting baby snakes, and so on. In form he moved more intensely into a positive maternal transference. He seemed very comfortably and contentedly ensconced in my maternal lap; tensions were strikingly absent in the sessions, he was not at all provocative, and in the countertransference I felt able to "relax" for almost the first time. He was not by any means "good" in his play content, however. In spite of the brief and "passing" references to good mothering, his murderous and smash-crash play still predominated, with a difference only in the accompanying affect; he was not frenetic; nor malevolently grandiose (even when crushing dozens of plastic cowboys and indians, for instance). Further, his content references to good mothering continued to alternate with references to bad mothering (a good mother snake, for instance, in the next scene was terrifying) although the affect that accompanied such negative references continued to be appropriate to good mothering.

His fantasy material remained crude—that is, unelaborated and disorganized, made up of a sequence of seemingly arbitrarily strung together still photographs of violent scenes, so to speak, instead of even brief but narrative moving pictures; but there was a slowly increasing variety of such fantasy precursors, and at this time in the analysis he began making more direct references to infantile neurosis material. Cockroaches were described as roaches that "sucked blood from cocks," something, by the way, he insisted was true; he claimed his mother had a "hairy cock" as well as "tits"; the play with mother dolls and baby dolls often had incestuous or sensuous connotations.

He also at this time began to claim I was his father, and asked to be taken home by me. In his yearnings for me as a nurturant parent, it felt more like he wanted me to be his mother. Unmistakable references to me as a male penis-bearing father figure were to first appear later.

Over the next 2 or 3 months, the material revolved primarily around his efforts at developing skills and mastery in play and in schoolwork. He was subject, however, to instant discouragement, in the face of the least obstacle or frustration or failure, and would promptly regress to smash–crashing, or to disorganized silliness, or to imperiosity. His references to mother's absence as central to his adaptive impotence grew, as did evidence of mutative perceptions of me as, in contrast, present in his life. He seemed to be trying to synthesize more differentiated mental images of himself, as an increasingly individuated and skilled coper, and of others, in particular of his mother as differentiated from me. In connection with this his material suggested some early efforts on his part to explain to himself why his mother rejected him, his usual belief being at this point it was because of his anal explosiveness; here, too, he seemed engaged in elaborating his world of mental images.

In our 9th month we had a session that began with his trying to create a narrative story accompanying his doll play. It involved the toy soldiers and some animal dolls, first the soldiers killing the animals, then the animals killing the soldiers. The best he could come up with was that the killers first lined up and got into position, then killed the other one by one, then afterward went and got milk to drink. In another version the soldiers were trying to throw a ball at the animals; when I asked, in an encouraging way, what the story was now, he said "I threw the ball, but nobody was there, so I had to catch it myself." As I began to underscore the reference to separation, his play speedily fell apart, and soldiers and animals were scattered around the room. But we then cleaned up, together, comfortably. That quite poignant reference to his feeling so alone, that seemed to come like an association from his preconscious, announced the theme that was central for the next few weeks, namely rejection and search. In one session he ran in, announced with great affect "I want my mother!," and was so upset he ran out again and did not return until our next day's session; of note, this was our second-to-last session before my summer vacation. In our next, and therefore prebreak session, he began by trying very hard to be organized and structured, playing a game with a war content but with a striking (for Jack) amount of ego control, speaking not just for his anger but also for his efforts at protecting me from that anger and holding on to me by pleasing me with behavior identified with me. He tried to make the presentation of the game more verbal than behavioral, again, I think, to please me. He met with but mixed success, however; the game did not come together, and increasingly it became more of a smash-crash equivalent to the negative transference. He began then to include my person in the activity, and hit me, gently at first, but soon hard enough that I fended him off and reflected back to him his anger at me over my pending vacation. He grew instantly upset, screamed he was not hitting hard, and soon was accusing me of wanting to hit him. He then ran to his social worker's office, tearfully complaining to her that I hated him. I followed him, and attempted to put into words what I saw as his hurt over the vacation break; but he "ignored" me. I wished him a pleasant break in a friendly manner, and left. Again, we can see his gains, his use of me as a means of achieving those gains, but how friable and fragile those gains were, in particular in terms of his inability to cope with the rage mobilized by passively experienced separations.

In our first session after the vacation, he again presented much rich material that predicted our focus for the next months. He arrived a few minutes late, clearly on purpose, but was so excited to see me he had then to run to tell his social worker about it. He ran back and began to write on the blackboard, to demonstrate how much better he was doing in school; it is also likely that in keeping with his self-object transference our reunion had triggered a hypomanic response. What he wrote was:

WO
YRecLess
Sally

He tried, then, without success to figure out what he had written. He was distracted by a fly, alternately threatening to kill it or save it; he did cripple it enough that it couldn't crawl away, and he said "See? It doesn't want to fly away, as it loves me." He kissed it. He then wrote a note to his social worker; he said he was writing to her, "I wanted you to give me a rifle but you didn't, as you were not here." What he put on paper was:

I wanted
As you my rifel
You to give me were not here
But you didn't.

The similarity to how he had written his name on the blackboard on our first session was most striking. The blend of preoedipal and oedipal material was also striking, in particular the depressive core that contributed a separation anxiety underpinning to his castration anxiety, a very frequent phenomena in deprived children. Striking also was again the extent to which a sense of organization—here, sequential verbal thought—was vulnerable to

separation. The admittedly ambivalent but largely positive illusory transference was in evidence as was its selfobject nature.

A few weeks later in our 11th month, there was an unexpected contact
from his aunt, and a visit with her was scheduled. Jack was ecstatic, and
showed it in increased phallic narcissistic activity; that is, he became
preoccupied with making paper airplanes, having me teach him how to make
them, making cleverer and fancier ones himself. It seemed that he had used his
aunt's return to the scene as a narcissistic support that made possible for him
more hypomanic aggressive self-actualizing behavior, a trend that had already
been surfacing from our work together but that now also took a boost from
this his first family contact in 4 years. I learned from the social worker that the
aunt had told her that Jack's mother was now remarried and living in Florida,
that the mother had no plans for reunion with Jack, and in fact she was telling
relatives that Jack was dead. (Interestingly I learned at about the same time
that he had been telling the other children in the cottage that his mother was
dead.) Although Jack did not tell me directly about what transpired in his visit
with his aunt, he did make a few seemingly tangential and vague references to
Florida, which led me to believe he and his aunt had discussed his mother and
he knew of her whereabouts.

The material over the next couple of months, during the fall of 1977,
including the first anniversary of the analysis, did not bring forth any new
content. It appeared to be a period of consolidation of earlier gains and
continued working through of material already introduced into our work
together. He alternated between structure and chaos, between being "good"
and being "bad," positive and negative transference trends, grandiosity and
impotence. He tried to learn how to play games by the rules, though with poor
results, as his tolerance level for frustration was still low and his cognitive
processes were vulnerable to uncomfortable affects. He made scattered and
inconstant references to more oedipally tinged sexual material, but these were
fleeting references on which he never elaborated. For instance on several
occasions he wrote profanities on the blackboard. He was in part showing off
how much better his spelling was. However, this seemed to occur when there
was adequate motivation from his drives; social motivation seemed far less in
evidence. I wrote myself a note in one session that his progression–regression
cycles seemed increasingly dynamic as opposed to merely structural; I was
seeing signal anxiety and defense more and structural collapse less.

On December 6 of 1977 during our 14th month, he came in and presented
a long complex fantasy about Santa Claus that was hard to follow. It seemed
to resemble one of his more typical ambitendent or split perceptions; that is,
the "story," or the sequence of photographs, alternated between a good Santa
Claus giving the good Jack lots of presents and the bad Santa Claus giving the
bad Jack nothing, so Jack in retaliation would beat him up or kill him. As
usual, it was as though he didn't even notice that his fantasy changed back and
forth between the expression of negatives and positives. As I reflected this

back to him, he came up with a variety in which he was bad, beating up Santa Claus and killing him, while Santa Claus was good, bringing him presents. It seemed to me he was struggling to break free from his rigidified tendency to experience only his own split all-good or all-bad introjects, from a projective mode of pseudointeraction to a truly interactive mode that was interpersonal, reactive, and adaptive. To try to help him develop this, I asked, "Would he bring you presents when you were so bad to him?" Jack replied, almost with surprise that I had even asked, "Of course!" I then asked, "If he beat you up and killed you, would you give him presents?" Jack answered: "Of course not! Never!" Again he seemed perplexed I had even asked. I then wondered out loud that Jack didn't seem to realize that he and Santa Claus, and all people, for that matter, were alike, that all people tend to want to be nice to those that are nice to them, and get angry at people that are bad to them—just like Jack, I emphasized. He seemed more thoughtful about that exchange than usual.

The next day Jack came in and instantly I could see that he was a changed boy. The content of his play was not too different: He continued to refer to Santa Claus, this time with Mr. and Mrs. Claus alternating between fighting and making love, and utilizing this to play out love versus hate, niceness versus badness. But it was the change in form that was striking. He seemed suddenly warmer, "softer," more empathic, more related, more likable. And when the Clauses were fighting or having sex there was a new inhibited and sublimated quality to the play. The violence was suggested, with attenuated gestures, rather than wallowed in, and there was a new kind of affective sincerity when one character, in the positive mode, was being kind, even empathic, to the other. Even more striking was the improved quality of his focus and reality relatedness, a change that seemed to have occurred overnight.

This change continued and soon was reflected more directly in the content of his play. He painted, but carefully and with skill. He played with racing cars, but had them stay within their lanes, and turn corners carefully. Violent, or grandiose, or sexual material continued to be more inhibited in its presentation. Previously, inhibition of impulse gratification or narcissistic demand, whether internally or externally originated (not that he was fully able to tell one from the other), was usually experienced as a dire threat to his desperately needed illusory grandiosity; now, with what I took to be early true object relatedness, he was finding strength instead in identification with a love object's skills, values, impulse control, and mastery. I decided that what I had also observed was that he had hatched; or, perhaps better put, he had made an observable change that resembled in all specifics that developmental phenomenon called "hatching," something that usually occurs in the middle of the 1st year of life. He was more alert; he maintained eye contact in a new way; he was perceptive of limits imposed by his surround and his situational context. He seemed suddenly more aware of me as a person, and took into greater account what he assumed my wishes or feelings to be. He was much less distractable. His fantasy material began to be more and more elaborated.

A couple of weeks later his social worker reported to me that his teacher had noted a sudden change as well, with a spurt in his capacity to focus, to attend to her, to do his work, and to learn. The cottage reported he was starting to play in a more socialized manner, learning how to play games truly by the rules.

Three weeks later there was a very heavy snow storm and I was unable to get in to see Jack for two appointments; he missed school, as well. In our next session his regression was striking; it gave me an opportunity to see him as he had been, to make even more clear the extent to which he had changed. This regression lasted for two sessions; in them he was as chaotic, violent, and as lost in his projections as he had ever been. By our third postinterruption session he had reconstituted his recent gains; as I said, it was remarkable to see these shifts occur before my very eyes.

The loss of his gains, associated as I assumed them to be with the temporary and unexpected loss of me (and his teacher) spoke not only for their vulnerability, but for the extent to which they were object dependent, surely in their origin, but also in their maintenance. Some important developmental milestone had been (belatedly) passed, it seemed, relating to his perception and use of objects. He had, it seemed, become suddenly capable of acknowledging separateness, and therefore of relating to others in a more object-related manner. Attending to, and then reacting accordingly to, diacritic perceptions of external reality seemed to be gaining in ascendancy over internal perceptions and projections. Internal and external reality had become much better structured, doing so in a mutually enhancing manner, and self and other seemed much better differentiated. I wrote a note to myself that confirmation of this would be an increase in infantile neurosis material and the appearance of a more oedipal transference; that is, the previously dyadic self–object material would be replaced by object-related material. Indeed this did occur. The maternal split transference was replaced by an ambivalent oedipal one, where I increasingly became a penis-bearing model and competitor, whose penis was bigger than his and therefore whose penis he wanted removed, but also whose strength was to be imitated and identified with.

DISCUSSION

In terms of the subject of this chapter, it is hypothesized that certain developmental processes were activated in the context of the analytic relationship. The question is raised as to the relative impact of the transference relationship as opposed to the so-called "real" relationship with the analyst in cases such as this. Issues appropriate to Jack's relationship with his mother were indeed transferred onto me, and these transferences were verbalized and brought into consciousness via reconstructive as well as transference interpretations. For instance, in the transference the repeated sequence that was first identified and then explicated in the first major interpretive process was: (1) demand for selfobject compliance transferred onto the analyst; (2) in response to the analyst's failure to gratify this demand, a sense of loss of the selfobject; (3) reactive mortification, collapse and rage; and (4) restitution via play in which the illusion of (malevolent) grandiosity is reestablished. This process reflected fairly standard analytic procedures: transference wish, frustration as the deprivation of the analytic situation is maintained, anxiety, defense, and then interpretation of the whole sequence. There was ample confirmatory material from Jack attesting to the efficacy of this insight-generating process. This material dealt primarily with dyadic issues in the early months of the analysis recounted above.

However, as Spitz (1956), Winnicott (1956), and more recently Settlage (1977) have discussed, the analytic situation has a "real" shape and character that resembles in some of its specifics certain aspects of the early mother–child dyadic relationship. For the so-called normal neurotic, who is adequately object related as a consequence of adequate early parenting, this aspect of the analytic situation is of significance primarily insofar as it makes possible participation in functional working and therapeutic alliances. But for the developmentally arrested child—or adult—who has not yet achieved object constancy the situation is different. An attentive, empathic, patient, and constant other person is a new experience, one which has an effect in and of itself beyond its functioning as a vehicle for an insight producing process. Careful and sensitive verbalization of this fact by the analyst, as part of the interpretive (in particular, of the character-analytic) process brings it to the fore and prevents treatment from becoming merely an exercise in gratification. We called it Jack's "struggle to figure out how to make use of me."

This "real" experience, I suggest, was an influence in Jack's move out of his autistic character disorder, into a belated symbiotic-like experience, through hatching, and into a state of improved object relatedness. In normal development, hatching can be viewed as an outcome of the establishment of the libidinal object, the positive investment in a mental image constructed out of an accumulation of memories of perceptions of gratifying and meaningful interactions. Such a process results in psychic structures—that is, positive (as well as negative) introjects out of which self and object images, drives, and interactive patterns are elaborated. When pleasurable there is also an affective motivation for the continuing experience of similar interactions; by this means the ego structures that make possible participation in such interactions are used and thereby further developed. Hatching, with its improved diacritic data collection, is part of that self-perpetuating, circular process. Jack, it would seem, was brought first into a positive narcissistic selfobject transference; to that extent a libidinal object was established, and a symbiotic-like experience with the analyst was evoked. This required development of improved ego skills for it to occur at all; once begun, it did to some degree feed itself. The interpretive aspects of the interaction seemed to have fostered its "real" dimensions.

It would seem that the coincidental similarity between certain aspects of the "real" analytic situation and the external supports upon which the normally developing psychic apparatus of the young child relies was a significant factor in his progress. But the "realness" of this "reality" requires closer scrutiny. Certain behavioral parallels between "good-enough" mothering and proper analytic technique are obvious: patience, acceptance, empathic understanding, and so on. (Of course, there are other aspects of adequate mothering that do not resemble analytic technique at all, such as feeding, hygiene, exclusivity, etc.; and mothers don't often see their newborns by appointment only, or charge a fee, or offer interpretations, etc.) However, to what extent is it still up to the analysand to project into the more maternal-like behaviors of the analyst those unique affective and subjective qualities that define the psychological "mother," to utilize a behavioral parallel to support what is still dynamically a process involving displacements from the primary object? Observations of mother–infant interactions suggest that in the course of development much of what makes mothering "good enough" is, over time, increasingly read into the mother's activities by the infant, especially when her activities are in compliance with his needs and expectations. For instance, relatively perfunctory responses of support by the mother—perfunctory as determined by third-party, objective scrutiny—can be seen to be very effective, given a history of good emotional investment by the mother in previous encounters. And something similar occurs in the treatment situation, of course. The issue of the roles of reality and illusion, both in development and in psychoanalytic treatment, needs further consideration (see Burland, Chapter 4, this volume).

What would seem to have occurred to the symptomatic expressions of Jack's autistic character disorder can be schematized as follows:

1. The unrelatedness: Jack was not suffering from an autistic psychosis; he did not apparently lack the inherent capacity to invest others with libidinal energies, nor did he lack the inherent capacity to develop the mental structures needed to carry through such investments. Nor can it be said he lacked the necessary motivation, something one must view as also being a vital part of one's natural endowment. What he lacked was the opportunity, due to environmental inadequacies. As a consequence, certain normally occurring developmental shifts failed to take place. His persistent autistic grandiose promiscuous hedonism reflects, then, a developmental failure as the result of an environmental failure. But, in addition, development being circular, lacking the experience of day-to-day, regularly recurring good-enough dyadic experiences, those ego structures that normally evolve from such interactions failed to develop, and a maladaptive ego weakness resulted, with impaired coping skills. His unrelatedness then became also a regressive self-protective device used in coping by means of autistic withdrawal and imperious grandiosity with a reality he could not confront progressively or constructively. In other words his ego developmental deficit became also a defense, a largely narcissistic defense, interestingly something described by Reich over 50 years ago (Reich, 1927). To change such a situation one needs to deal with the various elements of the complex dynamic. One has to count upon some dormant residual capacity for emotional investment and some motivation to do so; assuming they are present, one then needs to serve as an adequate if not inviting object for such an investment. In this case I believe that my analytic stance sufficed. To the extent that the unrelatedness serves as a defense, it needs to be interpreted. The "real" relationship to the analyst (keeping in mind that the analysand assigns that realness to the analyst) and the interpretive process combine then to offer an analysis that is both developmental and interpretive.

2. The pathological narcissism: As with his unrelatedness, Jack's reliance upon restitutive grandiosity both reflected a developmental interruption and served, later, a defensive function, protecting him—albeit not too well—from narcissistic mortification. This latter was particularly made necessary by the painful narcissistic challenges of rapprochement with which Jack could not at all cope, that is, the discovery of vulnerability, dependency, and loneliness. Here, too, the therapeutic process involved both an experiential and an interpretive aspect. As Kohut has suggested, the analyst does not actively encourage a positive narcissistic transference; instead, he allows it to evolve, and avoids trying to interpret it away too soon (Kohut, 1971). To bring Jack from his reliance upon grandiosity into a more stable and growth promoting overidealized transference was one of the major challenges early in treatment, leading to his use of me as a positive rather than a negative narcissistic extension. Out of his overidealization of me as a support to his infantile omnipotence, he was eventually able to use me in a more constructive, object-related manner for purposes of identification and individuation.

3. Cognition: The improvement in Jack's intellectual functioning reflected changes in self-image, motivation, and investment. Hatching made thinking pleasurable. Identification with the cognitive aspects of the analytic process, and with the example of my obvious investment in cognition as a tool for coping with life's challenges, played a role here as well.

4. Destructive aggression: Destructive fantasies and behavior are the result of many factors. Drive pressures, reflecting the impact of deprivation upon the original differentiation of the primitive id matrix, exert their influence; but even the most impulsive appearing behavior has to be understood as reflecting in part compromise formation, that is, ego activity. Whereas it is possible that some of the positive "real" aspects of our interaction might well have led to the elaboration of increased positive introjects, and therefore a shift in their positive:negative ratio, it is easier to identify changes in ego function to account for the lessening of Jack's direct expression of destructiveness. His growing use of reaction–formation and his identification with the nondestructive aims of the analyst, and in time, of his community, are testimony to the socializing effects of improved libidinal investments. Further, in the months that followed those described above, with increasing prominence of phallic–oedipal material, early superego functioning became evident as well, reflecting his efforts to cope now with ambivalence as opposed to splitting, his initial means of expressing his love–hate dichotomies. Finally, as the reality principle gained ascendancy over the pleasure principle, pragmatic and socialized adaptation became more prominent as an ego-organizing principle than merely pleasure–unpleasure.

These changes, visible within the office and without, resulted then from a complex, reverberating interaction between interpretive, "real" experiential and developmental processes, understandable, I suggest, on the basis of the theoretic and developmental hypotheses offered above. As to the "real" relationship, one is left with the metaphysical question: What is reality? Those qualities of the analyst and the analytic situation felt to have been therapeutic are labeled as "real" if they are visible and therefore capable of consensual validation; but this formulation omits the largely affective reasons why Jack chose to make therapeutic use of them. In "reality" my emotional investment in Jack was of neither the quality nor quantity one requires from a "good-enough" mother. The object toward which Jack reached out was the (idealized) infantile primary maternal object, the illusory object of which Winnicott (1960a) writes when he speaks of the mother's task in the first 6 months of life as supporting the infant's illusion that his wishes create a gratifying environment. That illusion is what gives the "average expectable environment" its most essential ingredient. This object, then, is inherent and constitutional rather than external; it is the dyadic partner we are all born expecting to interact with. When the actual dyadic partner is unable to support the illusion, is unable to resemble the expected partner sufficiently, the child "relates" instead to the internal processes, that is, remains (characterologically) autistic in the sense that I used that term previously. The process that Winnicott calls "disillusionment," which starts toward the end of the 1st year of life, consists of adapting to the differences between this internal image and the external objects with whom we all must live in reality. Object constancy requires that this disillusionment be successfully mastered; it is not surprising, by the way, that philosophy should concern itself as much as it does with this process of disillusionment (see Burland, 1976). This process stimulates ego growth, of course; but when there is no illusion, and therefore little disillusionment, there is a subsequent lessening of motivation for the development of adapative, reality-related ego skills. The mindless promiscuous hedonist has little use for them.

I would suggest that the difference between transference and the "real" relationship can be understood in terms of the differences between object-related and selfobject transferences. In the former, separation–individuation has proceeded to the point where object constancy has been more or less achieved, and interactions are with objects that are comfortably separate and autonomous; postrapprochement primary objects are the source of transference displacements. In such individuals the original selfobject relationships to the primary objects persist in the timeless unconscious but are evoked electively and adaptively, as in love relationships, esthetic experiences, and so on. Selfobject transferences, in the developmentally arrested and object-hungry patient such as Jack, are displacements from interactions with primary objects prior to the differentiation between inside and outside, between self and object. In such situations realness is very much in the eye of the observer, as the dyadic "other" is allowed no autonomy and is judged solely on the basis of the subject's needs and wishes. As is implied by Winnicott's use of the term "illusion," this initial dyadic partner is in fact an internal rather than an external object, supported though it is by sensitive external ministrations; that is, the dyadic partner's performance is measured against internal expectations. Jack's improvement, therefore, in a most fundamental sense, was possible because of certain internal assets and resources he was able to mobilize with the help of the analytic situation and its ability to support the illusion of the actualization of the facilitating internal expectations. Cure, even for the developmentally arrested, has to come ultimately from within; but that is in keeping with Mahler's discovery of the very active role of the infant in the developmental events of his life from its very beginning.

SUMMARY

Mahler has written that the adequate mother acts as a beacon, directing, organizing, and encouraging her infant's psychic development. In the absence of this function, the infant's psychic development is derailed. Multiple contacts with maternally deprived children revealed a resultant syndrome characterized by a failure to achieve object constancy, pathological narcissism, cognitive defect, and excessive destructive aggression. In this chapter the 1st year and a half of the analysis of such a child was recounted, with emphasis put upon the uncovering and working through of these issues. The significance of the parallels between certain aspects of proper analytic technique and certain functions of the "good-enough" mother were discussed, as were the differences between transference and the "real" relationship in the analytic situation.

REFERENCES

Beres, D., & Ober, S. (1950). The effects of extreme deprivation in infancy on psychic structure in adolescence: a study in ego development. *The Psychoanalytic Study of the Child, 5,* 212–235.

Burland, J. A. (1976). Conservatism and liberalism: A psychoanalytic examination of political belief. *International Journal of Psychoanalytic Psychotherapy, 5,* 369–396.

Burland, J. A. (1980). Psychoanalytic psychiatrist in the world of foster care. *Clinical Social Work Journal, 8* (1), 50–61.

Burland, J. A. (1984). Dysfunctional parenthood in a deprived population. In R. S. Cohen, B. J. Cohler, & S. H. Weissman (Eds.), *Parenthood: A psychodynamic perspective* (pp. 148–163). New York: Guilford.

Glover, E. (1968). *The birth of the ego.* New York: International Universities Press.

Hartmann, H. (1937). *Ego psychology and the problem of adaptation.* New York: International Universities Press, 1958.

Kohut, H. (1971). *The analysis of the self.* New York: International Universities Press.

Lax, R., Bach, S., & Burland, J. A. (Eds.). (1980). *Rapprochement: Critical subphase of separation-individuation.* New York: Jason Aronson.

Mahler, M., Pine, F., & Bergman, A. (1975). *The psychological birth of the human infant.* New York: Basic Books.

Parens, H. (1979). *The development of aggression in early childhood.* New York: Jason Aronson.

Reich, W. (1927). On the technique of character analysis. In *Character analysis* (pp. 39–137). New York: Orgone Institute Press, 1949.

Settlage, C. (1977). The psychoanalytic understanding of narcissistic and borderline personality disorders: Advances in developmental theory. In R. F. Lax, S. Bach, & J. A. Burland (Eds.), *Rapprochement: Critical subphase of separation-individuation* (pp. 77–100). New York: Jason Aronson.

Spitz, R. (1956). Transference: The analytic setting and its prototype. *International Journal of Psycho-Analysis, 37,* 380–385.

Spitz, R. (1965). *The first year of life.* New York: International Universities Press.

Winnicott, D. W. (1956). On transference. *International Journal of Psycho-Analysis, 37,* 389–397.

Winnicott, D. W. (1960a). The theory of the parent-infant relationship. In *The maturational process and the facilitating environment* (pp. 37–55). New York: International Universities Press, 1965.

Winnicott, D. W. (1960b). Ego distortion in terms of true and false self. In *The maturational process and the facilitating environment* (pp. 140–152). New York: International Universities Press, 1965.

Index

349